ATTACK ON TITAN 4

HAJIME ISAYAMA

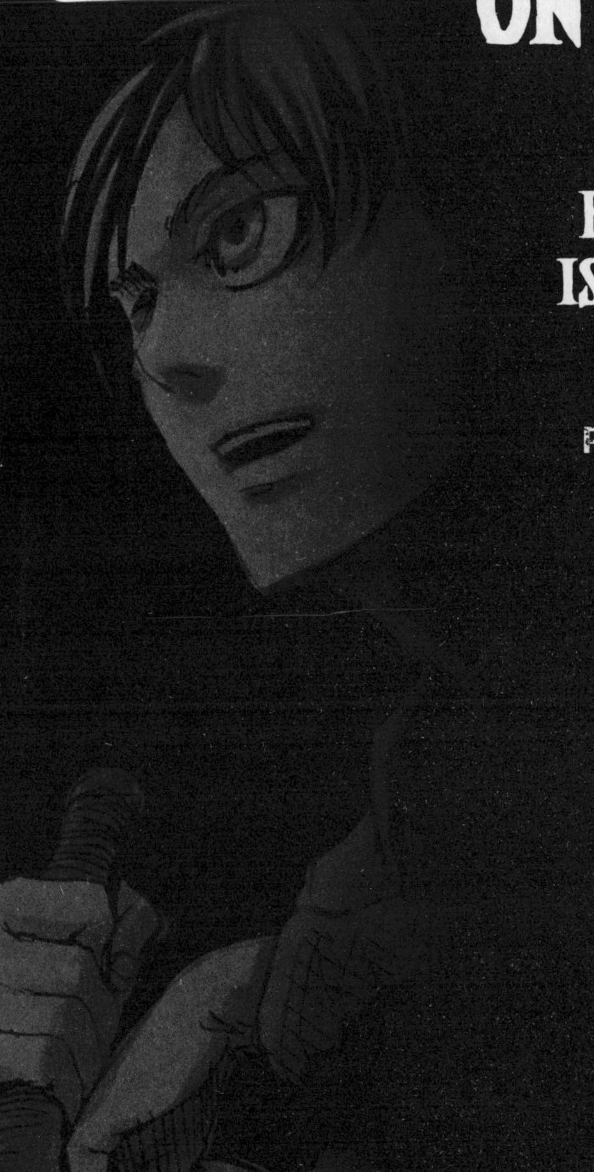

"Attack on Titan" Character Introduction

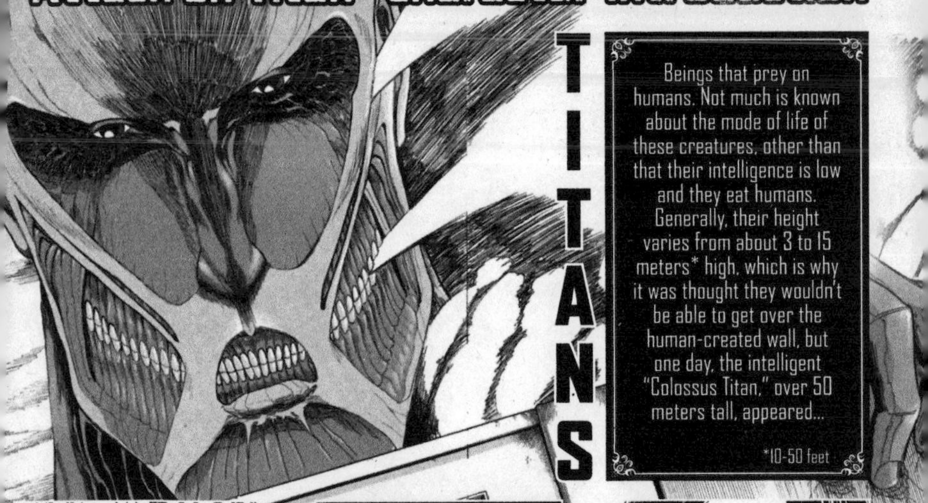

TITANS

Beings that prey on humans. Not much is known about the mode of life of these creatures, other than that their intelligence is low and they eat humans. Generally, their height varies from about 3 to 15 meters* high, which is why it was thought they wouldn't be able to get over the human-created wall, but one day, the intelligent "Colossus Titan," over 50 meters tall, appeared...

*10-50 feet

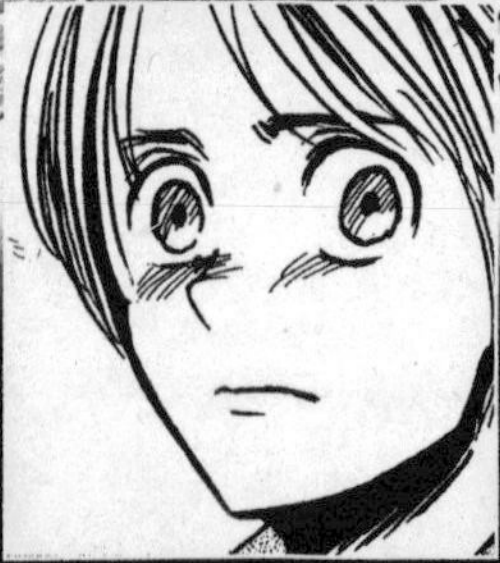

Armin Arlert
Eren and Mikasa's childhood friend. Armin is physically weak and feels that his two friends have protected him since they were children.

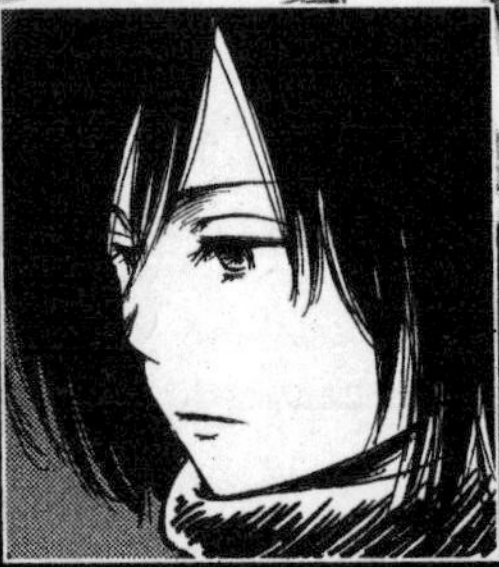

Mikasa Ackerman
Mikasa graduated at the top of her training corps. Her parents were murdered before her eyes when she was a child. Afterward, she was raised alongside Eren, whom she tenaciously tries to protect.

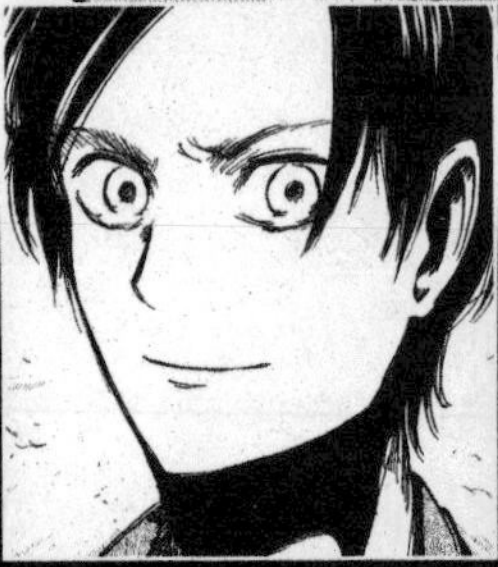

Eren Yeager
Longing for the world outside the wall, Eren aims to join the Survey Corps. For some reason, he is now able to turn himself into a Titan.

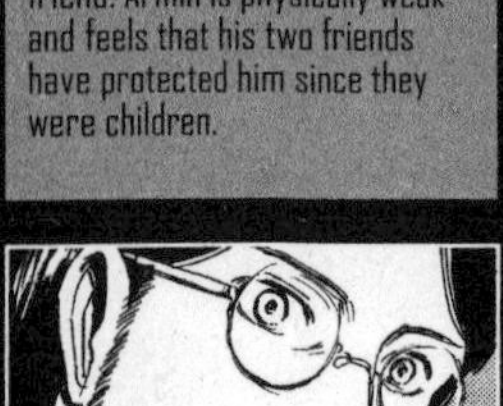

Grisha Yeager
A doctor and Eren's father. He went missing after the Titan attack five years ago.

A century ago, the human race built three secure concentric walls, each over 50 meters tall.* This successfully secured a safe, Titan-free territory for humans. However, five years ago, a huge Titan, taller than the outer wall, suddenly appeared. After it broke through the wall, many smaller Titans found their way in, forcing the humans to abandon their outer wall. Currently, the sphere of activity of the human race has been reduced to the area behind the second wall, "Wall Rose."

* 164 feet

Episode 14: Primitive Desire

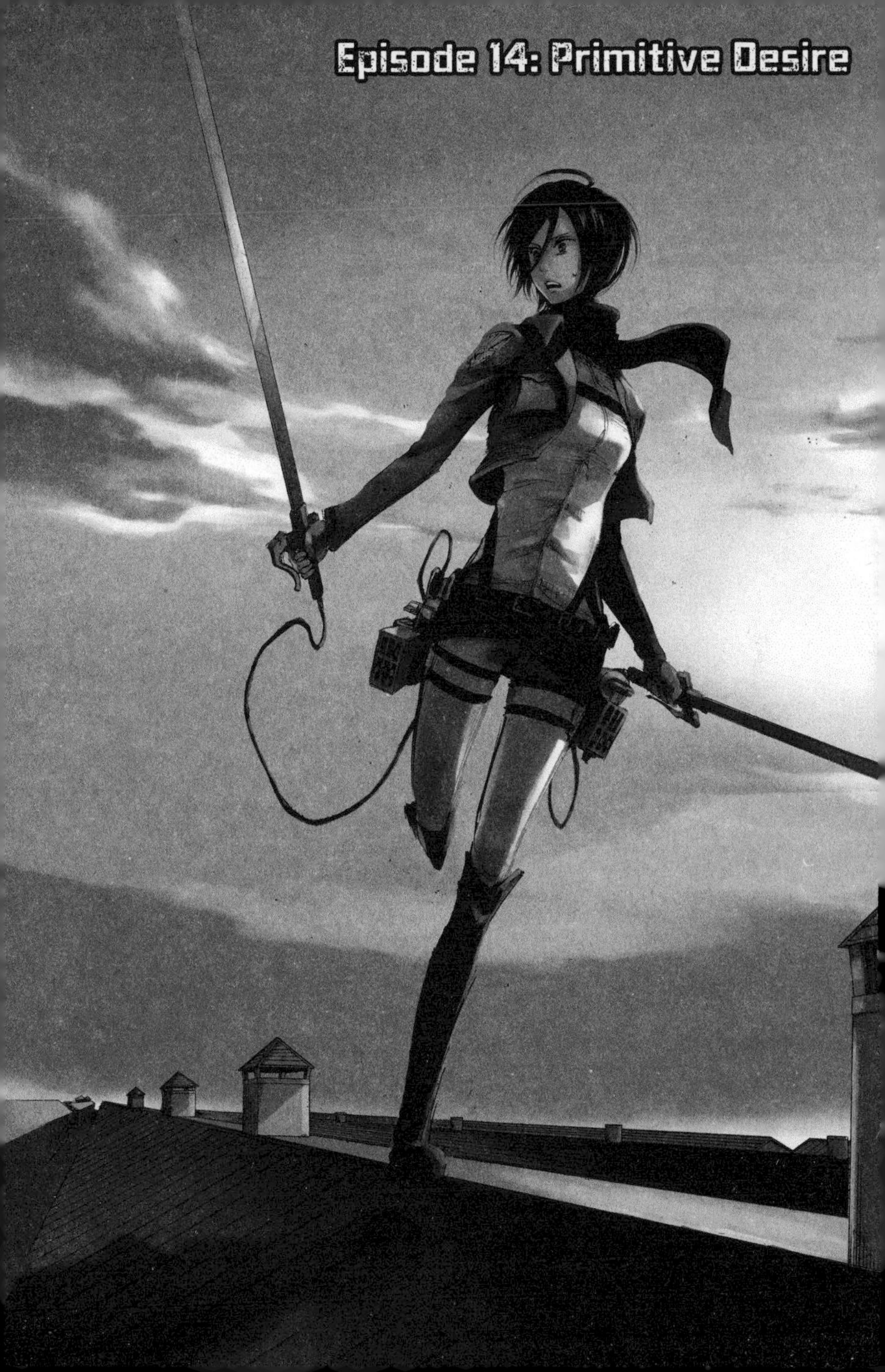

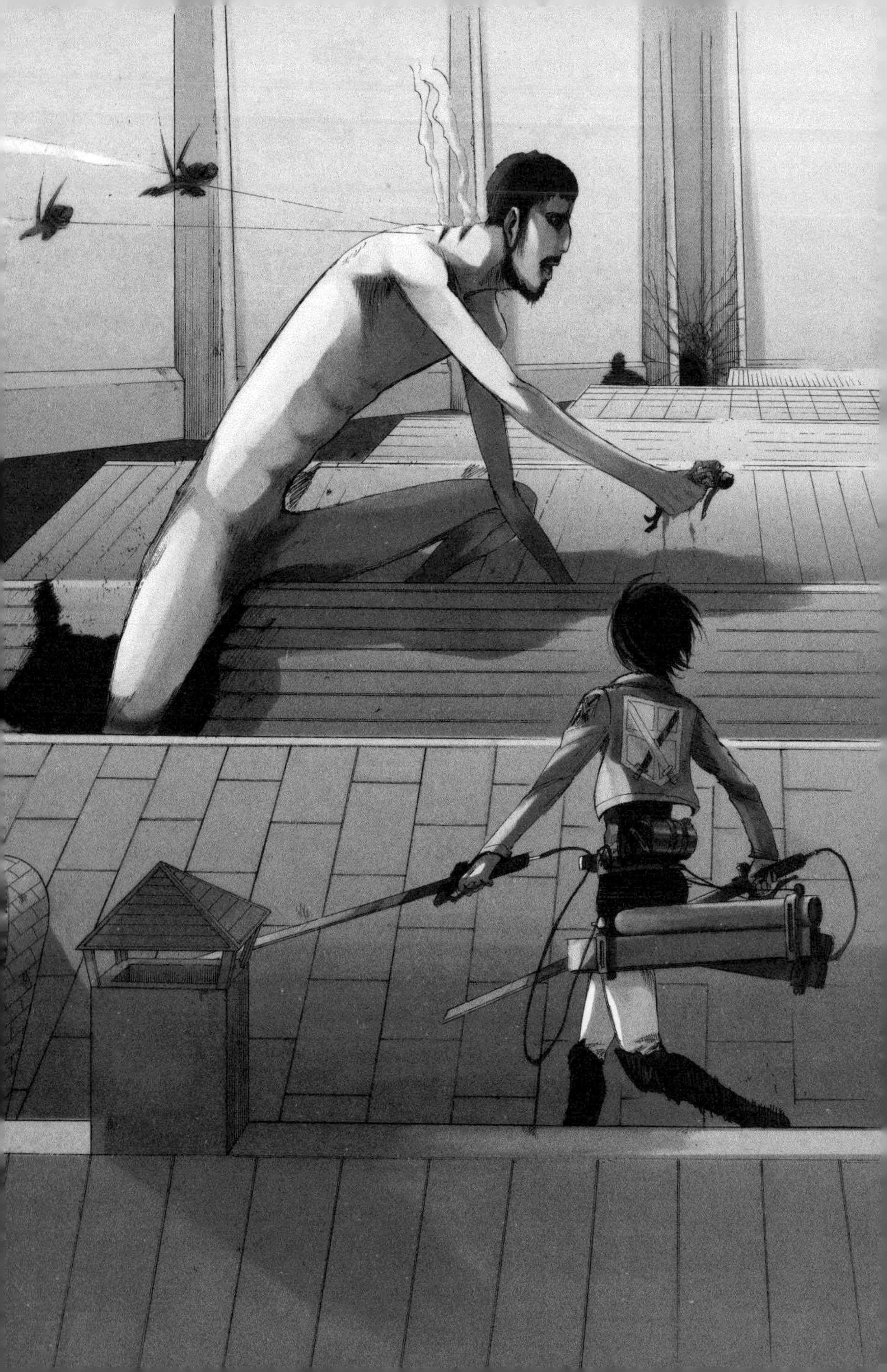

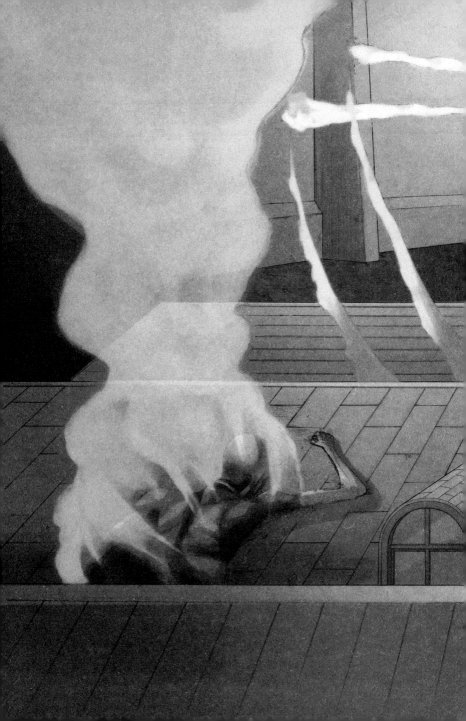

ATTACK on TITAN

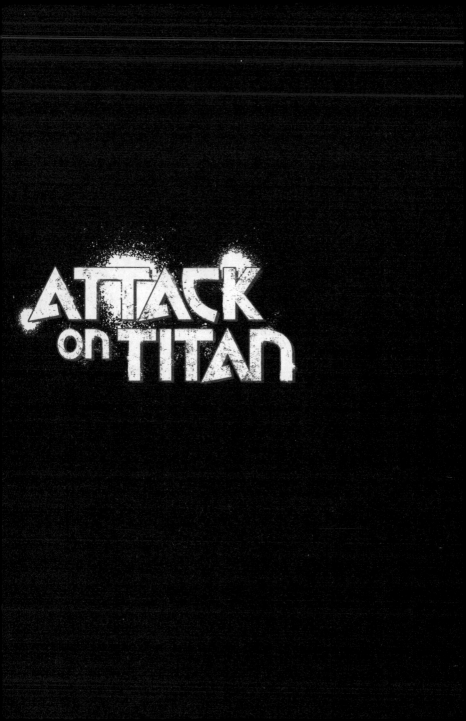

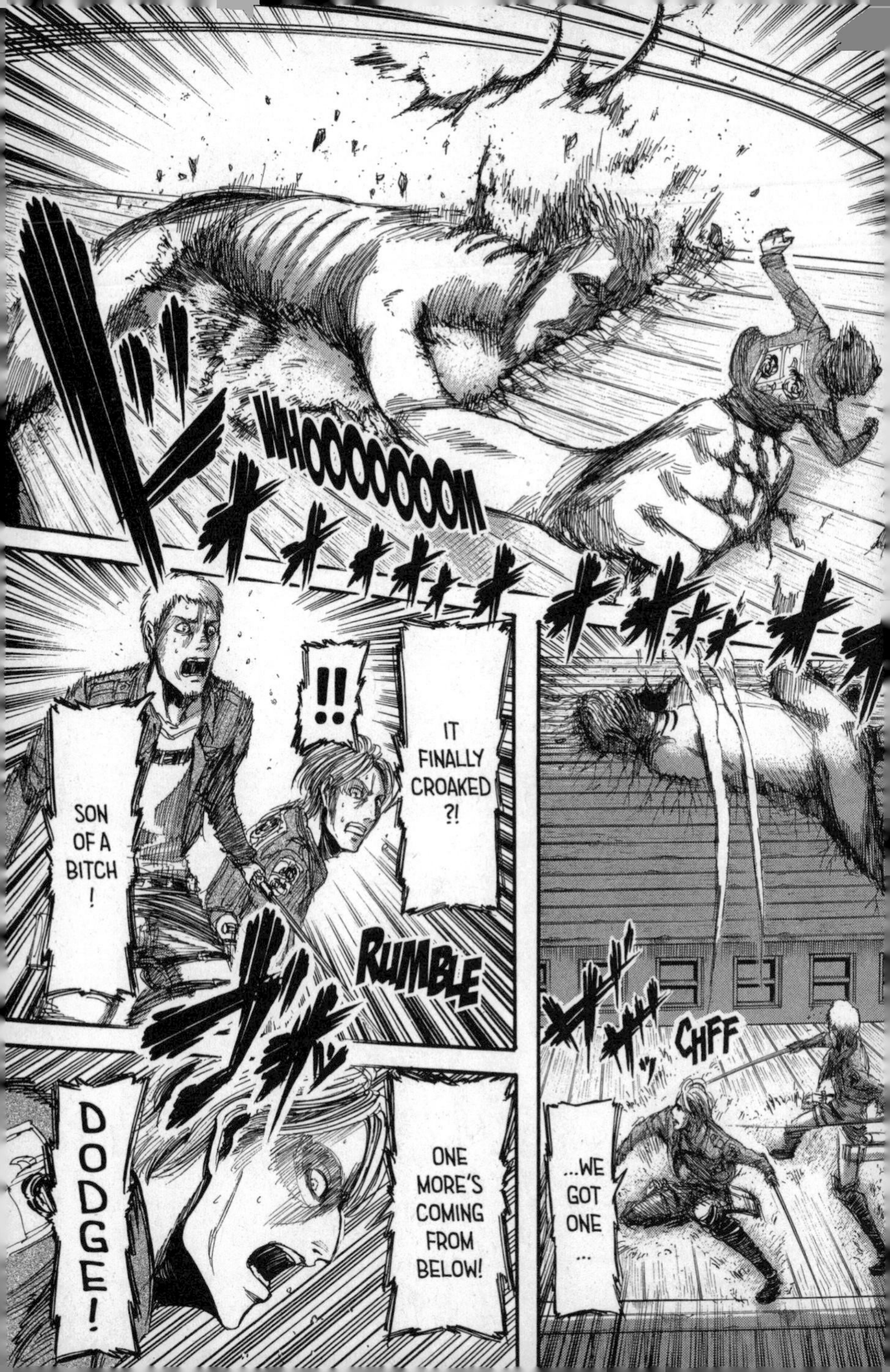
WHOOOOOOOM
CHFF
...WE GOT ONE...
!!
IT FINALLY CROAKED?!
SON OF A BITCH!
RUMBLE
ONE MORE'S COMING FROM BELOW!
DODGE!

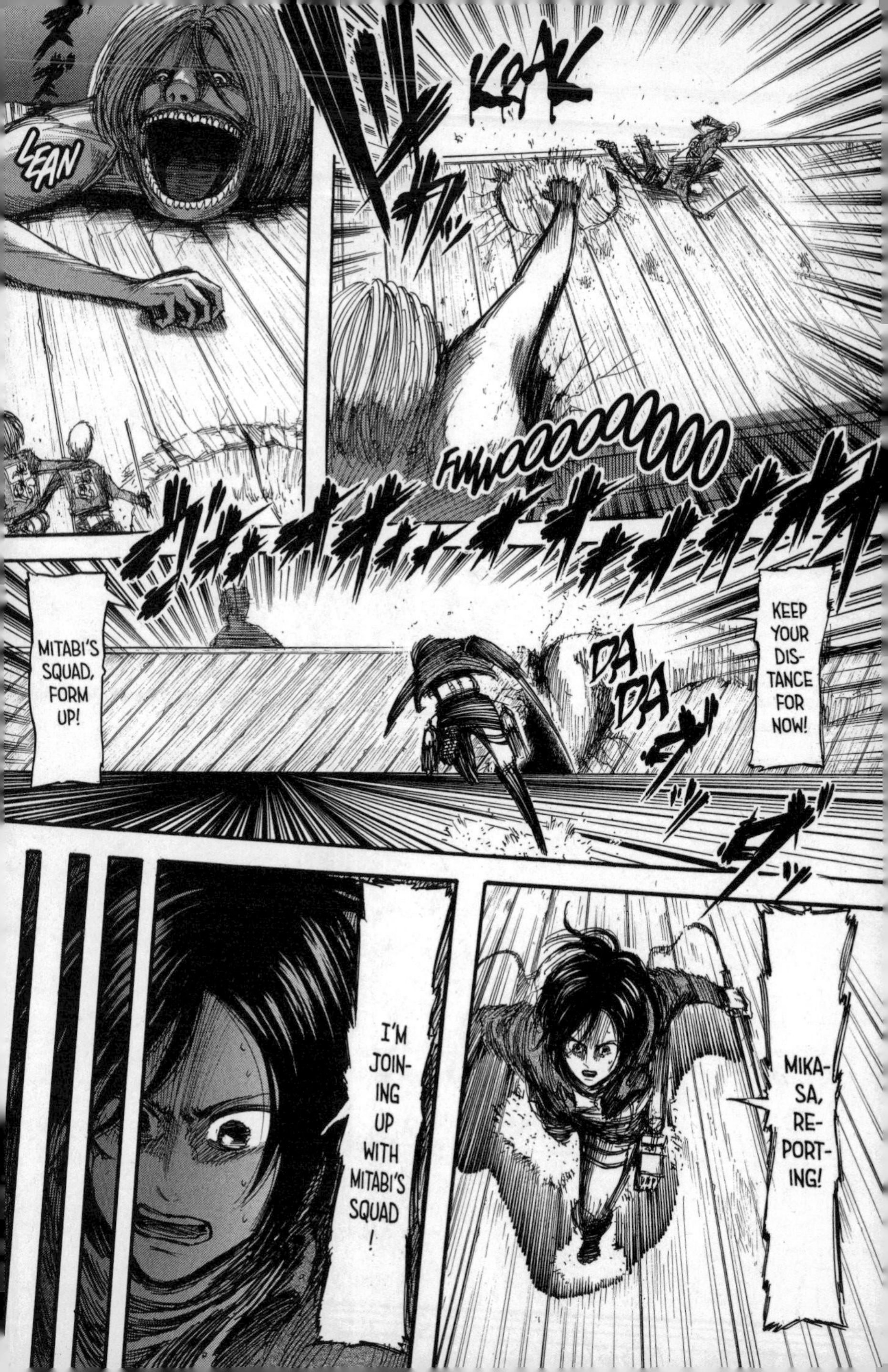
KRAK
FUWOOOOOOOOOO
LEAN
KEEP YOUR DIS-TANCE FOR NOW!
DA DA
MITABI'S SQUAD, FORM UP!
MIKA-SA, RE-PORT-ING!
I'M JOIN-ING UP WITH MITABI'S SQUAD!

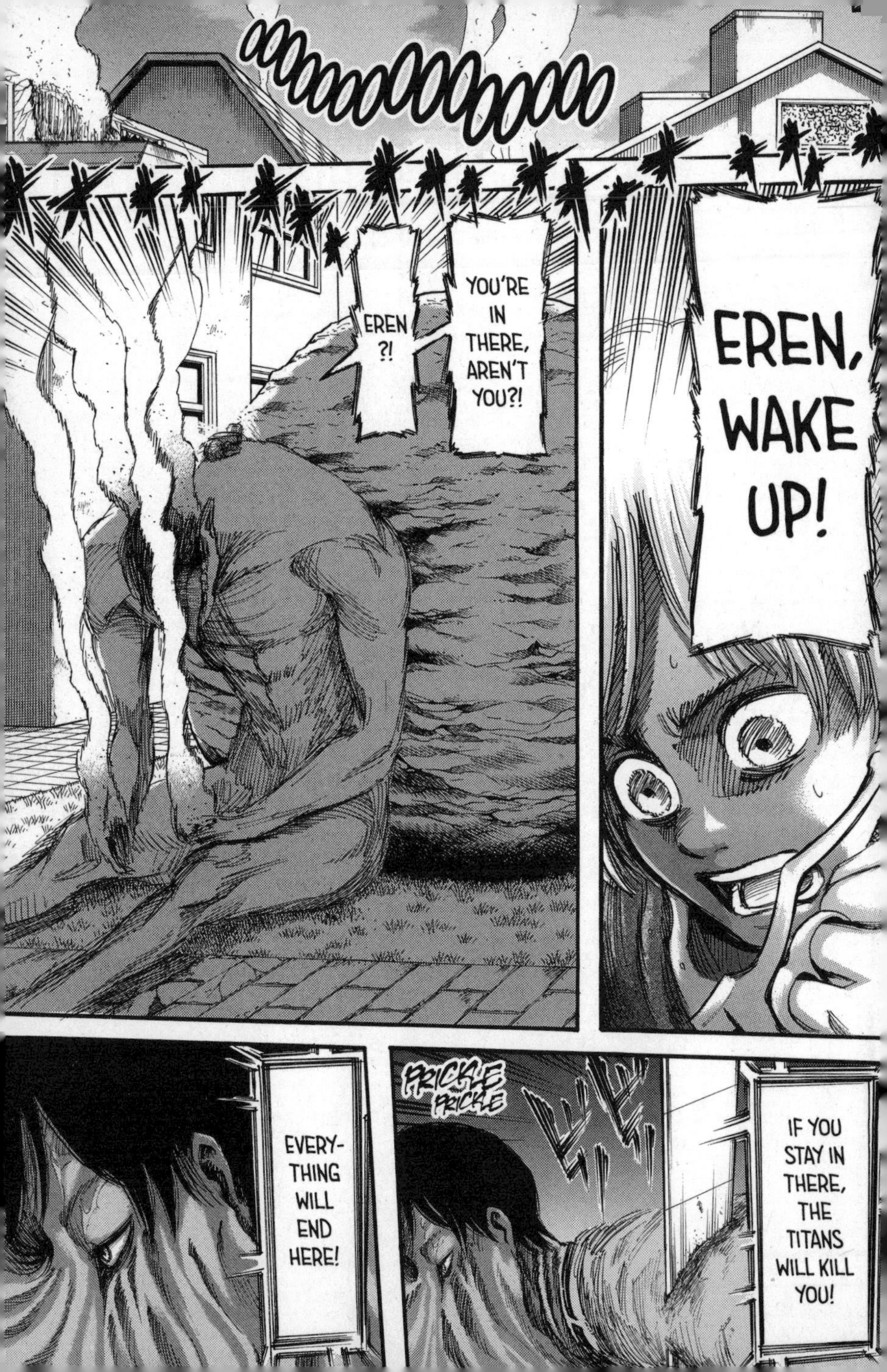
EREN, WAKE UP!
OOOOOOOOOOOOOOOO
YOU'RE IN THERE, AREN'T YOU?!
EREN ?!
PRICKLE PRICKLE
IF YOU STAY IN THERE, THE TITANS WILL KILL YOU!
EVERY-THING WILL END HERE!

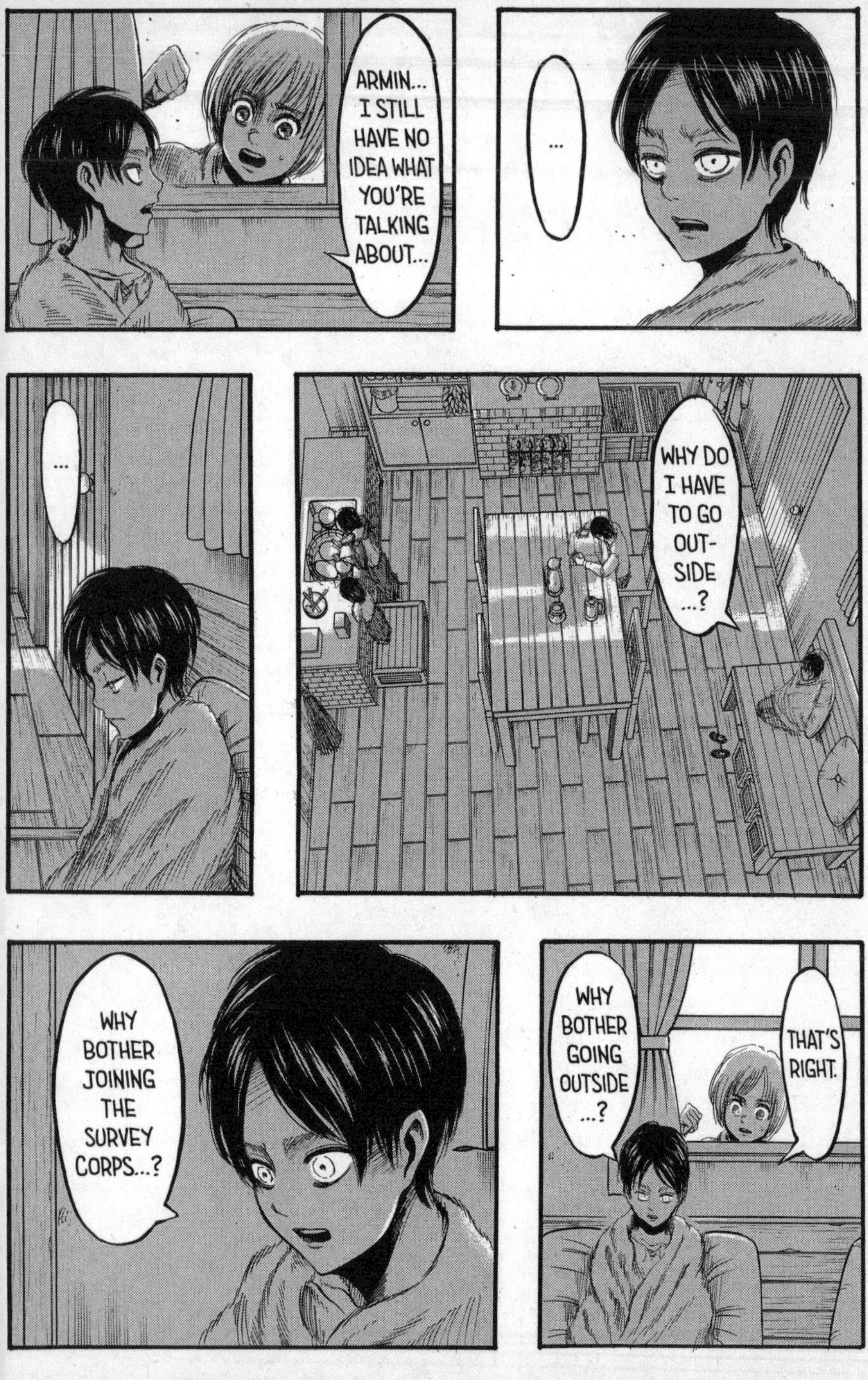
...
ARMIN... I STILL HAVE NO IDEA WHAT YOU'RE TALKING ABOUT...
WHY DO I HAVE TO GO OUT-SIDE ...?
...
THAT'S RIGHT.
WHY BOTHER GOING OUTSIDE ...?
WHY BOTHER JOINING THE SURVEY CORPS...?

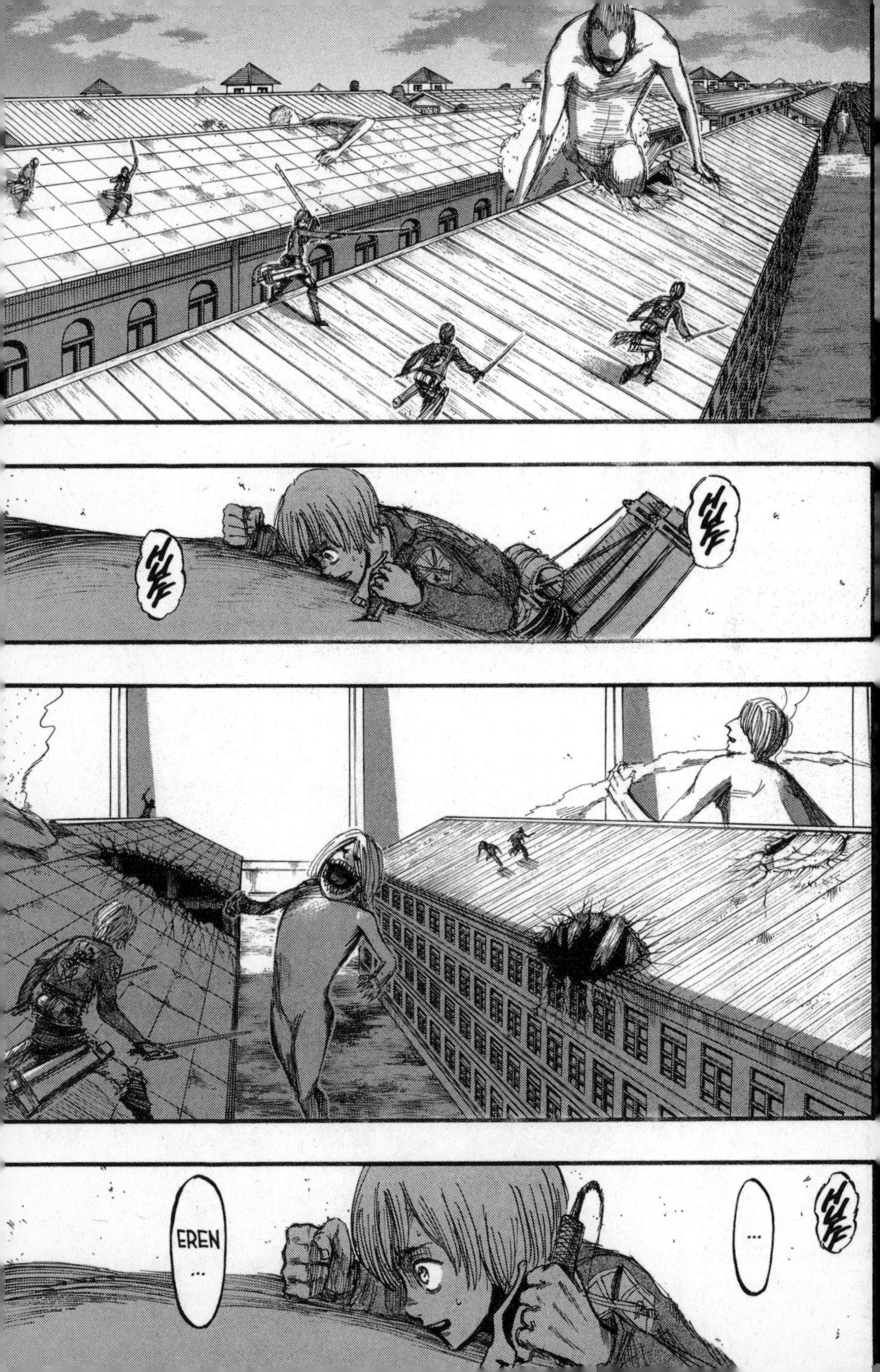
HUFF
HUFF
HUFF
...
EREN ...

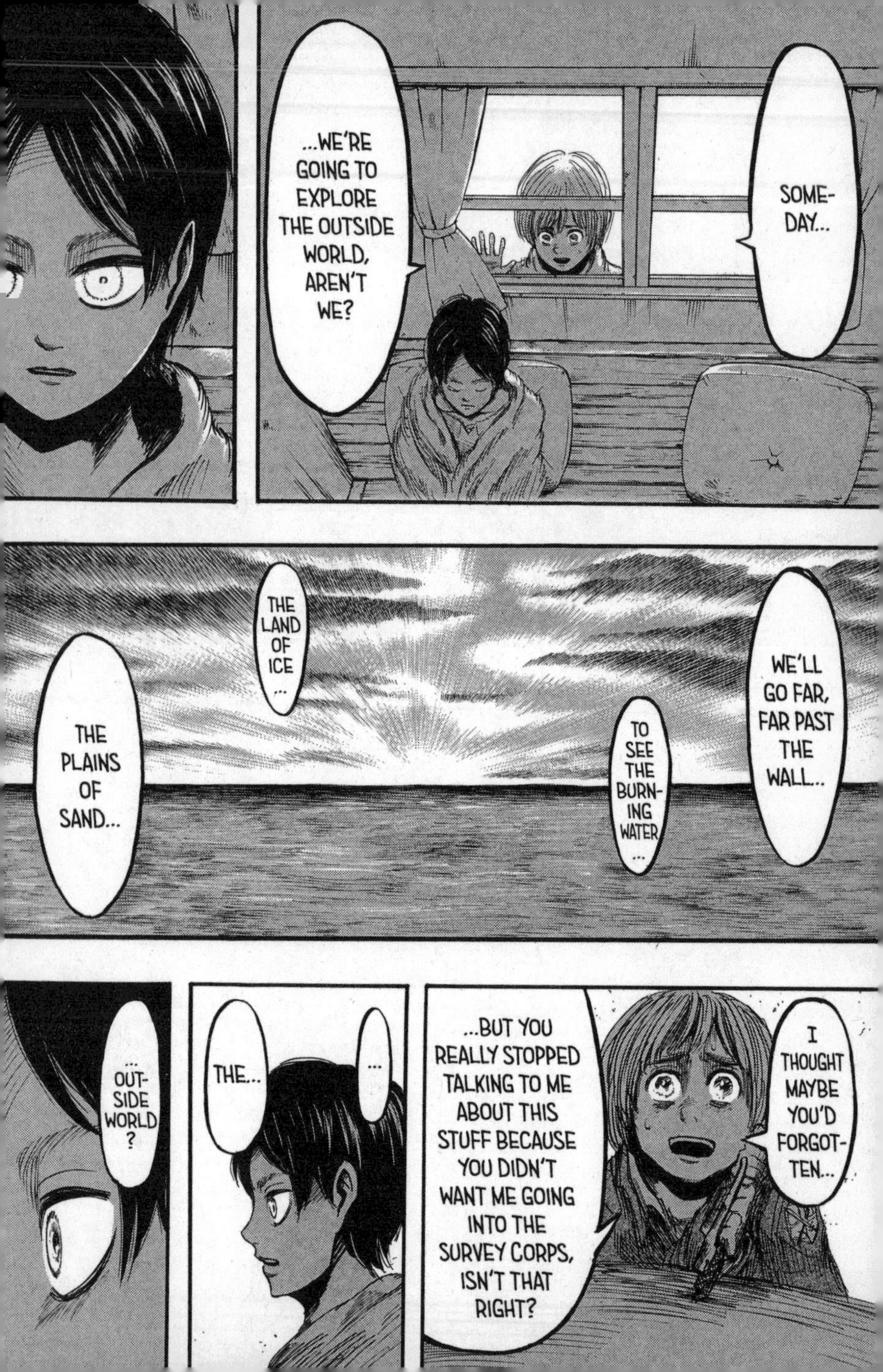
SOMEDAY...
...WE'RE GOING TO EXPLORE THE OUTSIDE WORLD, AREN'T WE?
WE'LL GO FAR, FAR PAST THE WALL...
TO SEE THE BURNING WATER...
THE LAND OF ICE...
THE PLAINS OF SAND...
I THOUGHT MAYBE YOU'D FORGOTTEN...
...BUT YOU REALLY STOPPED TALKING TO ME ABOUT THIS STUFF BECAUSE YOU DIDN'T WANT ME GOING INTO THE SURVEY CORPS, ISN'T THAT RIGHT?
...
THE...
...OUTSIDE WORLD?

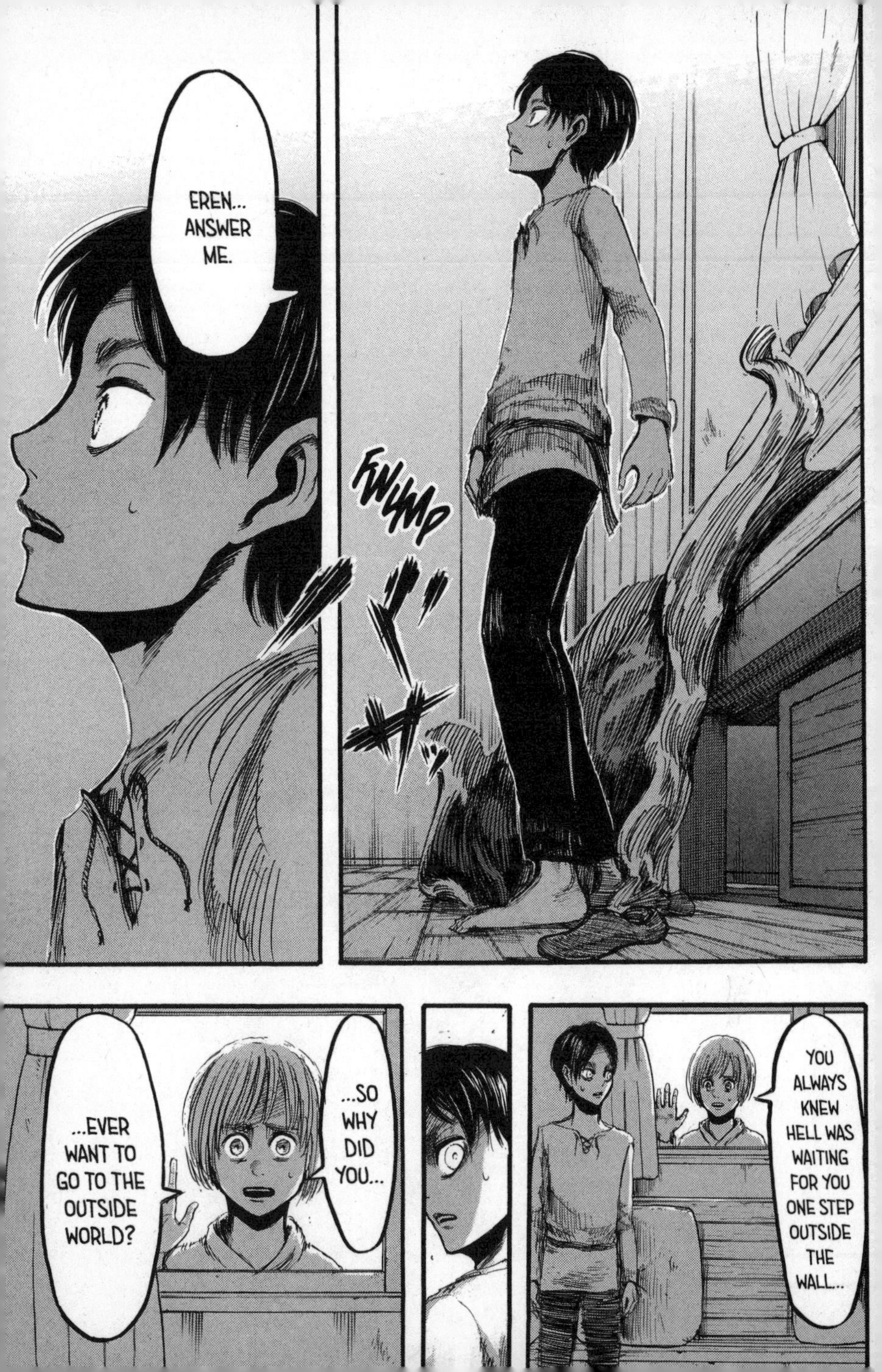
FWUMP
EREN... ANSWER ME.
YOU ALWAYS KNEW HELL WAS WAITING FOR YOU ONE STEP OUTSIDE THE WALL...
...SO WHY DID YOU...
...EVER WANT TO GO TO THE OUTSIDE WORLD?

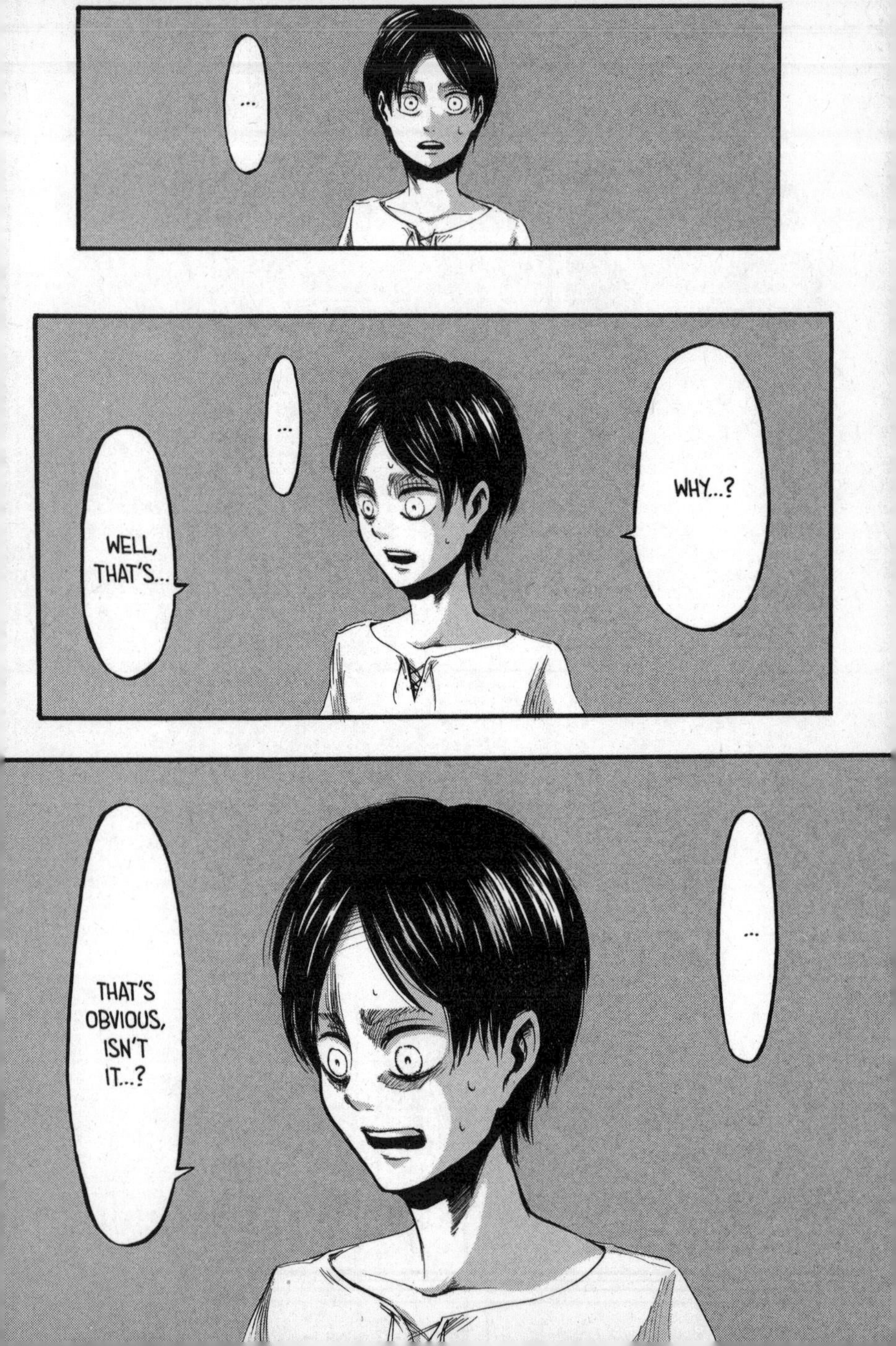
...
WHY...?
...
WELL, THAT'S...
...
THAT'S OBVIOUS, ISN'T IT...?

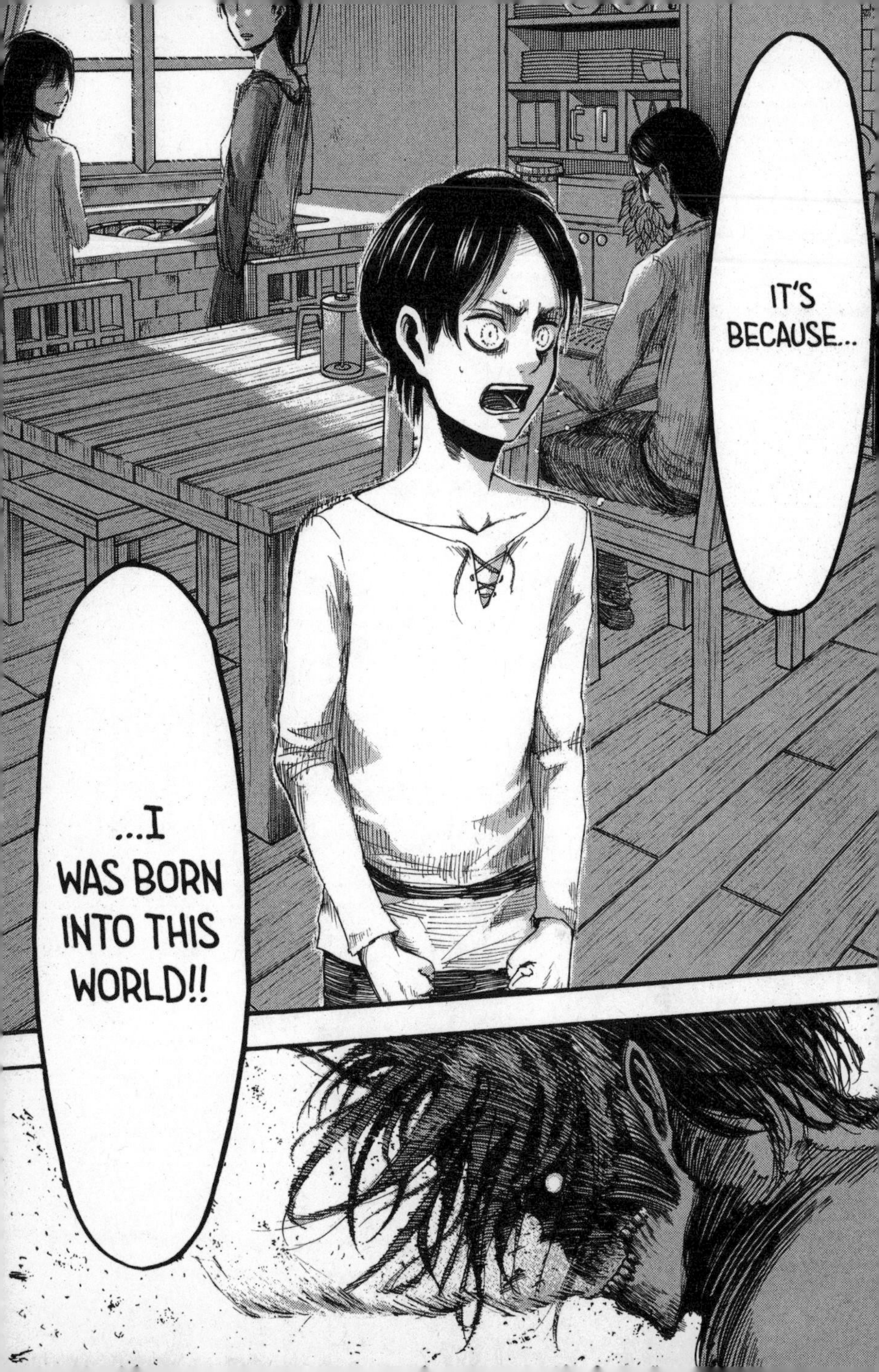
IT'S BECAUSE...
...I WAS BORN INTO THIS WORLD!!

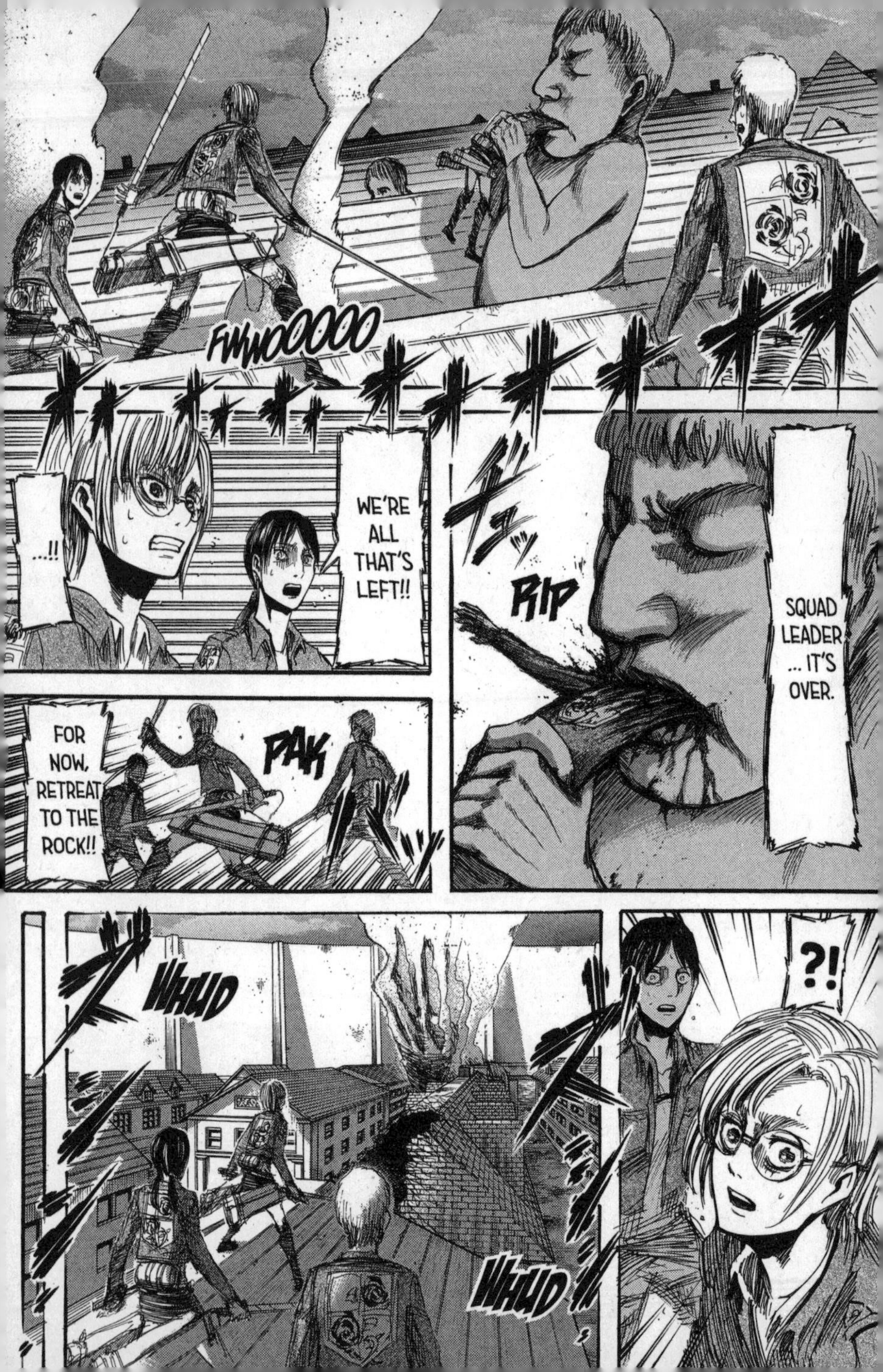

FWOOOOO
RIP
SQUAD LEADER ... IT'S OVER.
WE'RE ALL THAT'S LEFT!!
...!!
FOR NOW, RETREAT TO THE ROCK!!
PAK
?!
WHUD
WHUD

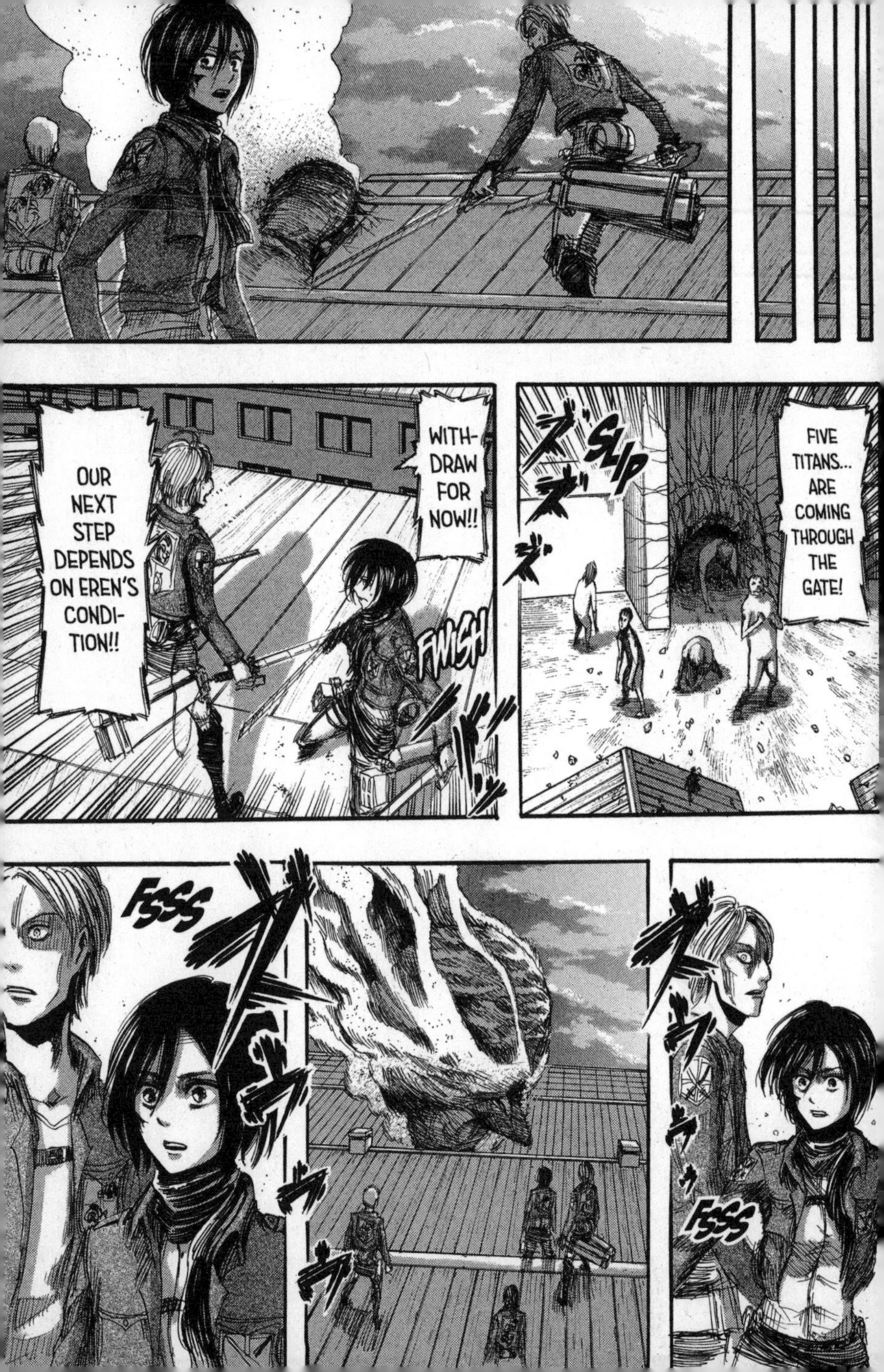
SLIP
FIVE TITANS... ARE COMING THROUGH THE GATE!
WITH-DRAW FOR NOW!!
OUR NEXT STEP DEPENDS ON EREN'S CONDI-TION!!
FWISH
FSSS
FSSS

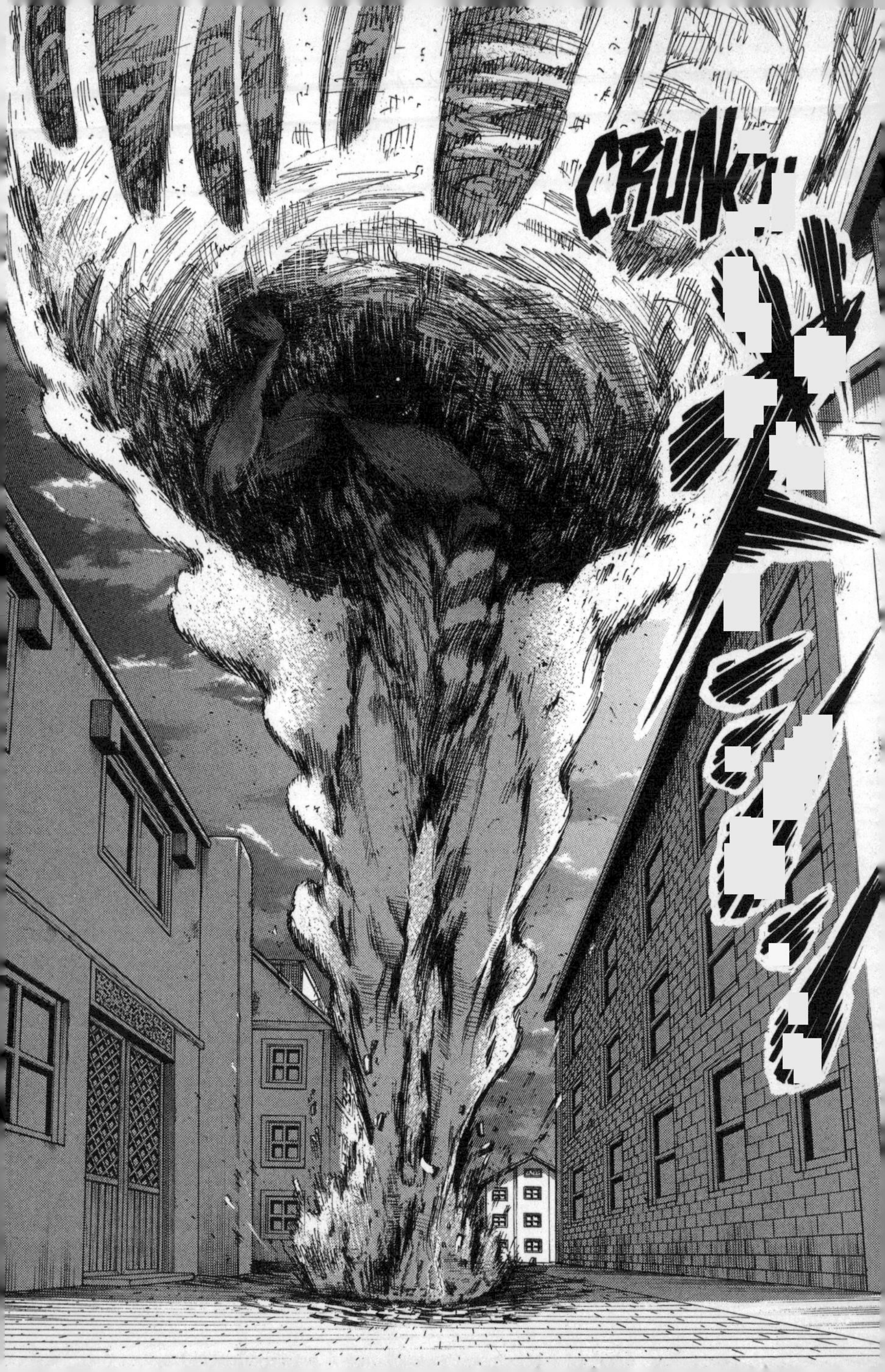
CRUNK

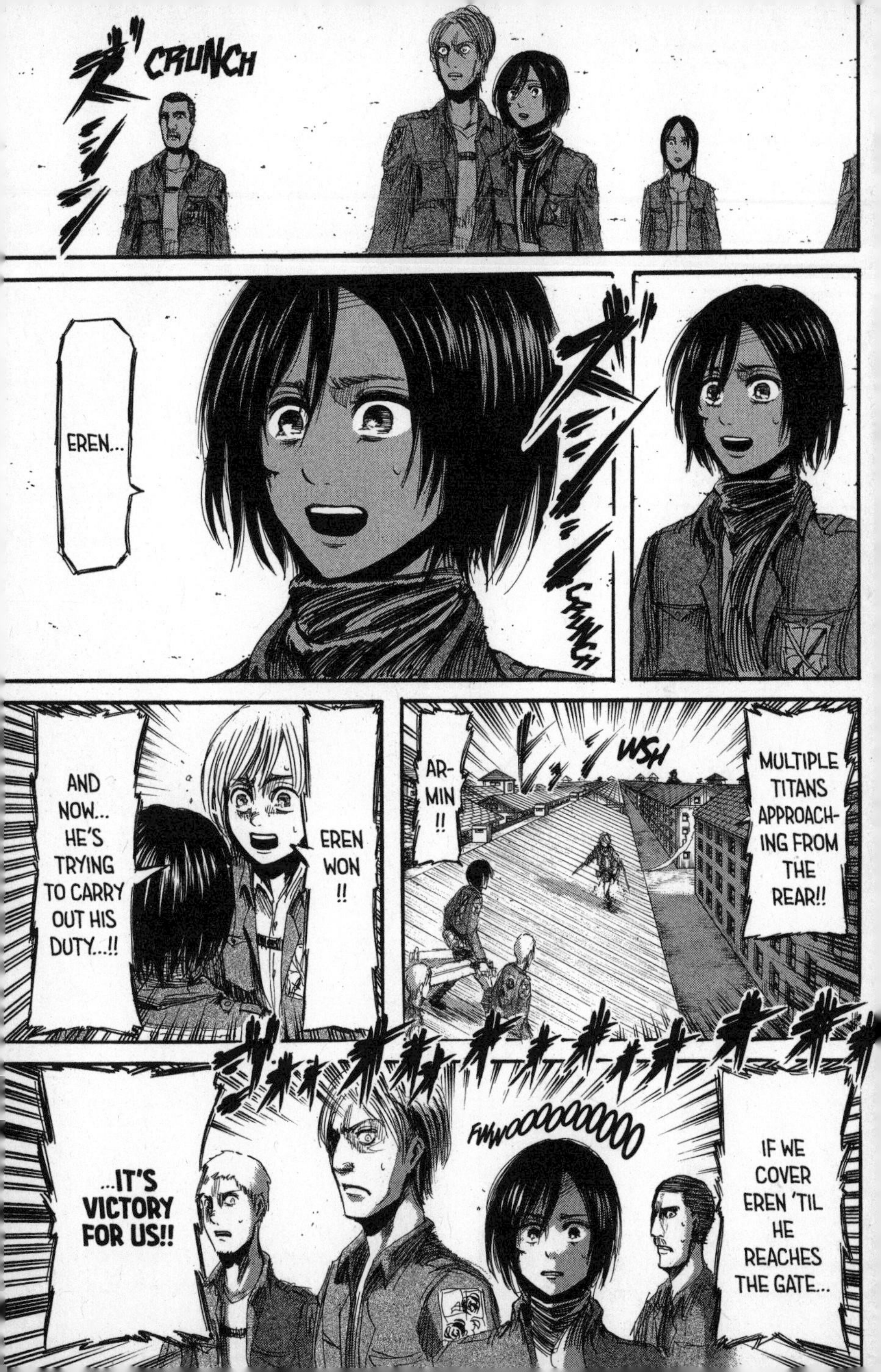
CRUNCH
CRUNCH
EREN...
MULTIPLE TITANS APPROACHING FROM THE REAR!!
WSH
ARMIN!!
EREN WON!!
AND NOW... HE'S TRYING TO CARRY OUT HIS DUTY...!!
FWWOOOOOOOOOO
IF WE COVER EREN 'TIL HE REACHES THE GATE...
...IT'S VICTORY FOR US!!

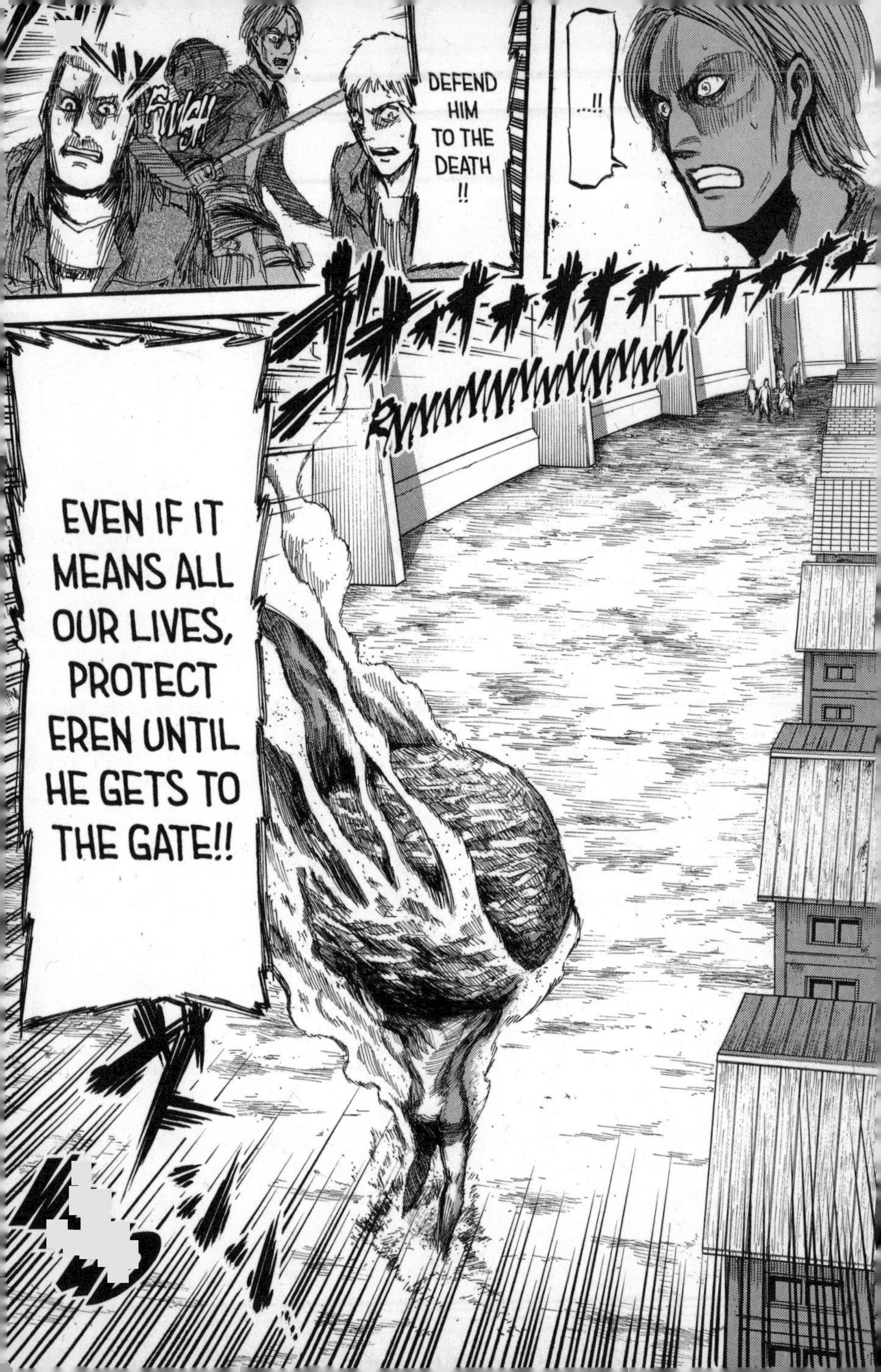
DEFEND HIM TO THE DEATH !!
...!!
FWSH
EVEN IF IT MEANS ALL OUR LIVES, PROTECT EREN UNTIL HE GETS TO THE GATE!!
RMMMMMMMMMMMMM

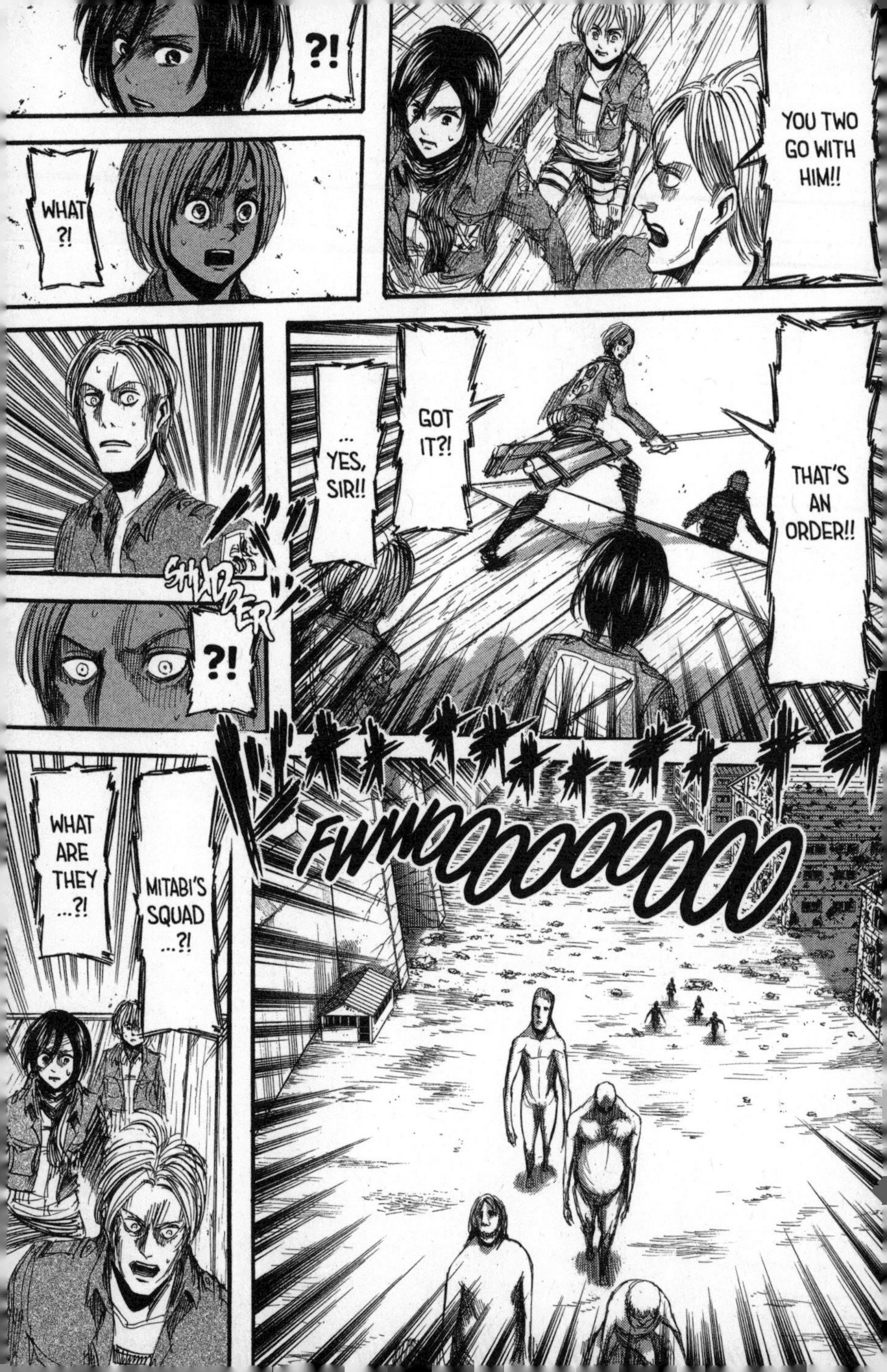
YOU TWO GO WITH HIM!!
?!
WHAT ?!
THAT'S AN ORDER!!
GOT IT?!
... YES, SIR!!
SHUDDER
?!
FWOOOOOOOOOO
MITABI'S SQUAD ...?!
WHAT ARE THEY ...?!

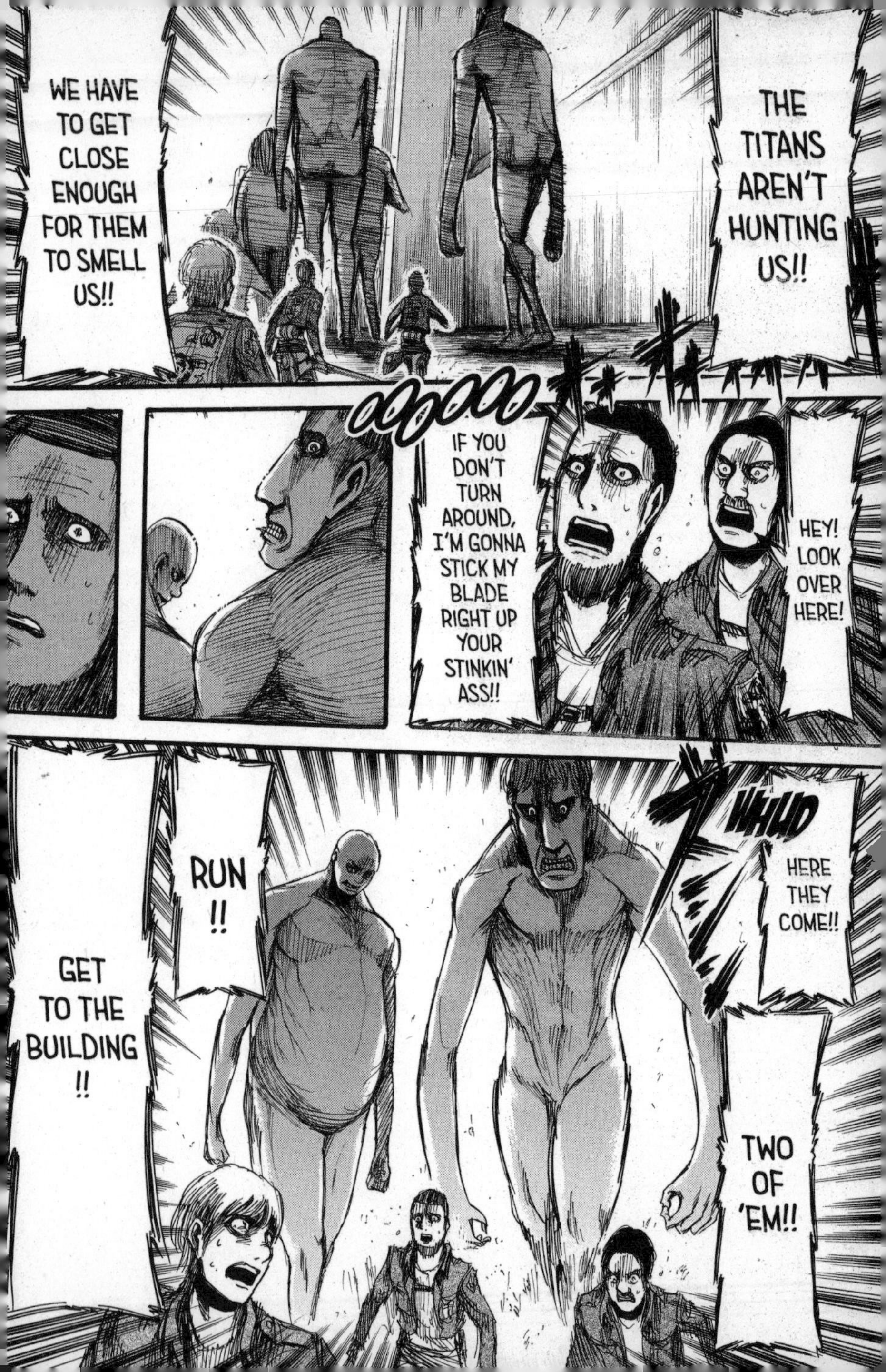
THE TITANS AREN'T HUNTING US!!
WE HAVE TO GET CLOSE ENOUGH FOR THEM TO SMELL US!!
HEY! LOOK OVER HERE!
IF YOU DON'T TURN AROUND, I'M GONNA STICK MY BLADE RIGHT UP YOUR STINKIN' ASS!!
HERE THEY COME!!
TWO OF 'EM!!
RUN !!
GET TO THE BUILDING !!

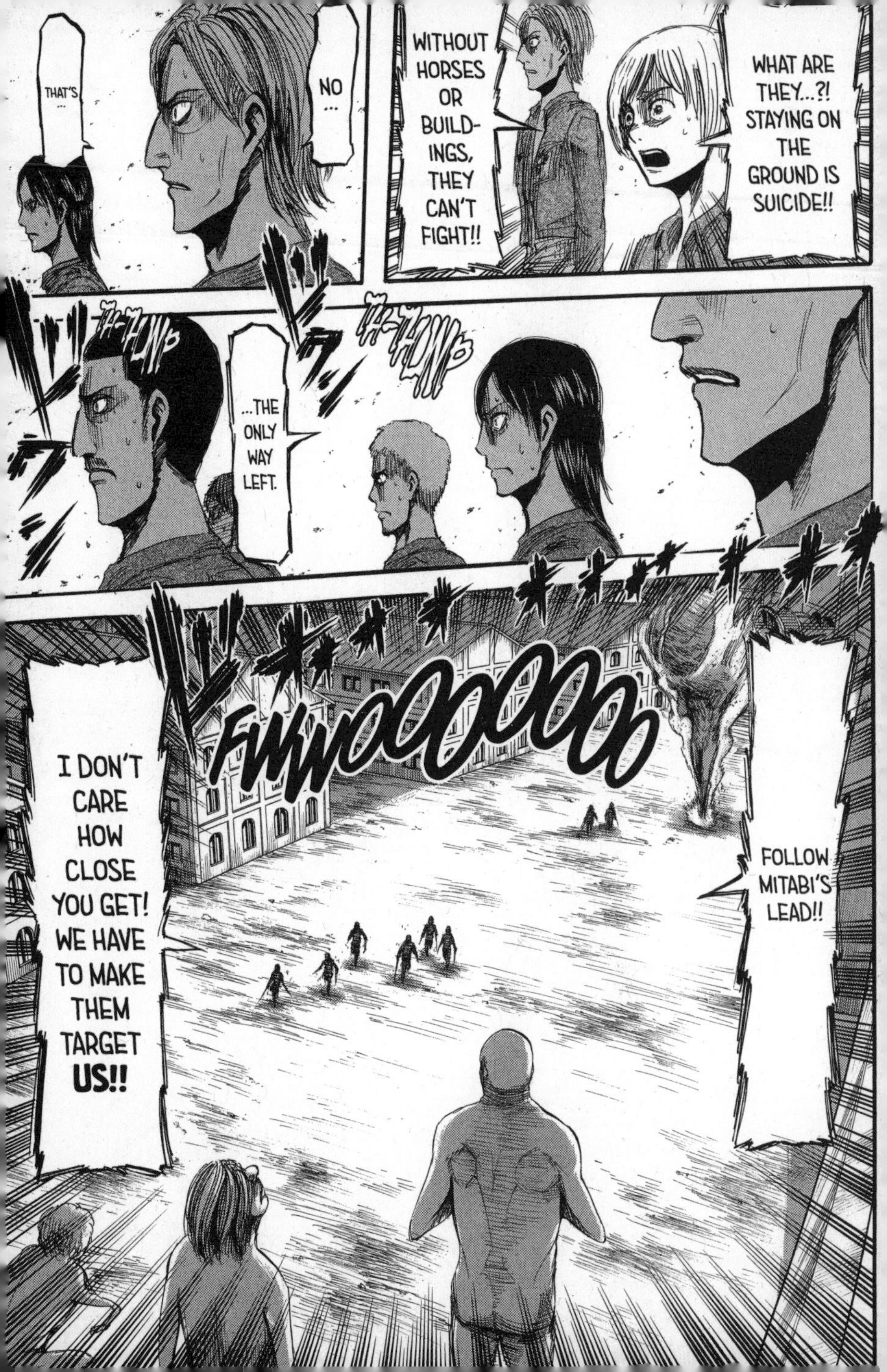
WHAT ARE THEY...?! STAYING ON THE GROUND IS SUICIDE!!
WITHOUT HORSES OR BUILD-INGS, THEY CAN'T FIGHT!!
NO ...
THAT'S ...
...THE ONLY WAY LEFT.
FWOOOOOOO
FOLLOW MITABI'S LEAD!!
I DON'T CARE HOW CLOSE YOU GET! WE HAVE TO MAKE THEM TARGET **US!!**

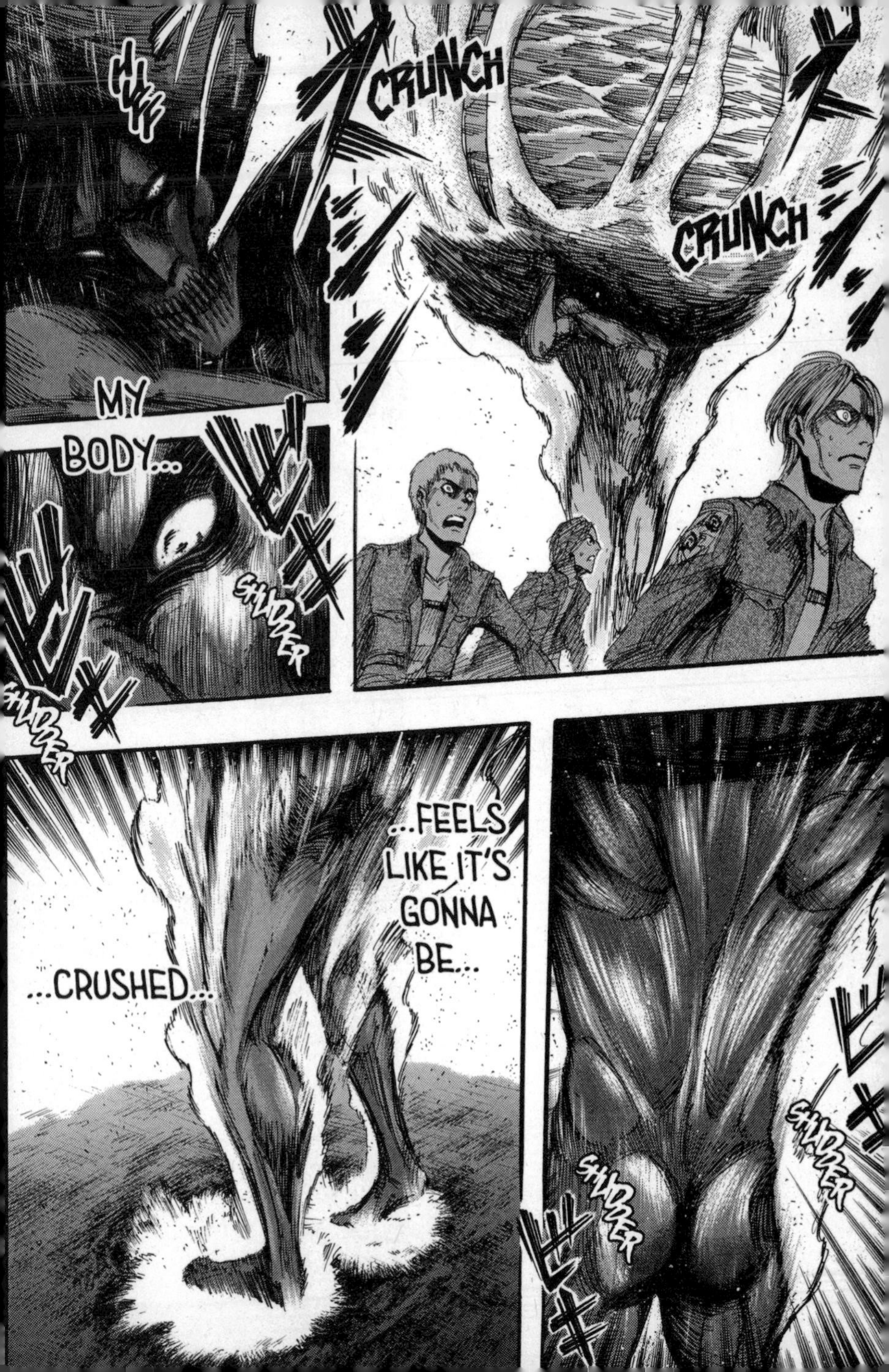
CRUNCH
CRUNCH
HUFF
MY BODY...
SHUDDER
SHUDDER
SHUDDER
SHUDDER
...FEELS LIKE IT'S GONNA BE...
...CRUSHED...

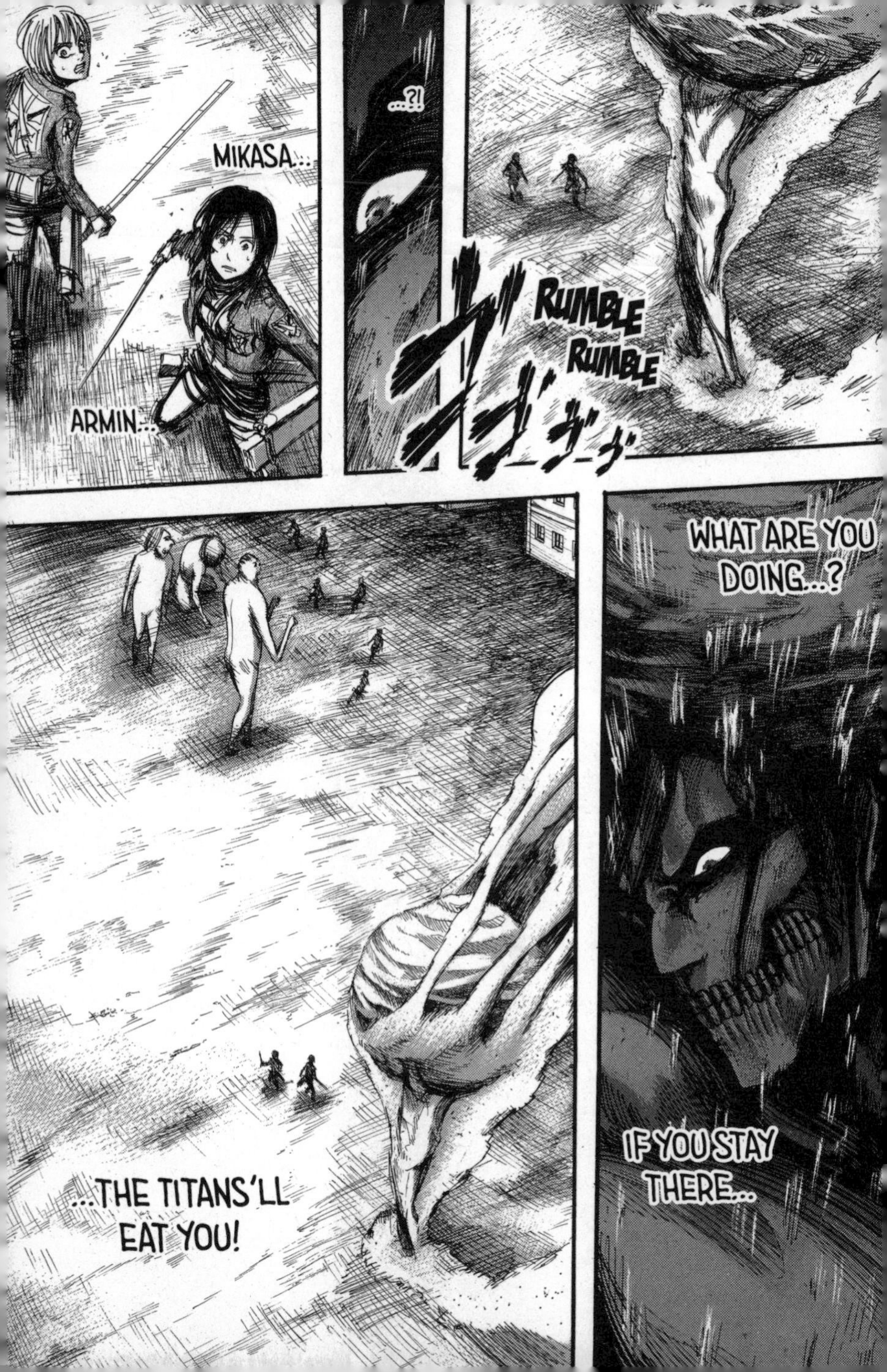
RUMBLE
RUMBLE
...?!
MIKASA...
ARMIN...
WHAT ARE YOU DOING...?
IF YOU STAY THERE...
...THE TITANS'LL EAT YOU!

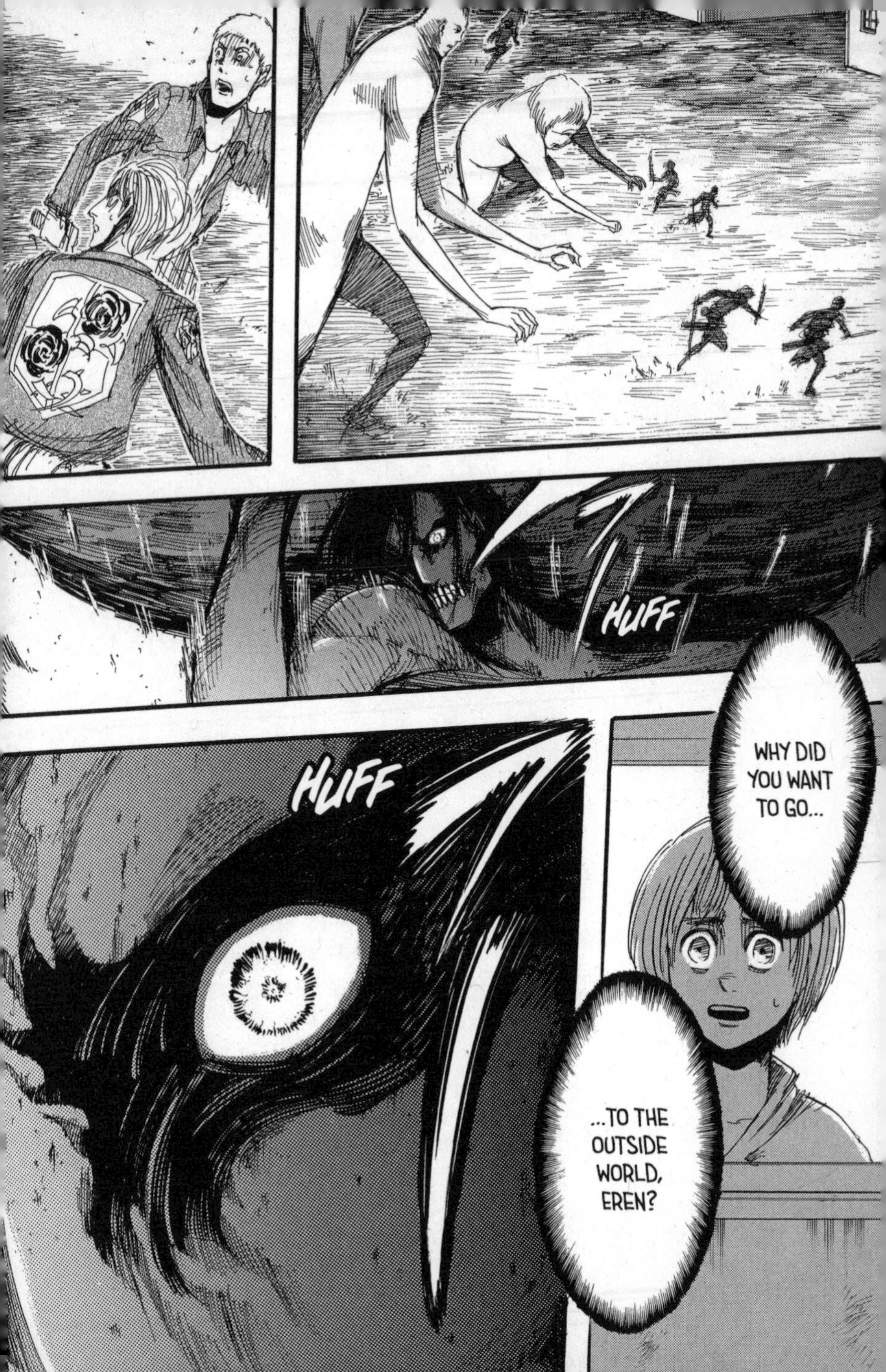
HUFF
WHY DID YOU WANT TO GO...
...TO THE OUTSIDE WORLD, EREN?
HUFF

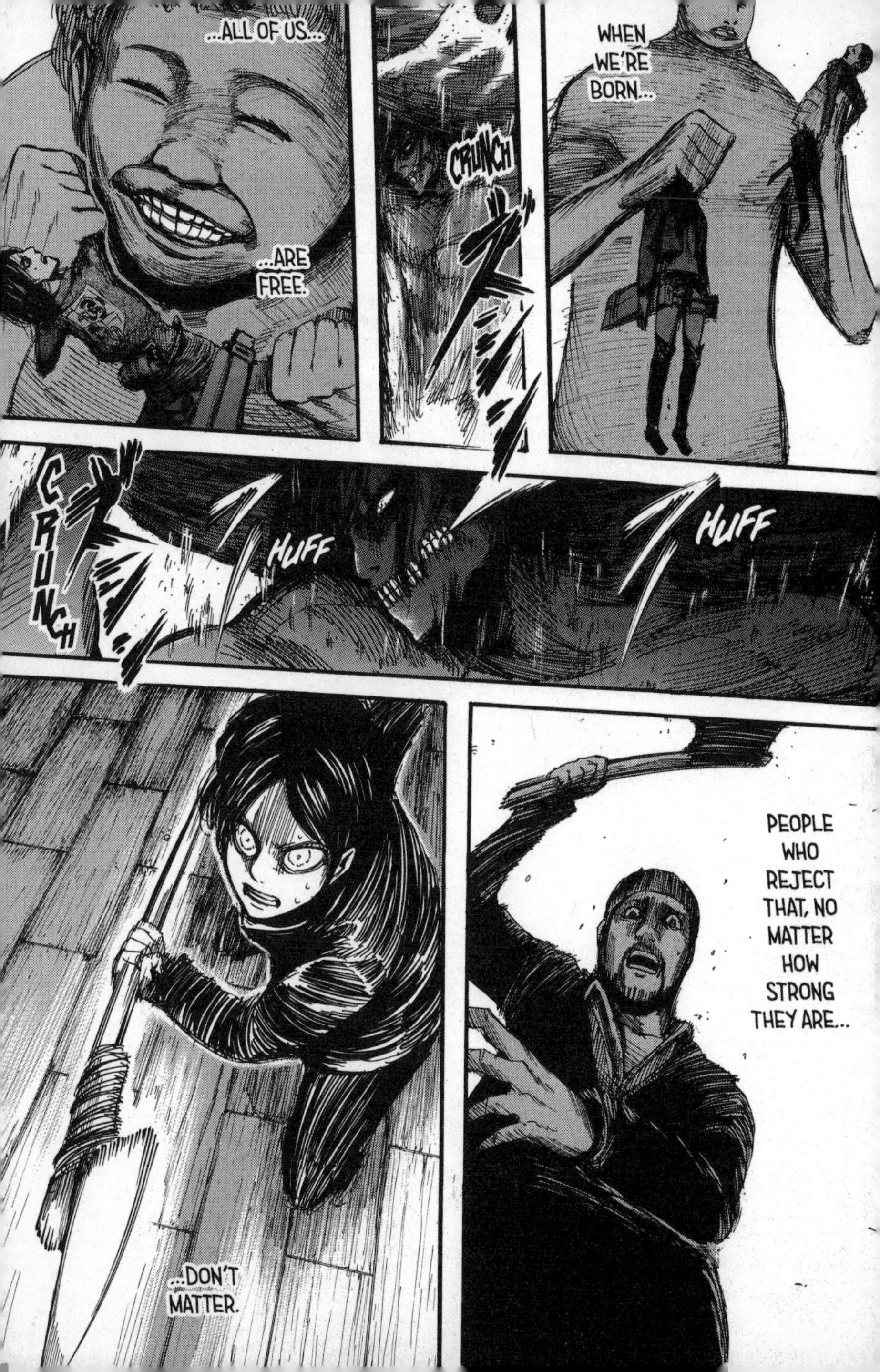
WHEN WE'RE BORN...
CRUNCH
...ALL OF US...
...ARE FREE.
HUFF
HUFF
CRUNCH
PEOPLE WHO REJECT THAT, NO MATTER HOW STRONG THEY ARE...
...DON'T MATTER.

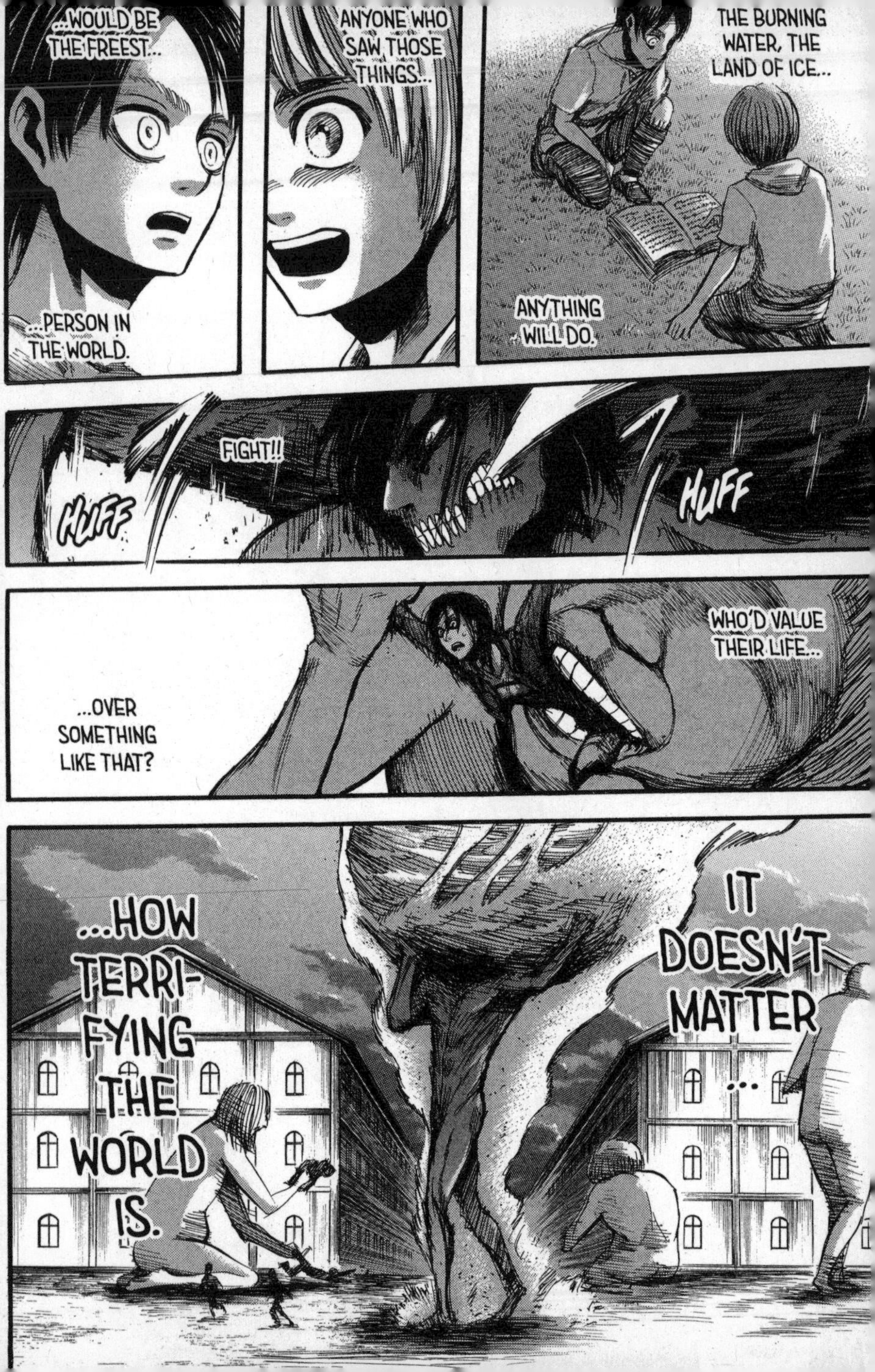
THE BURNING WATER, THE LAND OF ICE...
ANYTHING WILL DO.
ANYONE WHO SAW THOSE THINGS...
...WOULD BE THE FREEST...
...PERSON IN THE WORLD.
HUFF
FIGHT!!
HUFF
WHO'D VALUE THEIR LIFE...
...OVER SOMETHING LIKE THAT?
IT DOESN'T MATTER...
...HOW TERRI-FYING THE WORLD IS.

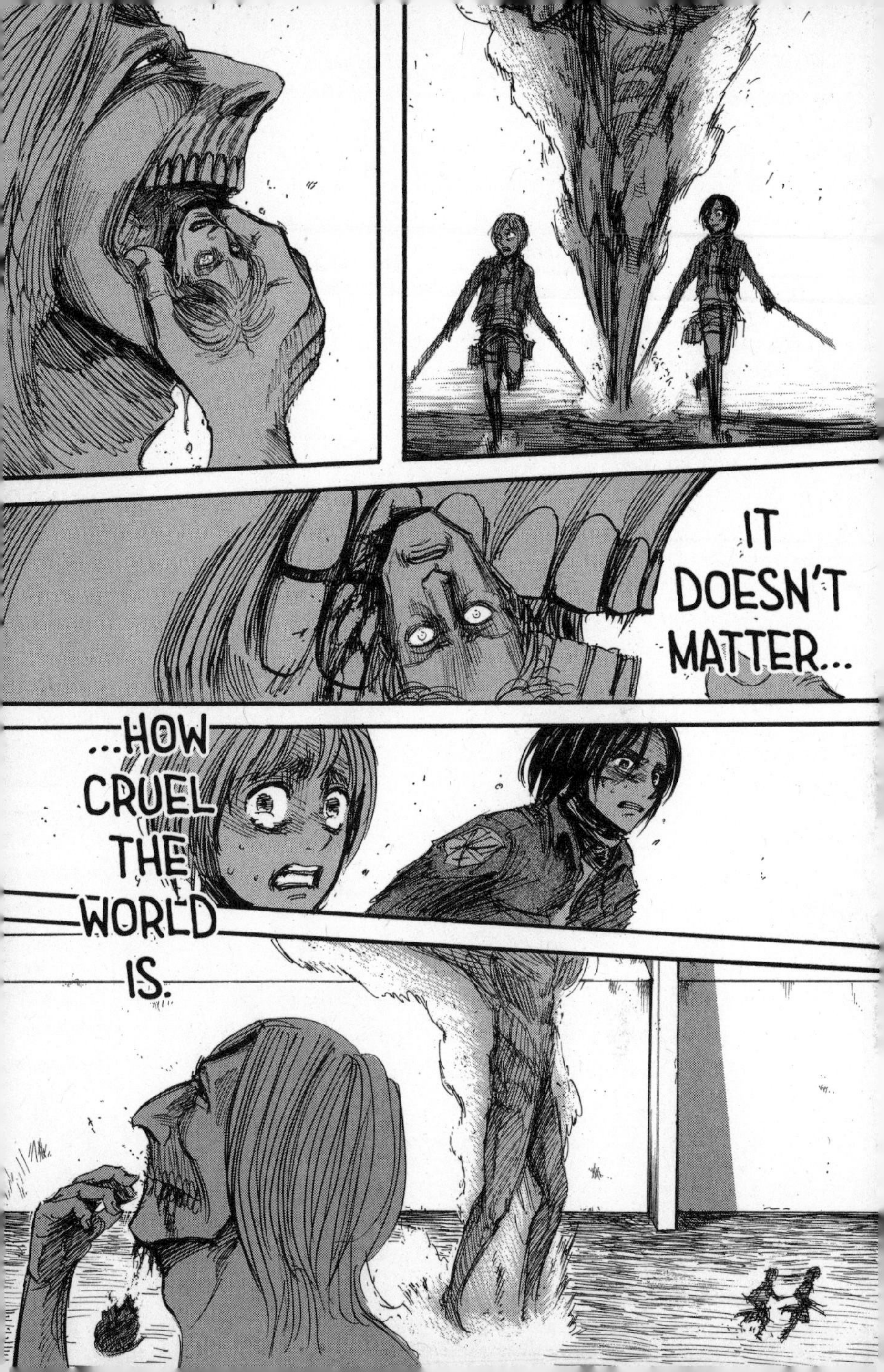
IT DOESN'T MATTER...
...HOW CRUEL THE WORLD IS.

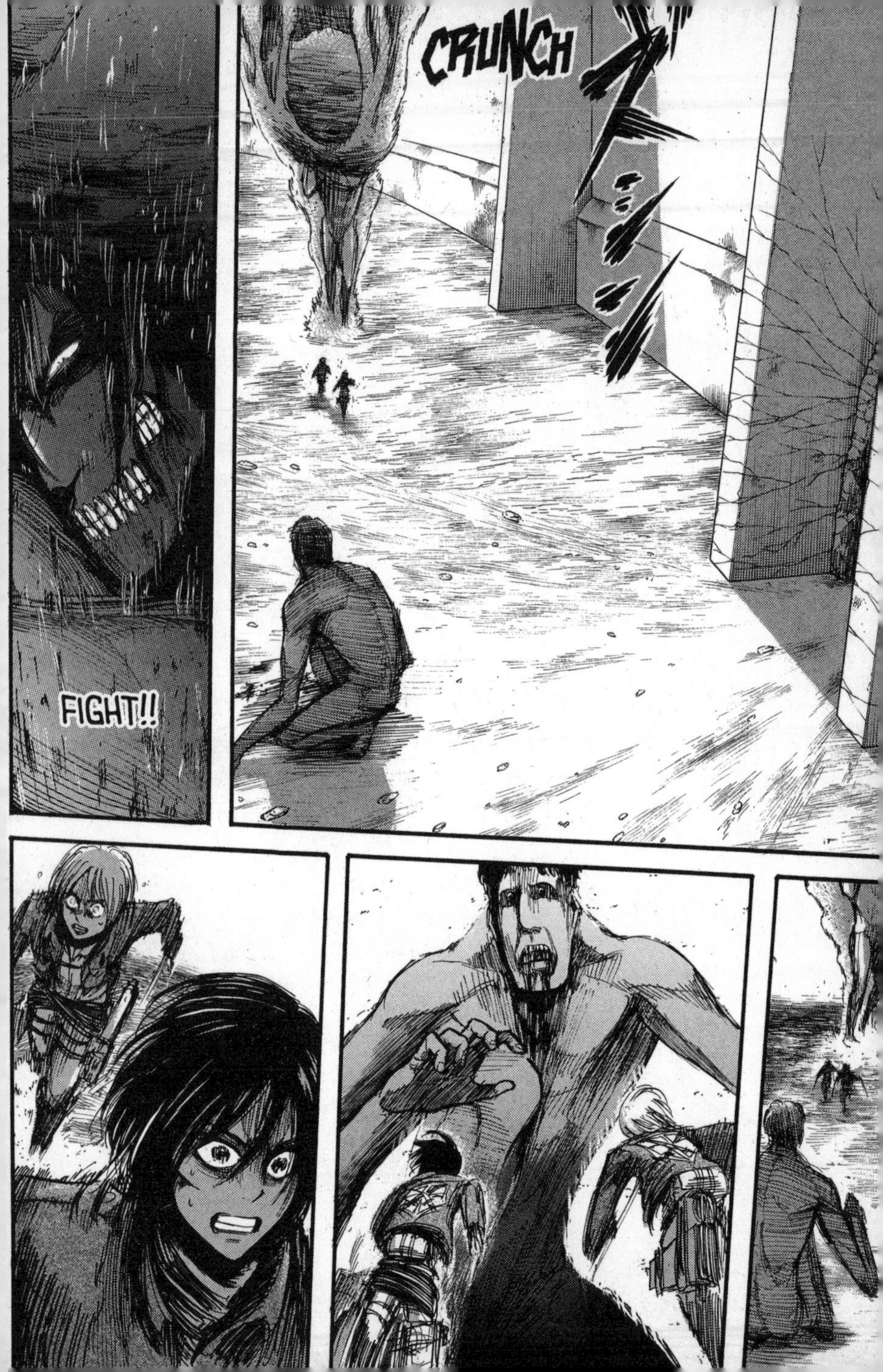
CRUNCH
FIGHT!!

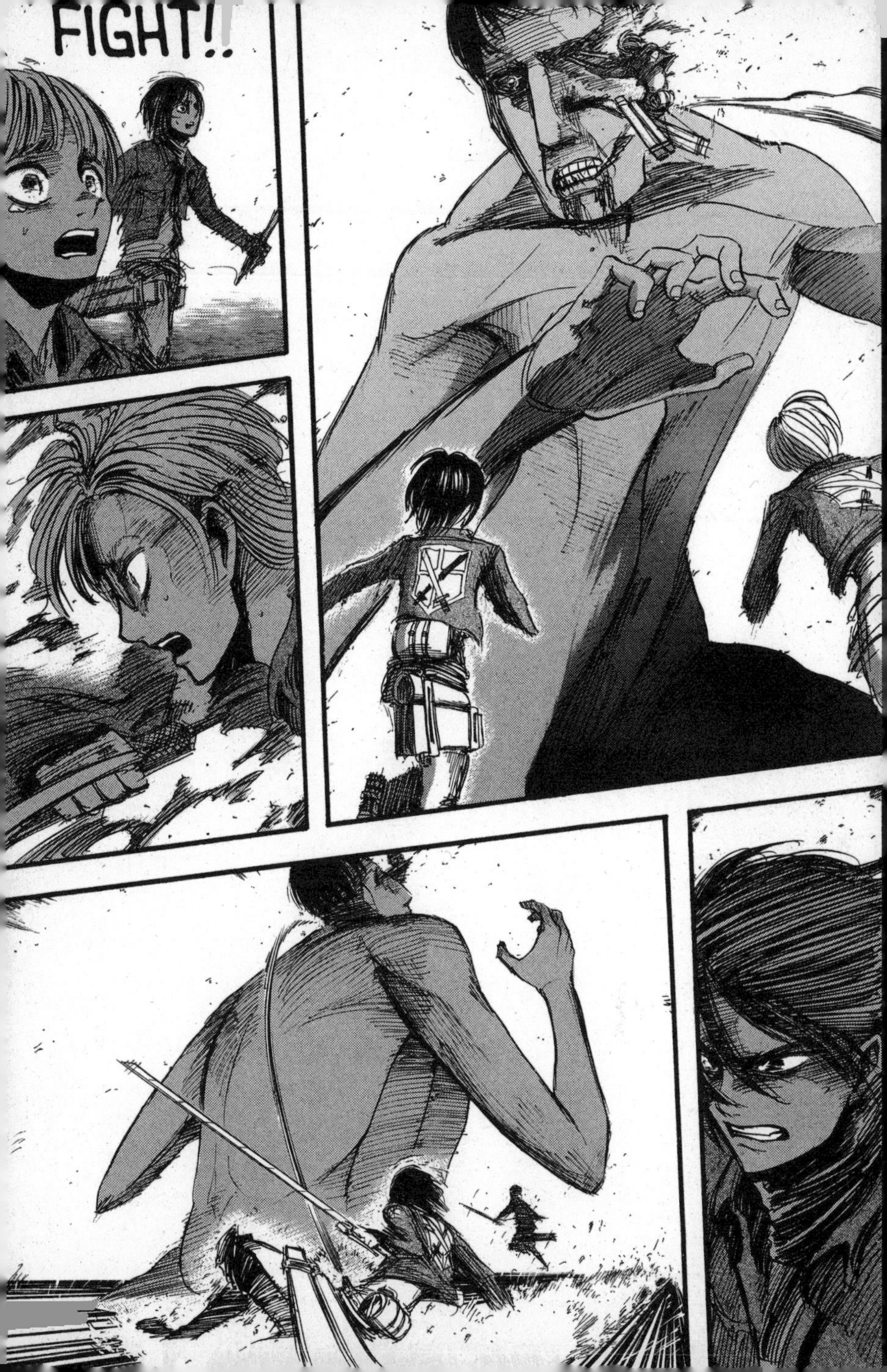
FIGHT!!

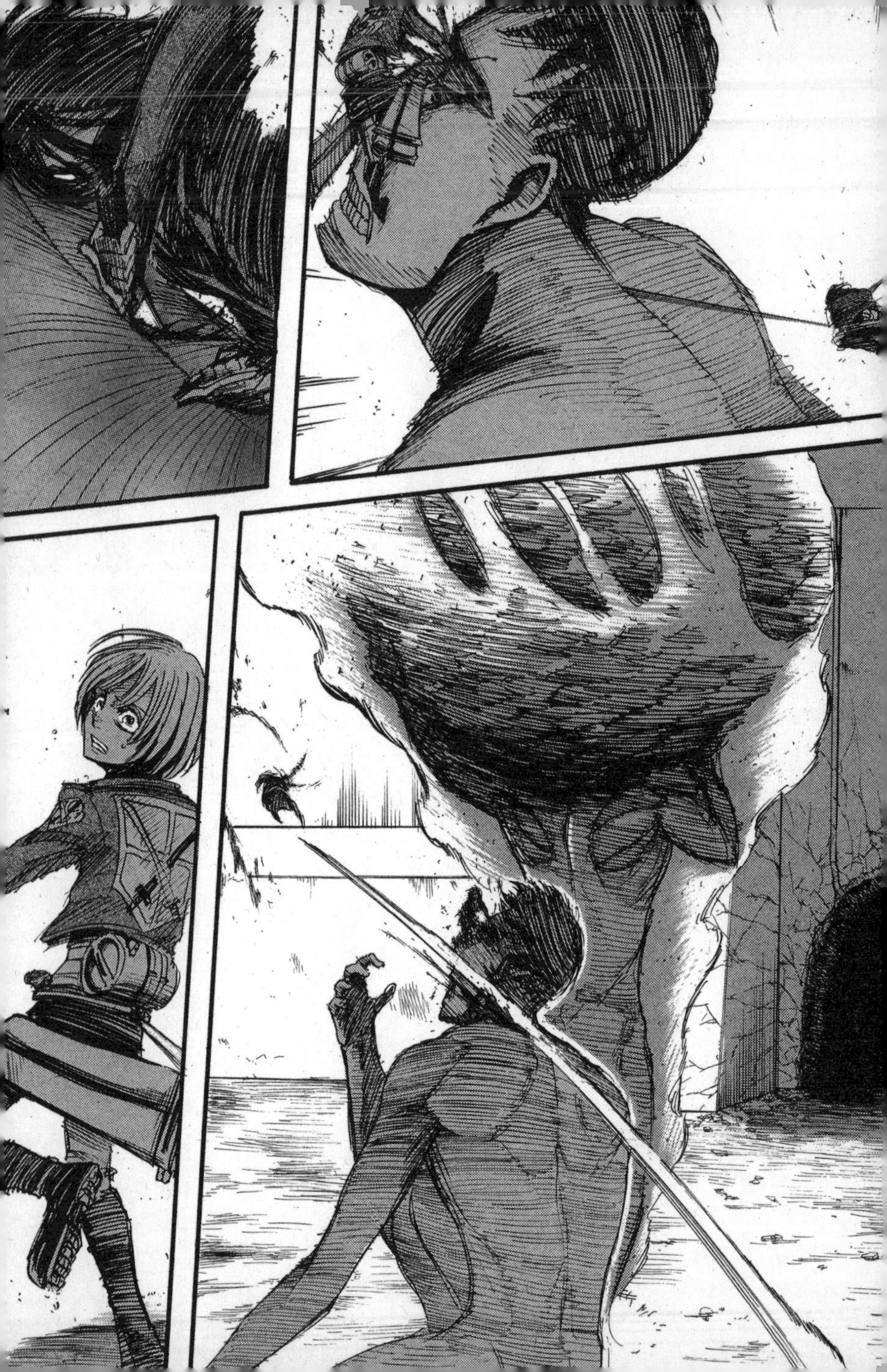

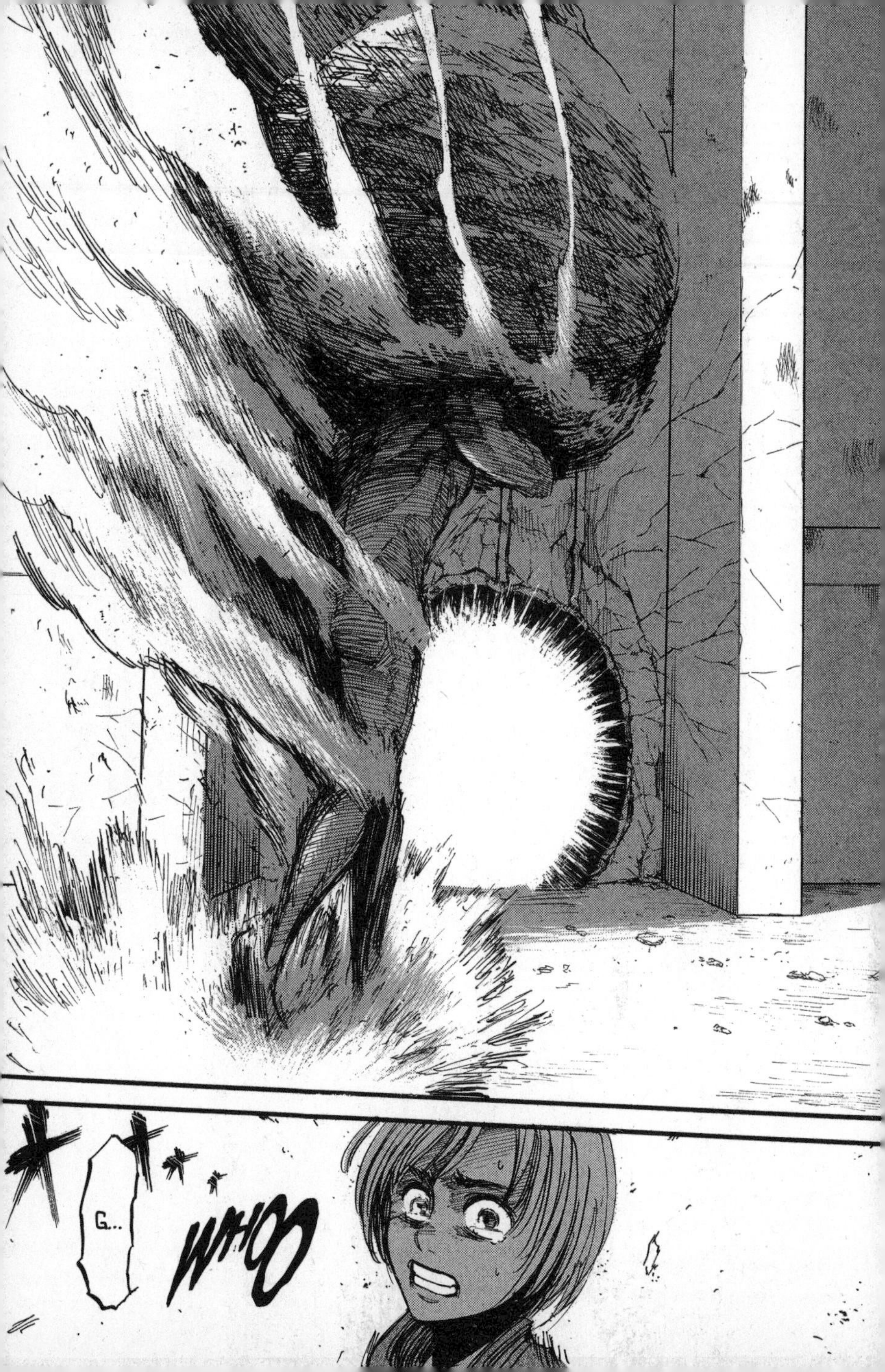
G...
WHOO

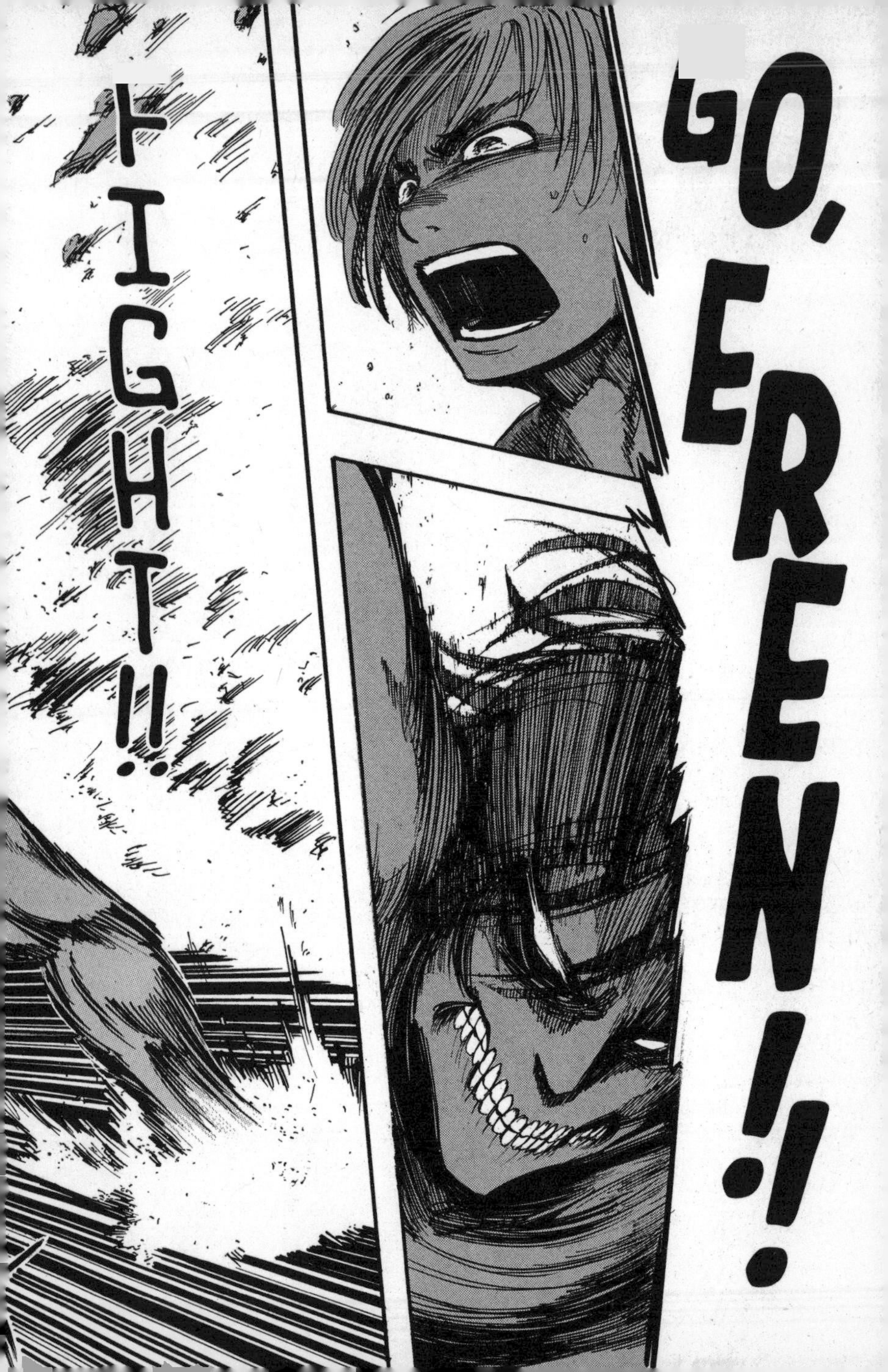
GO, EREN!!
FIGHT!!

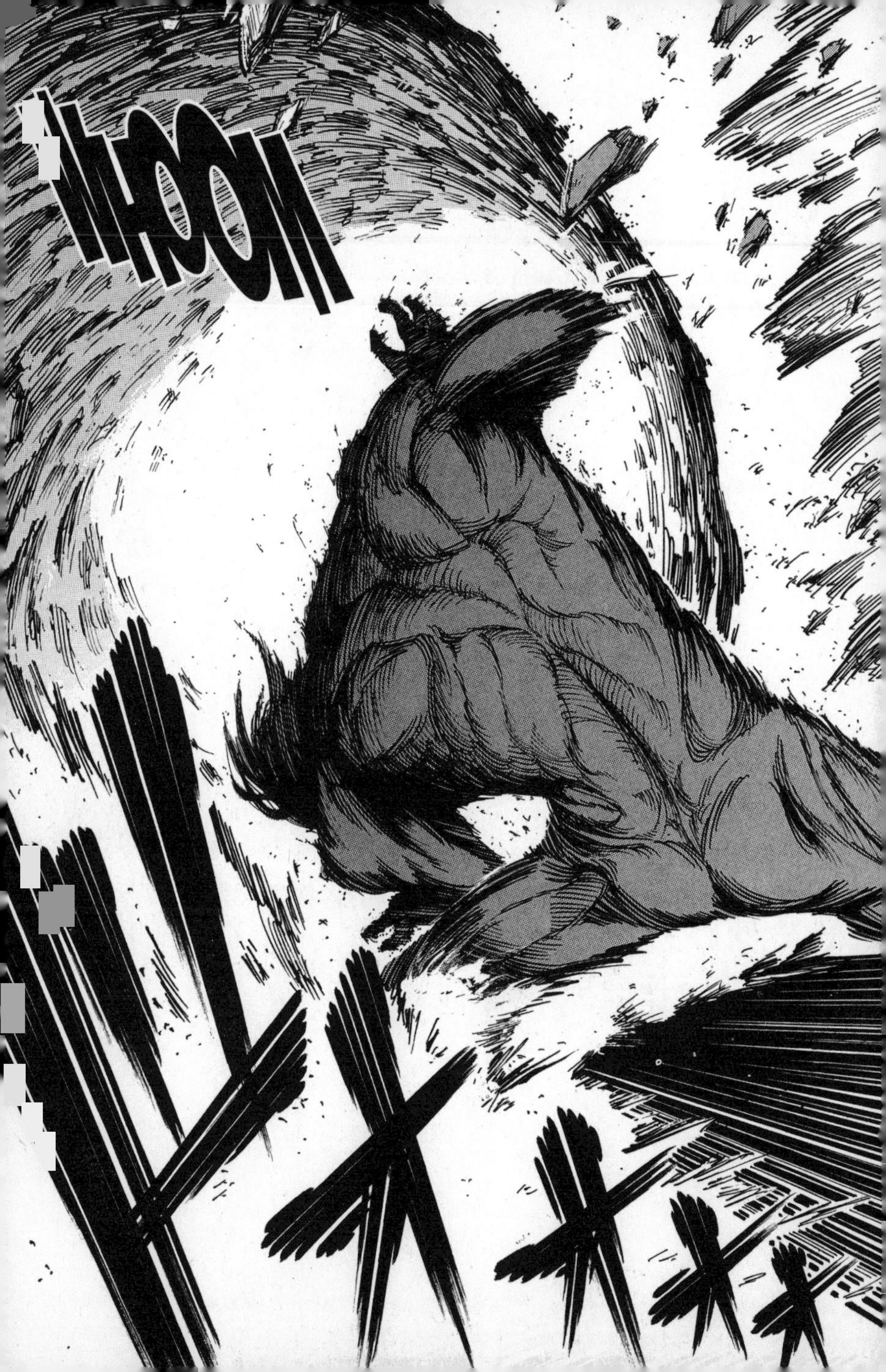
WHOOM

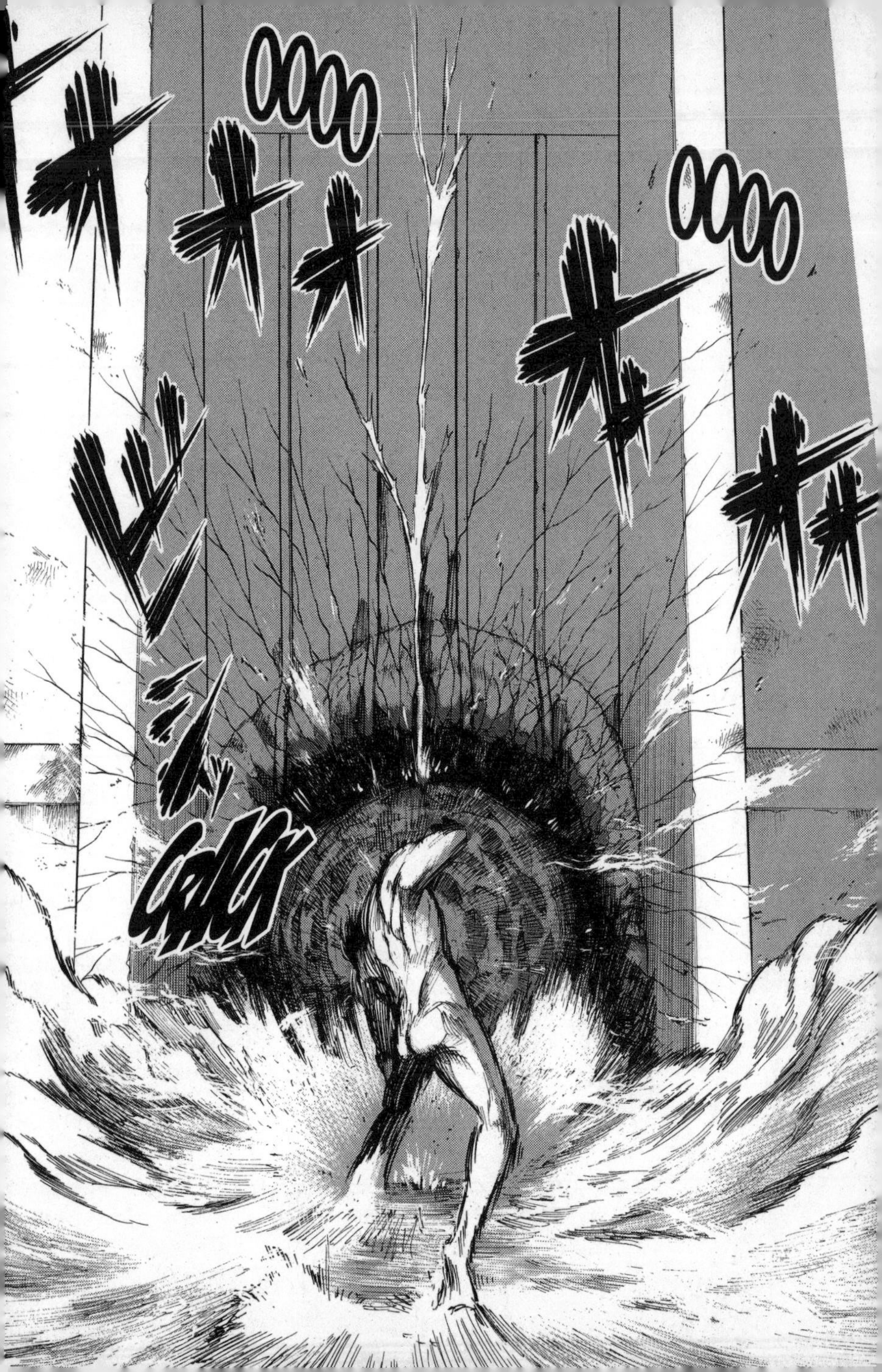
OOOO
OOOO
CRACK

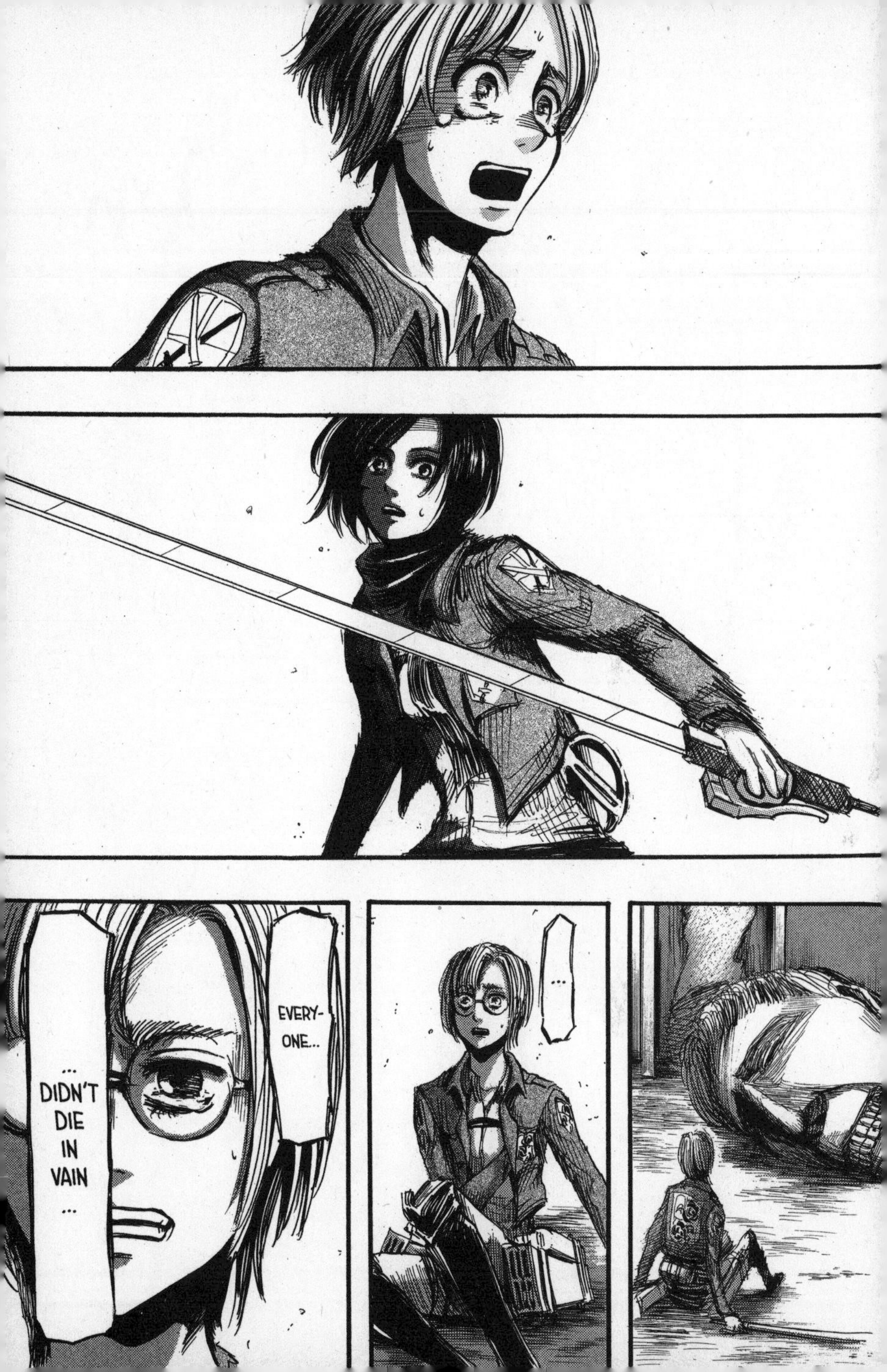
...
EVERY-
ONE...
...
DIDN'T
DIE
IN
VAIN
...

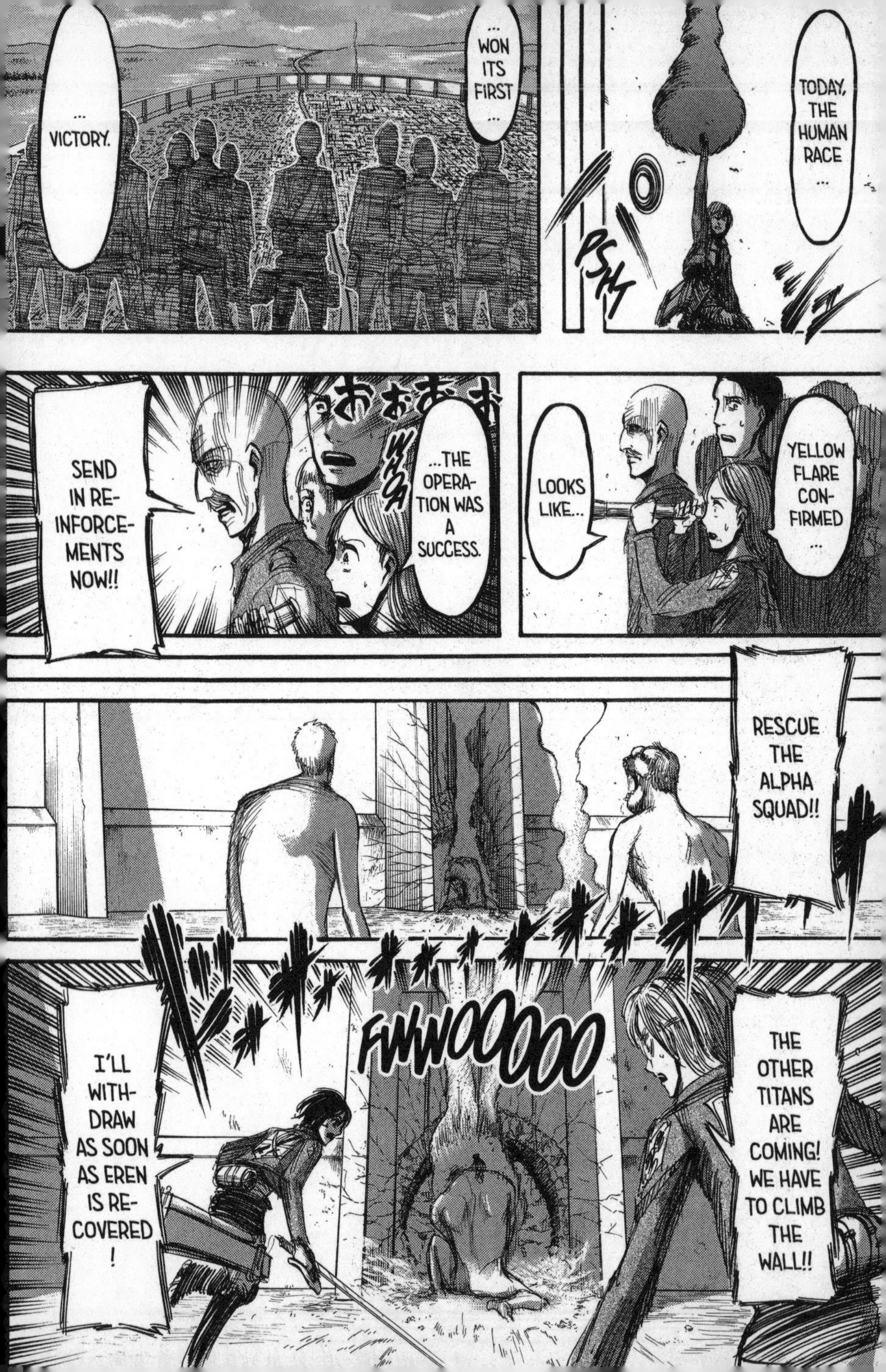
TODAY, THE HUMAN RACE ...
PSHH
... WON ITS FIRST ...
... VICTORY.
YELLOW FLARE CON-FIRMED ...
LOOKS LIKE...
...THE OPERA-TION WAS A SUCCESS.
SEND IN RE-INFORCE-MENTS NOW!!
RESCUE THE ALPHA SQUAD!!
THE OTHER TITANS ARE COMING! WE HAVE TO CLIMB THE WALL!!
FWWOOOOOO
I'LL WITH-DRAW AS SOON AS EREN IS RE-COVERED!

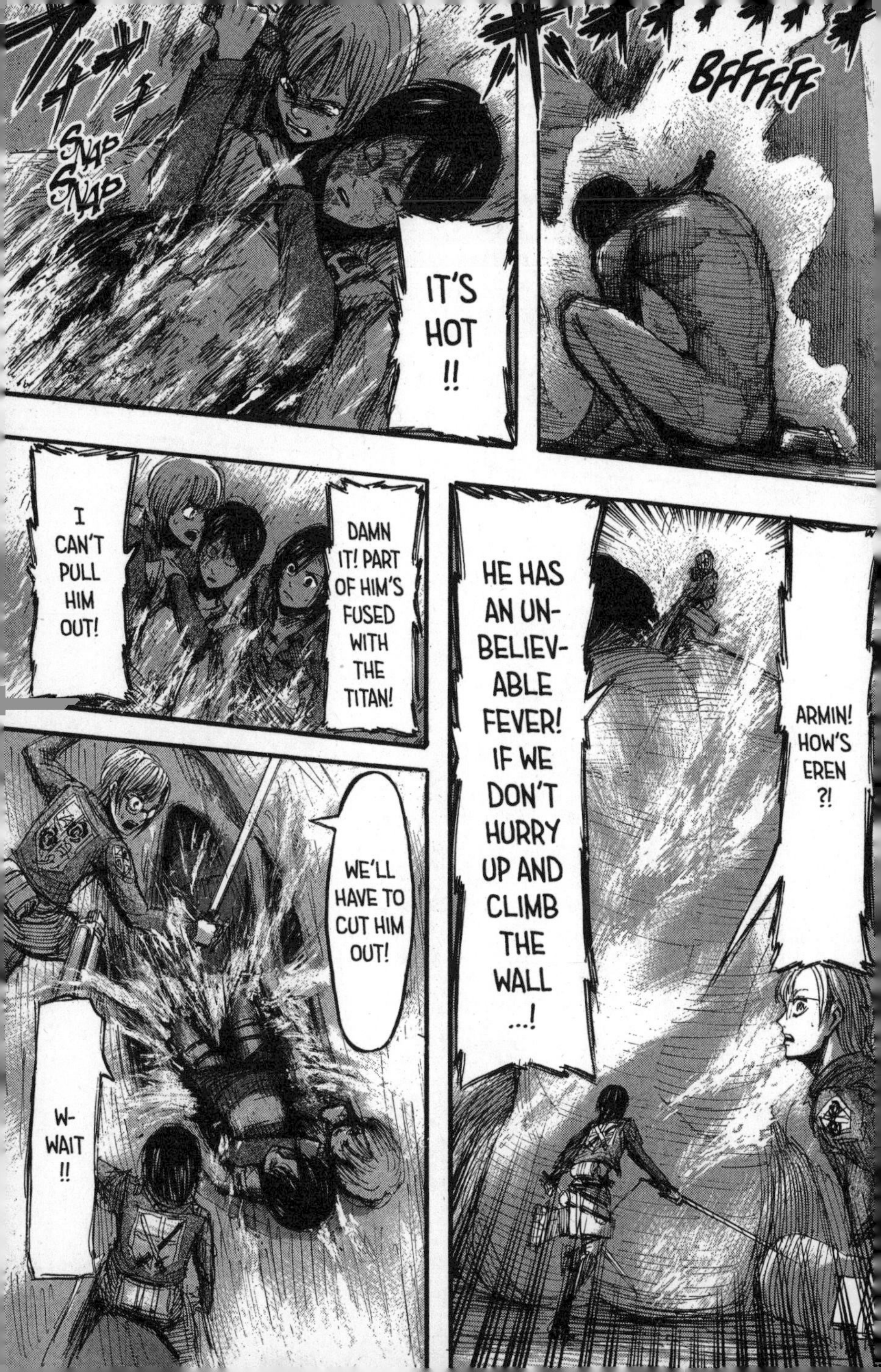
BFFFFFF
SNAP SNAP
IT'S HOT !!
ARMIN! HOW'S EREN ?!
HE HAS AN UN-BELIEV-ABLE FEVER! IF WE DON'T HURRY UP AND CLIMB THE WALL ...!
DAMN IT! PART OF HIM'S FUSED WITH THE TITAN!
I CAN'T PULL HIM OUT!
WE'LL HAVE TO CUT HIM OUT!
W-WAIT !!

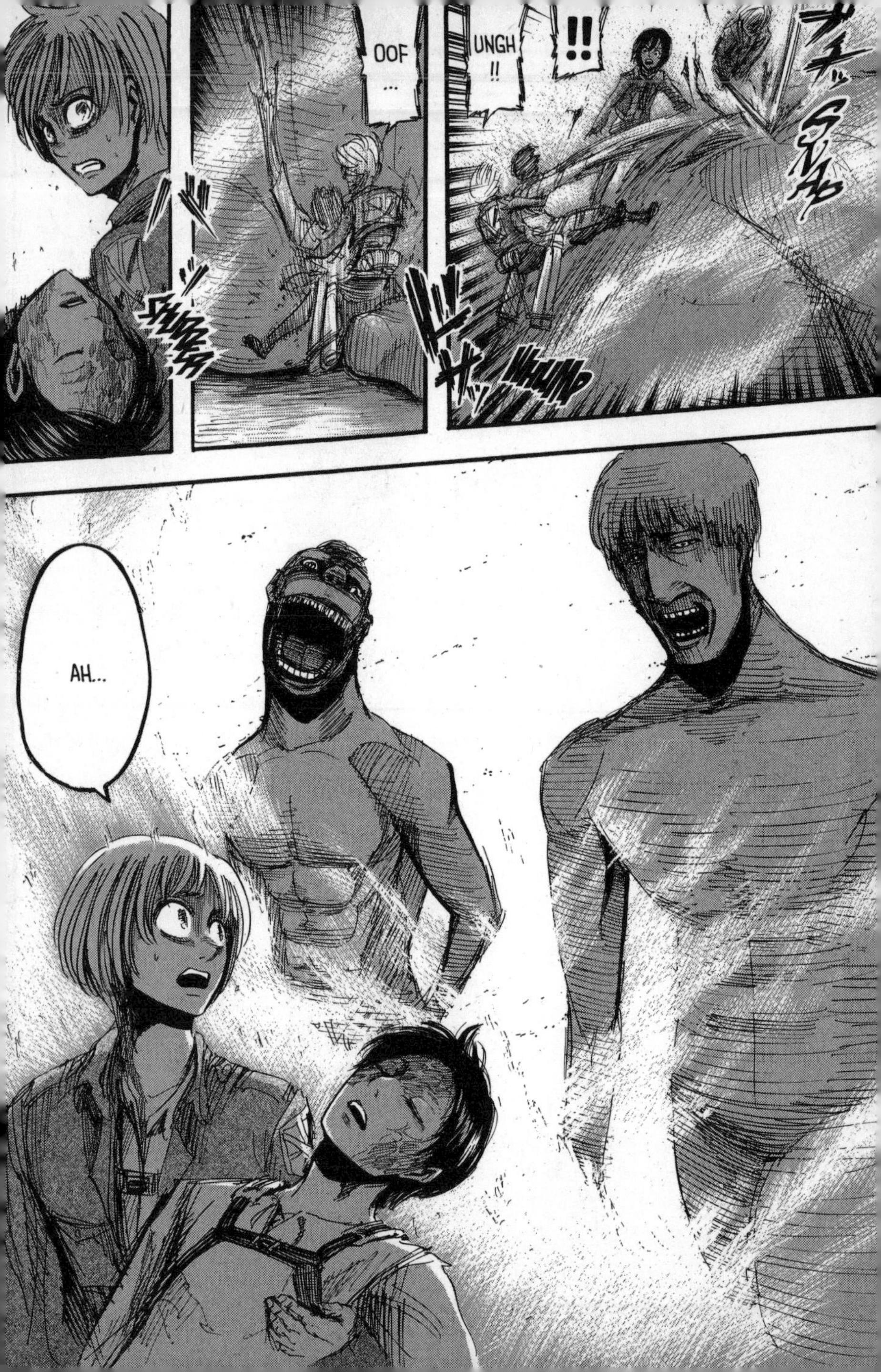
!!
SNAP
WHUMP
UNGH !!
OOF ...
AH...

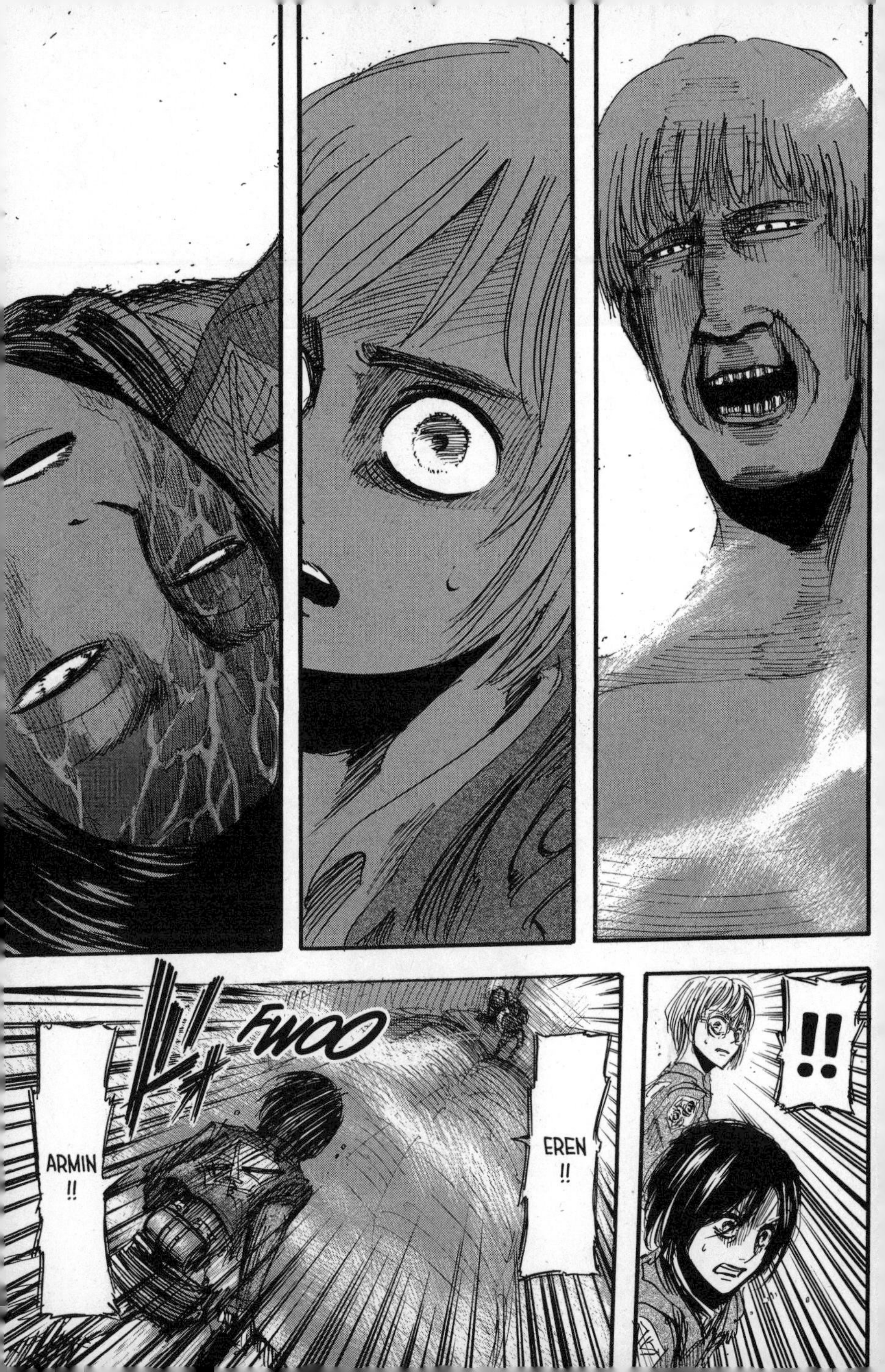
!!
FWOO
EREN !!
ARMIN !!

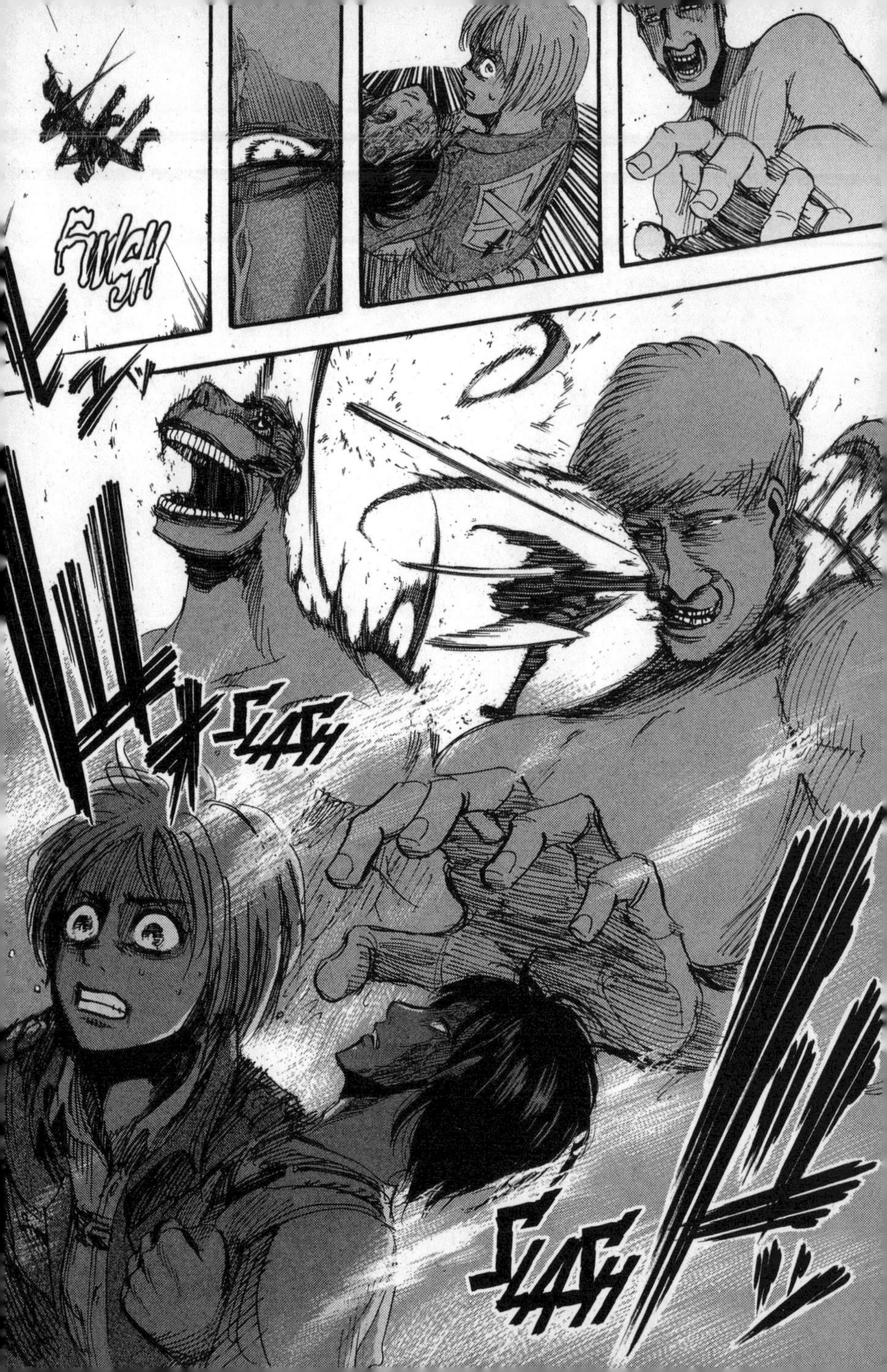

Fwagh
SLASH
SLASH

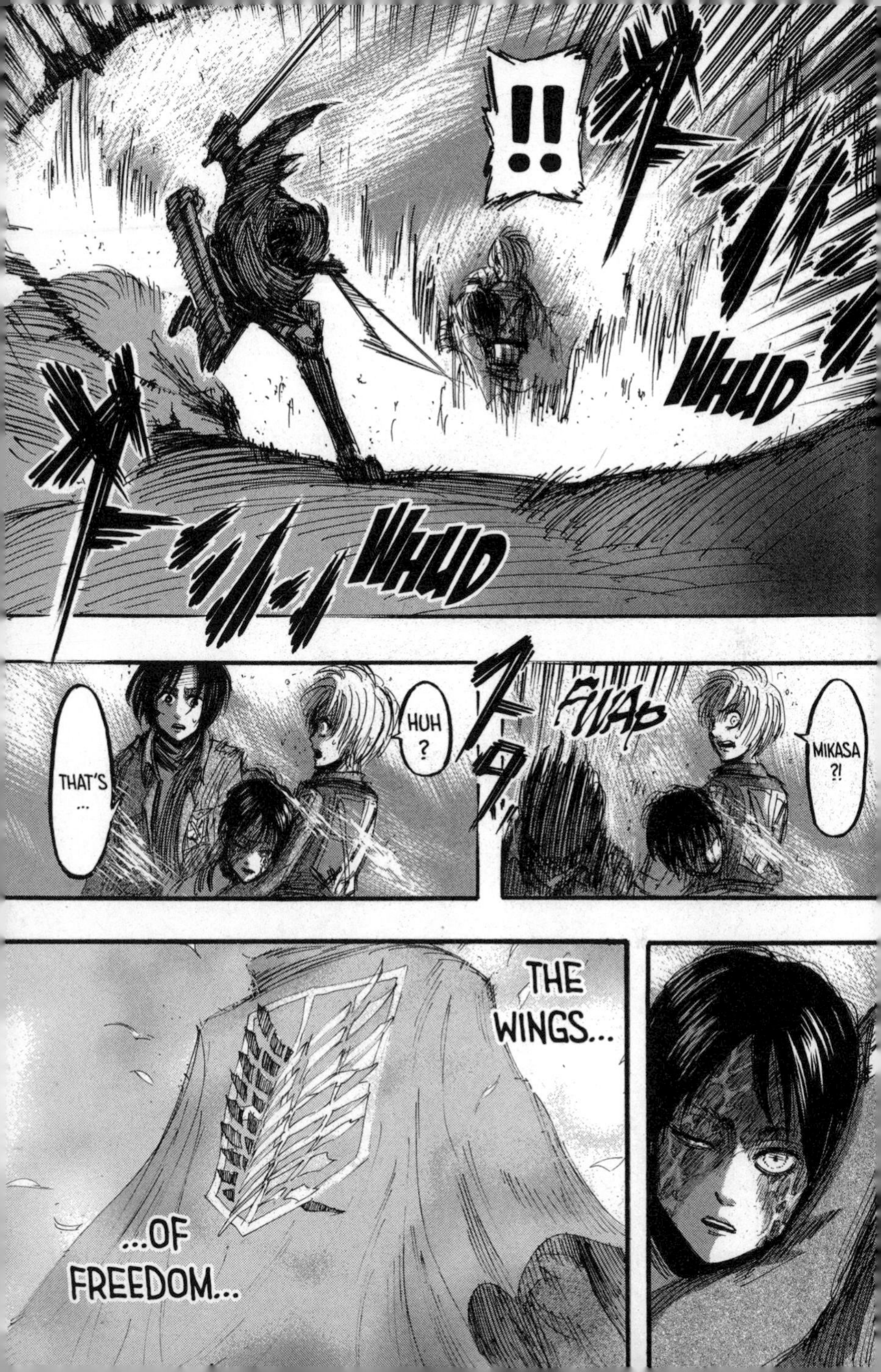
!!
WHUD
WHUD
FWAP
MIKASA ?!
HUH ?
THAT'S ...
THE WINGS...
...OF FREEDOM...

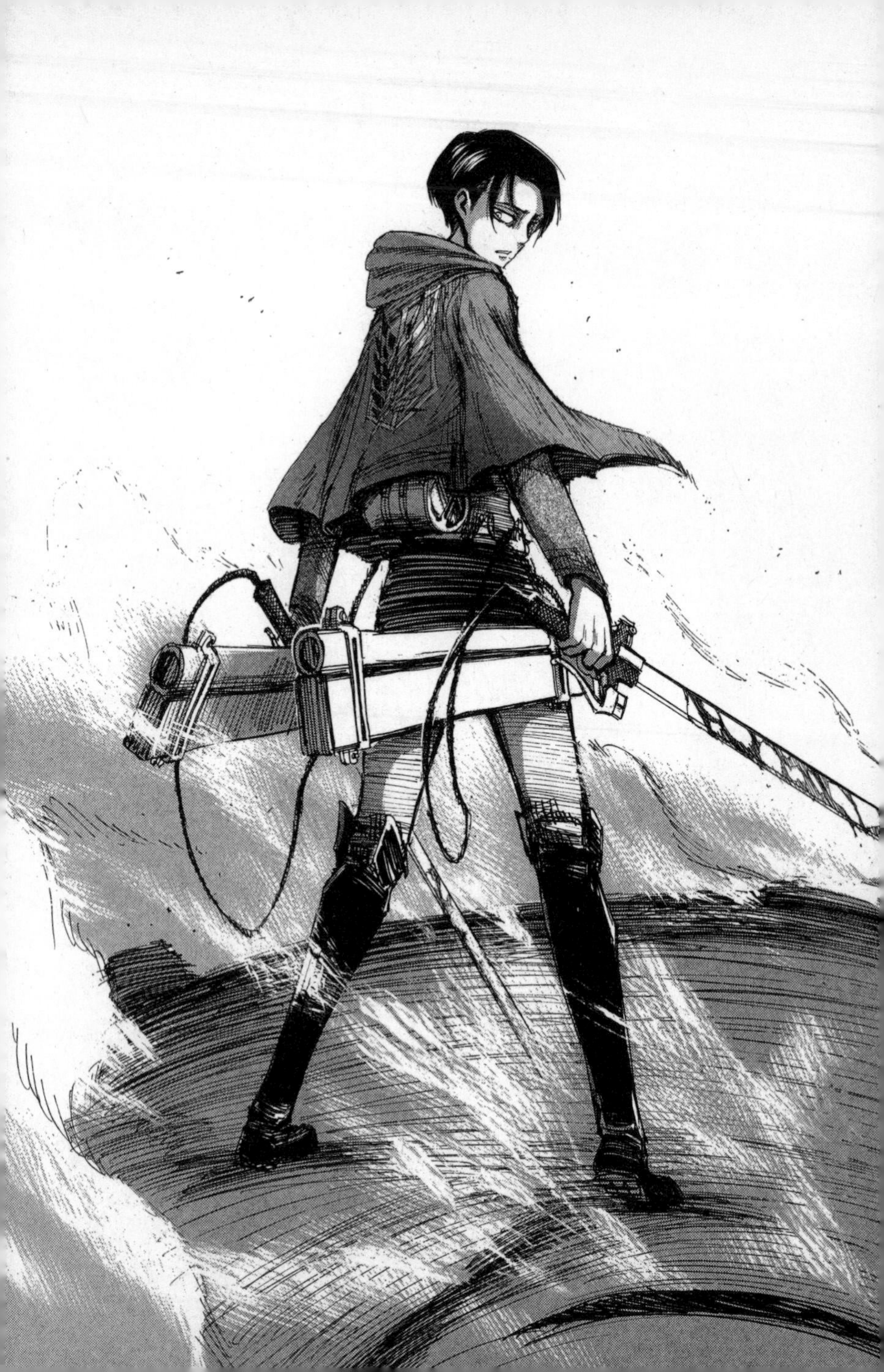

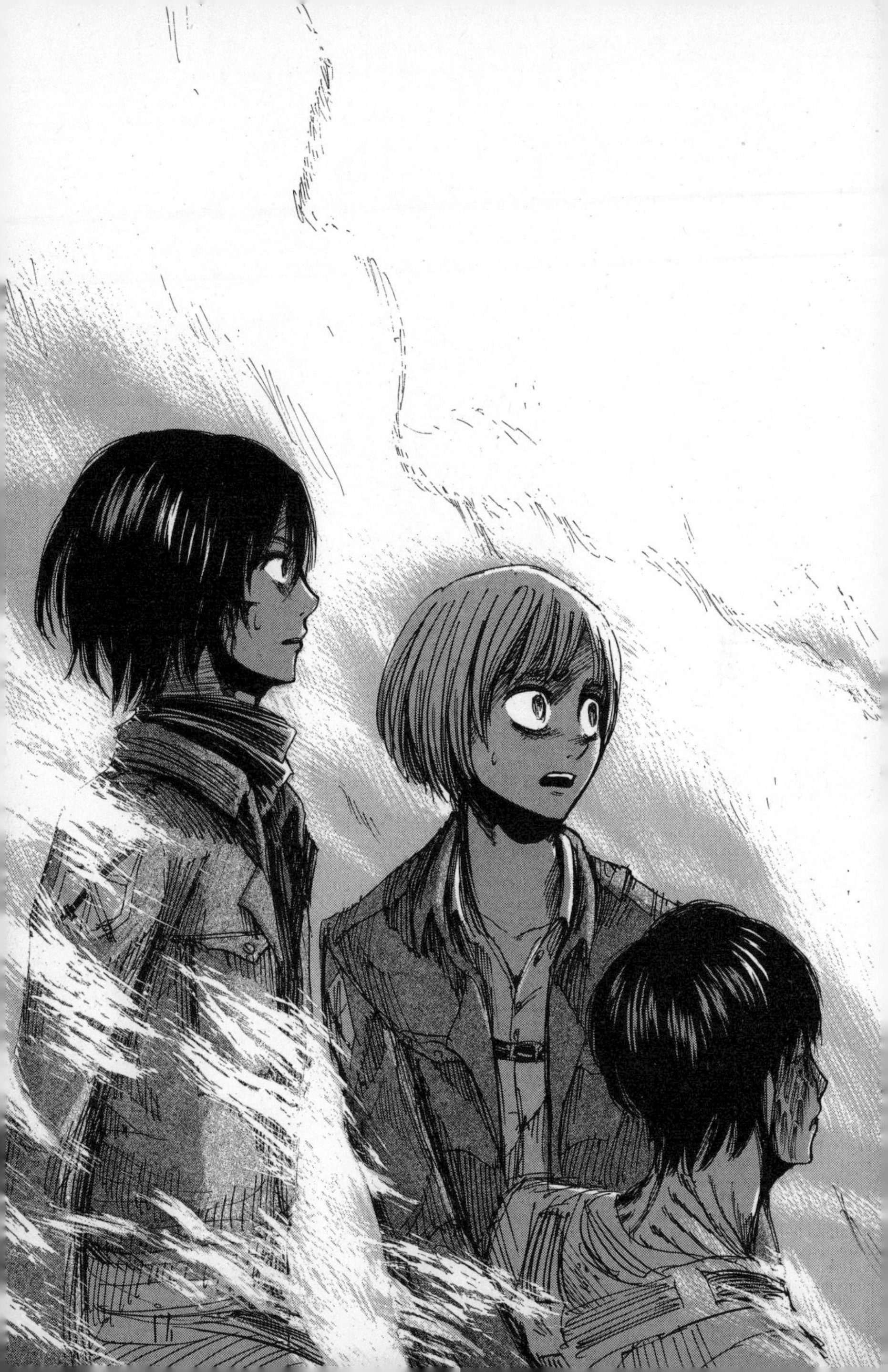

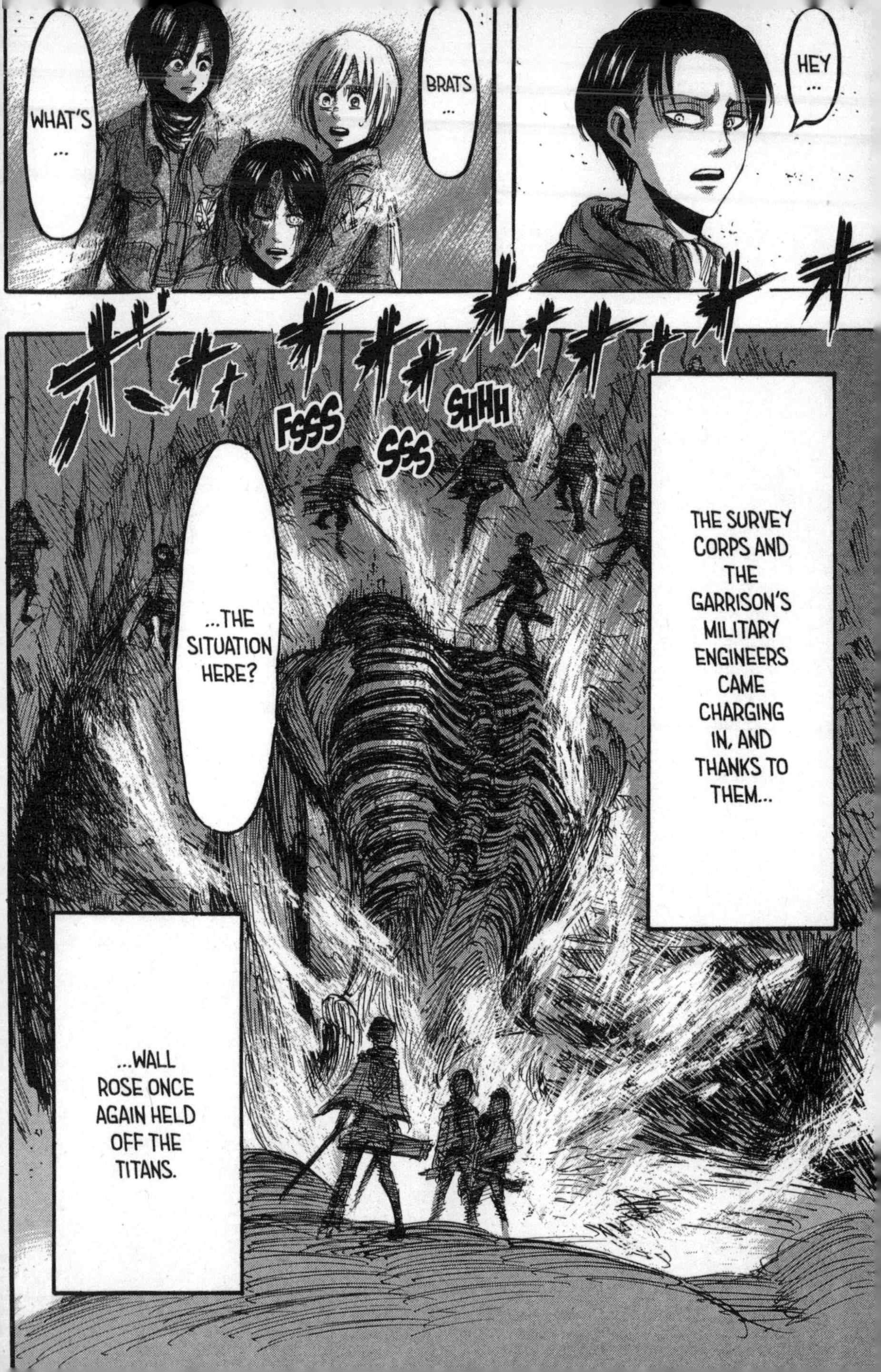
HEY ...
BRATS ...
WHAT'S ...
SHHH
SSS
FSSS
...THE SITUATION HERE?
THE SURVEY CORPS AND THE GARRISON'S MILITARY ENGINEERS CAME CHARGING IN, AND THANKS TO THEM...
...WALL ROSE ONCE AGAIN HELD OFF THE TITANS.

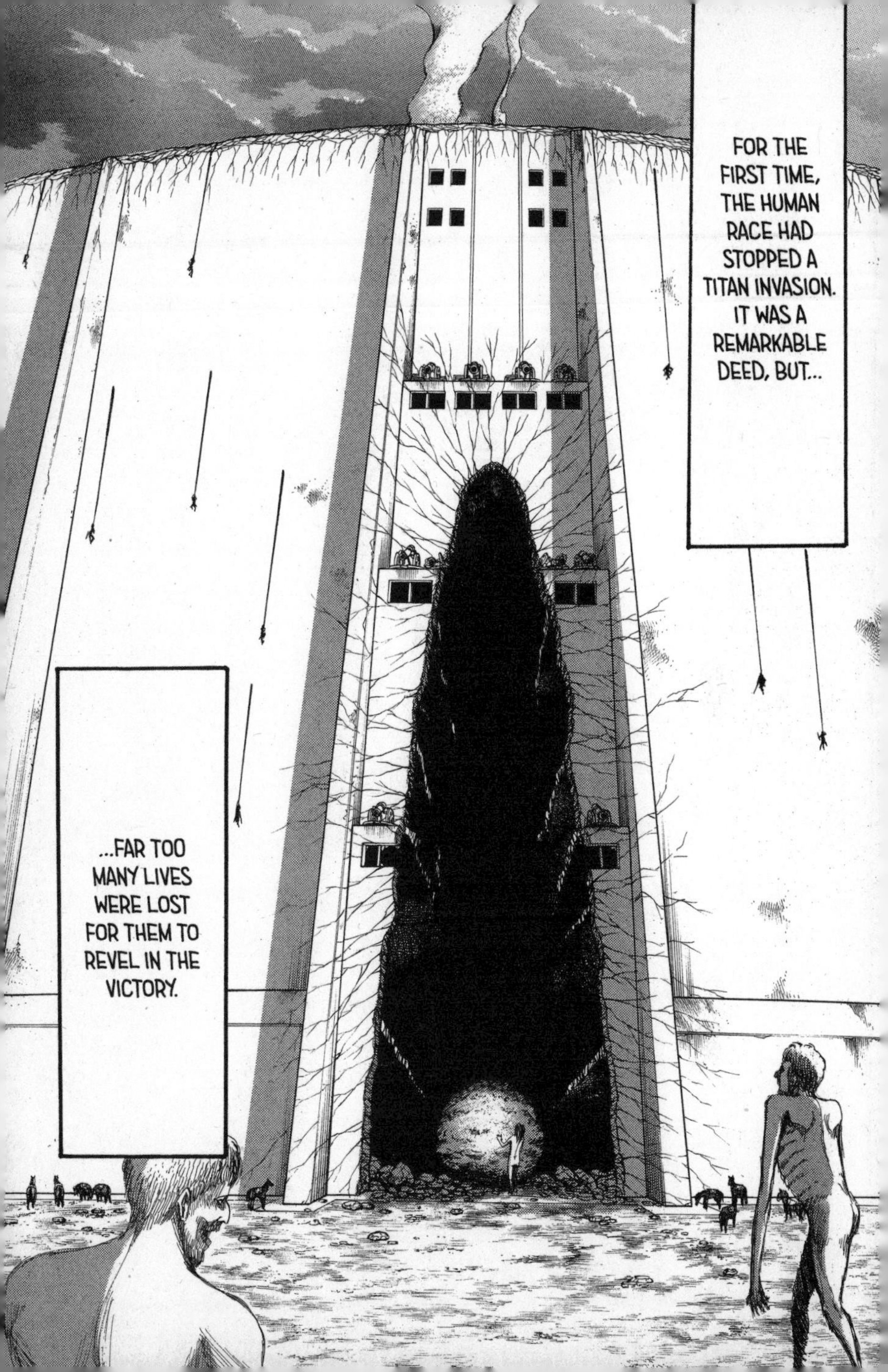
FOR THE FIRST TIME, THE HUMAN RACE HAD STOPPED A TITAN INVASION. IT WAS A REMARKABLE DEED, BUT...
...FAR TOO MANY LIVES WERE LOST FOR THEM TO REVEL IN THE VICTORY.

ATTACK on TITAN

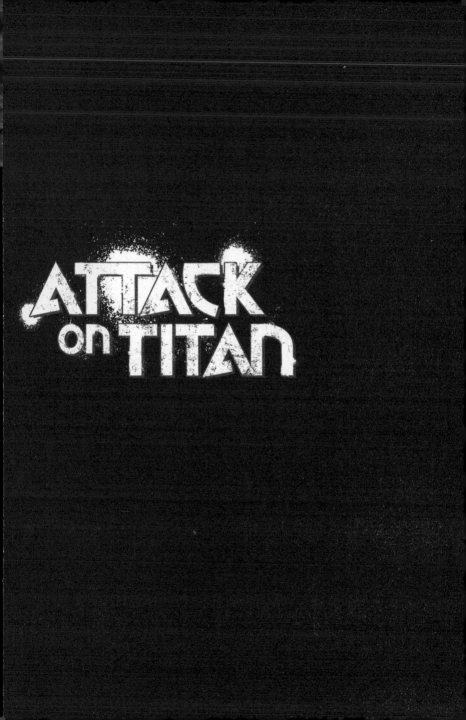

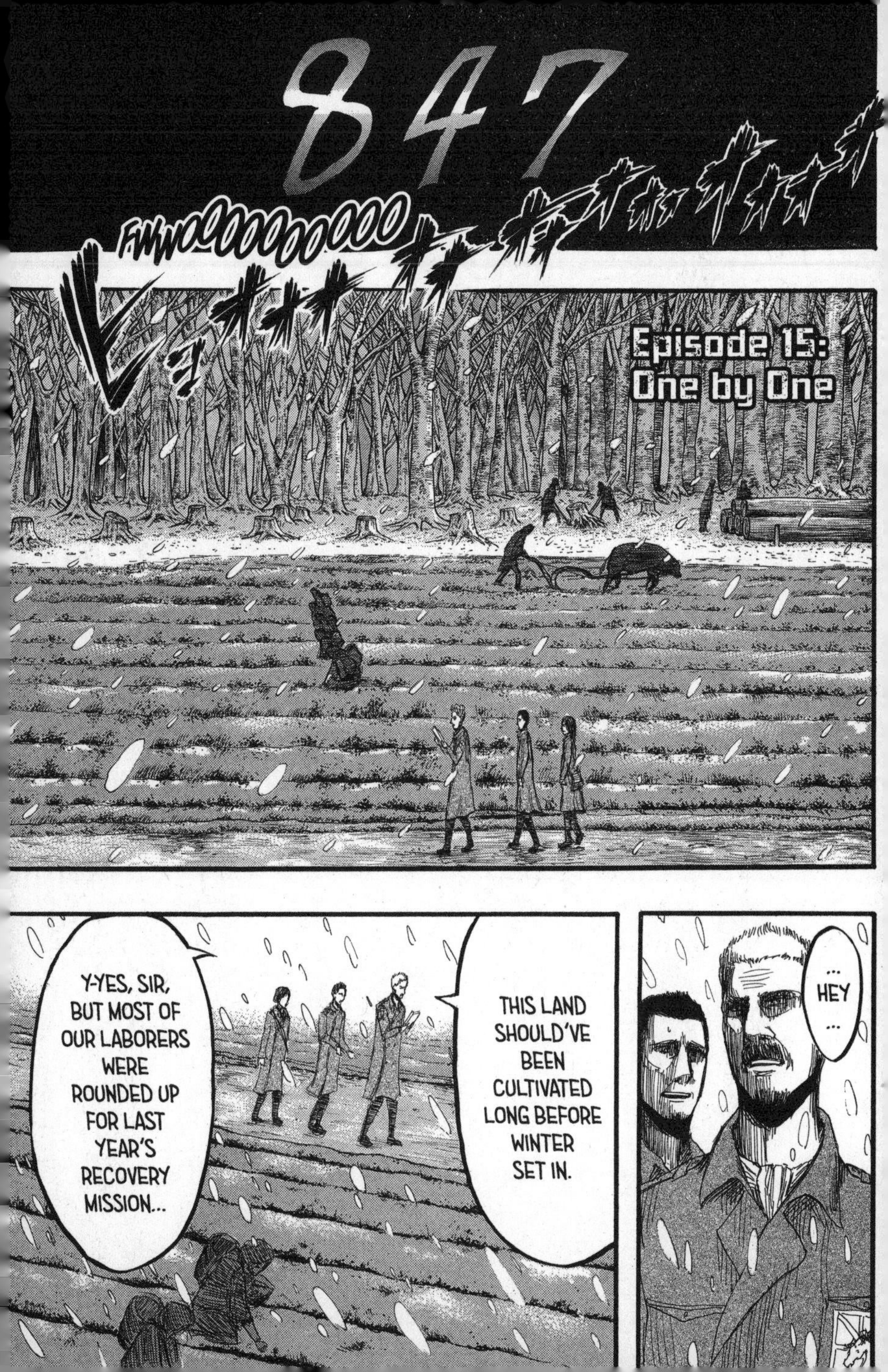
847
FWWOOOOOOOOOO
Episode 15: One by One
... HEY ...
THIS LAND SHOULD'VE BEEN CULTIVATED LONG BEFORE WINTER SET IN.
Y-YES, SIR, BUT MOST OF OUR LABORERS WERE ROUNDED UP FOR LAST YEAR'S RECOVERY MISSION...

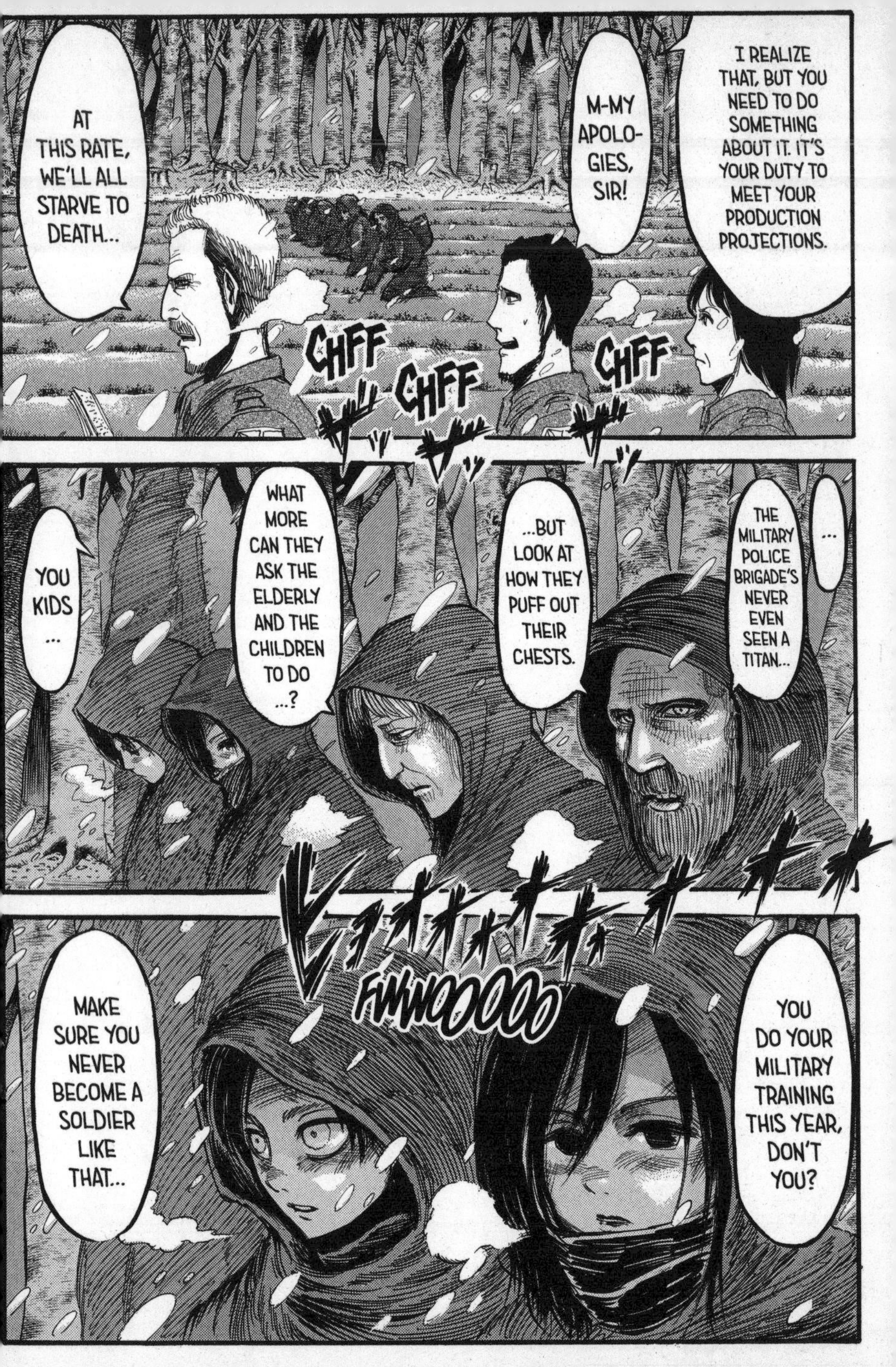
I REALIZE THAT, BUT YOU NEED TO DO SOMETHING ABOUT IT. IT'S YOUR DUTY TO MEET YOUR PRODUCTION PROJECTIONS.
M-MY APOLOGIES, SIR!
AT THIS RATE, WE'LL ALL STARVE TO DEATH...
CHFF
CHFF
CHFF
...
THE MILITARY POLICE BRIGADE'S NEVER EVEN SEEN A TITAN...
...BUT LOOK AT HOW THEY PUFF OUT THEIR CHESTS.
WHAT MORE CAN THEY ASK THE ELDERLY AND THE CHILDREN TO DO ...?
YOU KIDS ...
YOU DO YOUR MILITARY TRAINING THIS YEAR, DON'T YOU?
FWWOOOOOO
MAKE SURE YOU NEVER BECOME A SOLDIER LIKE THAT...

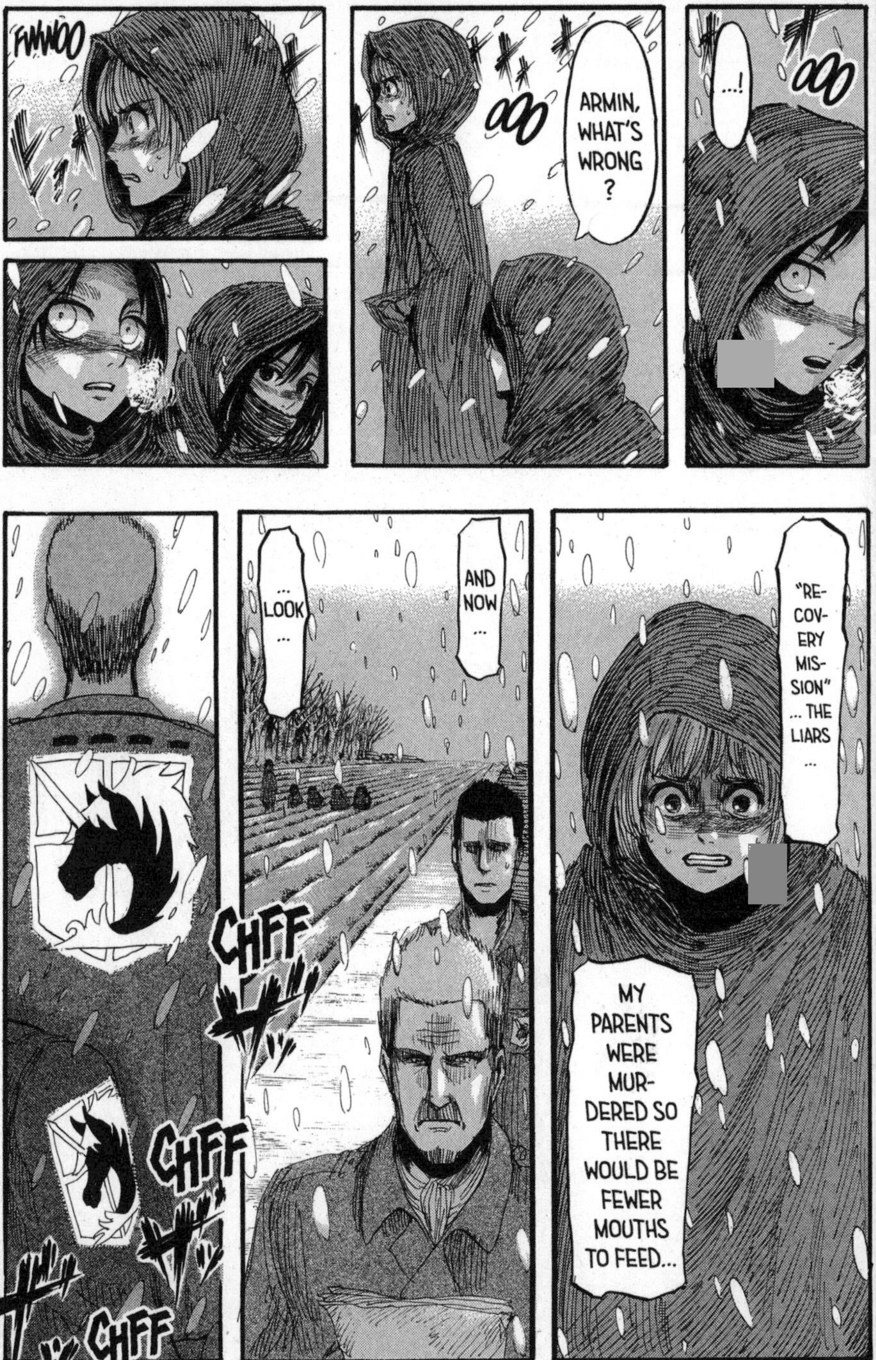

...!
OOO
OOO
ARMIN, WHAT'S WRONG?
FWWOO
"RE-COVERY MISSION" ... THE LIARS ...
MY PARENTS WERE MURDERED SO THERE WOULD BE FEWER MOUTHS TO FEED...
AND NOW ...
... LOOK ...
CHFF
CHFF
CHFF

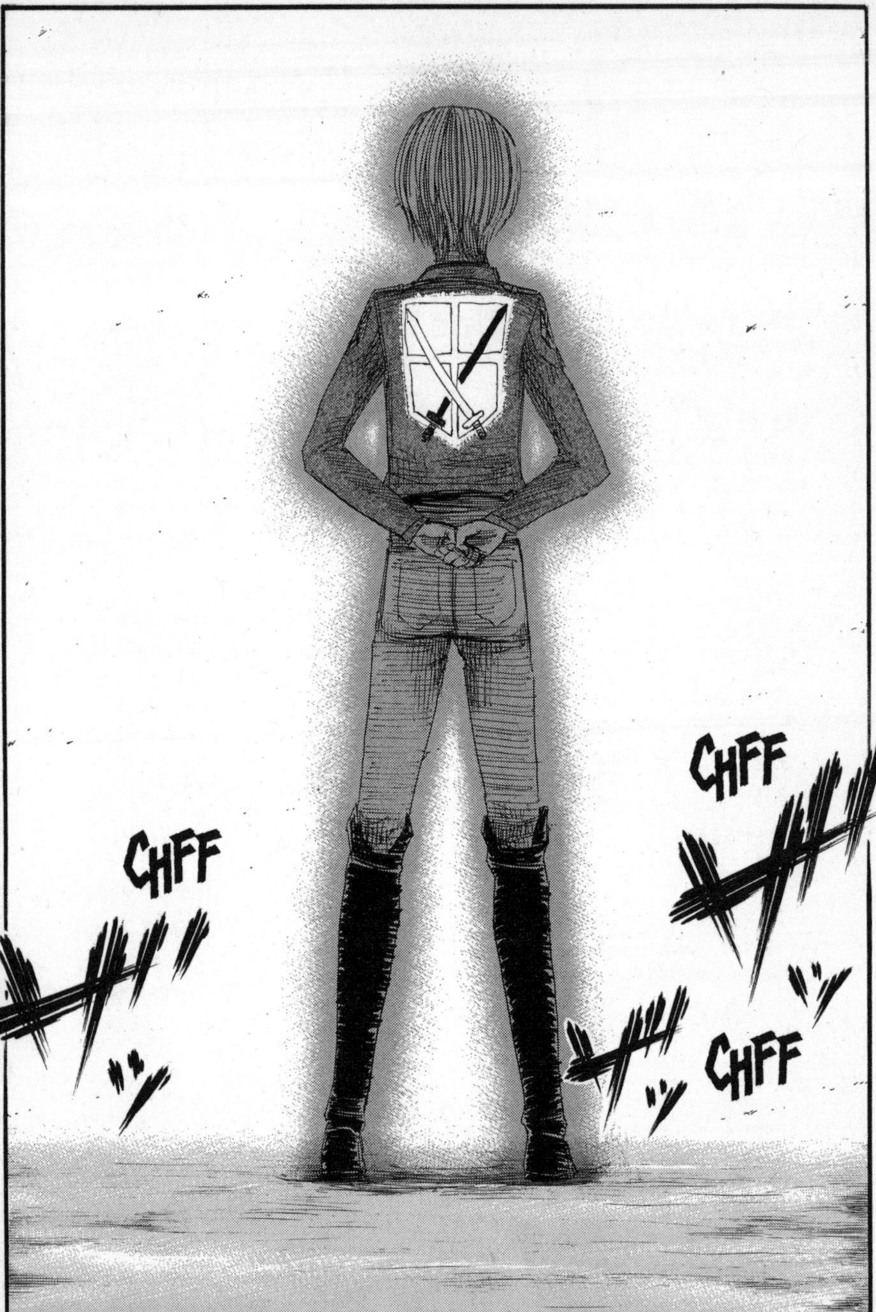
CHFF
CHFF
CHFF

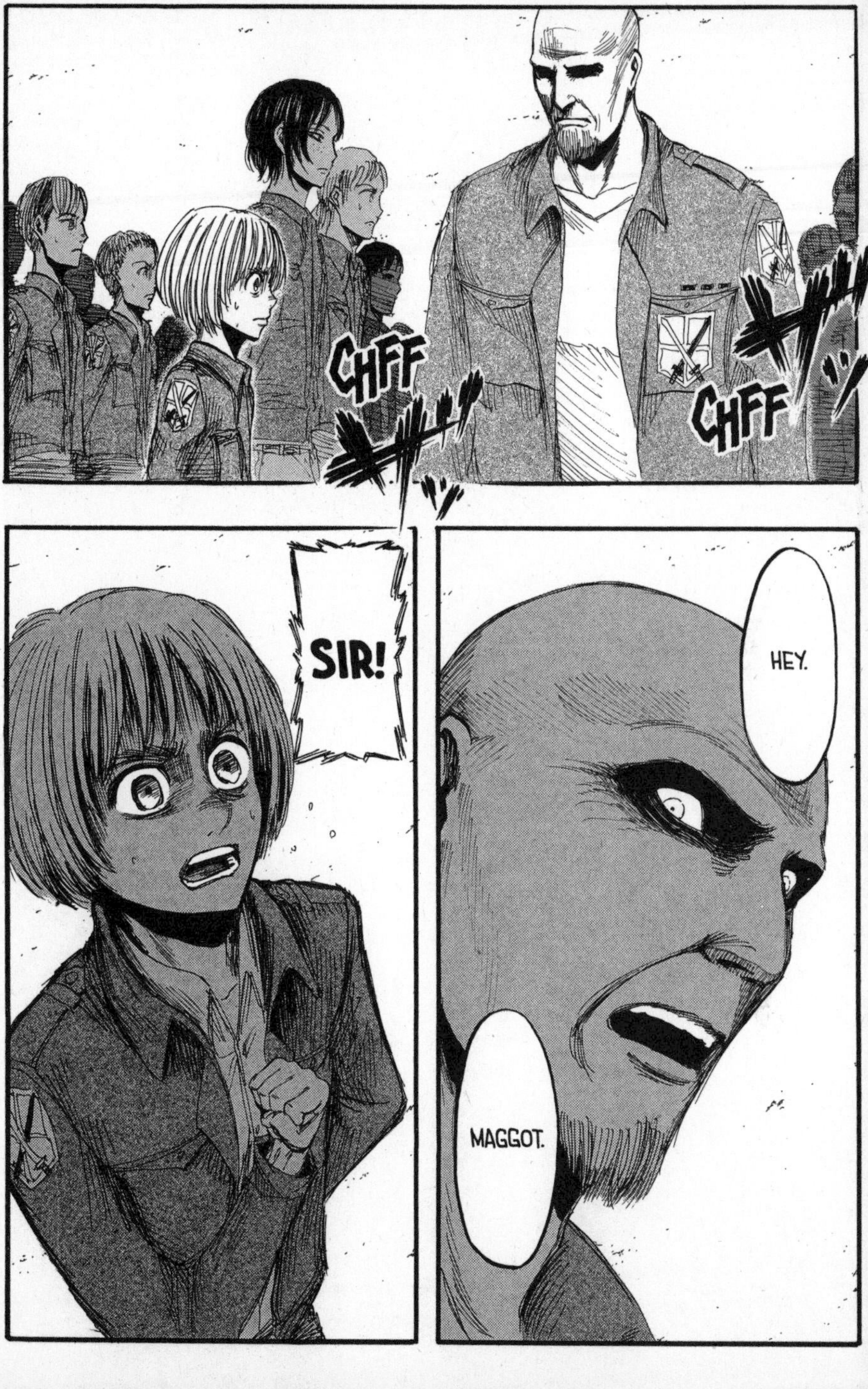
CHFF
CHFF
HEY.
MAGGOT.
SIR!

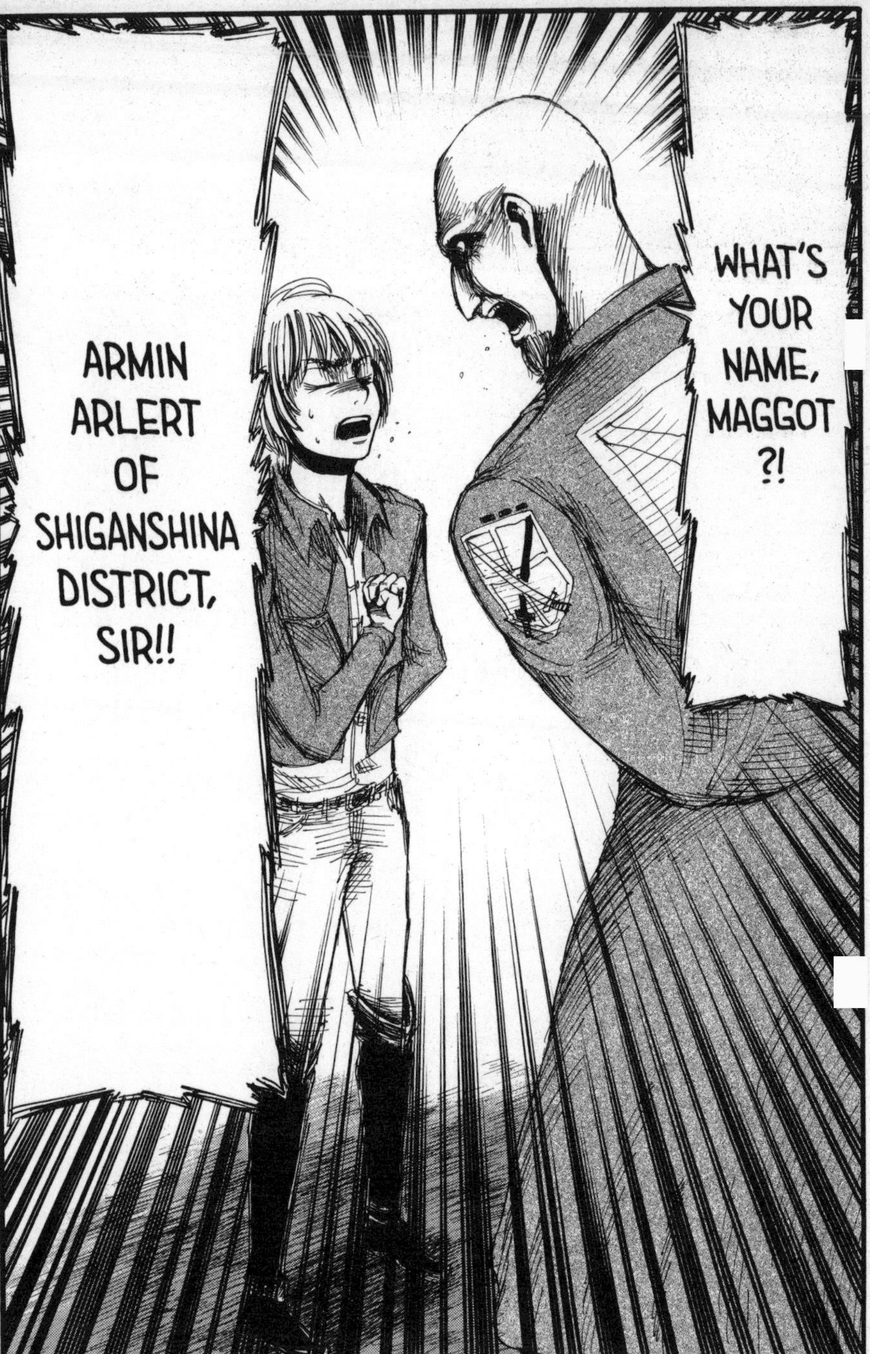
WHAT'S YOUR NAME, MAGGOT ?!
ARMIN ARLERT OF SHIGANSHINA DISTRICT, SIR!!

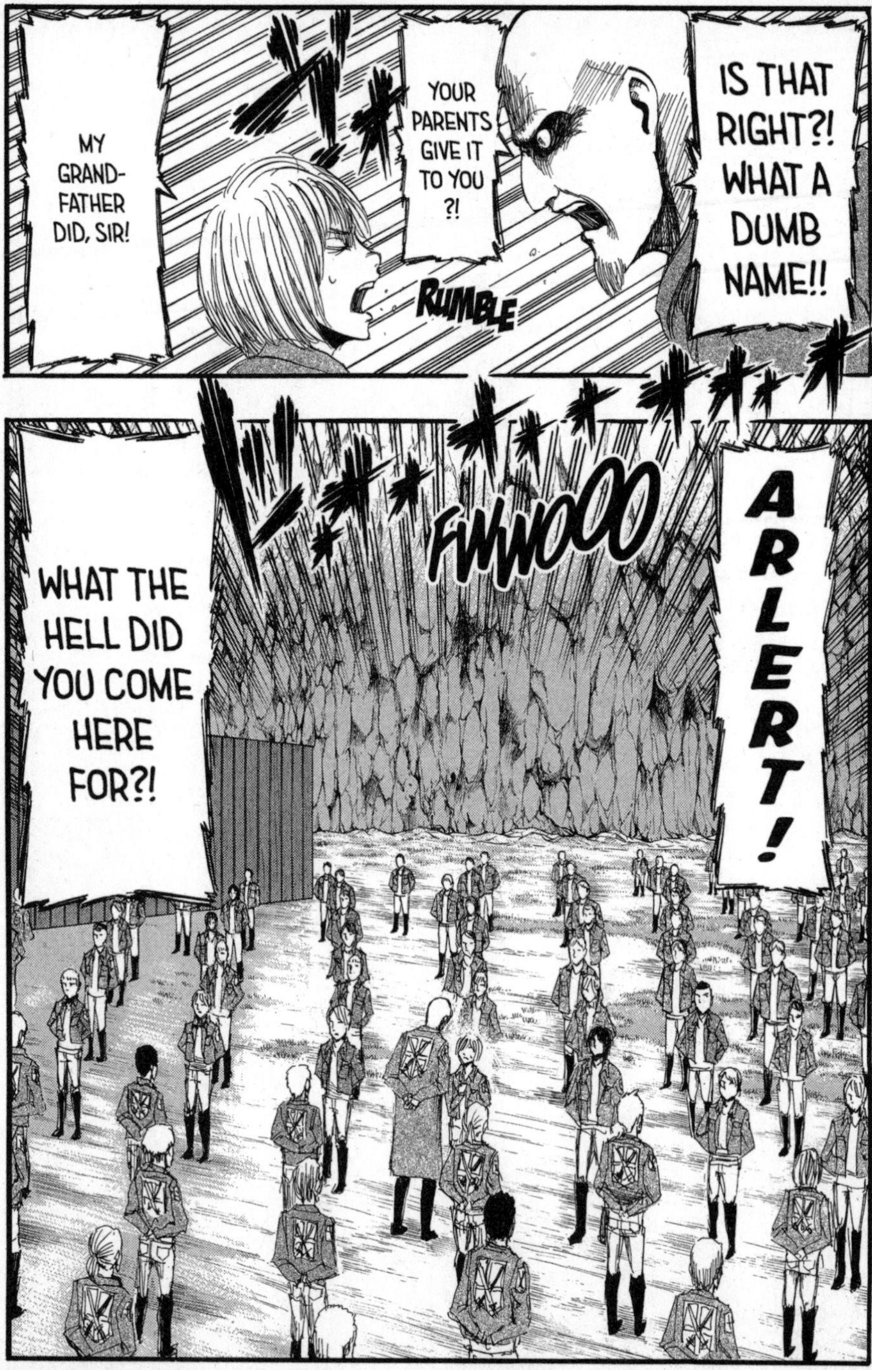
IS THAT RIGHT?! WHAT A DUMB NAME!!
YOUR PARENTS GIVE IT TO YOU ?!
RUMBLE
MY GRAND-FATHER DID, SIR!
ARLERT!
FWWOOO
WHAT THE HELL DID YOU COME HERE FOR?!

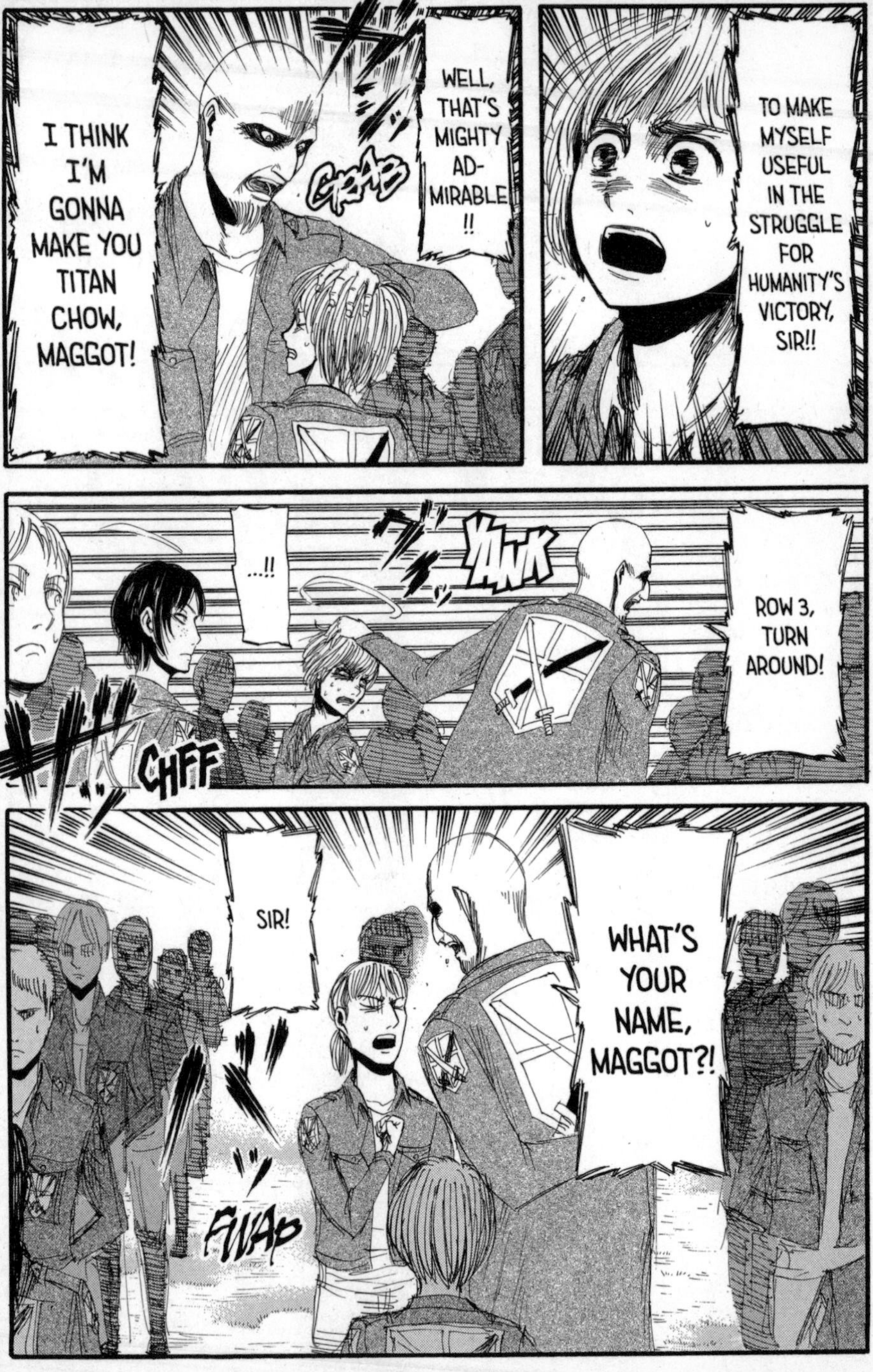
TO MAKE MYSELF USEFUL IN THE STRUGGLE FOR HUMANITY'S VICTORY, SIR!!
WELL, THAT'S MIGHTY AD-MIRABLE!!
GRAB
I THINK I'M GONNA MAKE YOU TITAN CHOW, MAGGOT!
ROW 3, TURN AROUND!
YANK
...!!
CHFF
WHAT'S YOUR NAME, MAGGOT?!
SIR!
FWAP

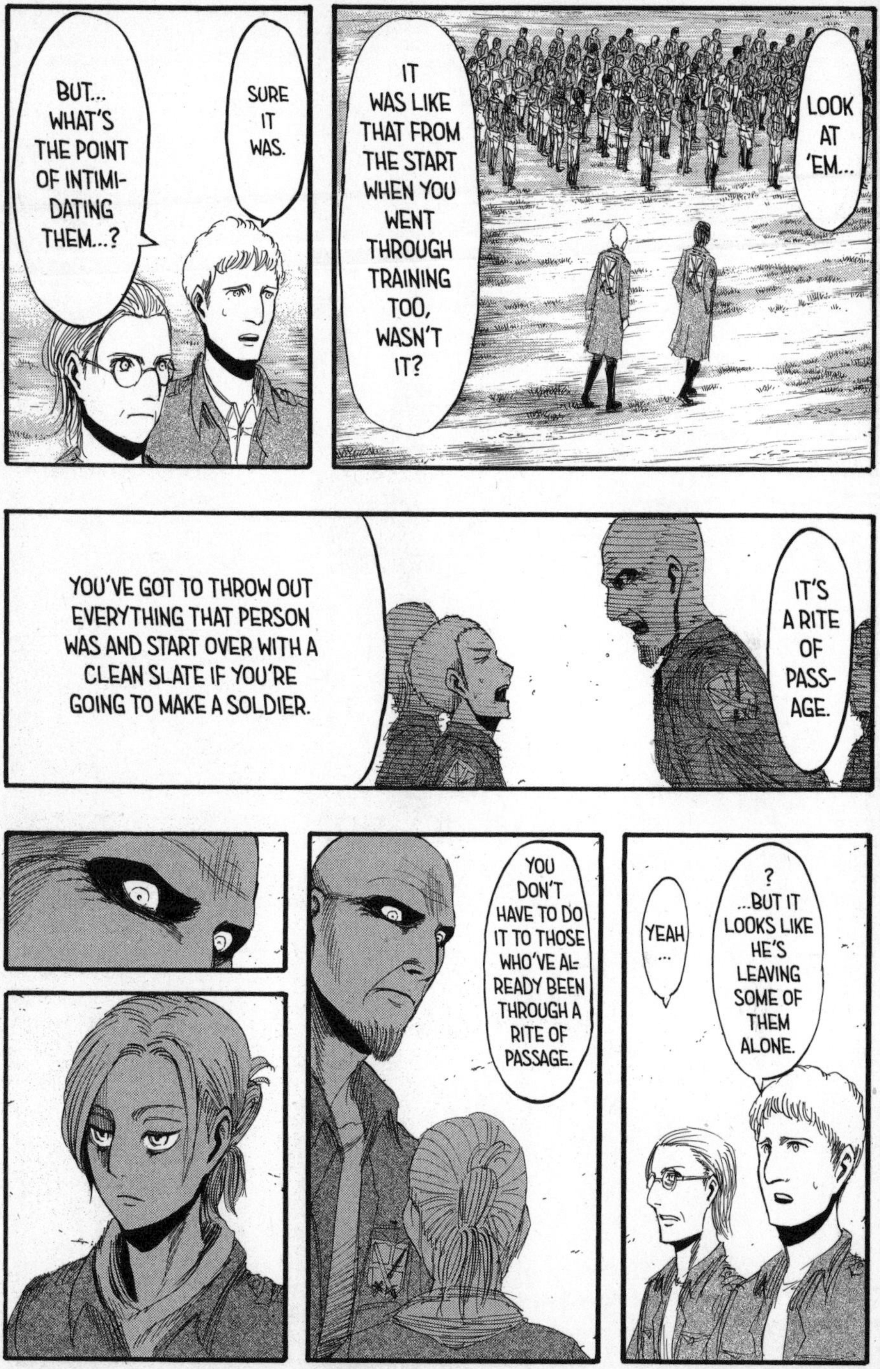
LOOK AT 'EM...
IT WAS LIKE THAT FROM THE START WHEN YOU WENT THROUGH TRAINING TOO, WASN'T IT?
SURE IT WAS.
BUT... WHAT'S THE POINT OF INTIMIDATING THEM...?
IT'S A RITE OF PASSAGE.
YOU'VE GOT TO THROW OUT EVERYTHING THAT PERSON WAS AND START OVER WITH A CLEAN SLATE IF YOU'RE GOING TO MAKE A SOLDIER.
? ...BUT IT LOOKS LIKE HE'S LEAVING SOME OF THEM ALONE.
YEAH...
YOU DON'T HAVE TO DO IT TO THOSE WHO'VE ALREADY BEEN THROUGH A RITE OF PASSAGE.

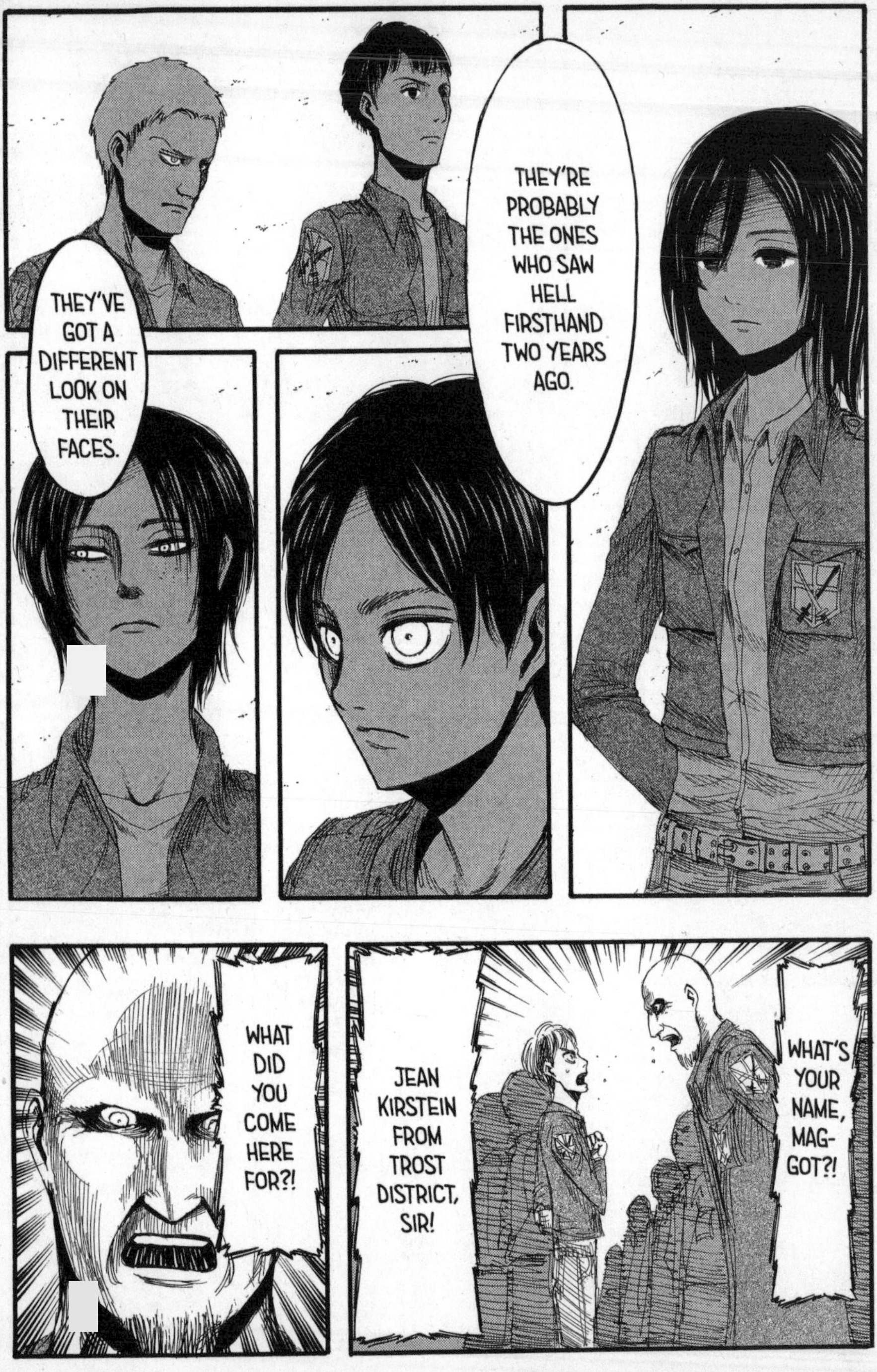
THEY'RE PROBABLY THE ONES WHO SAW HELL FIRSTHAND TWO YEARS AGO.
THEY'VE GOT A DIFFERENT LOOK ON THEIR FACES.
WHAT'S YOUR NAME, MAG-GOT?!
JEAN KIRSTEIN FROM TROST DISTRICT, SIR!
WHAT DID YOU COME HERE FOR?!

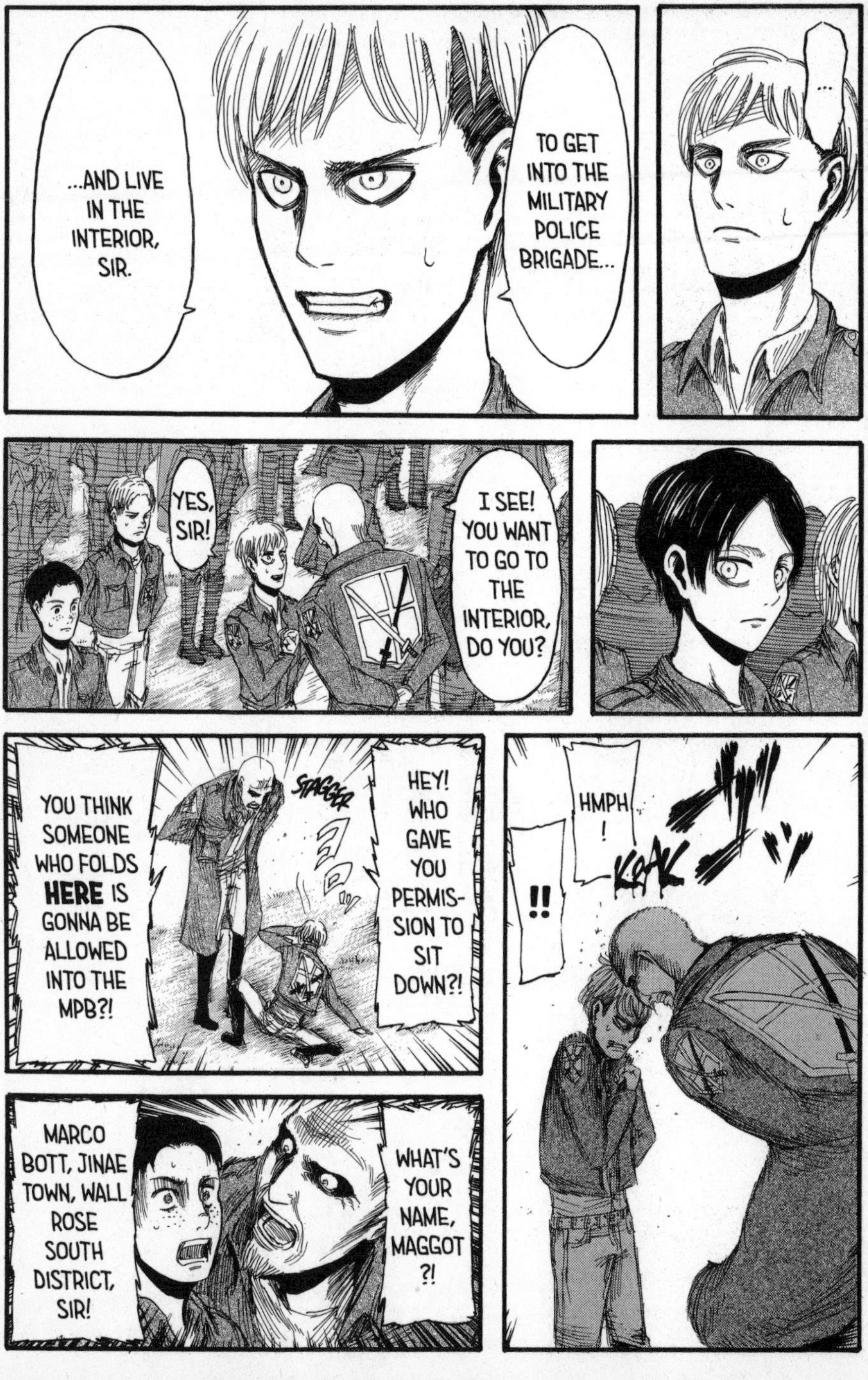
...
TO GET INTO THE MILITARY POLICE BRIGADE...
...AND LIVE IN THE INTERIOR, SIR.
I SEE! YOU WANT TO GO TO THE INTERIOR, DO YOU?
YES, SIR!
HMPH!
KRAK
!!
HEY! WHO GAVE YOU PERMISSION TO SIT DOWN?!
STAGGER
YOU THINK SOMEONE WHO FOLDS **HERE** IS GONNA BE ALLOWED INTO THE MPB?!
WHAT'S YOUR NAME, MAGGOT?!
MARCO BOTT, JINAE TOWN, WALL ROSE SOUTH DISTRICT, SIR!

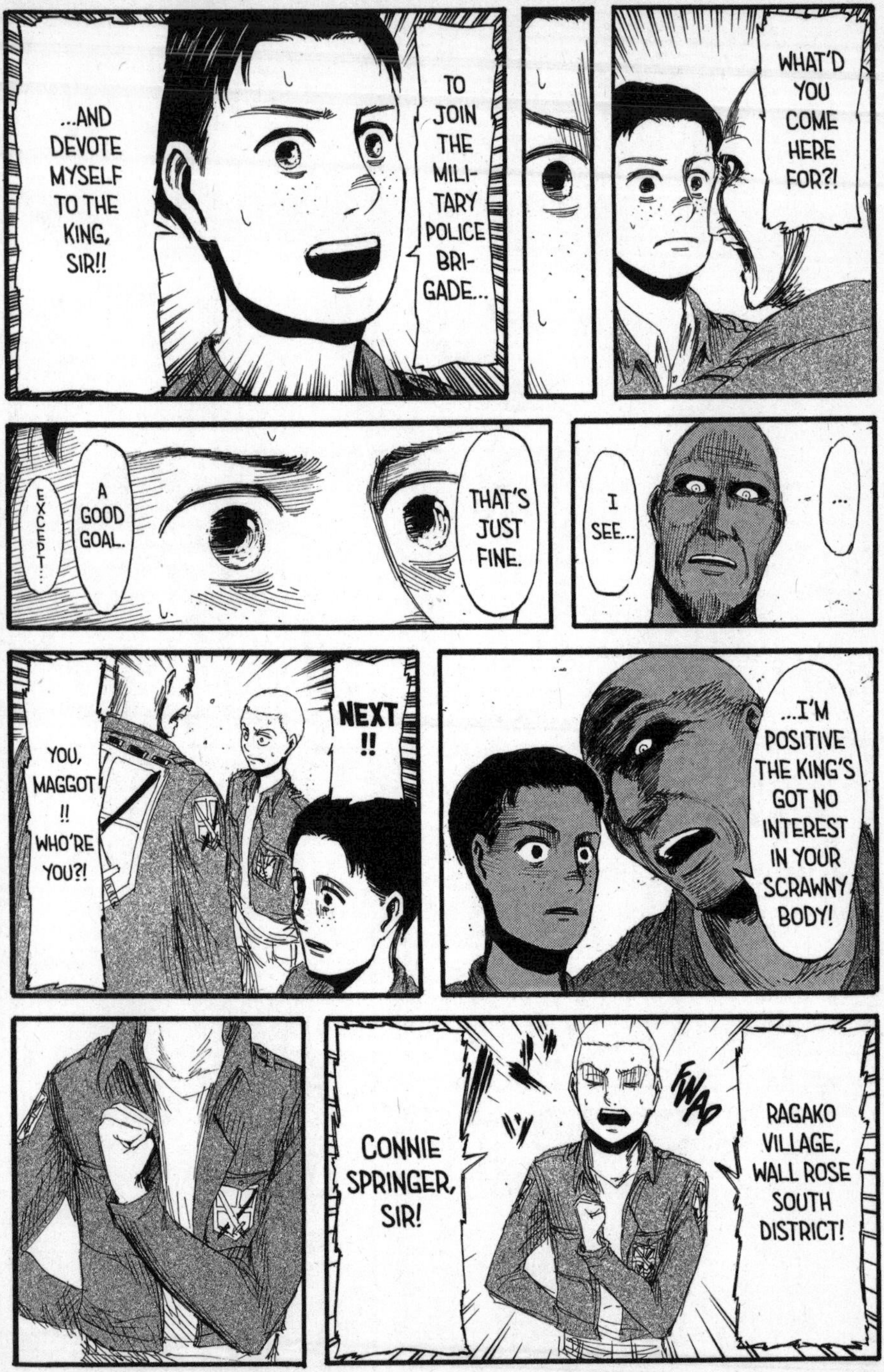
WHAT'D YOU COME HERE FOR?!
TO JOIN THE MILITARY POLICE BRIGADE...
...AND DEVOTE MYSELF TO THE KING, SIR!!
...
I SEE...
THAT'S JUST FINE.
A GOOD GOAL.
EXCEPT...
...I'M POSITIVE THE KING'S GOT NO INTEREST IN YOUR SCRAWNY BODY!
NEXT!!
YOU, MAGGOT!! WHO'RE YOU?!
RAGAKO VILLAGE, WALL ROSE SOUTH DISTRICT!
CONNIE SPRINGER, SIR!

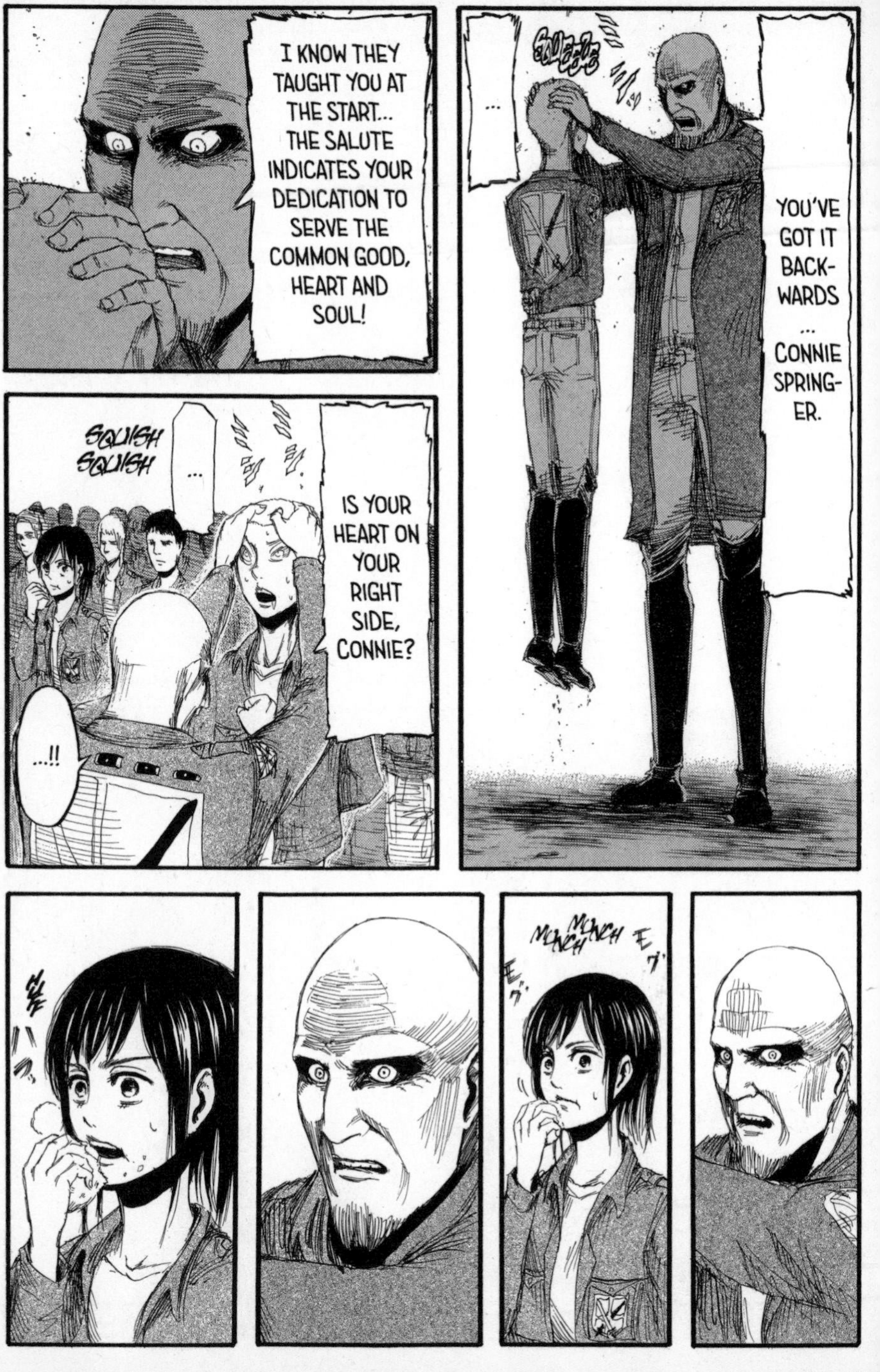
SQUEEZE
...
YOU'VE GOT IT BACKWARDS... CONNIE SPRINGER.
I KNOW THEY TAUGHT YOU AT THE START... THE SALUTE INDICATES YOUR DEDICATION TO SERVE THE COMMON GOOD, HEART AND SOUL!
IS YOUR HEART ON YOUR RIGHT SIDE, CONNIE?
...
SQUISH SQUISH
...!!
MUNCH MUNCH
モグ
モグ

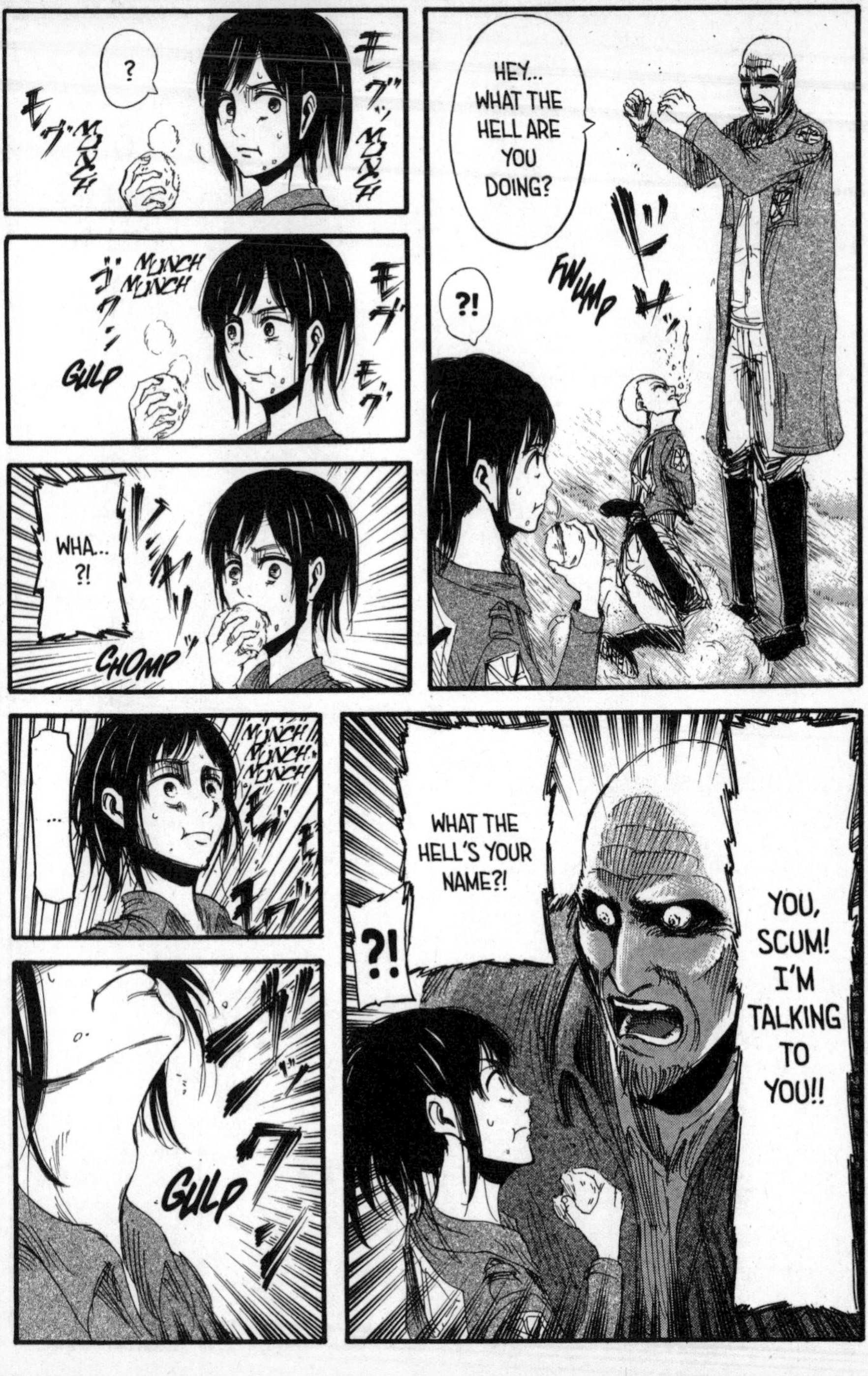
HEY... WHAT THE HELL ARE YOU DOING?
FWUMP
?!
MUNCH MUNCH
?
MUNCH MUNCH
GULP
CHOMP
WHA... ?!
YOU, SCUM! I'M TALKING TO YOU!!
WHAT THE HELL'S YOUR NAME?!
?!
MUNCH MUNCH MUNCH
...
GULP

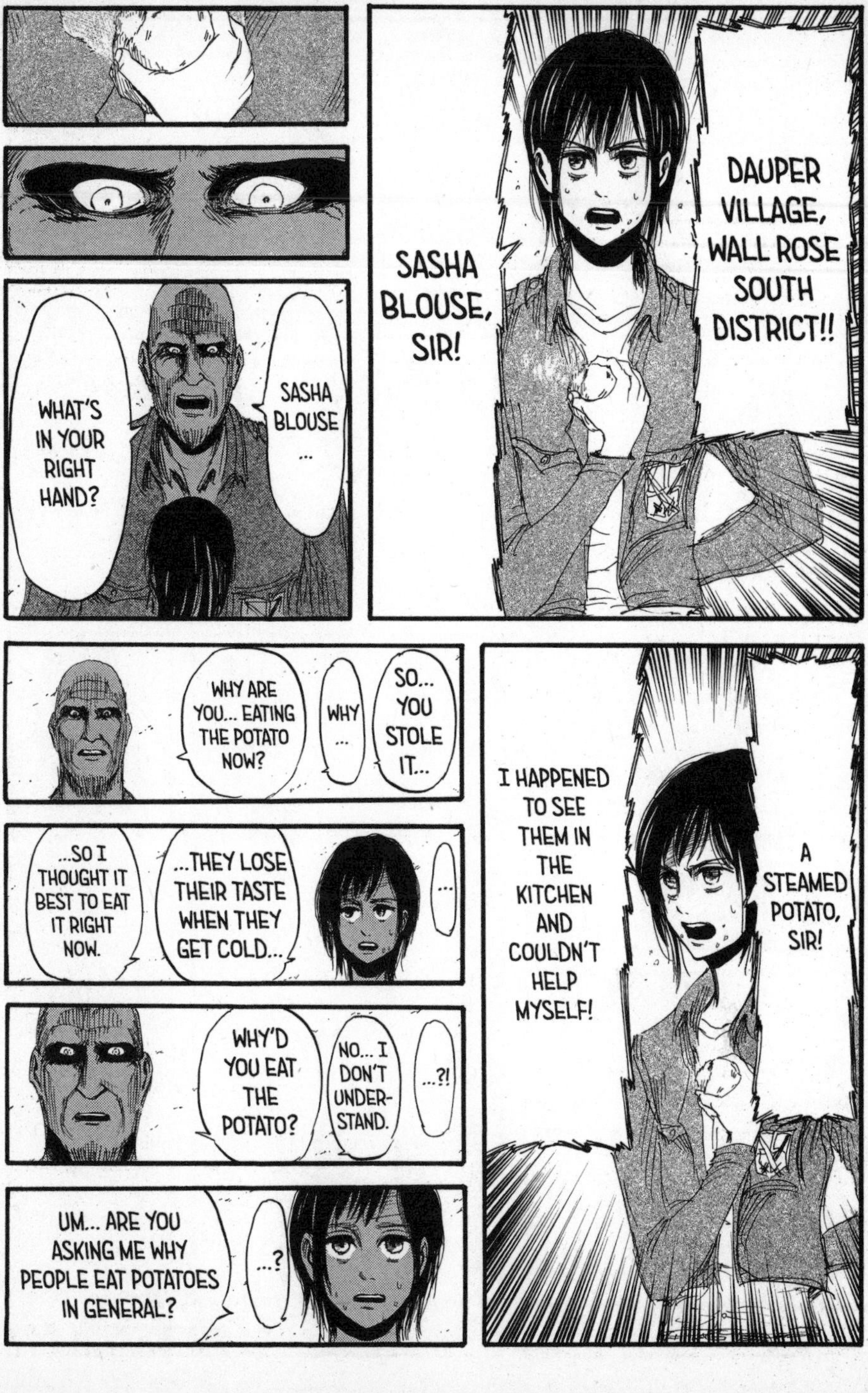
DAUPER VILLAGE, WALL ROSE SOUTH DISTRICT!!
SASHA BLOUSE, SIR!
SASHA BLOUSE ...
WHAT'S IN YOUR RIGHT HAND?
A STEAMED POTATO, SIR!
I HAPPENED TO SEE THEM IN THE KITCHEN AND COULDN'T HELP MYSELF!
SO... YOU STOLE IT...
WHY ...
WHY ARE YOU... EATING THE POTATO NOW?
...
...THEY LOSE THEIR TASTE WHEN THEY GET COLD...
...SO I THOUGHT IT BEST TO EAT IT RIGHT NOW.
...?!
NO... I DON'T UNDER-STAND.
WHY'D YOU EAT THE POTATO?
...?
UM... ARE YOU ASKING ME WHY PEOPLE EAT POTATOES IN GENERAL?

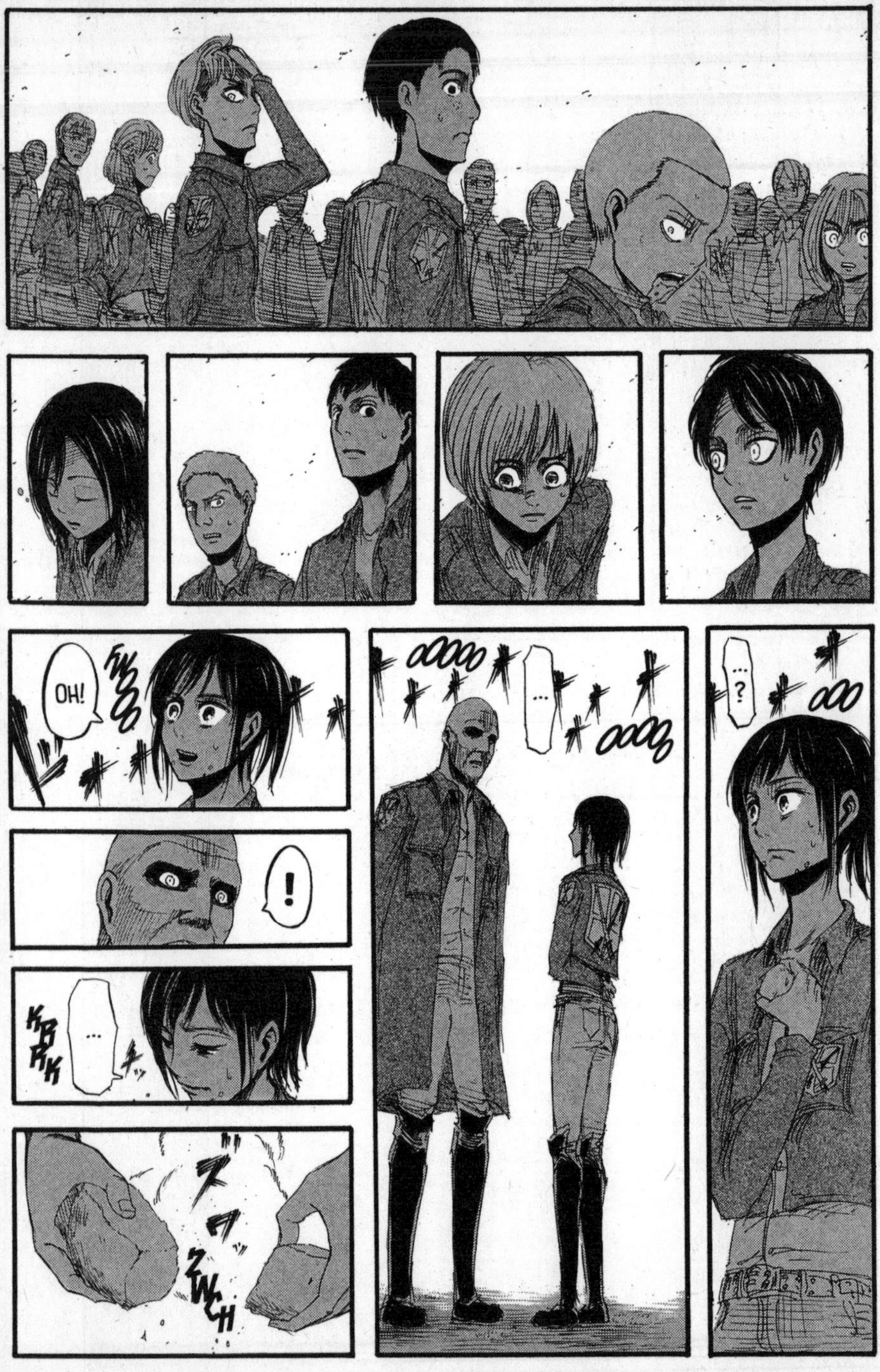
…?
…
OH!
!
KRRK
…
ZWCH

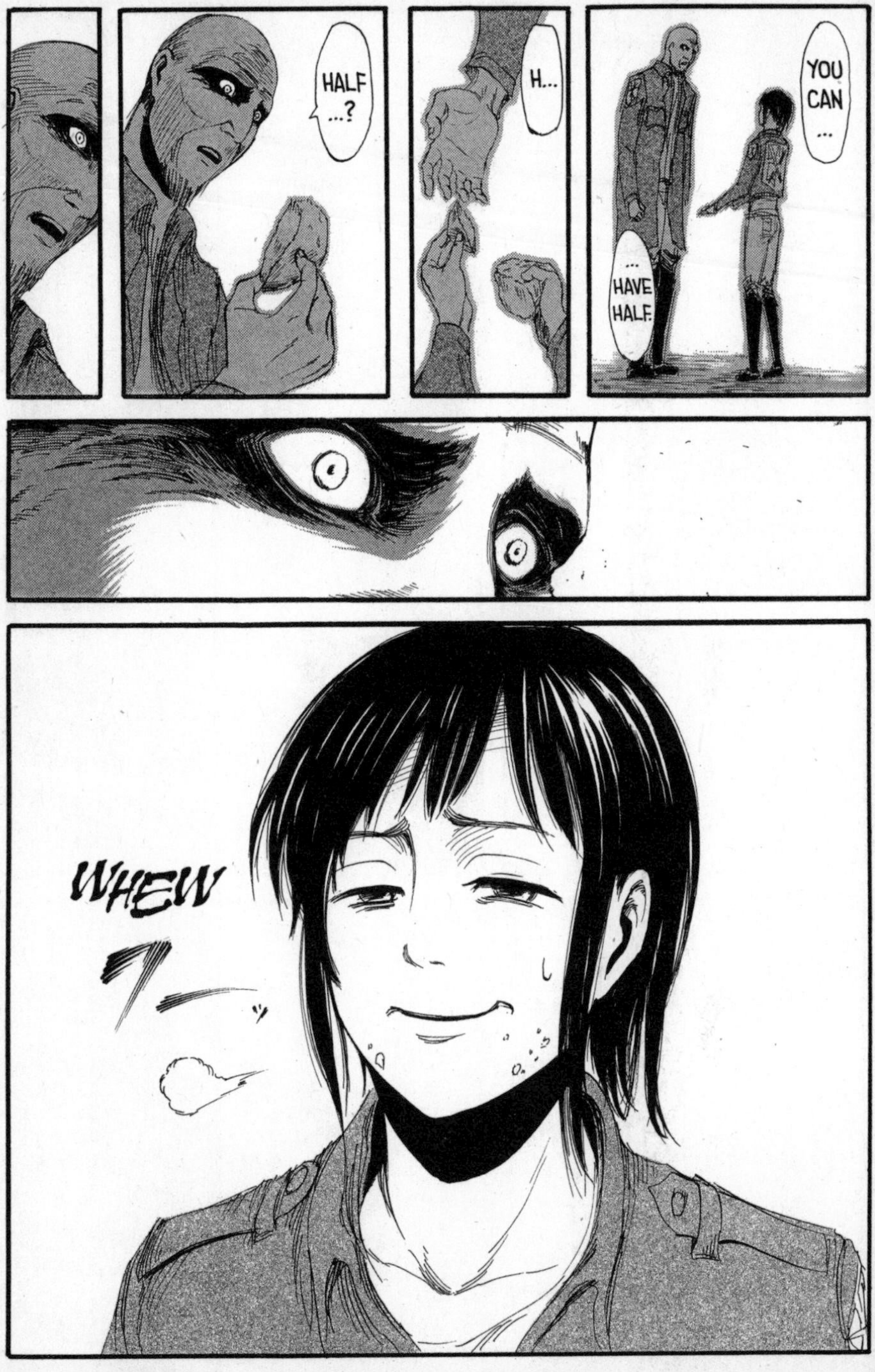
YOU CAN ...
... HAVE HALF.
H...
HALF ...?
WHEW

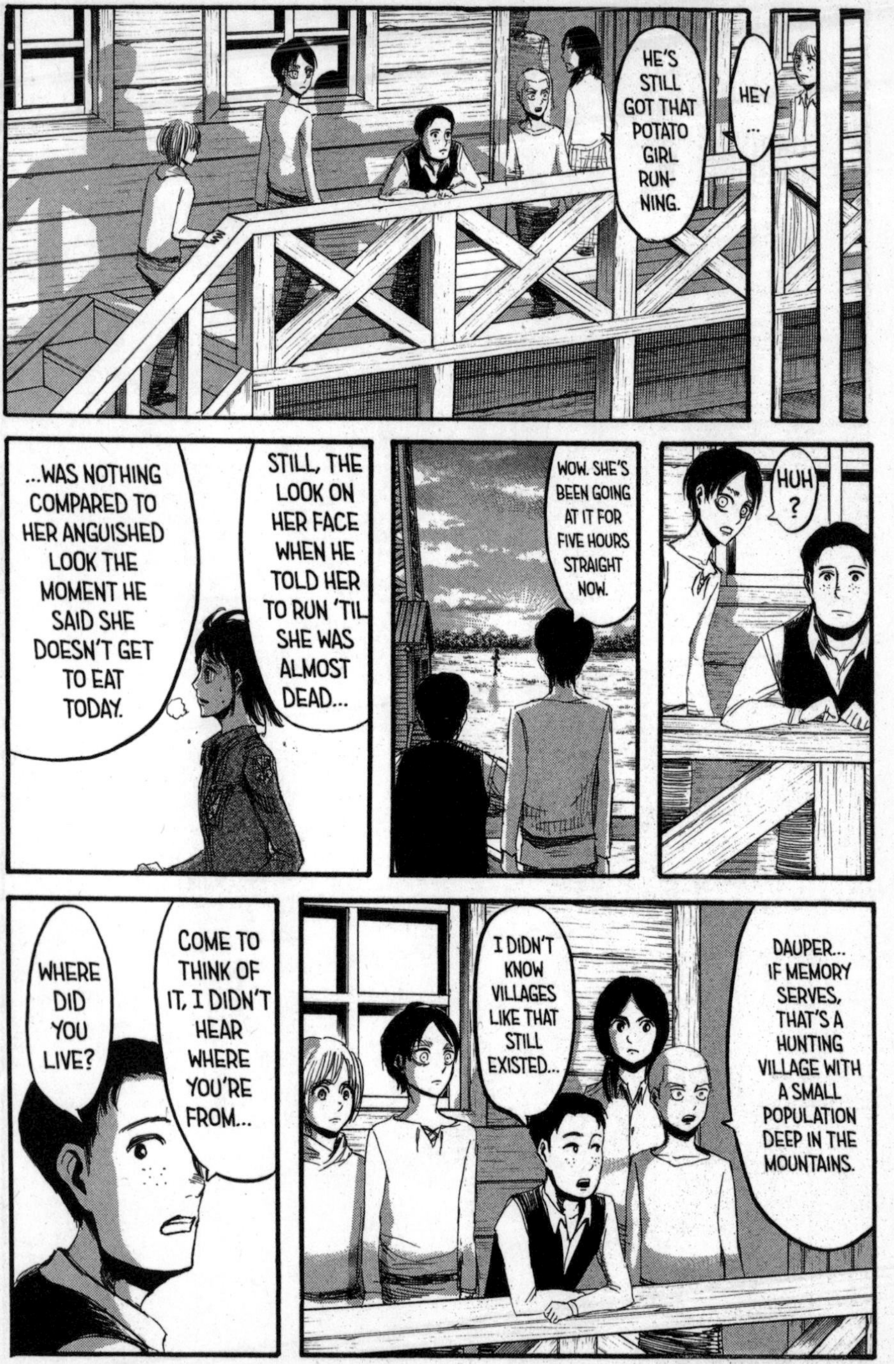
HEY ...
HE'S STILL GOT THAT POTATO GIRL RUN-NING.
HUH ?
WOW. SHE'S BEEN GOING AT IT FOR FIVE HOURS STRAIGHT NOW.
STILL, THE LOOK ON HER FACE WHEN HE TOLD HER TO RUN 'TIL SHE WAS ALMOST DEAD...
...WAS NOTHING COMPARED TO HER ANGUISHED LOOK THE MOMENT HE SAID SHE DOESN'T GET TO EAT TODAY.
DAUPER... IF MEMORY SERVES, THAT'S A HUNTING VILLAGE WITH A SMALL POPULATION DEEP IN THE MOUNTAINS.
I DIDN'T KNOW VILLAGES LIKE THAT STILL EXISTED...
COME TO THINK OF IT, I DIDN'T HEAR WHERE YOU'RE FROM...
WHERE DID YOU LIVE?

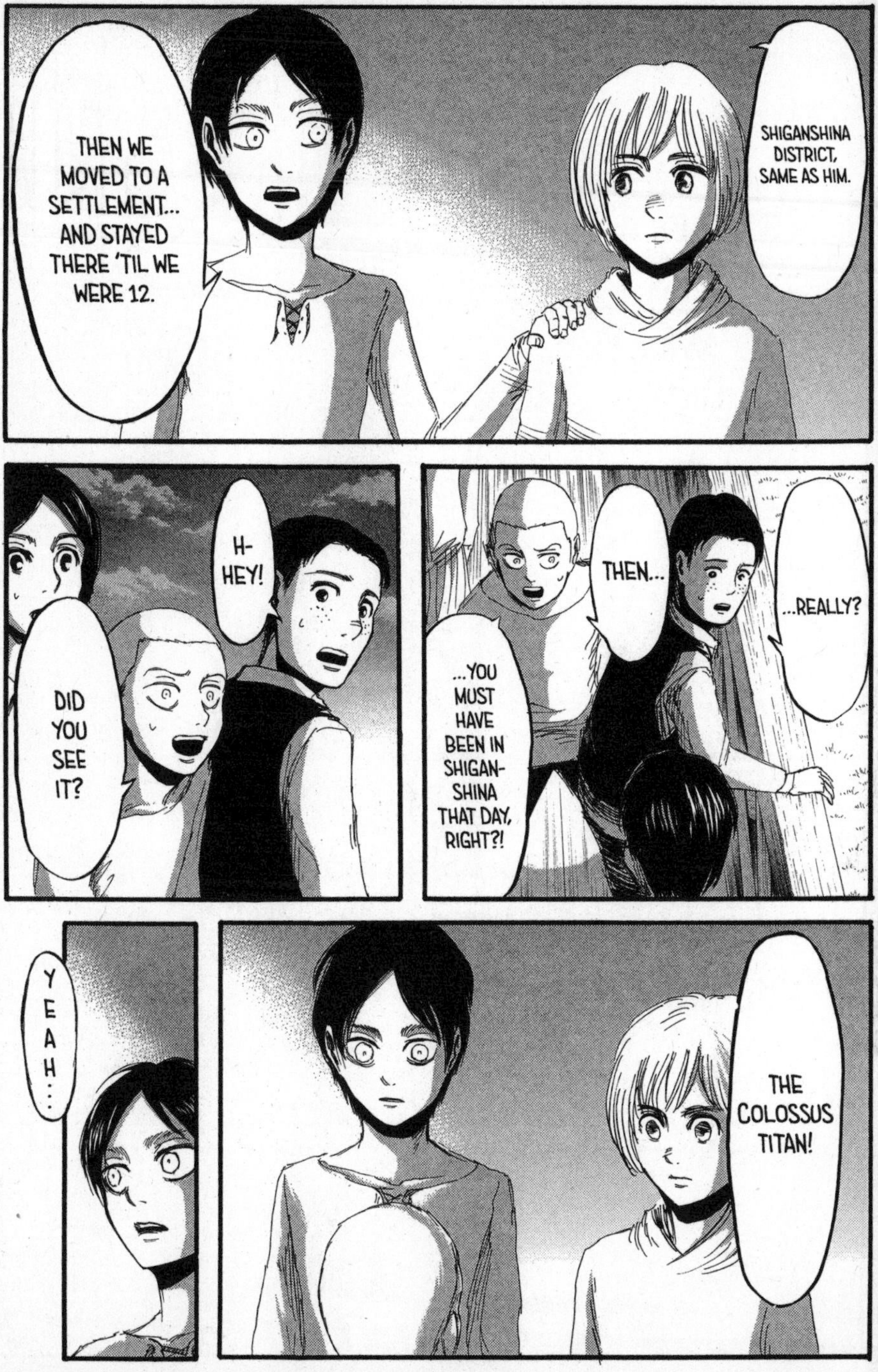
SHIGANSHINA DISTRICT, SAME AS HIM.
THEN WE MOVED TO A SETTLEMENT... AND STAYED THERE 'TIL WE WERE 12.
...REALLY?
THEN...
...YOU MUST HAVE BEEN IN SHIGAN-SHINA THAT DAY, RIGHT?!
H-HEY!
DID YOU SEE IT?
THE COLOSSUS TITAN!
YEAH...

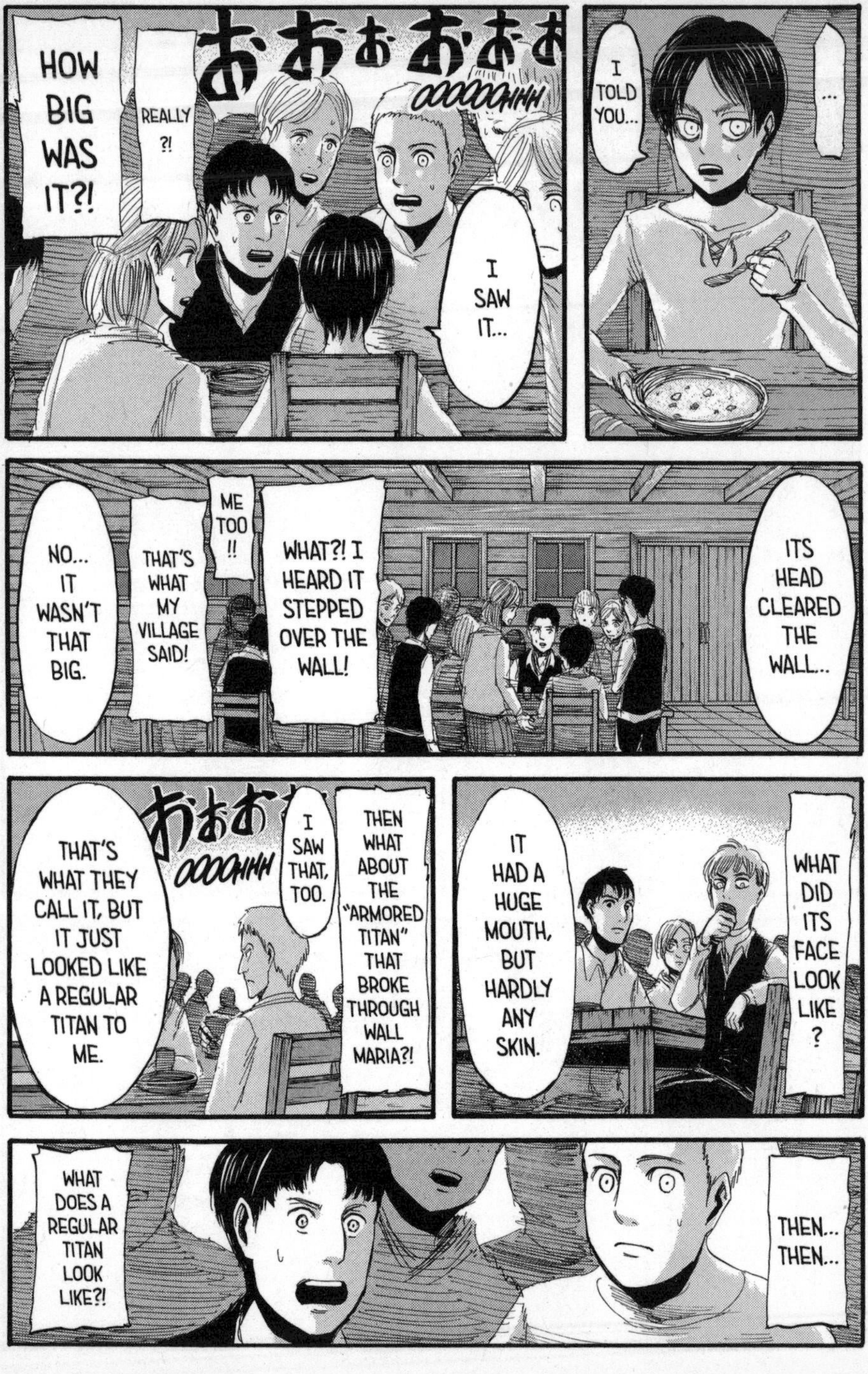
...
I TOLD YOU...
おおぉおおぉ
OOOOOOHHH
I SAW IT...
REALLY?!
HOW BIG WAS IT?!
ITS HEAD CLEARED THE WALL...
WHAT?! I HEARD IT STEPPED OVER THE WALL!
ME TOO!!
THAT'S WHAT MY VILLAGE SAID!
NO... IT WASN'T THAT BIG.
WHAT DID ITS FACE LOOK LIKE?
IT HAD A HUGE MOUTH, BUT HARDLY ANY SKIN.
THEN WHAT ABOUT THE "ARMORED TITAN" THAT BROKE THROUGH WALL MARIA?!
I SAW THAT, TOO.
おぉお
OOOOHHH
THAT'S WHAT THEY CALL IT, BUT IT JUST LOOKED LIKE A REGULAR TITAN TO ME.
THEN... THEN...
WHAT DOES A REGULAR TITAN LOOK LIKE?!

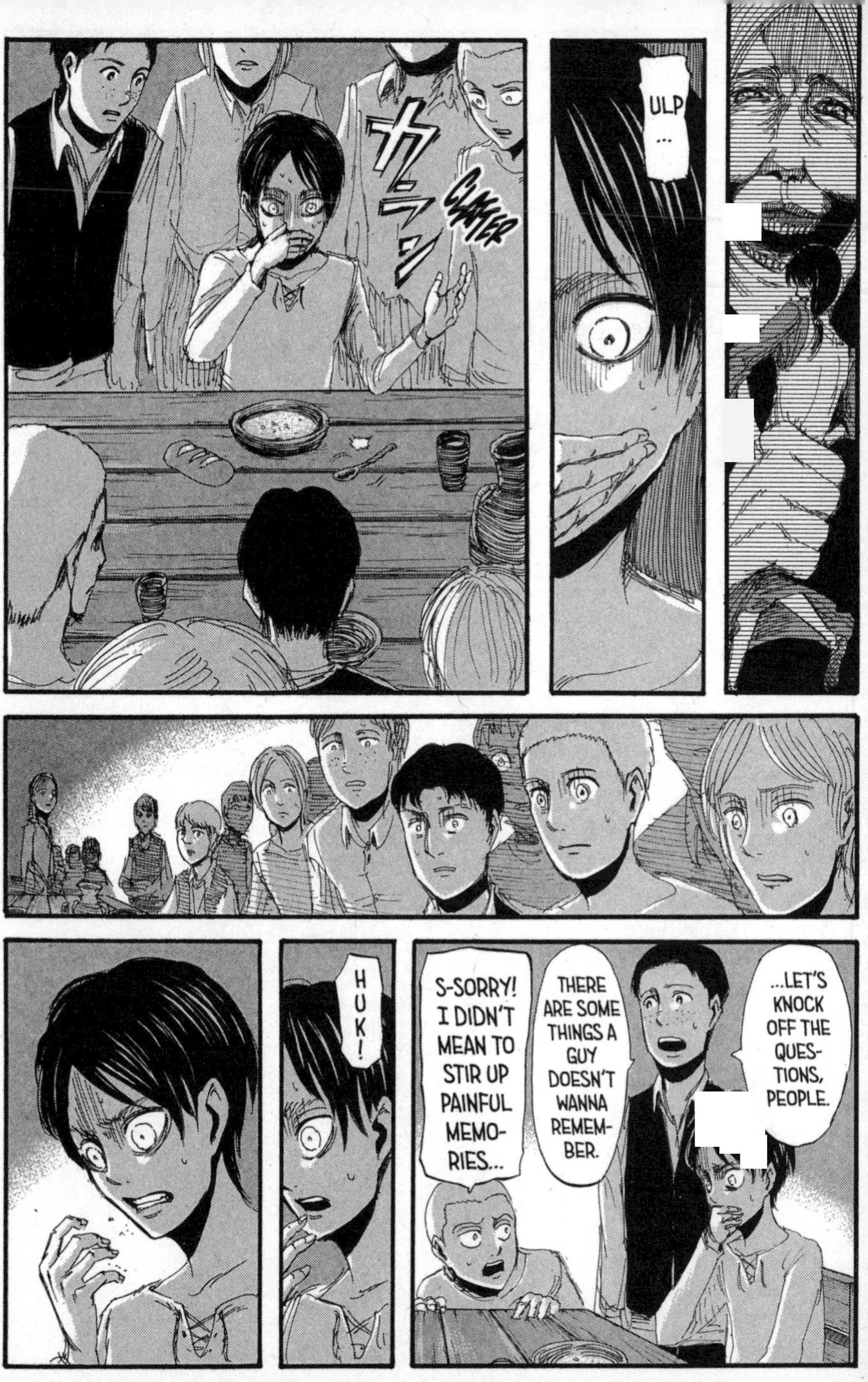
ULP ...
カラン
CLATTER
...LET'S KNOCK OFF THE QUESTIONS, PEOPLE.
THERE ARE SOME THINGS A GUY DOESN'T WANNA REMEMBER.
S-SORRY! I DIDN'T MEAN TO STIR UP PAINFUL MEMORIES...
HUK!

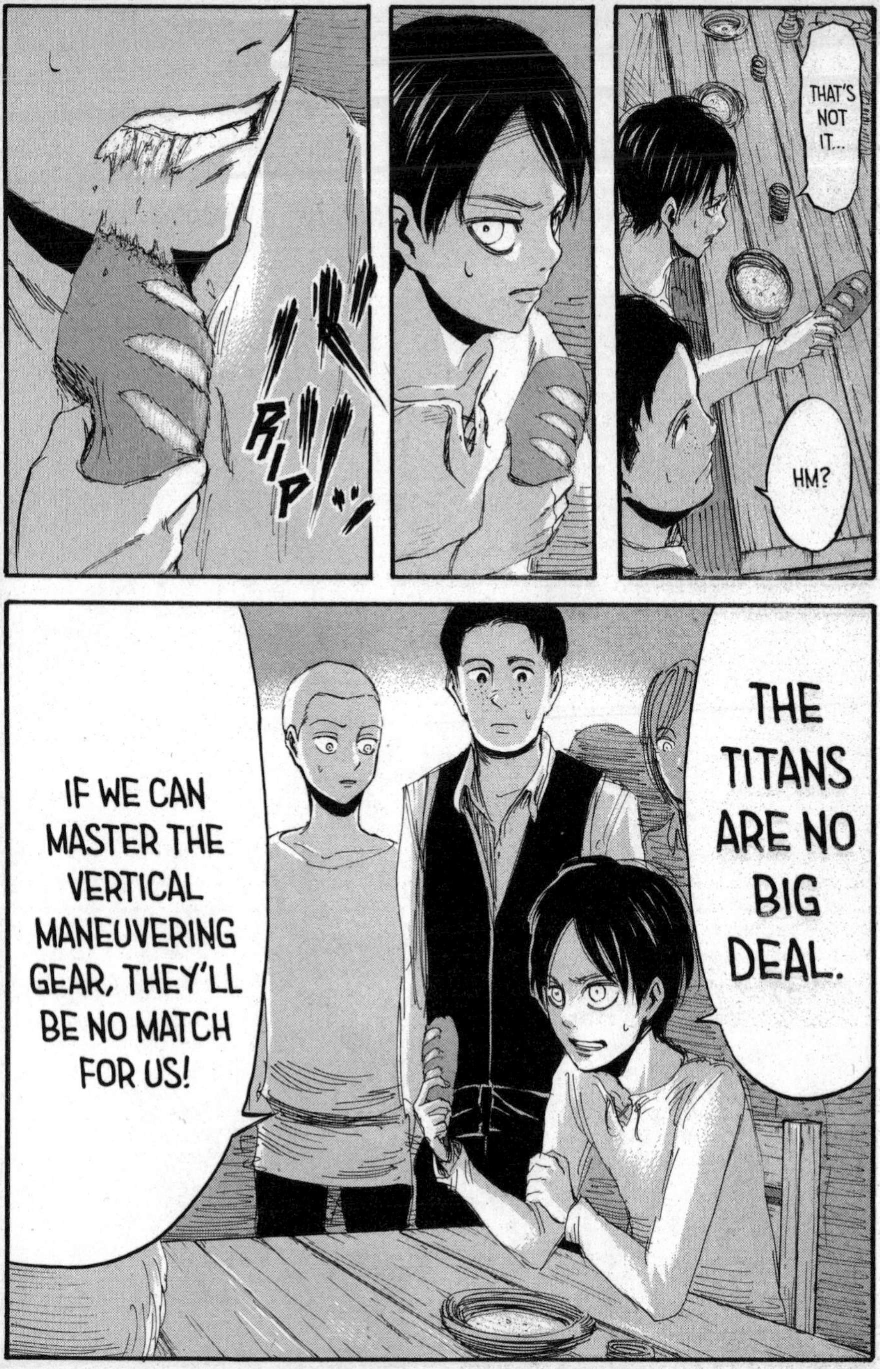
THAT'S NOT IT...
HM?
RIP
THE TITANS ARE NO BIG DEAL.
IF WE CAN MASTER THE VERTICAL MANEUVERING GEAR, THEY'LL BE NO MATCH FOR US!

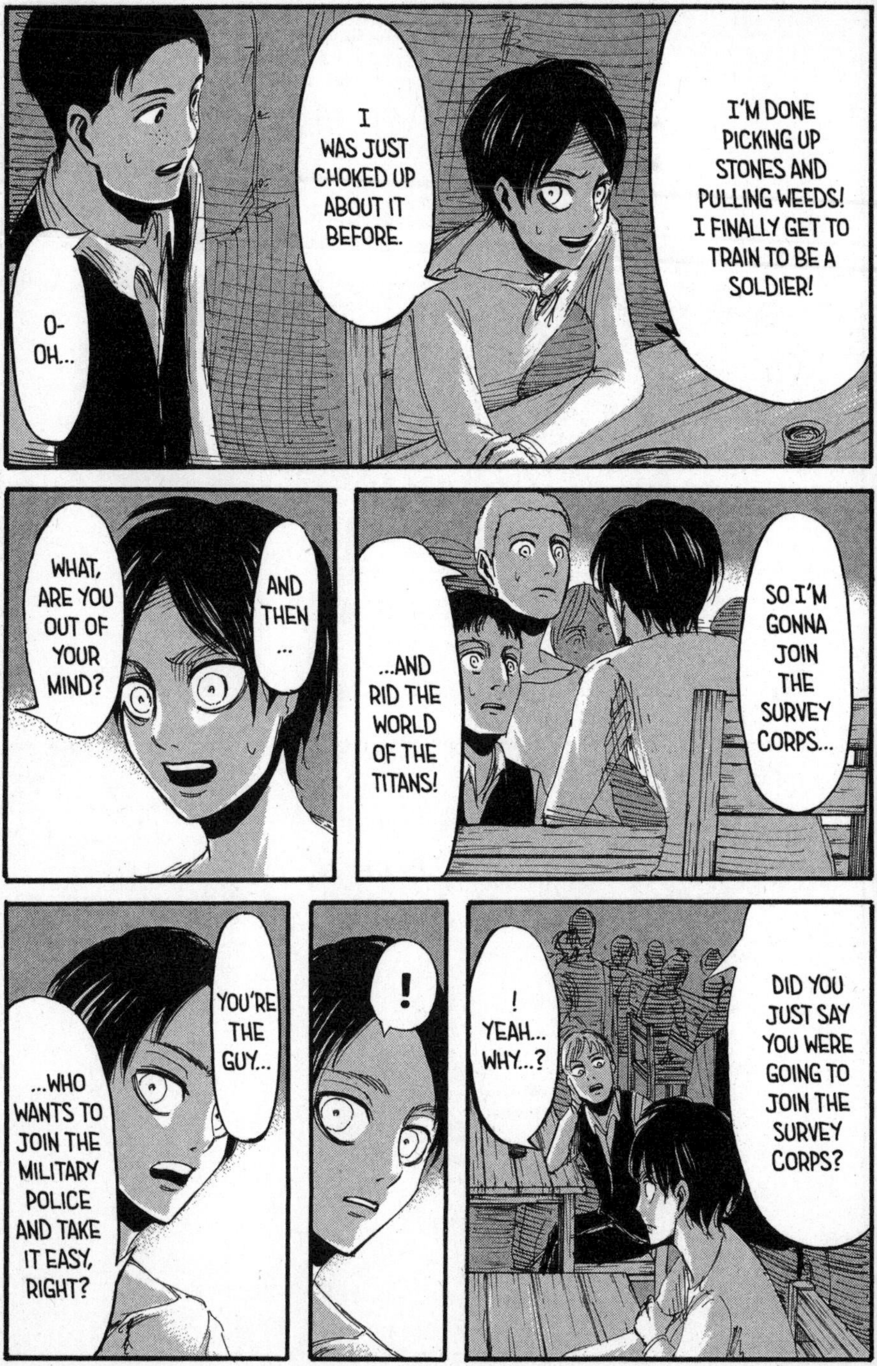
I'M DONE PICKING UP STONES AND PULLING WEEDS! I FINALLY GET TO TRAIN TO BE A SOLDIER!
I WAS JUST CHOKED UP ABOUT IT BEFORE.
O-OH...
SO I'M GONNA JOIN THE SURVEY CORPS...
...AND RID THE WORLD OF THE TITANS!
AND THEN ...
WHAT, ARE YOU OUT OF YOUR MIND?
DID YOU JUST SAY YOU WERE GOING TO JOIN THE SURVEY CORPS?
! YEAH... WHY...?
!
YOU'RE THE GUY...
...WHO WANTS TO JOIN THE MILITARY POLICE AND TAKE IT EASY, RIGHT?

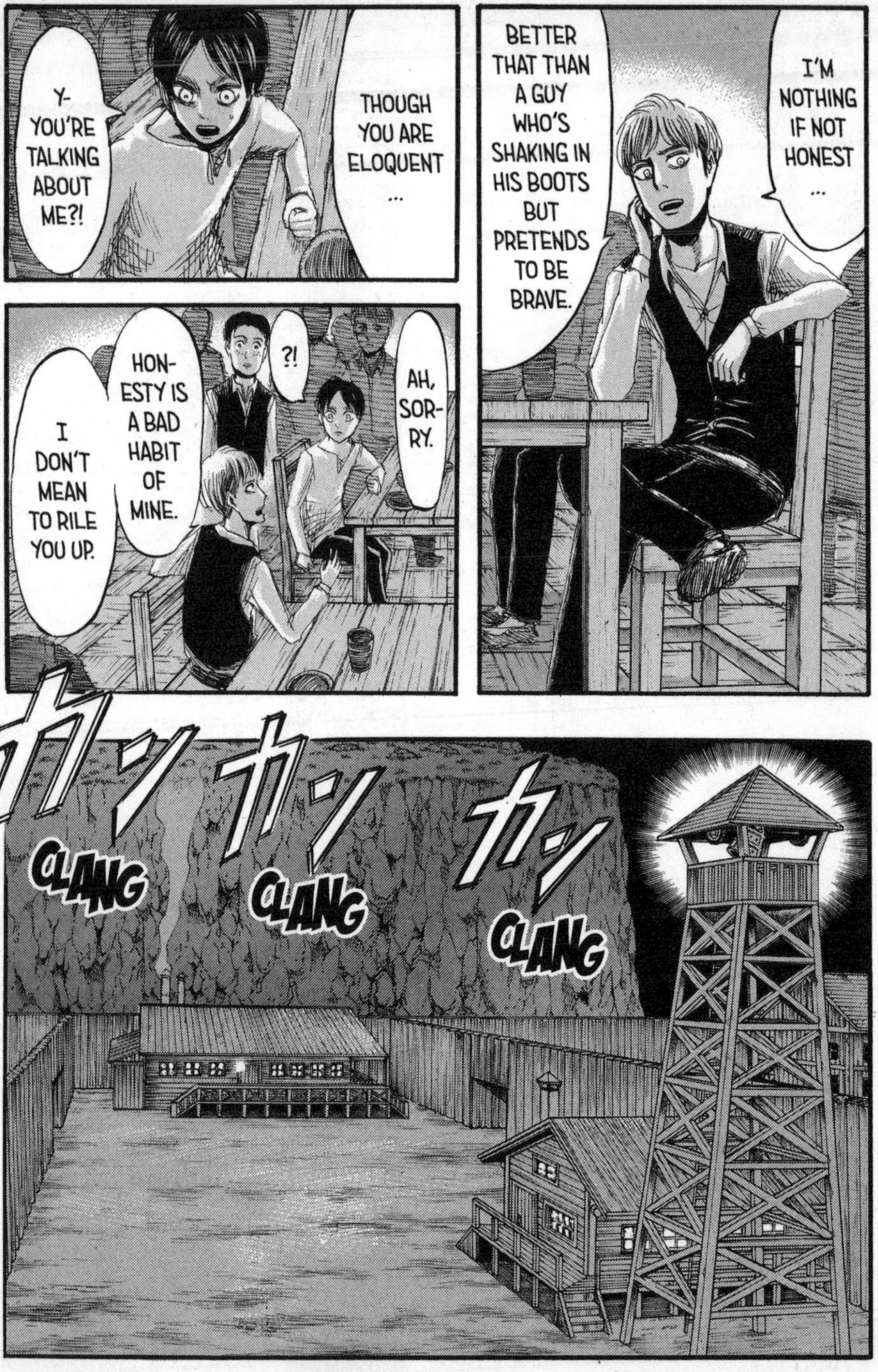
I'M NOTHING IF NOT HONEST ...
BETTER THAT THAN A GUY WHO'S SHAKING IN HIS BOOTS BUT PRETENDS TO BE BRAVE.
THOUGH YOU ARE ELOQUENT ...
Y- YOU'RE TALKING ABOUT ME?!
AH, SOR-RY.
?!
HON-ESTY IS A BAD HABIT OF MINE.
I DON'T MEAN TO RILE YOU UP.
カン
CLANG
カン
CLANG
カッ
CLANG

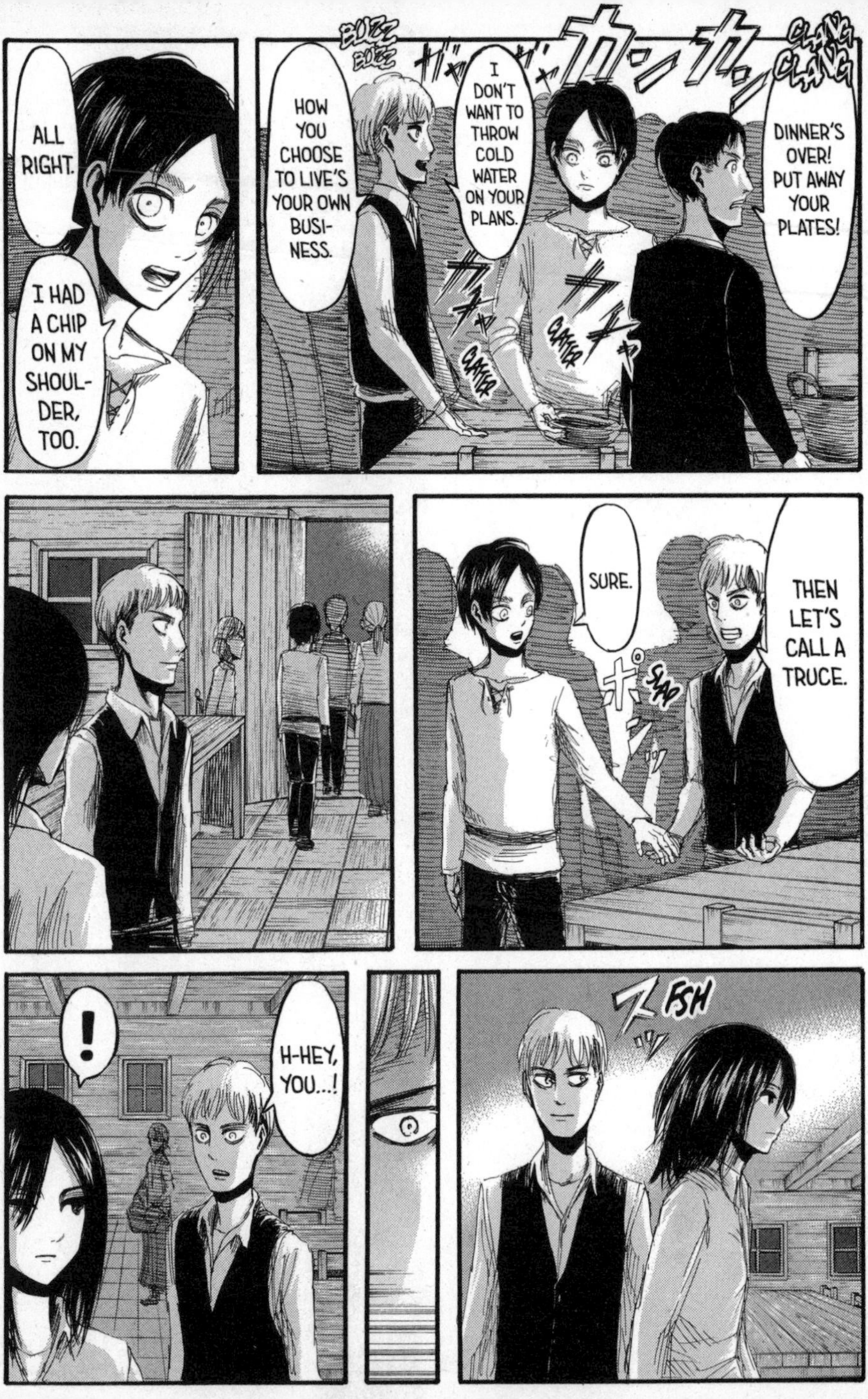
CLANG CLANG
DINNER'S OVER! PUT AWAY YOUR PLATES!
BUZZ BUZZ
I DON'T WANT TO THROW COLD WATER ON YOUR PLANS.
HOW YOU CHOOSE TO LIVE'S YOUR OWN BUSINESS.
CLAKKER
CLAKKER
ALL RIGHT.
I HAD A CHIP ON MY SHOULDER, TOO.
THEN LET'S CALL A TRUCE.
SURE.
SLAP
FSH
H-HEY, YOU...!
!

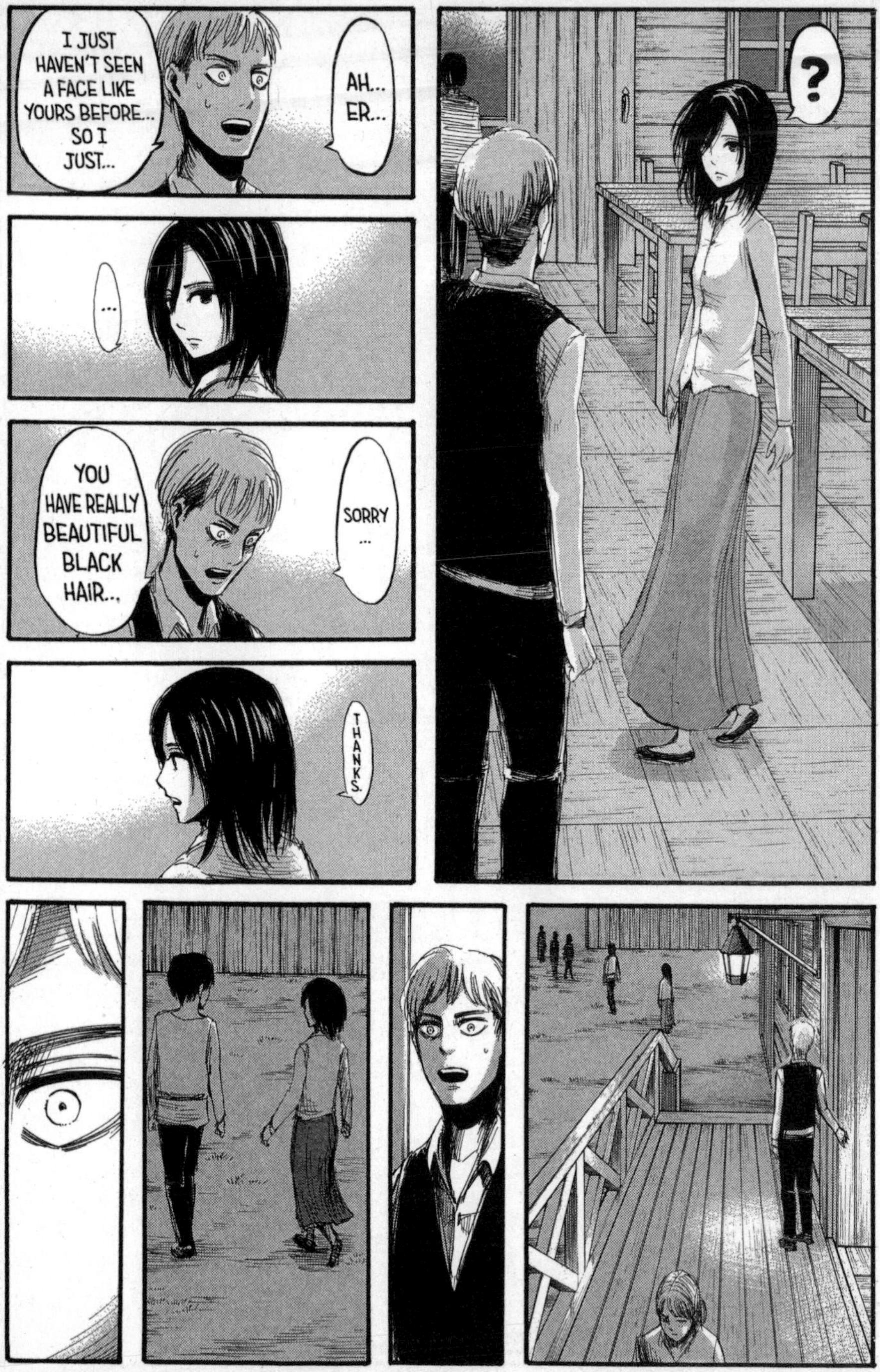
?
AH... ER...
I JUST HAVEN'T SEEN A FACE LIKE YOURS BEFORE... SO I JUST...
...
SORRY...
YOU HAVE REALLY BEAUTIFUL BLACK HAIR...
THANKS.

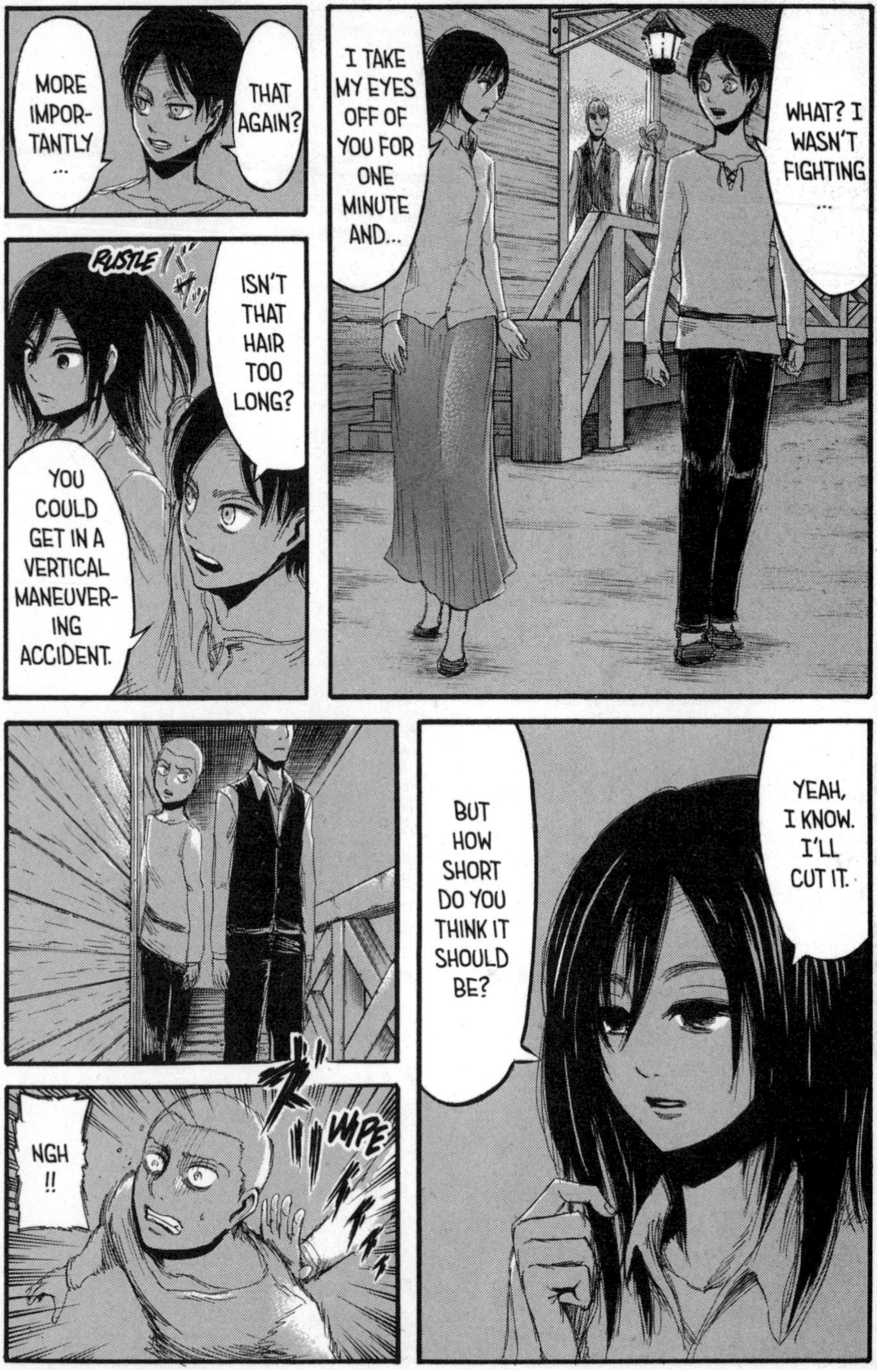
WHAT? I WASN'T FIGHTING ...
I TAKE MY EYES OFF OF YOU FOR ONE MINUTE AND...
THAT AGAIN?
MORE IMPOR-TANTLY ...
RUSTLE
ISN'T THAT HAIR TOO LONG?
YOU COULD GET IN A VERTICAL MANEUVER-ING ACCIDENT.
YEAH, I KNOW. I'LL CUT IT.
BUT HOW SHORT DO YOU THINK IT SHOULD BE?
WIPE
NGH !!

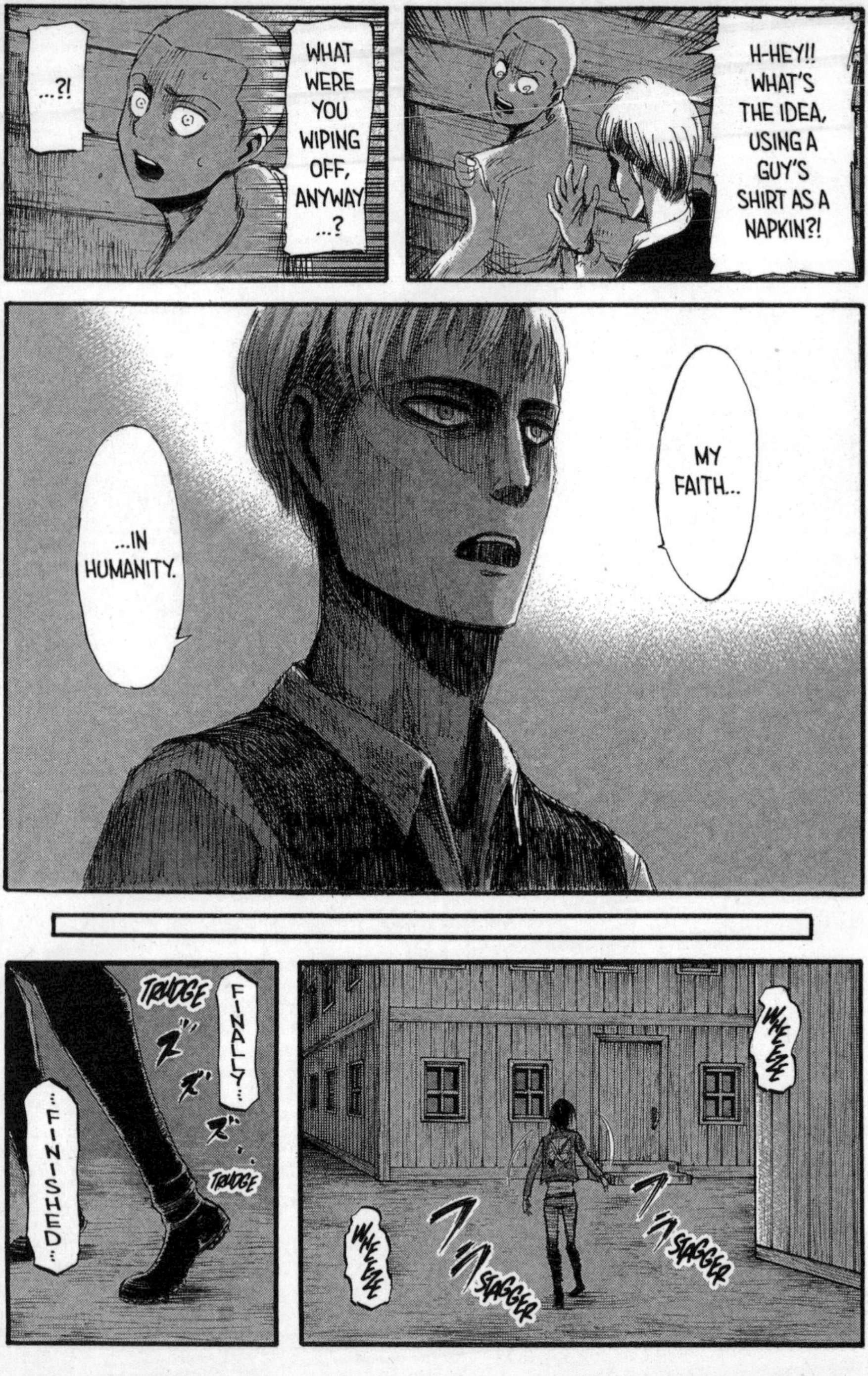
H-HEY!! WHAT'S THE IDEA, USING A GUY'S SHIRT AS A NAPKIN?!
WHAT WERE YOU WIPING OFF, ANYWAY...?
...?!
MY FAITH...
...IN HUMANITY.
WHEEZE
STAGGER
STAGGER
WHEEZE
FINALLY...
TRUDGE
...FINISHED...
TRUDGE

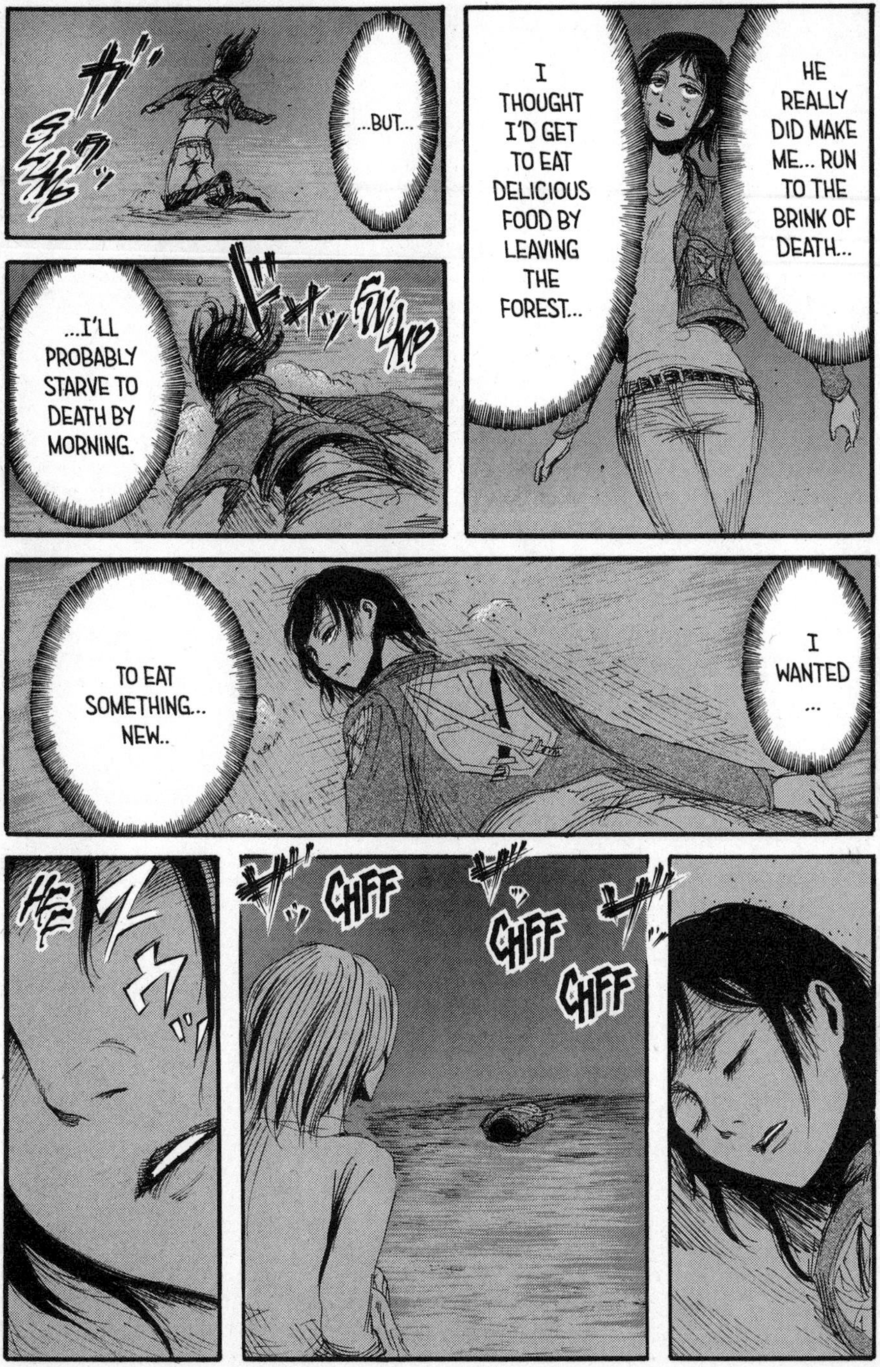
HE REALLY DID MAKE ME... RUN TO THE BRINK OF DEATH...
I THOUGHT I'D GET TO EAT DELICIOUS FOOD BY LEAVING THE FOREST...
...BUT...
...I'LL PROBABLY STARVE TO DEATH BY MORNING.
FWUMP
I WANTED ...
TO EAT SOMETHING... NEW..
CHFF
CHFF
CHFF

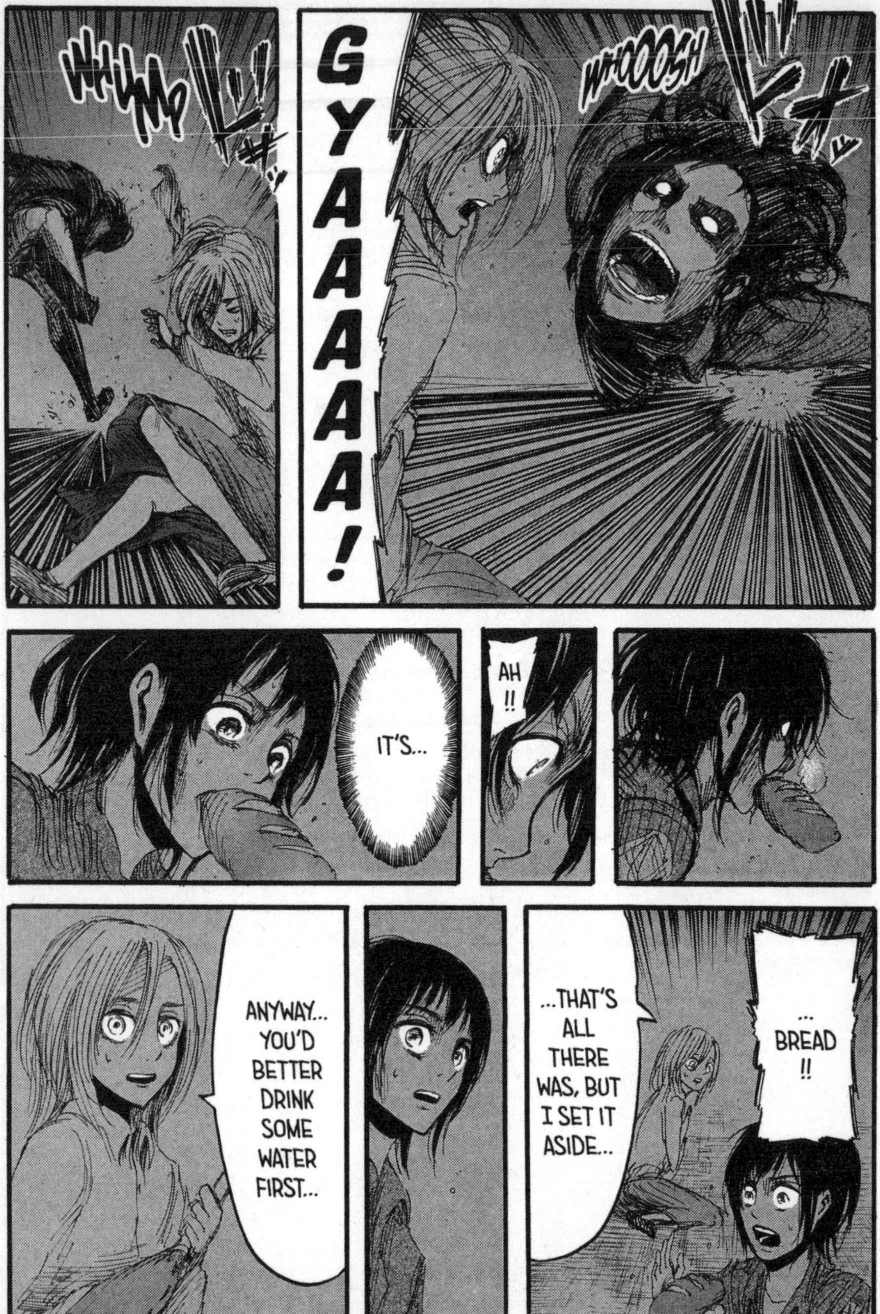
WHOOOSH
GYAAAAA!
WHUMP
AH !!
IT'S...
... BREAD !!
...THAT'S ALL THERE WAS, BUT I SET IT ASIDE...
ANYWAY... YOU'D BETTER DRINK SOME WATER FIRST...

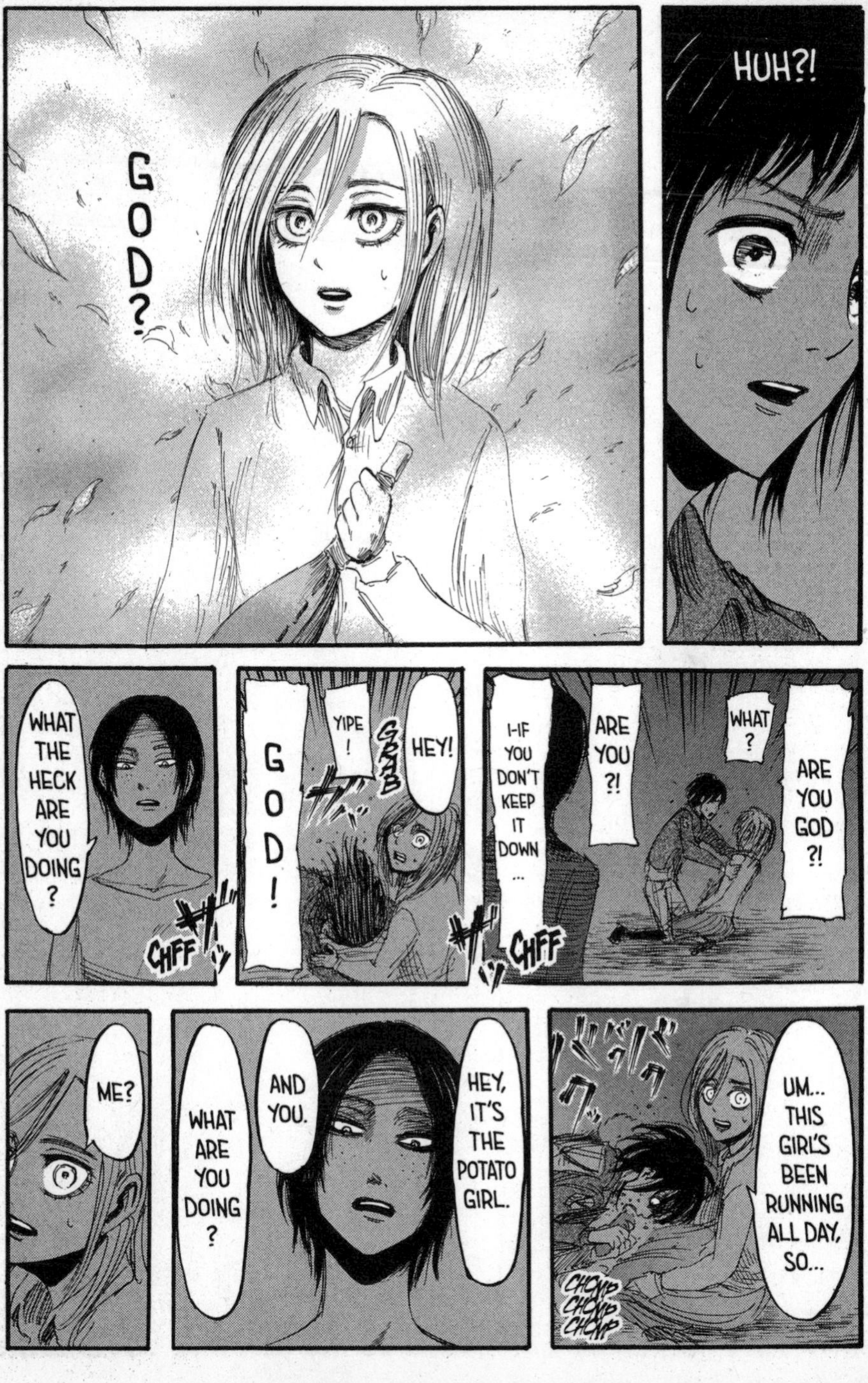
HUH?!
GOD?
ARE YOU GOD?!
WHAT?
ARE YOU?!
I-IF YOU DON'T KEEP IT DOWN ...
CHFF
HEY!
GRAB
YIPE!
GOD!
CHFF
WHAT THE HECK ARE YOU DOING?
UM... THIS GIRL'S BEEN RUNNING ALL DAY, SO...
CHOMP CHOMP CHOMP
HEY, IT'S THE POTATO GIRL.
AND YOU.
WHAT ARE YOU DOING?
ME?

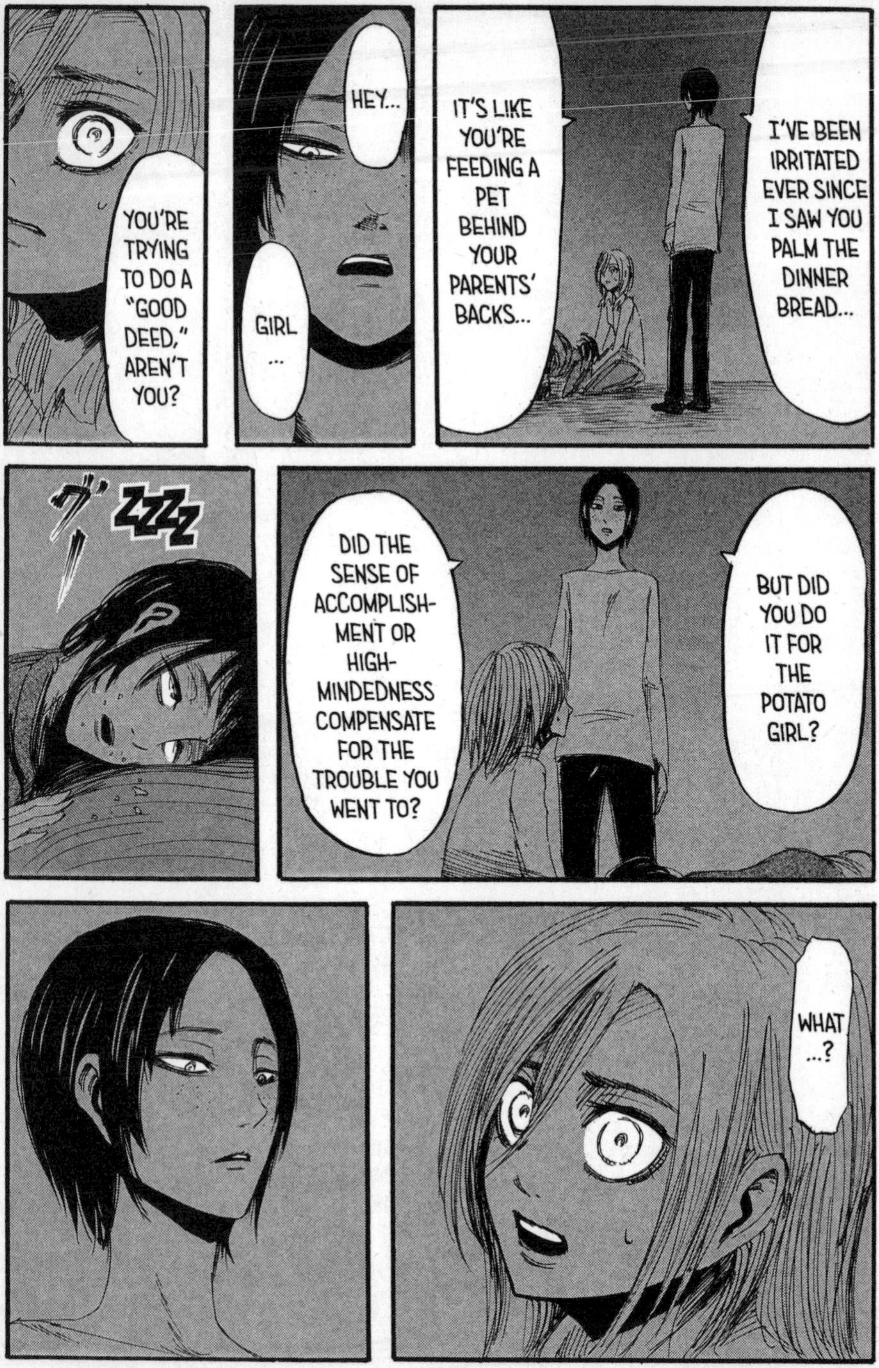
I'VE BEEN IRRITATED EVER SINCE I SAW YOU PALM THE DINNER BREAD...
IT'S LIKE YOU'RE FEEDING A PET BEHIND YOUR PARENTS' BACKS...
HEY...
GIRL ...
YOU'RE TRYING TO DO A "GOOD DEED," AREN'T YOU?
BUT DID YOU DO IT FOR THE POTATO GIRL?
DID THE SENSE OF ACCOMPLISHMENT OR HIGH-MINDEDNESS COMPENSATE FOR THE TROUBLE YOU WENT TO?
ZZZZ
WHAT ...?

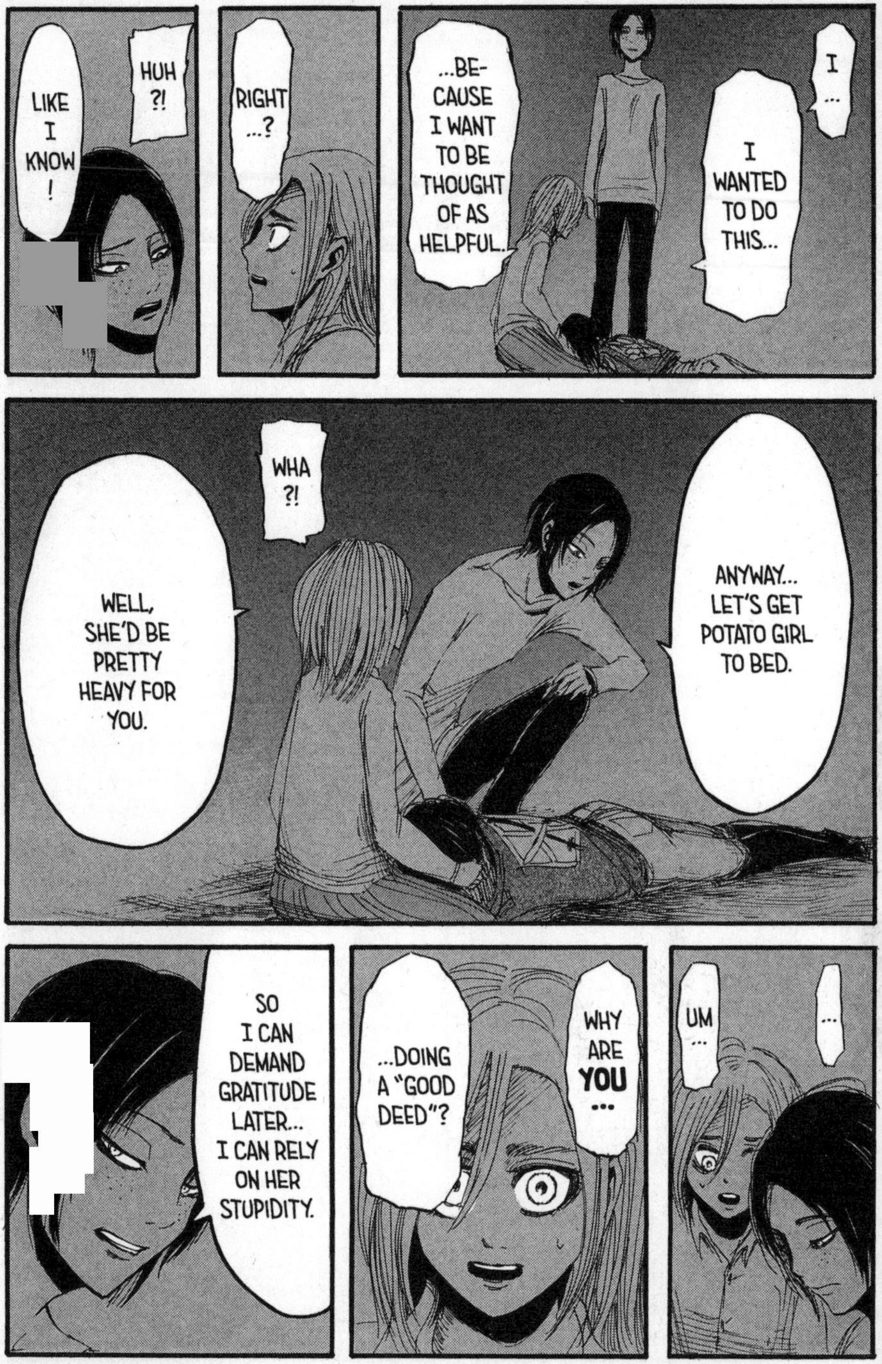
I ...
I WANTED TO DO THIS...
...BE-CAUSE I WANT TO BE THOUGHT OF AS HELPFUL.
RIGHT ...?
HUH ?!
LIKE I KNOW !
ANYWAY... LET'S GET POTATO GIRL TO BED.
WHA ?!
WELL, SHE'D BE PRETTY HEAVY FOR YOU.
...
UM ...
WHY ARE YOU ...
...DOING A "GOOD DEED"?
SO I CAN DEMAND GRATITUDE LATER... I CAN RELY ON HER STUPIDITY.

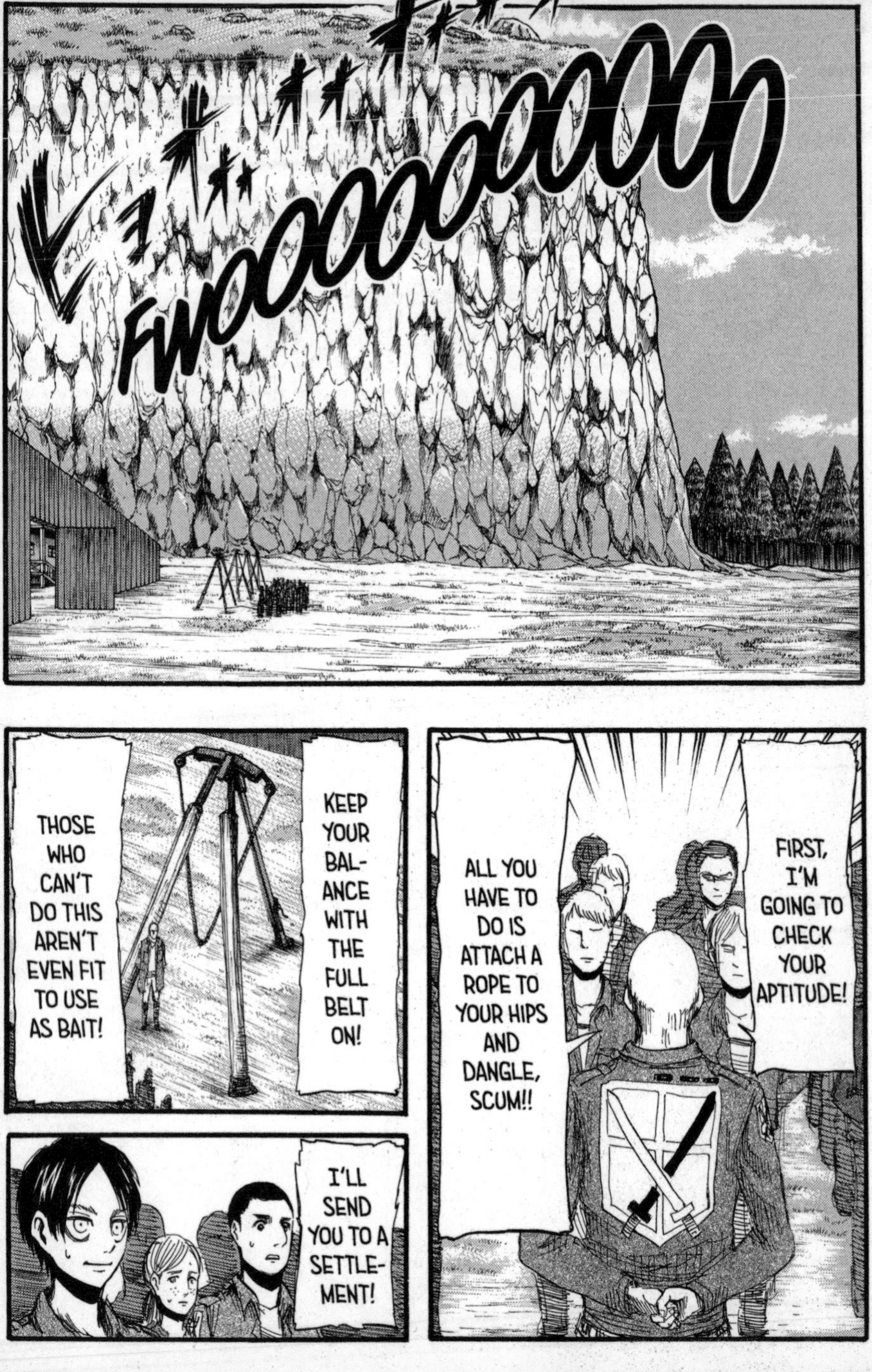
FWOOOOOOOOOO
FIRST, I'M GOING TO CHECK YOUR APTITUDE!
ALL YOU HAVE TO DO IS ATTACH A ROPE TO YOUR HIPS AND DANGLE, SCUM!!
KEEP YOUR BAL-ANCE WITH THE FULL BELT ON!
THOSE WHO CAN'T DO THIS AREN'T EVEN FIT TO USE AS BAIT!
I'LL SEND YOU TO A SETTLE-MENT!

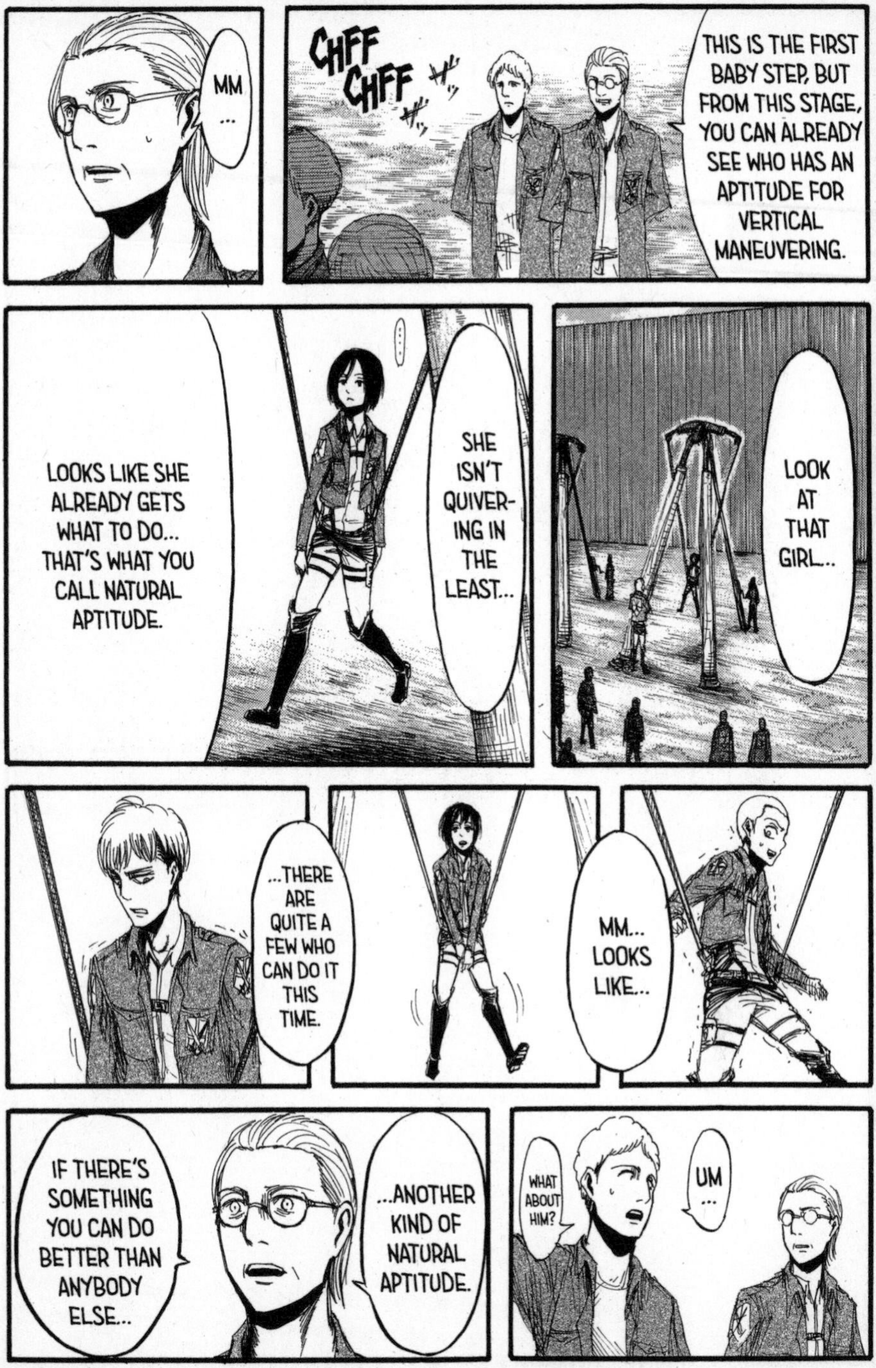
CHFF CHFF
THIS IS THE FIRST BABY STEP, BUT FROM THIS STAGE, YOU CAN ALREADY SEE WHO HAS AN APTITUDE FOR VERTICAL MANEUVERING.
MM ...
LOOK AT THAT GIRL...
...
SHE ISN'T QUIVERING IN THE LEAST...
LOOKS LIKE SHE ALREADY GETS WHAT TO DO... THAT'S WHAT YOU CALL NATURAL APTITUDE.
MM... LOOKS LIKE...
...THERE ARE QUITE A FEW WHO CAN DO IT THIS TIME.
UM ...
WHAT ABOUT HIM?
...ANOTHER KIND OF NATURAL APTITUDE.
IF THERE'S SOMETHING YOU CAN DO BETTER THAN ANYBODY ELSE...

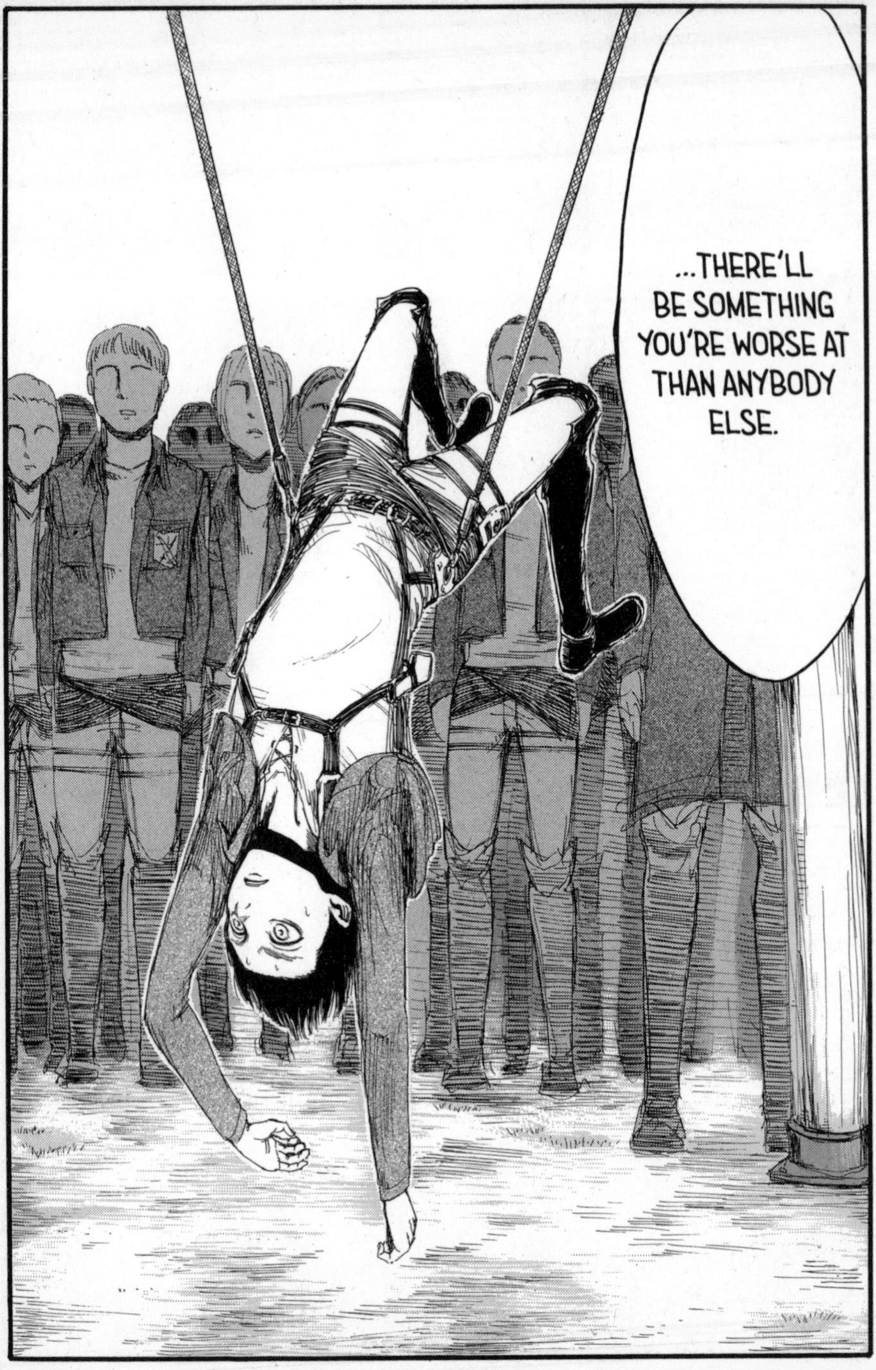
...THERE'LL BE SOMETHING YOU'RE WORSE AT THAN ANYBODY ELSE.

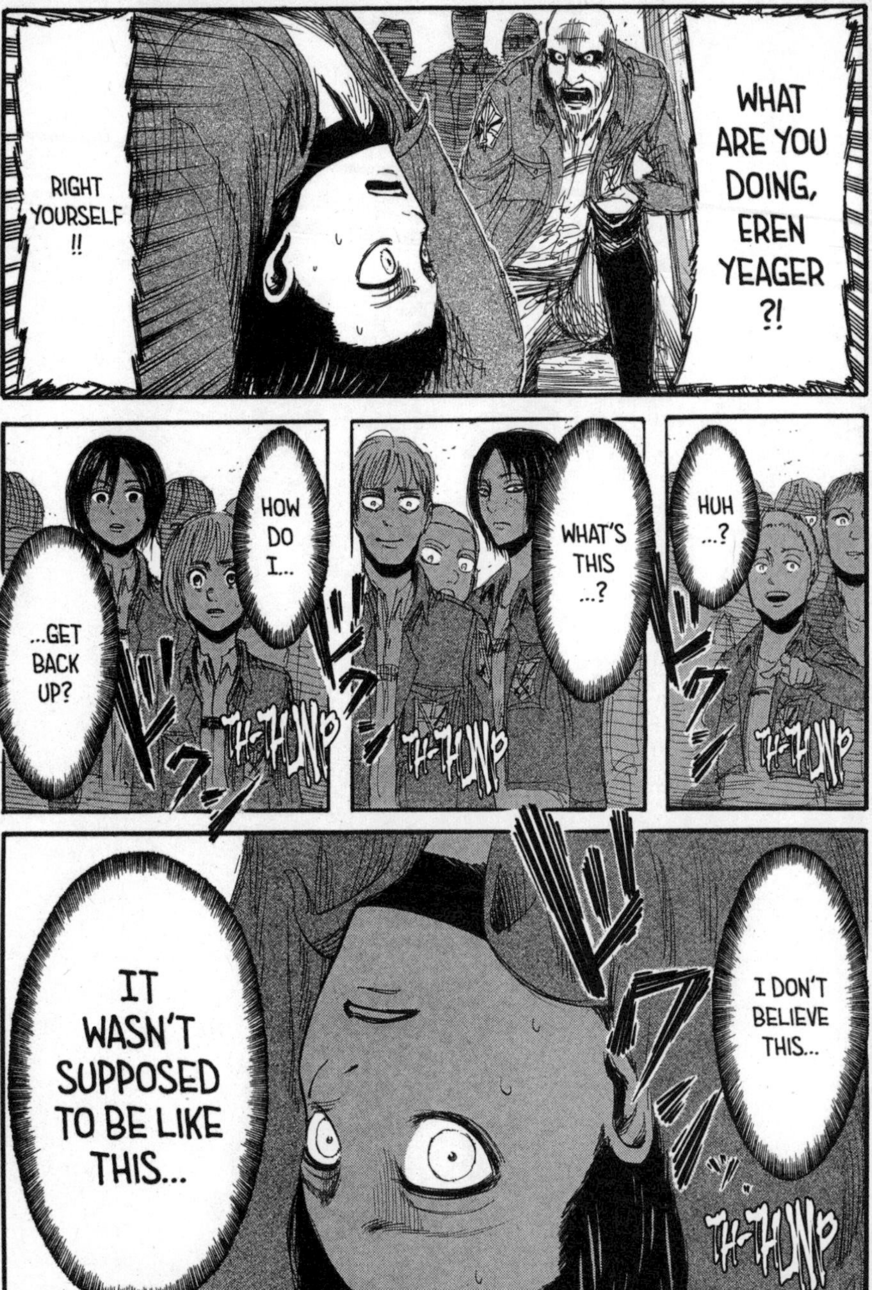
WHAT ARE YOU DOING, EREN YEAGER?!
RIGHT YOURSELF!!
HUH...?
TH-THUMP
WHAT'S THIS...?
TH-THUMP
HOW DO I...
...GET BACK UP?
TH-THUMP
I DON'T BELIEVE THIS...
TH-THUMP
IT WASN'T SUPPOSED TO BE LIKE THIS...

ATTACK on TITAN

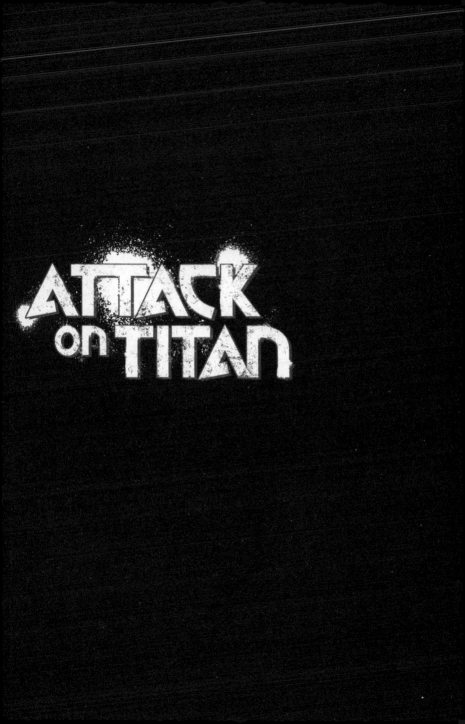

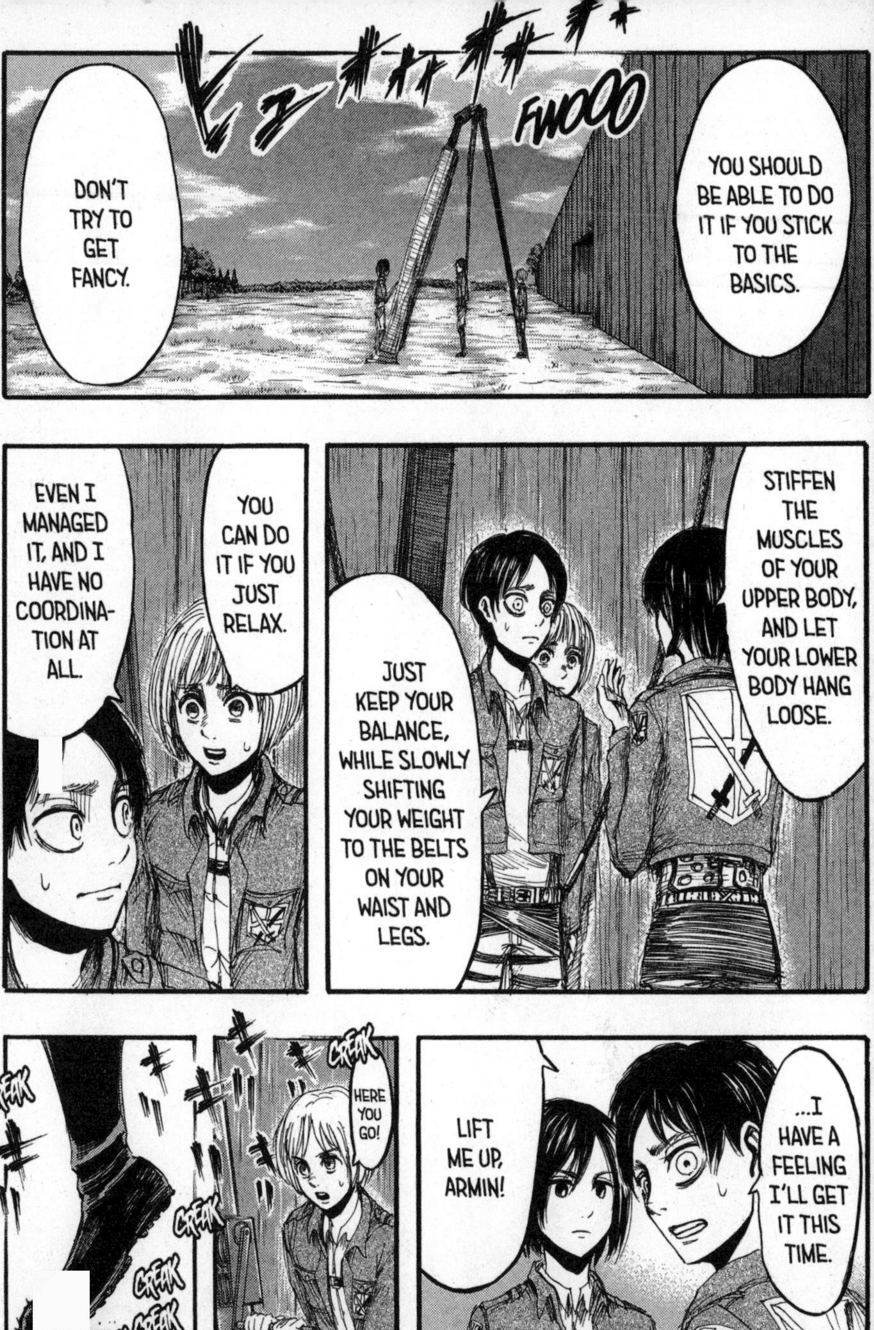
FWOOO
YOU SHOULD BE ABLE TO DO IT IF YOU STICK TO THE BASICS.
DON'T TRY TO GET FANCY.
STIFFEN THE MUSCLES OF YOUR UPPER BODY, AND LET YOUR LOWER BODY HANG LOOSE.
JUST KEEP YOUR BALANCE, WHILE SLOWLY SHIFTING YOUR WEIGHT TO THE BELTS ON YOUR WAIST AND LEGS.
YOU CAN DO IT IF YOU JUST RELAX.
EVEN I MANAGED IT, AND I HAVE NO COORDINATION AT ALL.
...I HAVE A FEELING I'LL GET IT THIS TIME.
LIFT ME UP, ARMIN!
CREAK
HERE YOU GO!
CREAK
CREAK
CREAK
CREAK CREAK

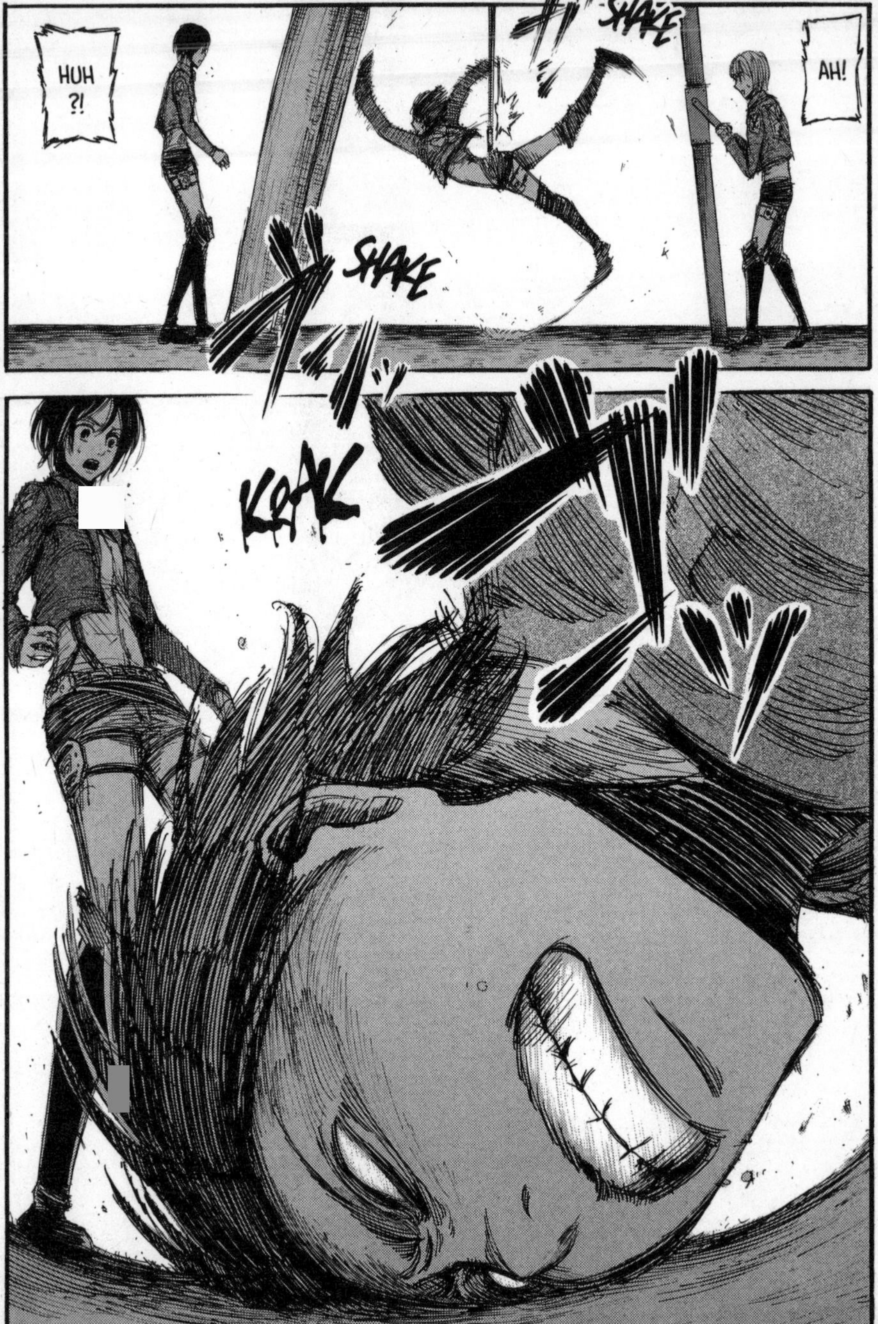
AH!
SHAKE
HUH ?!
SHAKE
KRAK

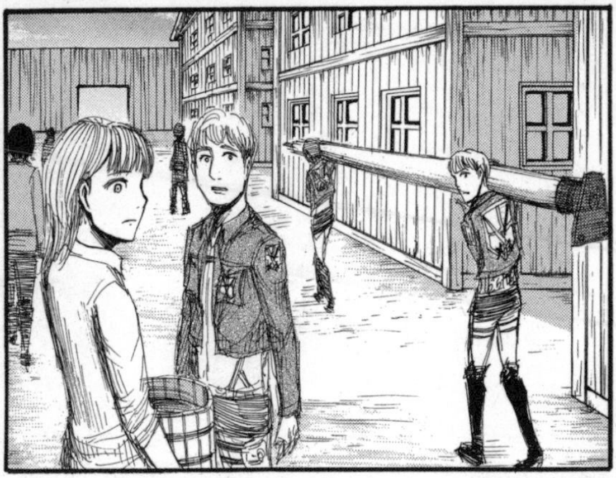

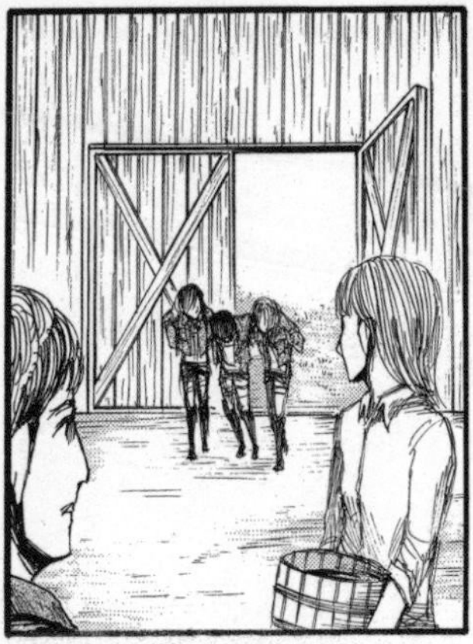

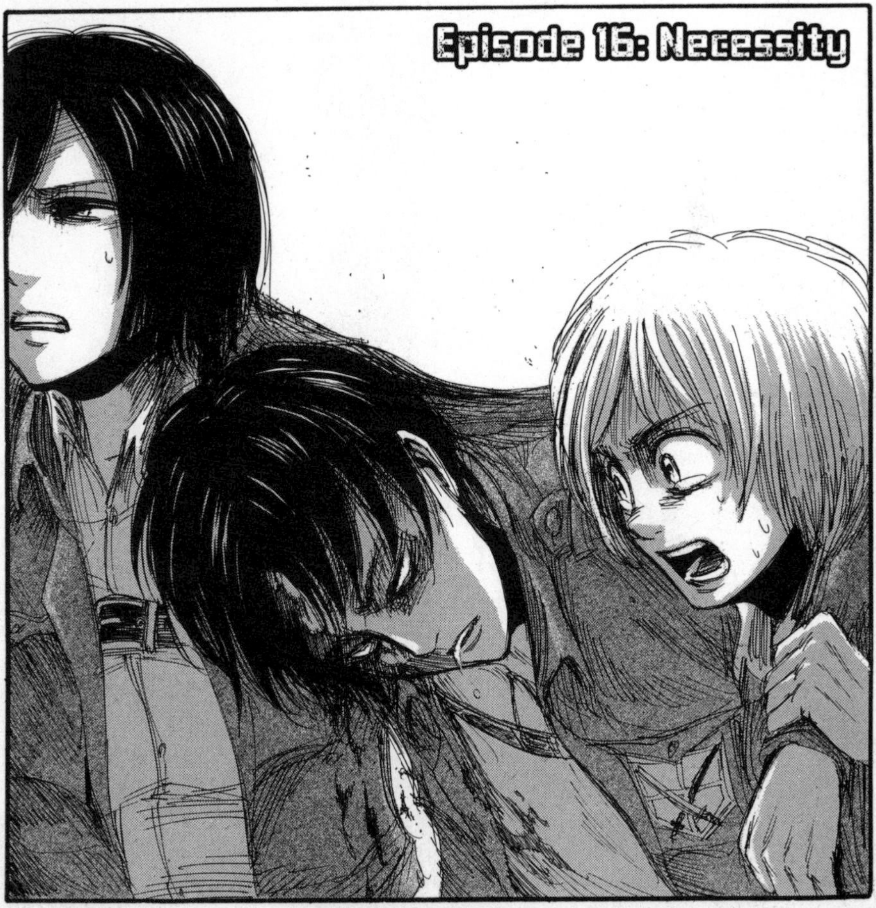
Episode 16: Necessity

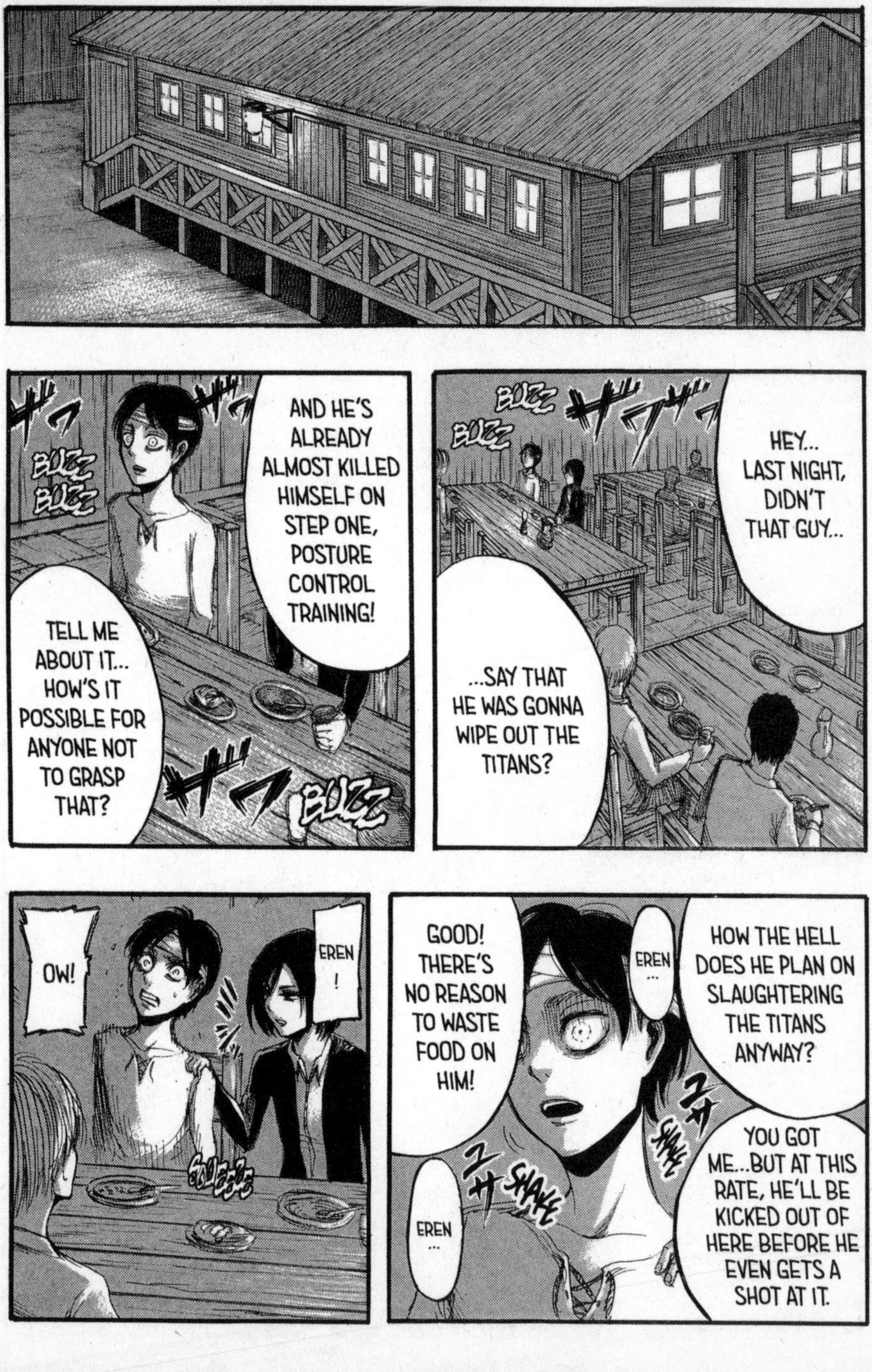
BUZZ
BUZZ
HEY... LAST NIGHT, DIDN'T THAT GUY...
...SAY THAT HE WAS GONNA WIPE OUT THE TITANS?
BUZZ
BUZZ
AND HE'S ALREADY ALMOST KILLED HIMSELF ON STEP ONE, POSTURE CONTROL TRAINING!
TELL ME ABOUT IT... HOW'S IT POSSIBLE FOR ANYONE NOT TO GRASP THAT?
BUZZ
HOW THE HELL DOES HE PLAN ON SLAUGHTERING THE TITANS ANYWAY?
EREN...
GOOD! THERE'S NO REASON TO WASTE FOOD ON HIM!
SHAKE
YOU GOT ME...BUT AT THIS RATE, HE'LL BE KICKED OUT OF HERE BEFORE HE EVEN GETS A SHOT AT IT.
SHAKE
EREN...
EREN!
OW!
SQUEEZE

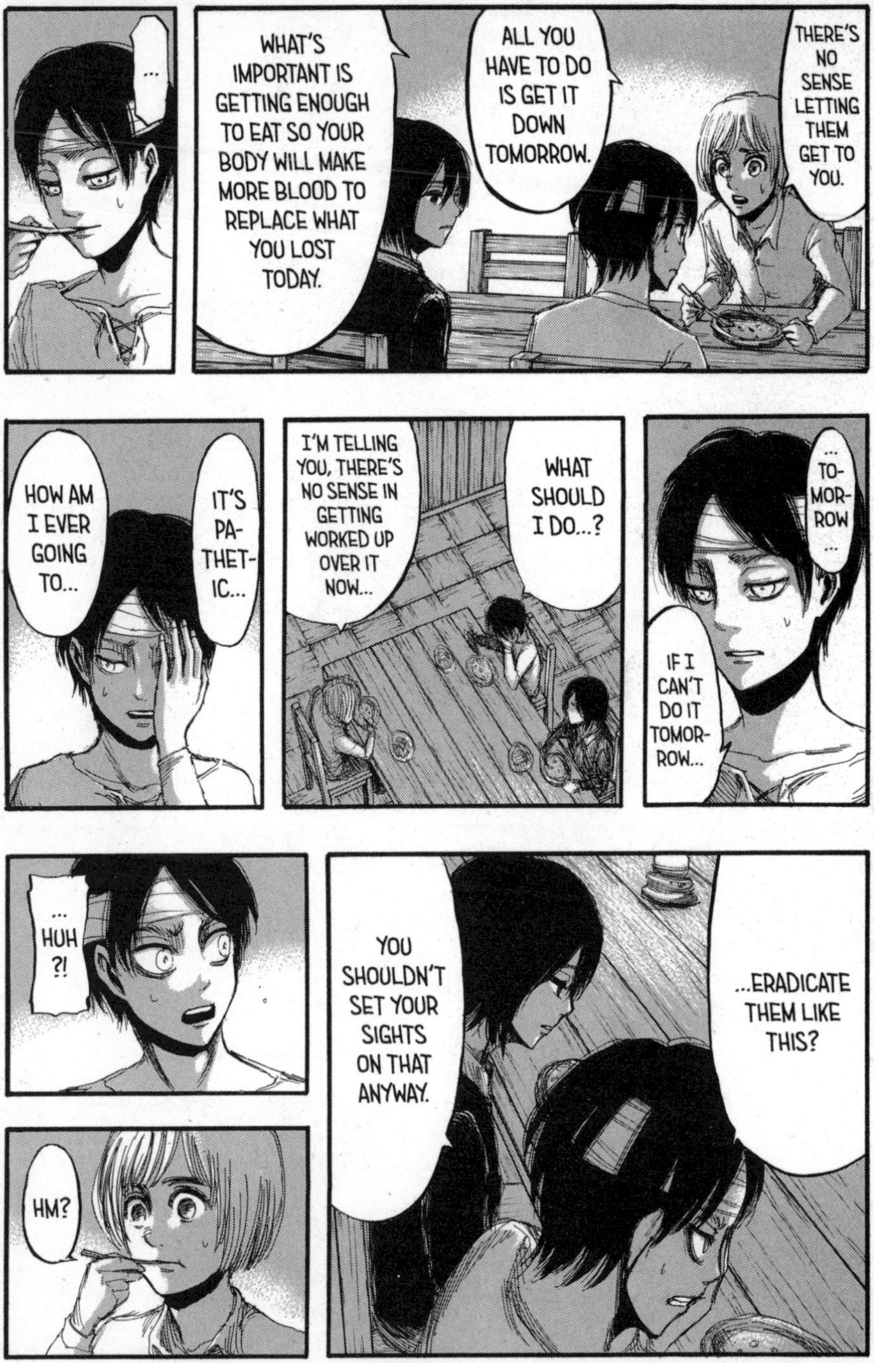
THERE'S NO SENSE LETTING THEM GET TO YOU.
ALL YOU HAVE TO DO IS GET IT DOWN TOMORROW.
WHAT'S IMPORTANT IS GETTING ENOUGH TO EAT SO YOUR BODY WILL MAKE MORE BLOOD TO REPLACE WHAT YOU LOST TODAY.
...
... TO-MOR-ROW ...
IF I CAN'T DO IT TOMOR-ROW...
WHAT SHOULD I DO...?
I'M TELLING YOU, THERE'S NO SENSE IN GETTING WORKED UP OVER IT NOW...
IT'S PA-THET-IC...
HOW AM I EVER GOING TO...
...ERADICATE THEM LIKE THIS?
YOU SHOULDN'T SET YOUR SIGHTS ON THAT ANYWAY.
... HUH ?!
HM?

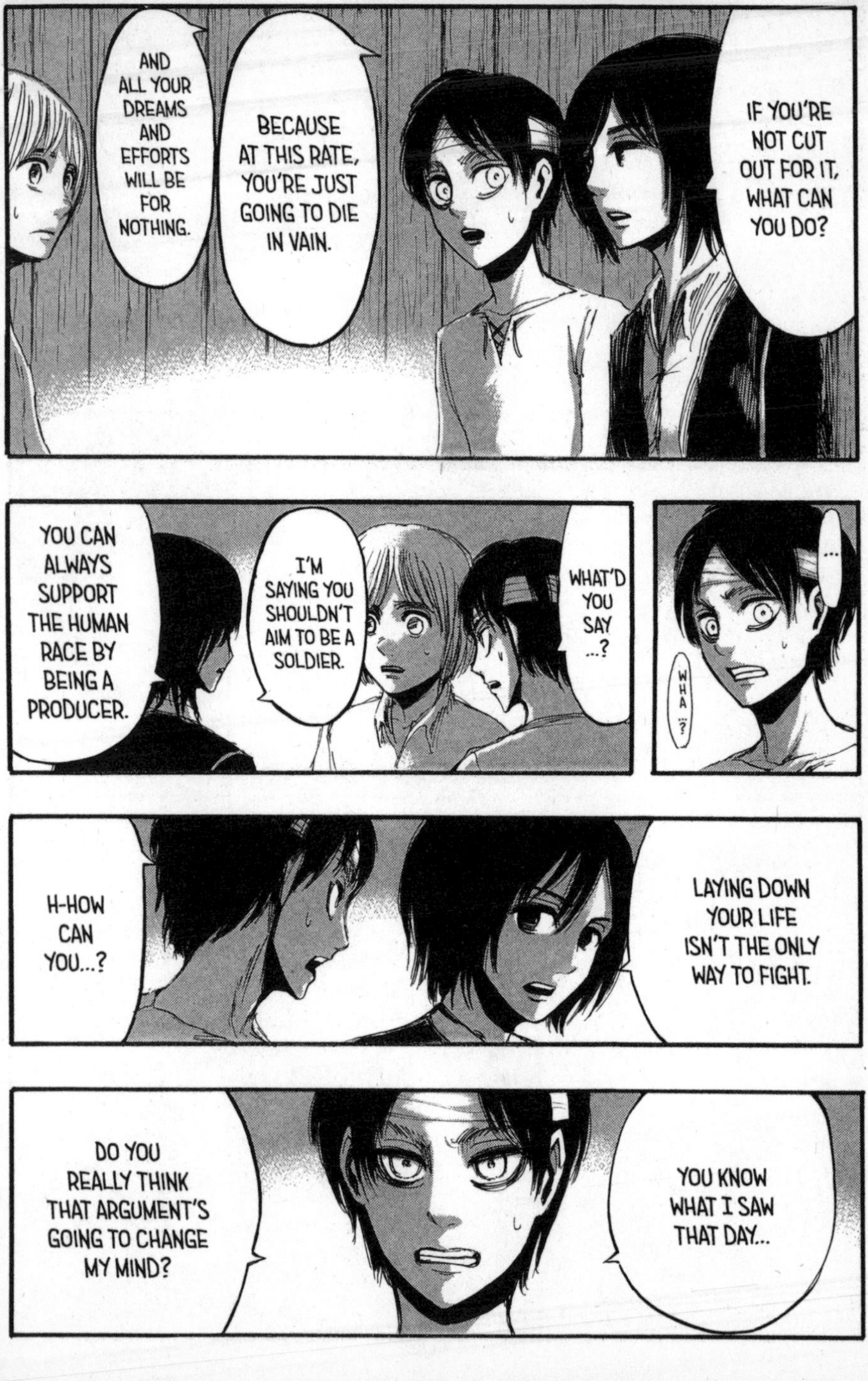
IF YOU'RE NOT CUT OUT FOR IT, WHAT CAN YOU DO?
BECAUSE AT THIS RATE, YOU'RE JUST GOING TO DIE IN VAIN.
AND ALL YOUR DREAMS AND EFFORTS WILL BE FOR NOTHING.
...
WHA...?
WHAT'D YOU SAY...?
I'M SAYING YOU SHOULDN'T AIM TO BE A SOLDIER.
YOU CAN ALWAYS SUPPORT THE HUMAN RACE BY BEING A PRODUCER.
LAYING DOWN YOUR LIFE ISN'T THE ONLY WAY TO FIGHT.
H-HOW CAN YOU...?
YOU KNOW WHAT I SAW THAT DAY...
DO YOU REALLY THINK THAT ARGUMENT'S GOING TO CHANGE MY MIND?

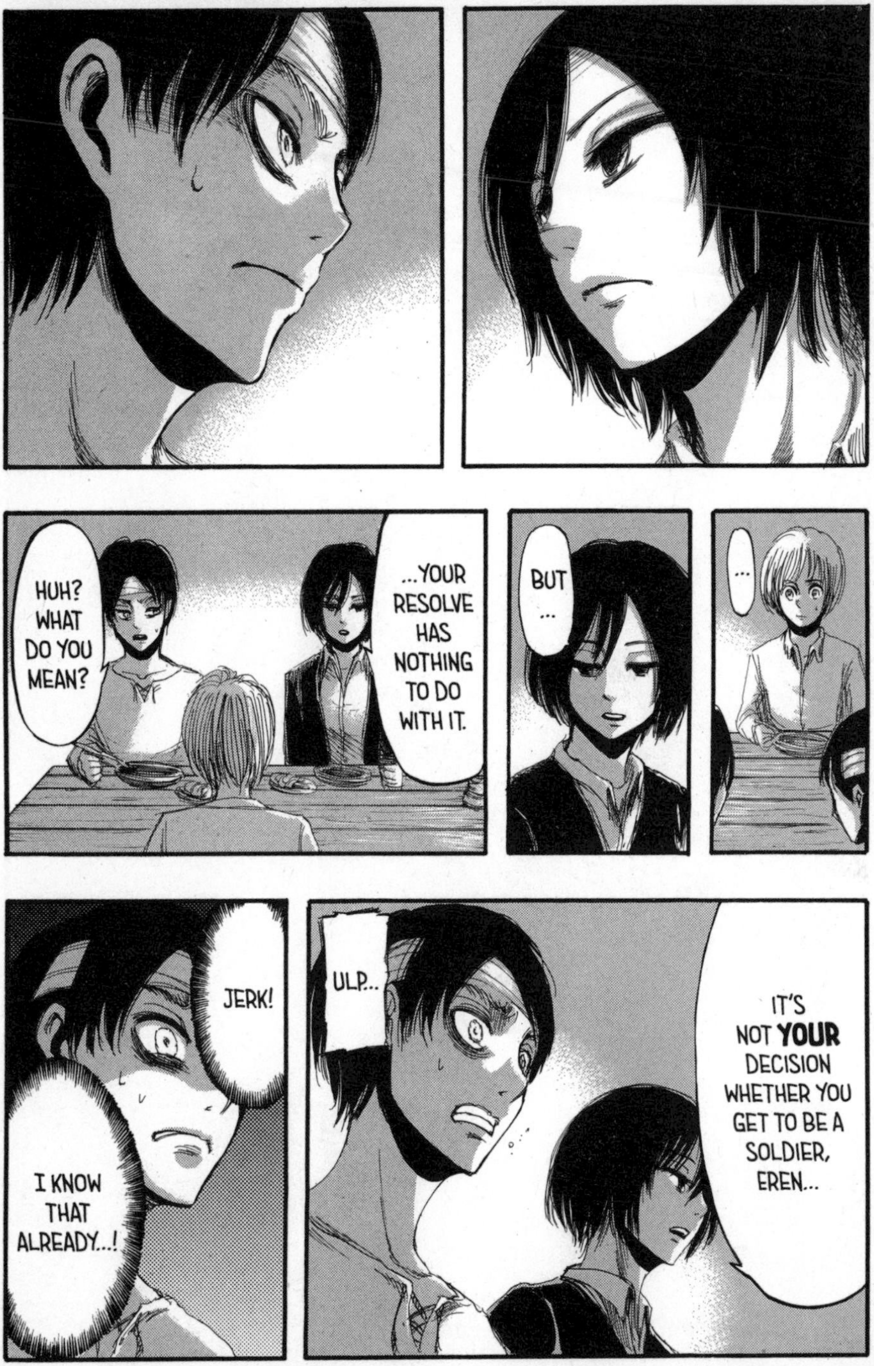
...
BUT ...
...YOUR RESOLVE HAS NOTHING TO DO WITH IT.
HUH? WHAT DO YOU MEAN?
IT'S NOT **YOUR** DECISION WHETHER YOU GET TO BE A SOLDIER, EREN...
ULP...
JERK!
I KNOW THAT ALREADY...!

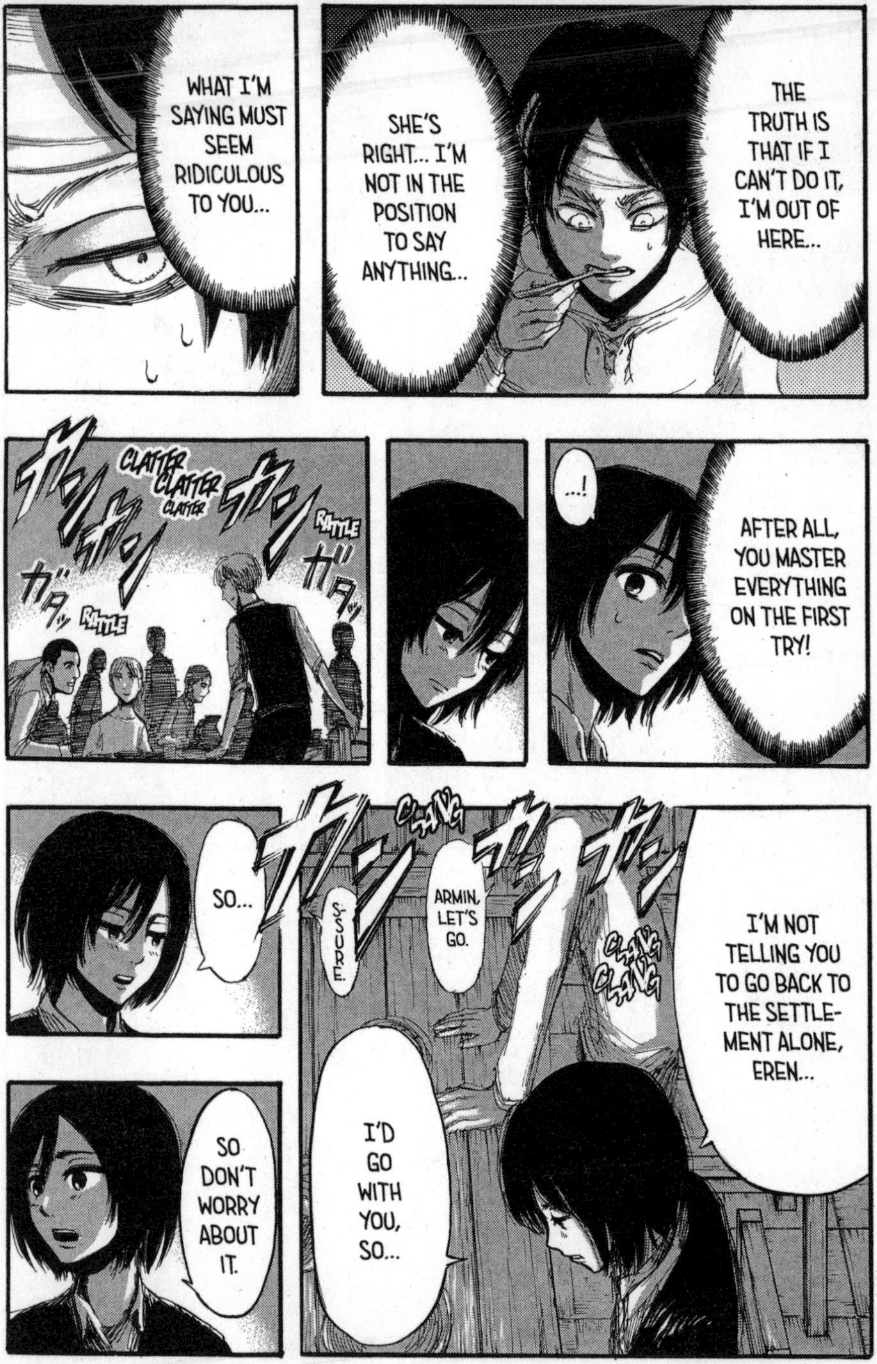
THE TRUTH IS THAT IF I CAN'T DO IT, I'M OUT OF HERE...
SHE'S RIGHT... I'M NOT IN THE POSITION TO SAY ANYTHING...
WHAT I'M SAYING MUST SEEM RIDICULOUS TO YOU...
AFTER ALL, YOU MASTER EVERYTHING ON THE FIRST TRY!
...!
RATTLE
CLATTER
CLATTER
CLATTER
RATTLE
I'M NOT TELLING YOU TO GO BACK TO THE SETTLE-MENT ALONE, EREN...
CLANG
CLANG
CLANG
ARMIN, LET'S GO.
S-SURE.
I'D GO WITH YOU, SO...
SO...
SO DON'T WORRY ABOUT IT.

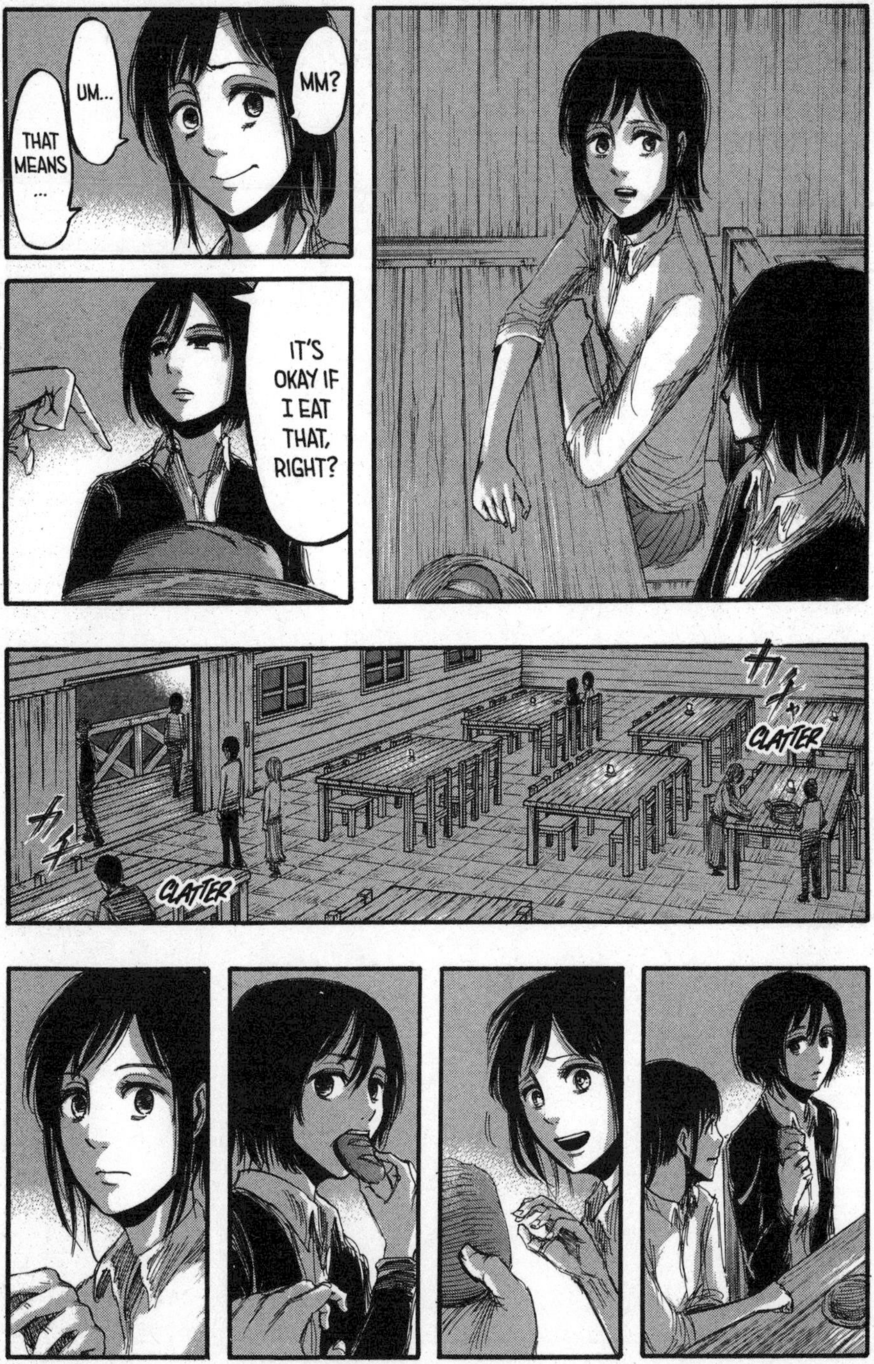
MM?
UM...
THAT MEANS ...
IT'S OKAY IF I EAT THAT, RIGHT?
CLATTER
CLATTER

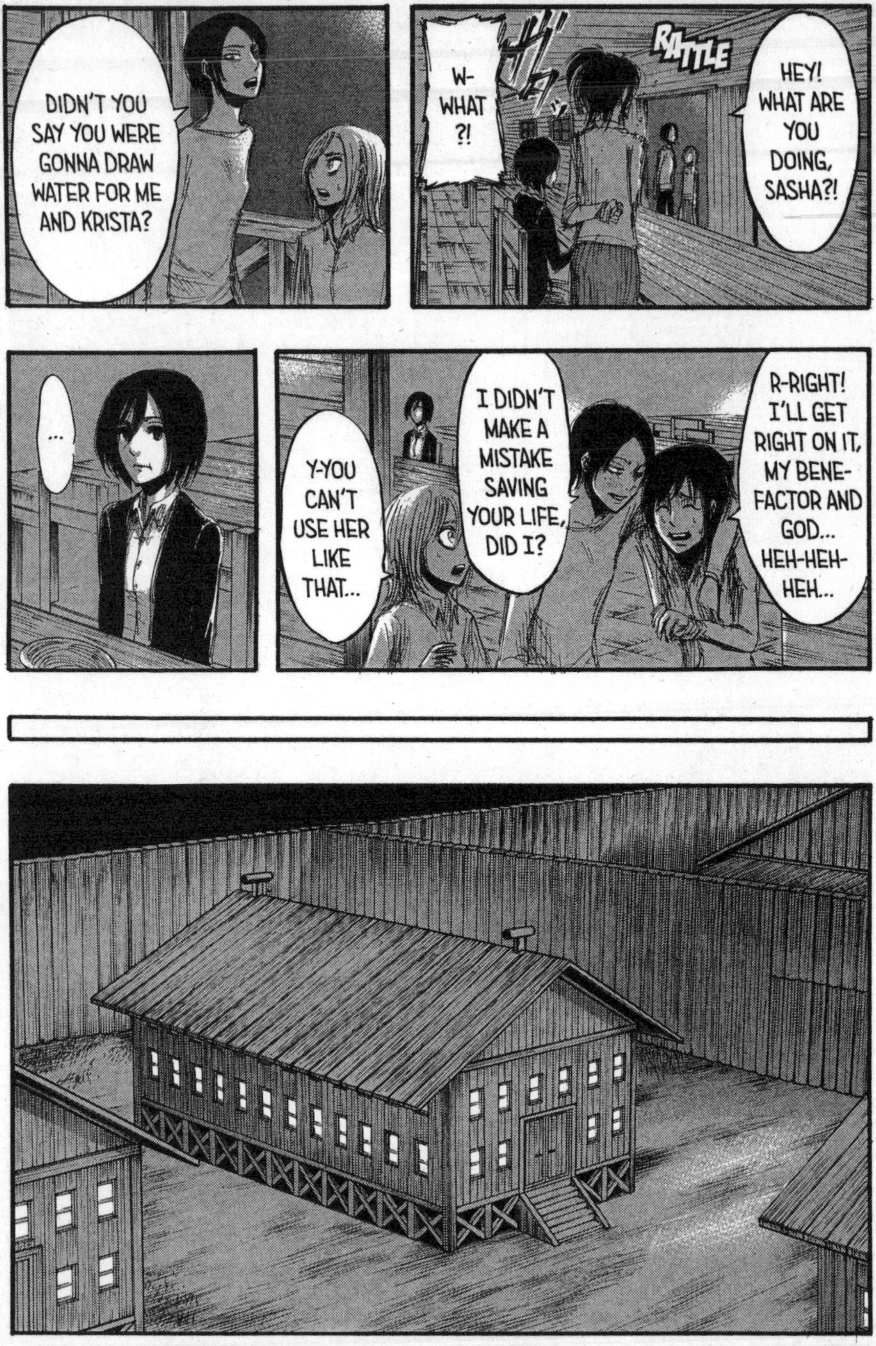
HEY! WHAT ARE YOU DOING, SASHA?!
RATTLE
W-WHAT?!
DIDN'T YOU SAY YOU WERE GONNA DRAW WATER FOR ME AND KRISTA?
R-RIGHT! I'LL GET RIGHT ON IT, MY BENE-FACTOR AND GOD... HEH-HEH-HEH...
I DIDN'T MAKE A MISTAKE SAVING YOUR LIFE, DID I?
Y-YOU CAN'T USE HER LIKE THAT...
...

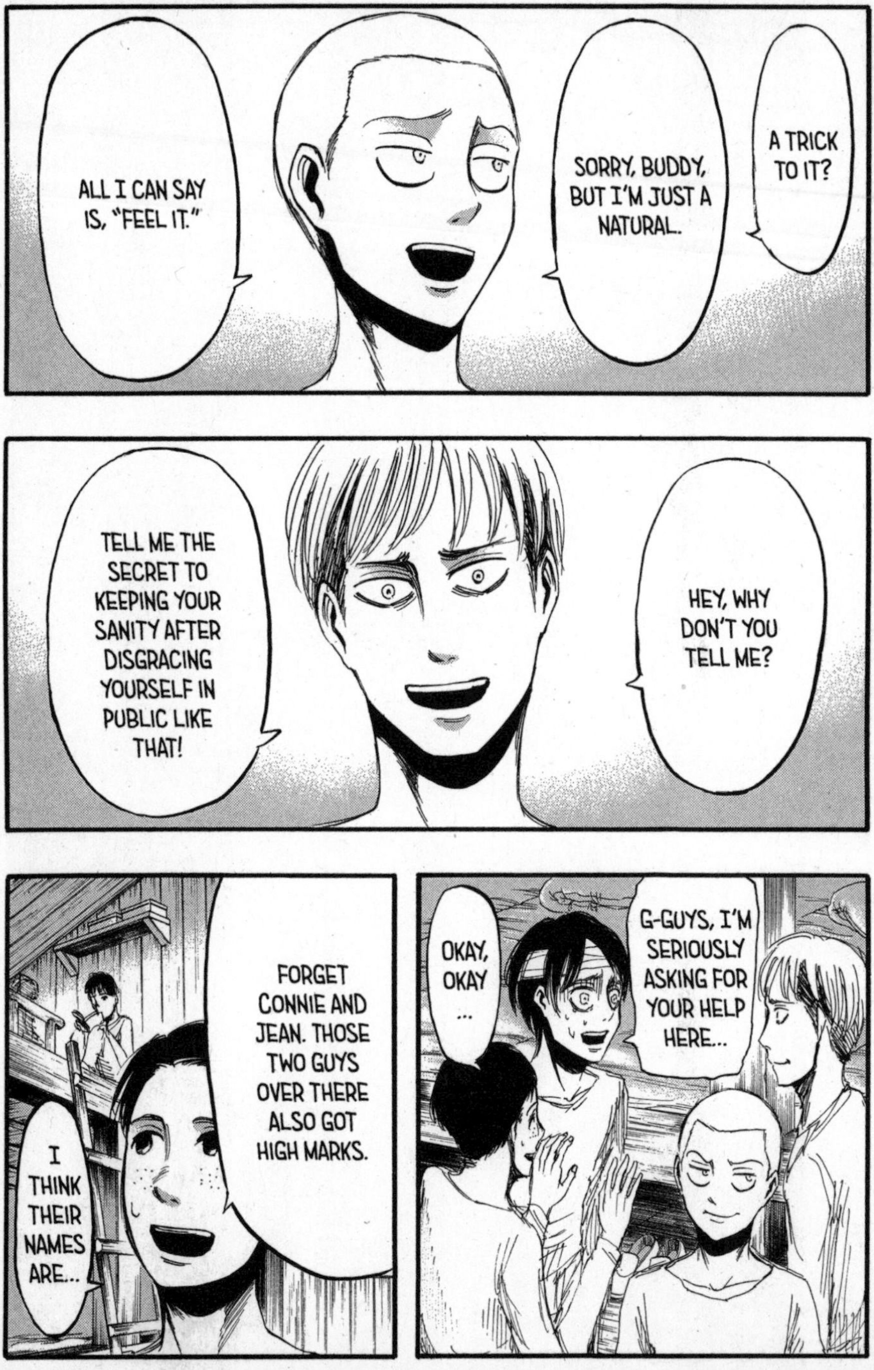
A TRICK TO IT?
SORRY, BUDDY, BUT I'M JUST A NATURAL.
ALL I CAN SAY IS, "FEEL IT."
HEY, WHY DON'T YOU TELL ME?
TELL ME THE SECRET TO KEEPING YOUR SANITY AFTER DISGRACING YOURSELF IN PUBLIC LIKE THAT!
G-GUYS, I'M SERIOUSLY ASKING FOR YOUR HELP HERE...
OKAY, OKAY ...
FORGET CONNIE AND JEAN. THOSE TWO GUYS OVER THERE ALSO GOT HIGH MARKS.
I THINK THEIR NAMES ARE...

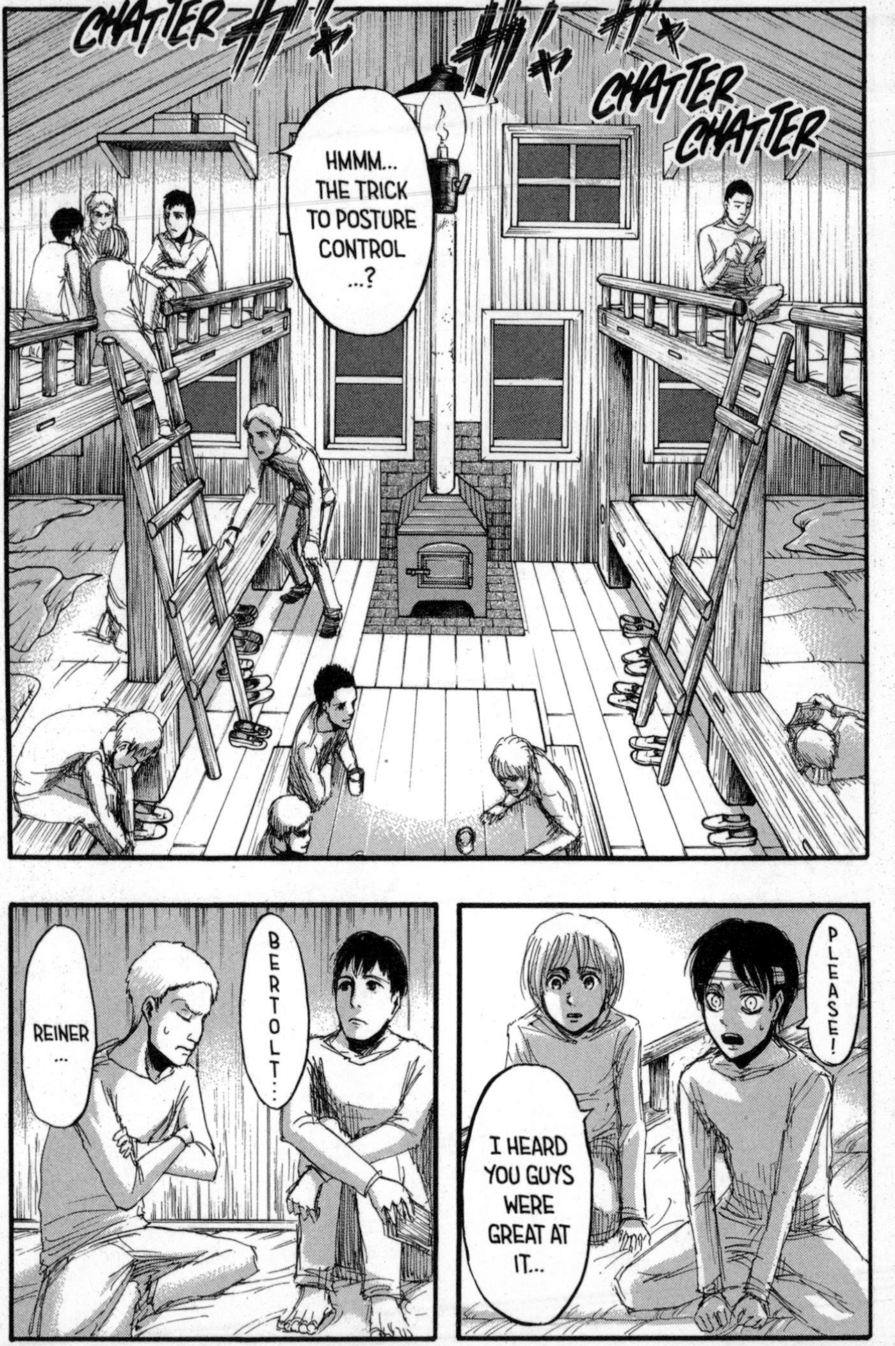
CHATTER
CHATTER
CHATTER
HMMM... THE TRICK TO POSTURE CONTROL ...?
CHATTER
PLEASE!
I HEARD YOU GUYS WERE GREAT AT IT...
BERTOLT...
REINER ...

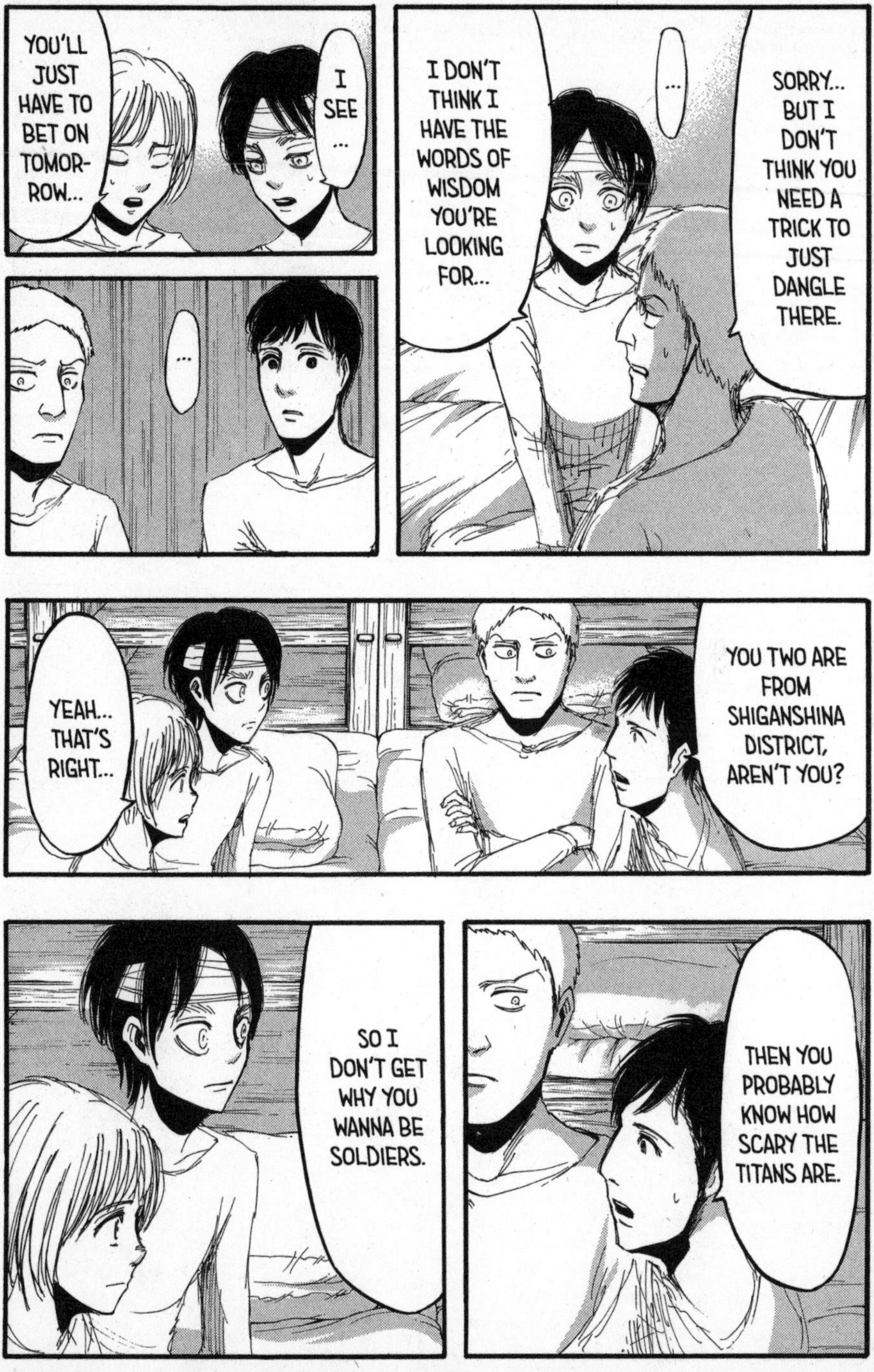
SORRY... BUT I DON'T THINK YOU NEED A TRICK TO JUST DANGLE THERE.
...
I DON'T THINK I HAVE THE WORDS OF WISDOM YOU'RE LOOKING FOR...
I SEE ...
YOU'LL JUST HAVE TO BET ON TOMOR-ROW...
...
YOU TWO ARE FROM SHIGANSHINA DISTRICT, AREN'T YOU?
YEAH... THAT'S RIGHT...
THEN YOU PROBABLY KNOW HOW SCARY THE TITANS ARE.
SO I DON'T GET WHY YOU WANNA BE SOLDIERS.

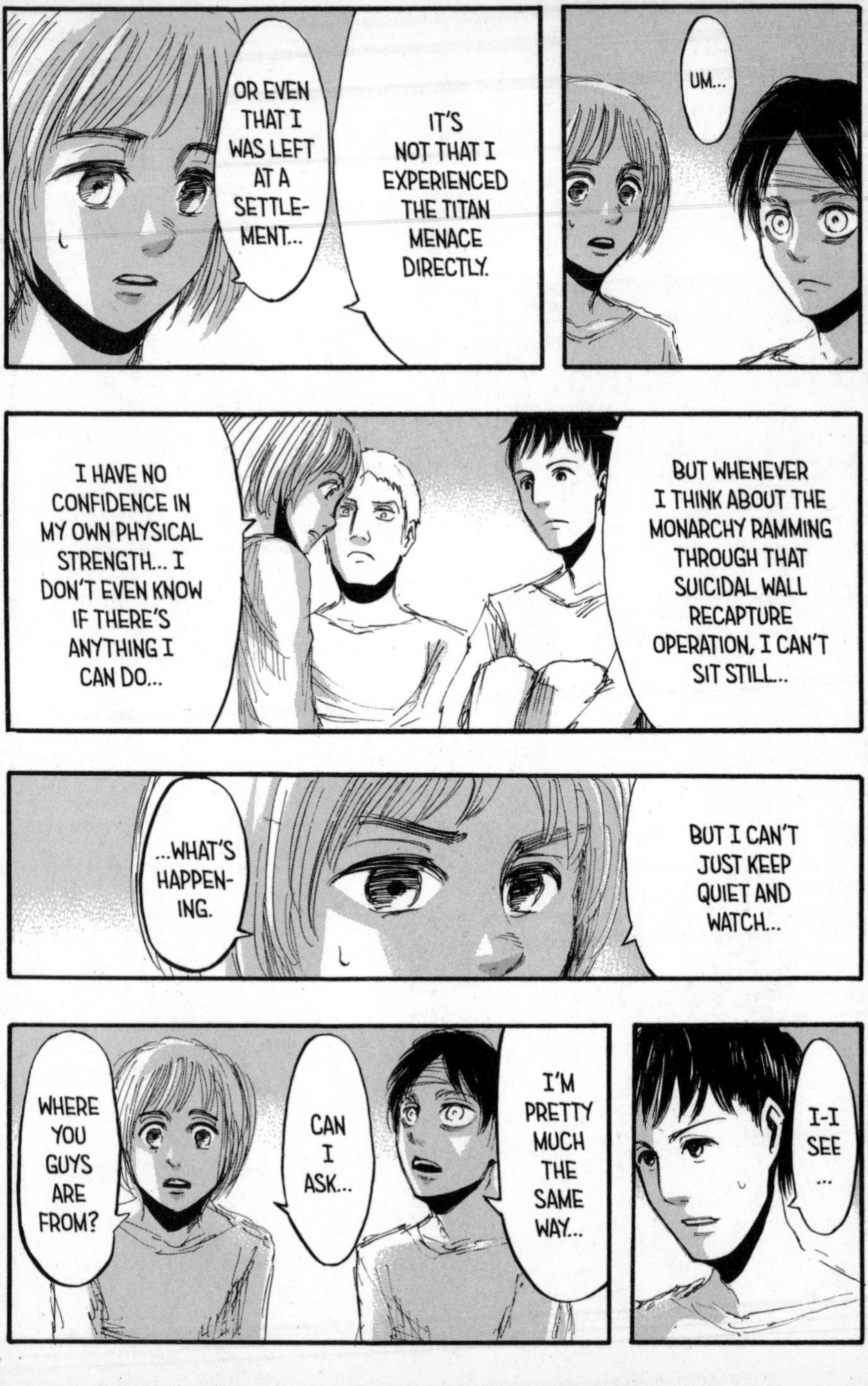
UM...
IT'S NOT THAT I EXPERIENCED THE TITAN MENACE DIRECTLY.
OR EVEN THAT I WAS LEFT AT A SETTLE-MENT...
BUT WHENEVER I THINK ABOUT THE MONARCHY RAMMING THROUGH THAT SUICIDAL WALL RECAPTURE OPERATION, I CAN'T SIT STILL...
I HAVE NO CONFIDENCE IN MY OWN PHYSICAL STRENGTH... I DON'T EVEN KNOW IF THERE'S ANYTHING I CAN DO...
BUT I CAN'T JUST KEEP QUIET AND WATCH...
...WHAT'S HAPPEN-ING.
I-I SEE ...
I'M PRETTY MUCH THE SAME WAY...
CAN I ASK...
WHERE YOU GUYS ARE FROM?

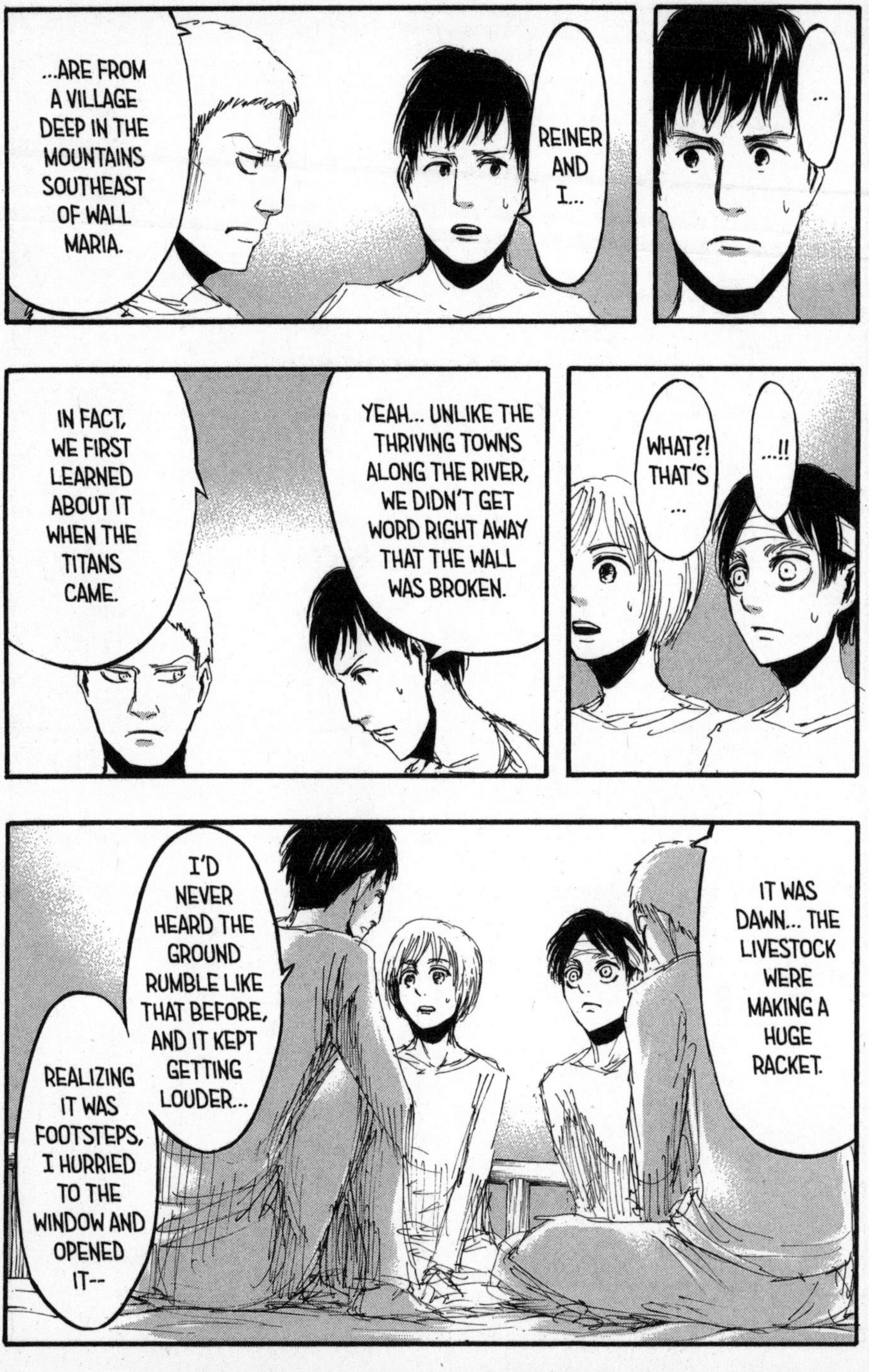
...
REINER AND I...
...ARE FROM A VILLAGE DEEP IN THE MOUNTAINS SOUTHEAST OF WALL MARIA.
...!!
WHAT?! THAT'S ...
YEAH... UNLIKE THE THRIVING TOWNS ALONG THE RIVER, WE DIDN'T GET WORD RIGHT AWAY THAT THE WALL WAS BROKEN.
IN FACT, WE FIRST LEARNED ABOUT IT WHEN THE TITANS CAME.
IT WAS DAWN... THE LIVESTOCK WERE MAKING A HUGE RACKET.
I'D NEVER HEARD THE GROUND RUMBLE LIKE THAT BEFORE, AND IT KEPT GETTING LOUDER...
REALIZING IT WAS FOOTSTEPS, I HURRIED TO THE WINDOW AND OPENED IT--

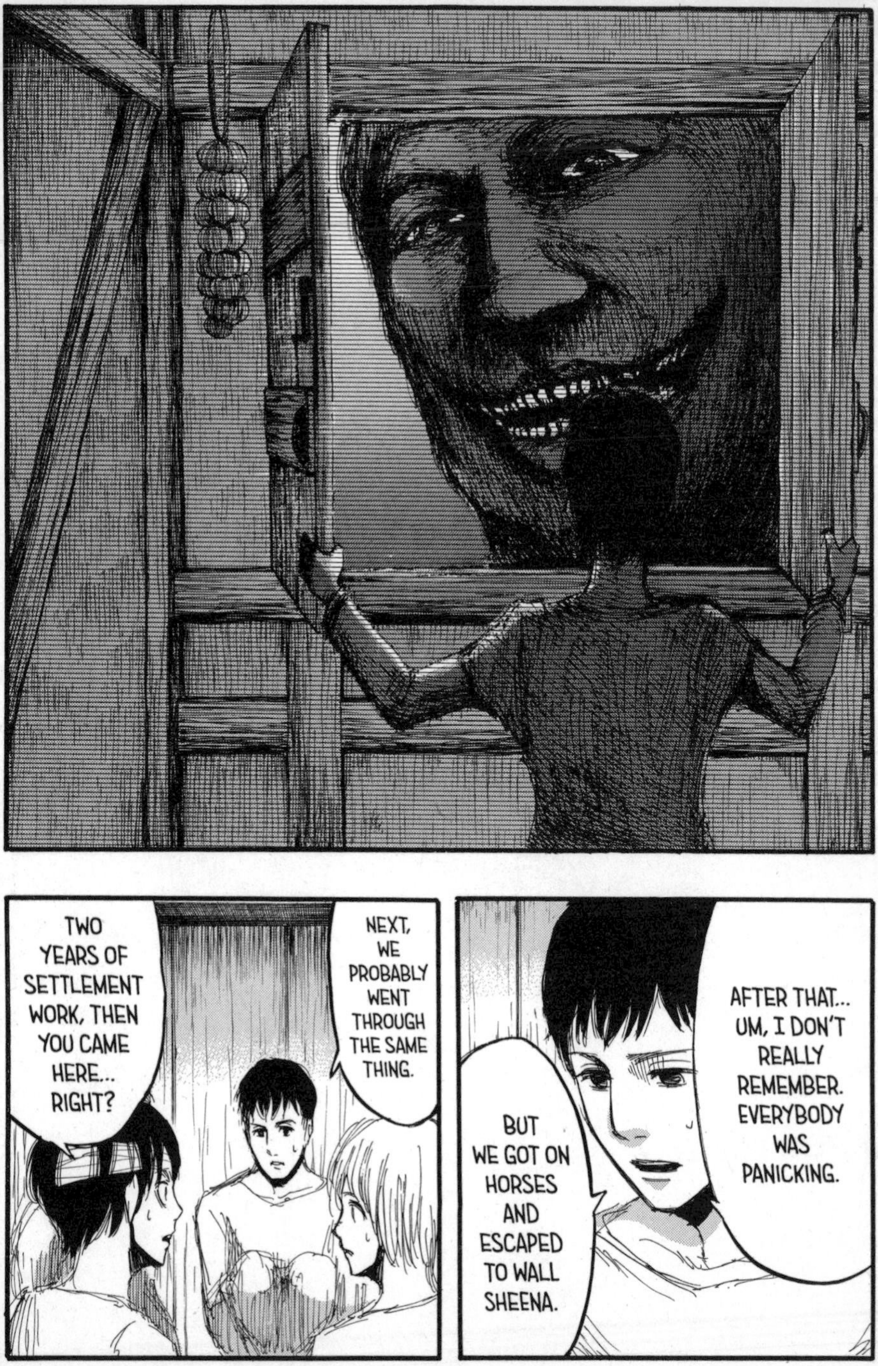
AFTER THAT... UM, I DON'T REALLY REMEMBER. EVERYBODY WAS PANICKING.
BUT WE GOT ON HORSES AND ESCAPED TO WALL SHEENA.
NEXT, WE PROBABLY WENT THROUGH THE SAME THING.
TWO YEARS OF SETTLEMENT WORK, THEN YOU CAME HERE... RIGHT?

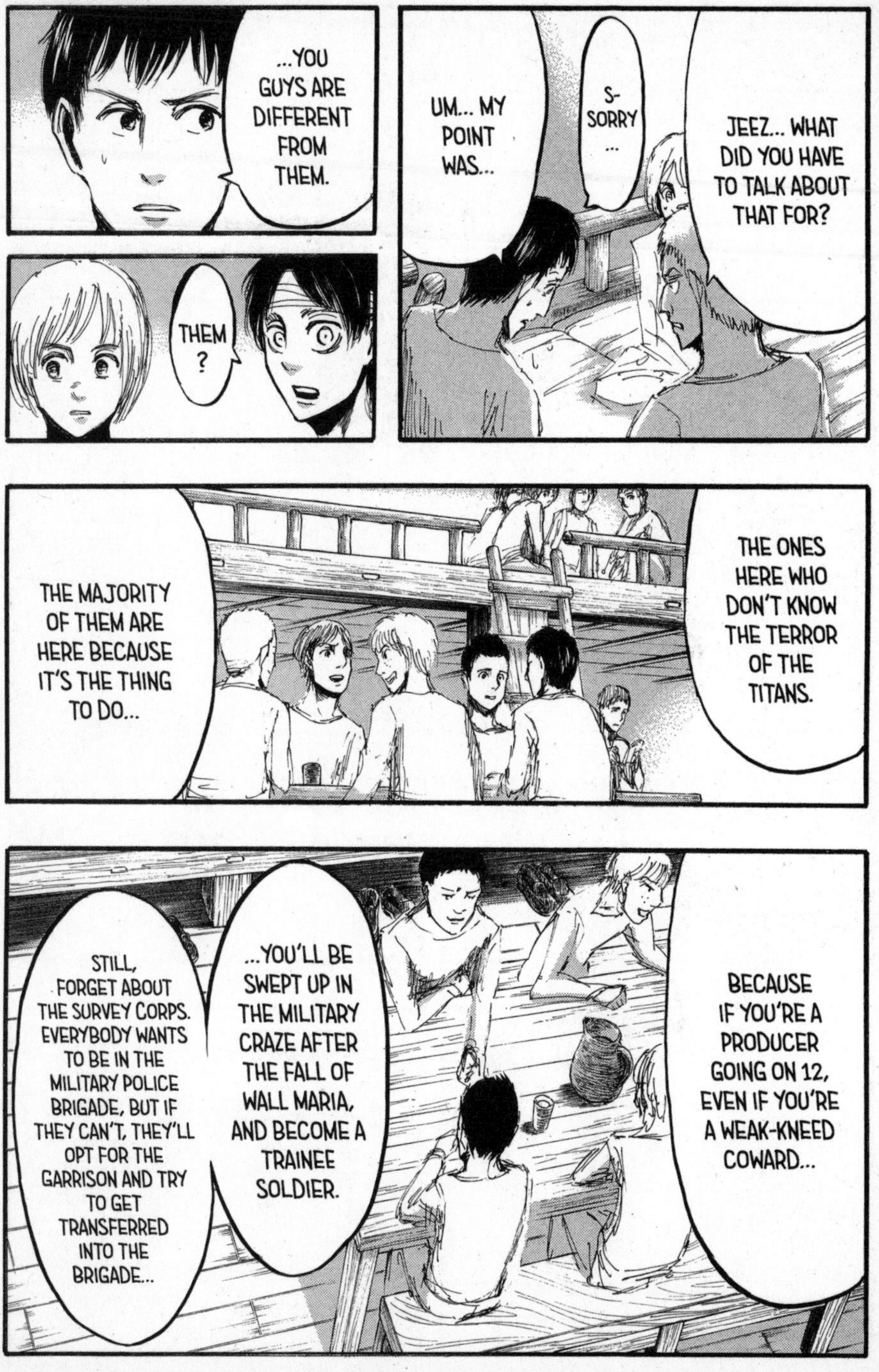
JEEZ... WHAT DID YOU HAVE TO TALK ABOUT THAT FOR?
S-SORRY...
UM... MY POINT WAS...
...YOU GUYS ARE DIFFERENT FROM THEM.
THEM?
THE ONES HERE WHO DON'T KNOW THE TERROR OF THE TITANS.
THE MAJORITY OF THEM ARE HERE BECAUSE IT'S THE THING TO DO...
BECAUSE IF YOU'RE A PRODUCER GOING ON 12, EVEN IF YOU'RE A WEAK-KNEED COWARD...
...YOU'LL BE SWEPT UP IN THE MILITARY CRAZE AFTER THE FALL OF WALL MARIA, AND BECOME A TRAINEE SOLDIER.
STILL, FORGET ABOUT THE SURVEY CORPS. EVERYBODY WANTS TO BE IN THE MILITARY POLICE BRIGADE, BUT IF THEY CAN'T, THEY'LL OPT FOR THE GARRISON AND TRY TO GET TRANSFERRED INTO THE BRIGADE...

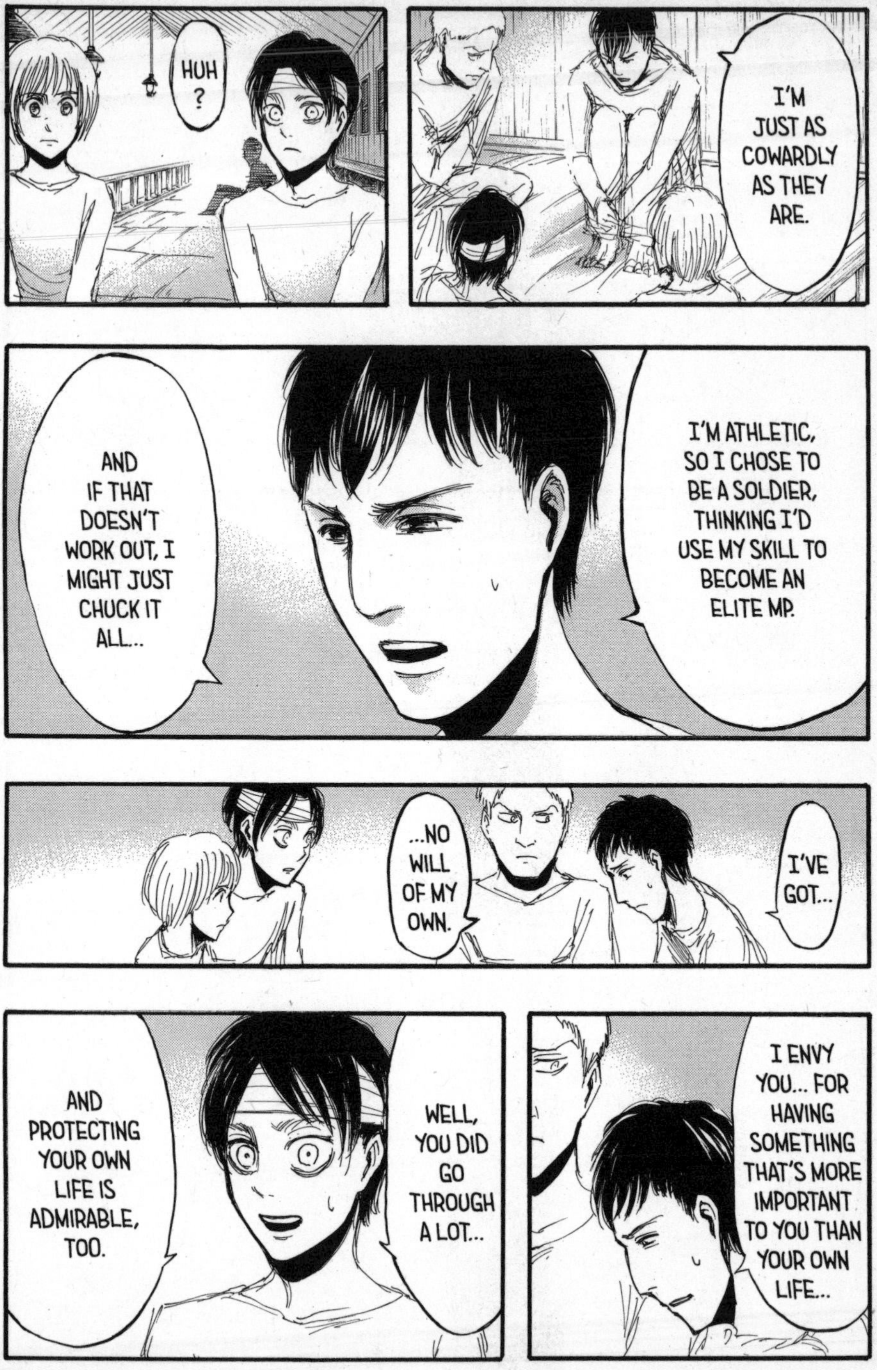
I'M JUST AS COWARDLY AS THEY ARE.
HUH?
I'M ATHLETIC, SO I CHOSE TO BE A SOLDIER, THINKING I'D USE MY SKILL TO BECOME AN ELITE MP.
AND IF THAT DOESN'T WORK OUT, I MIGHT JUST CHUCK IT ALL...
I'VE GOT...
...NO WILL OF MY OWN.
I ENVY YOU... FOR HAVING SOMETHING THAT'S MORE IMPORTANT TO YOU THAN YOUR OWN LIFE...
WELL, YOU DID GO THROUGH A LOT...
AND PROTECTING YOUR OWN LIFE IS ADMIRABLE, TOO.

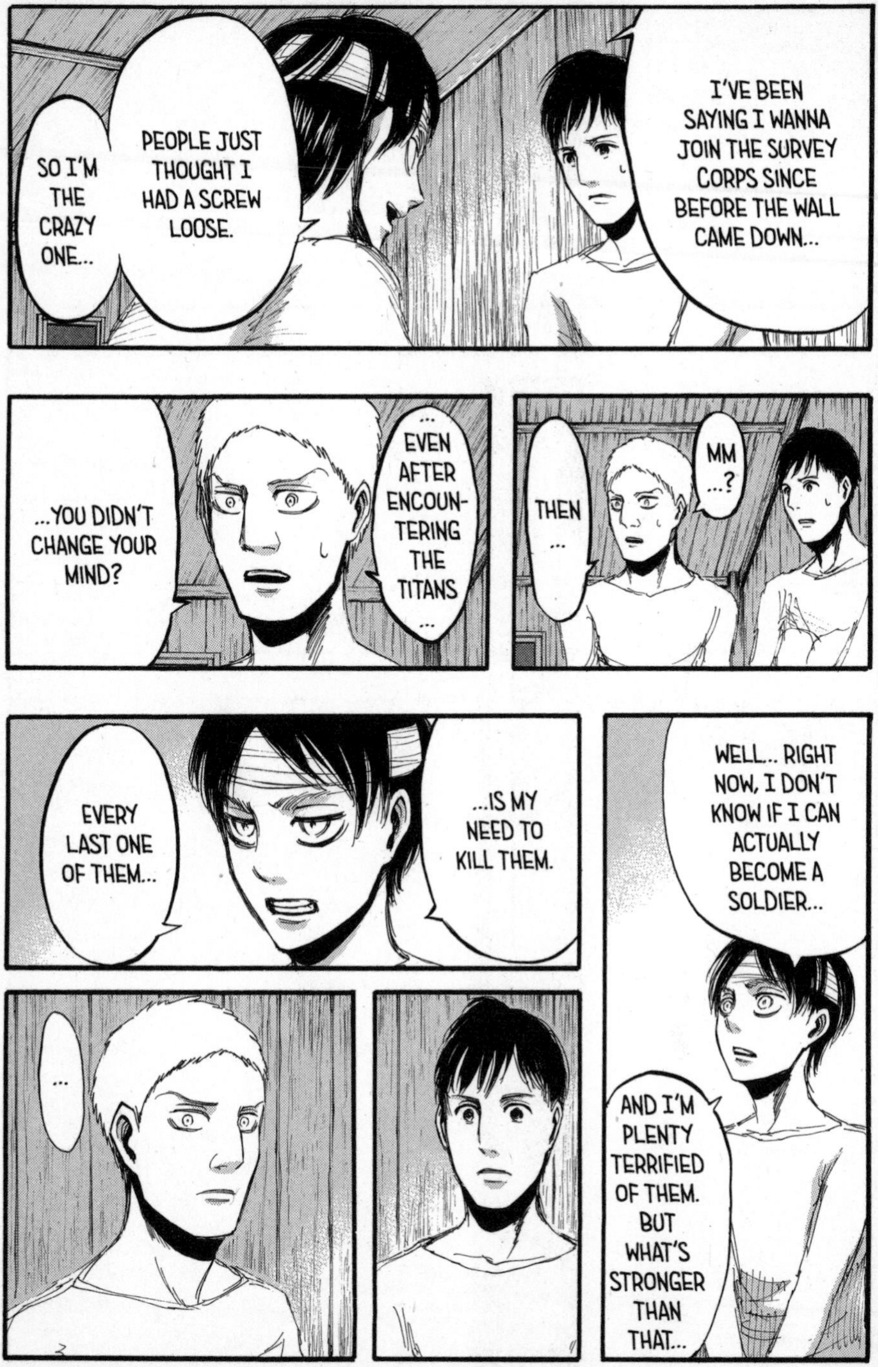
I'VE BEEN SAYING I WANNA JOIN THE SURVEY CORPS SINCE BEFORE THE WALL CAME DOWN...
PEOPLE JUST THOUGHT I HAD A SCREW LOOSE.
SO I'M THE CRAZY ONE...
MM ...?
THEN ...
... EVEN AFTER ENCOUN-TERING THE TITANS ...
...YOU DIDN'T CHANGE YOUR MIND?
WELL... RIGHT NOW, I DON'T KNOW IF I CAN ACTUALLY BECOME A SOLDIER...
AND I'M PLENTY TERRIFIED OF THEM. BUT WHAT'S STRONGER THAN THAT...
...IS MY NEED TO KILL THEM.
EVERY LAST ONE OF THEM...
...

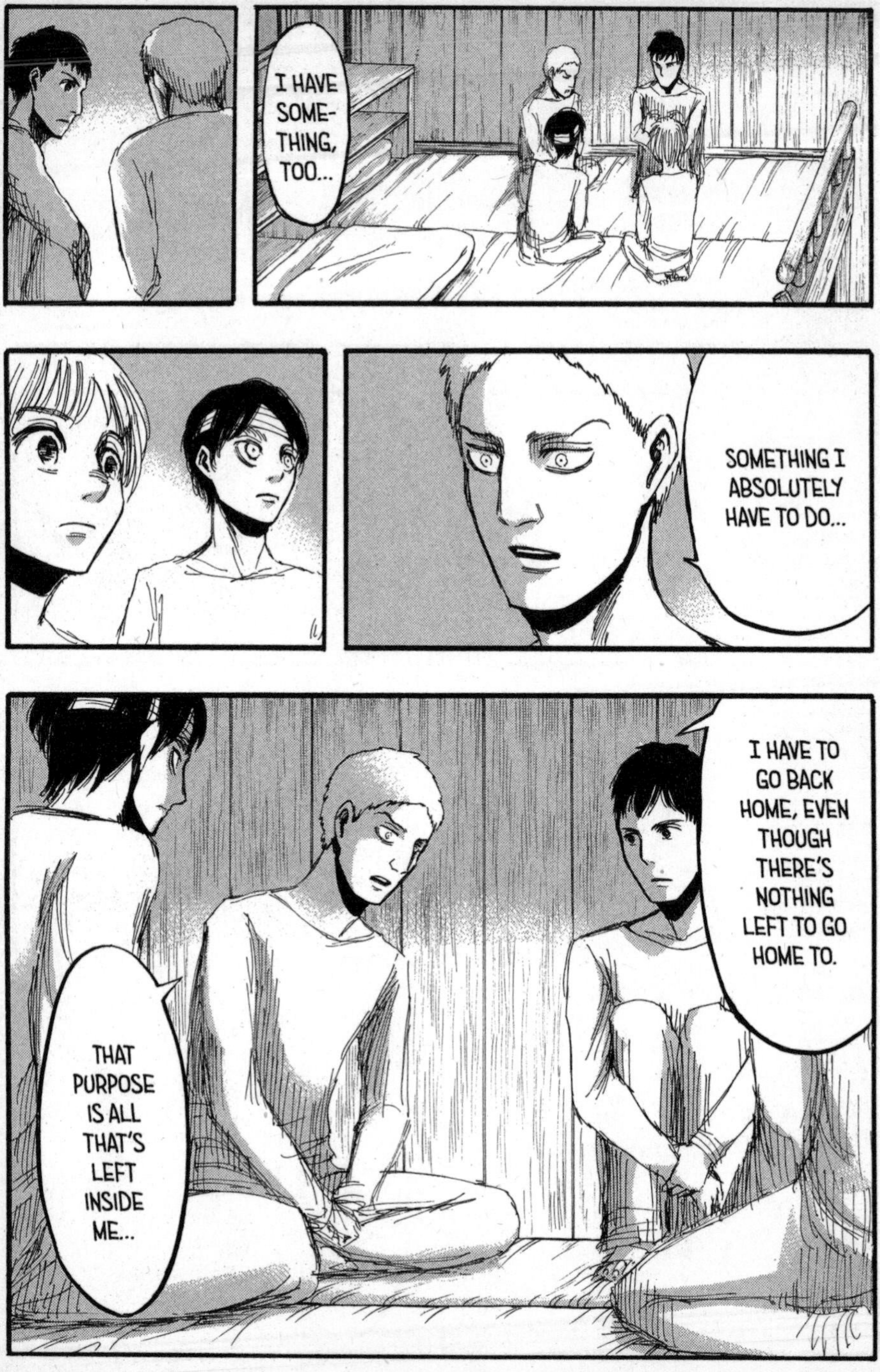
I HAVE SOME-THING, TOO...
SOMETHING I ABSOLUTELY HAVE TO DO...
I HAVE TO GO BACK HOME, EVEN THOUGH THERE'S NOTHING LEFT TO GO HOME TO.
THAT PURPOSE IS ALL THAT'S LEFT INSIDE ME...

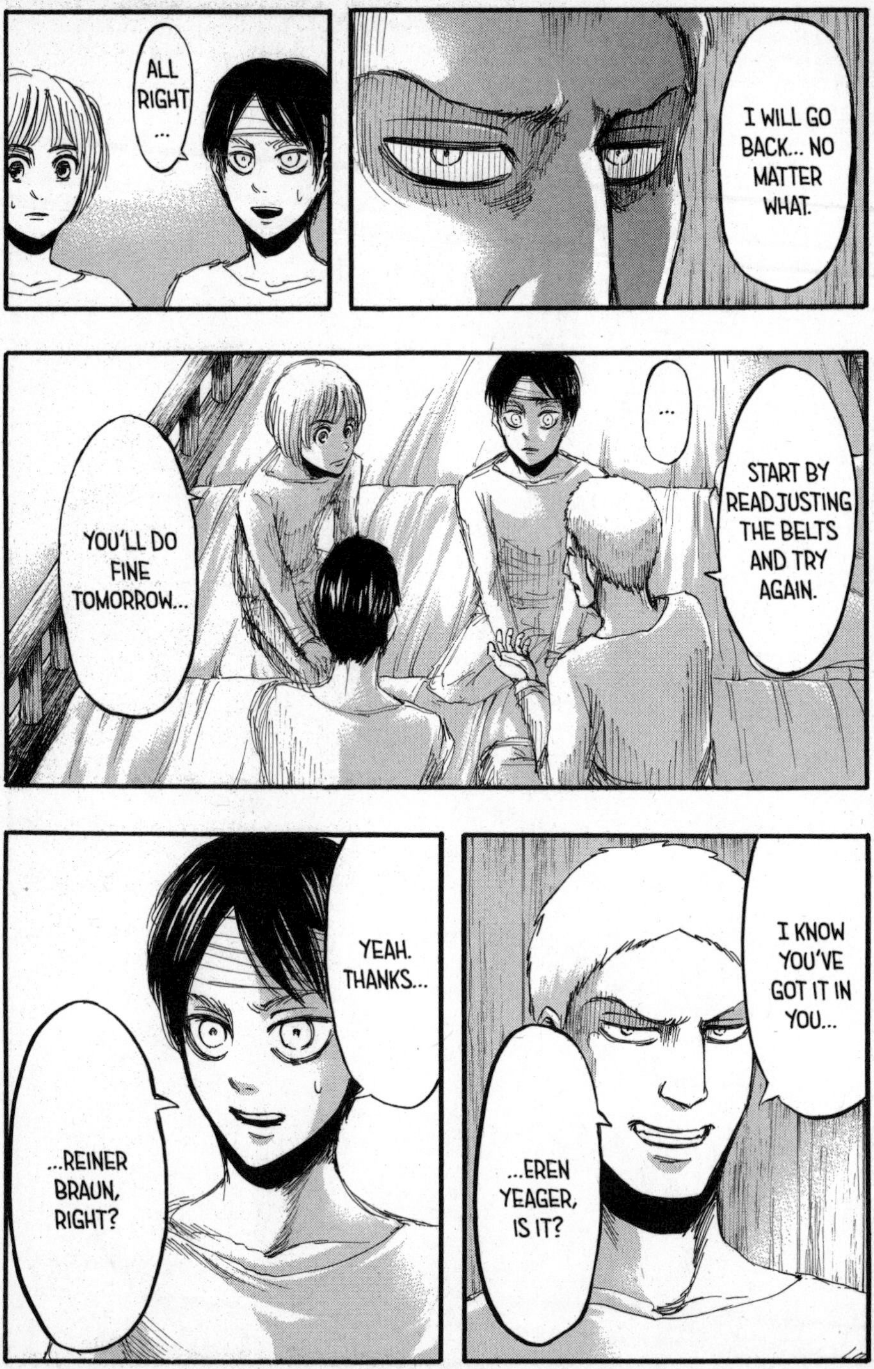
I WILL GO BACK... NO MATTER WHAT.
ALL RIGHT ...
START BY READJUSTING THE BELTS AND TRY AGAIN.
...
YOU'LL DO FINE TOMORROW...
I KNOW YOU'VE GOT IT IN YOU...
...EREN YEAGER, IS IT?
YEAH. THANKS...
...REINER BRAUN, RIGHT?

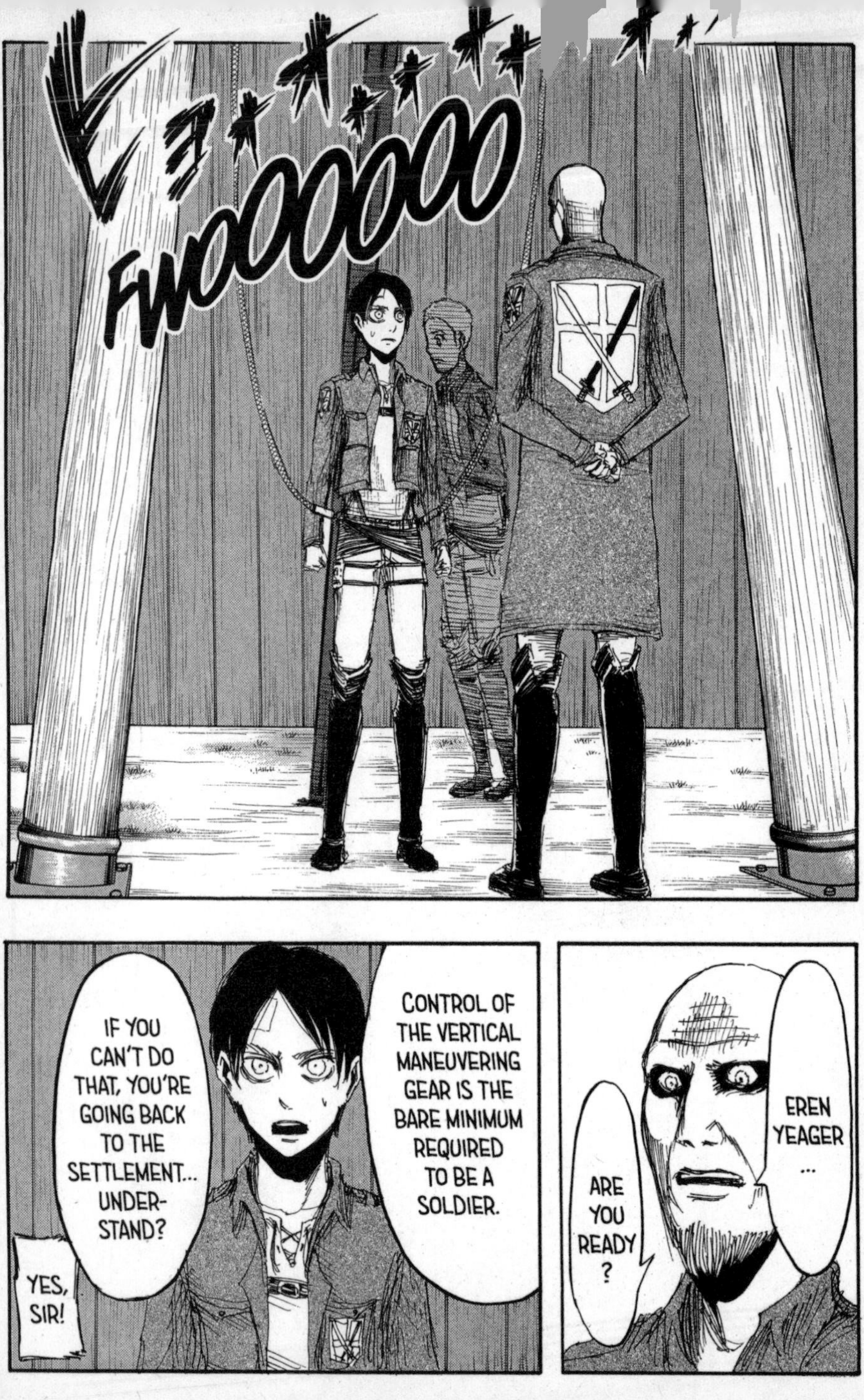
FWOOOOOO
EREN YEAGER ...
ARE YOU READY ?
CONTROL OF THE VERTICAL MANEUVERING GEAR IS THE BARE MINIMUM REQUIRED TO BE A SOLDIER.
IF YOU CAN'T DO THAT, YOU'RE GOING BACK TO THE SETTLEMENT... UNDER-STAND?
YES, SIR!

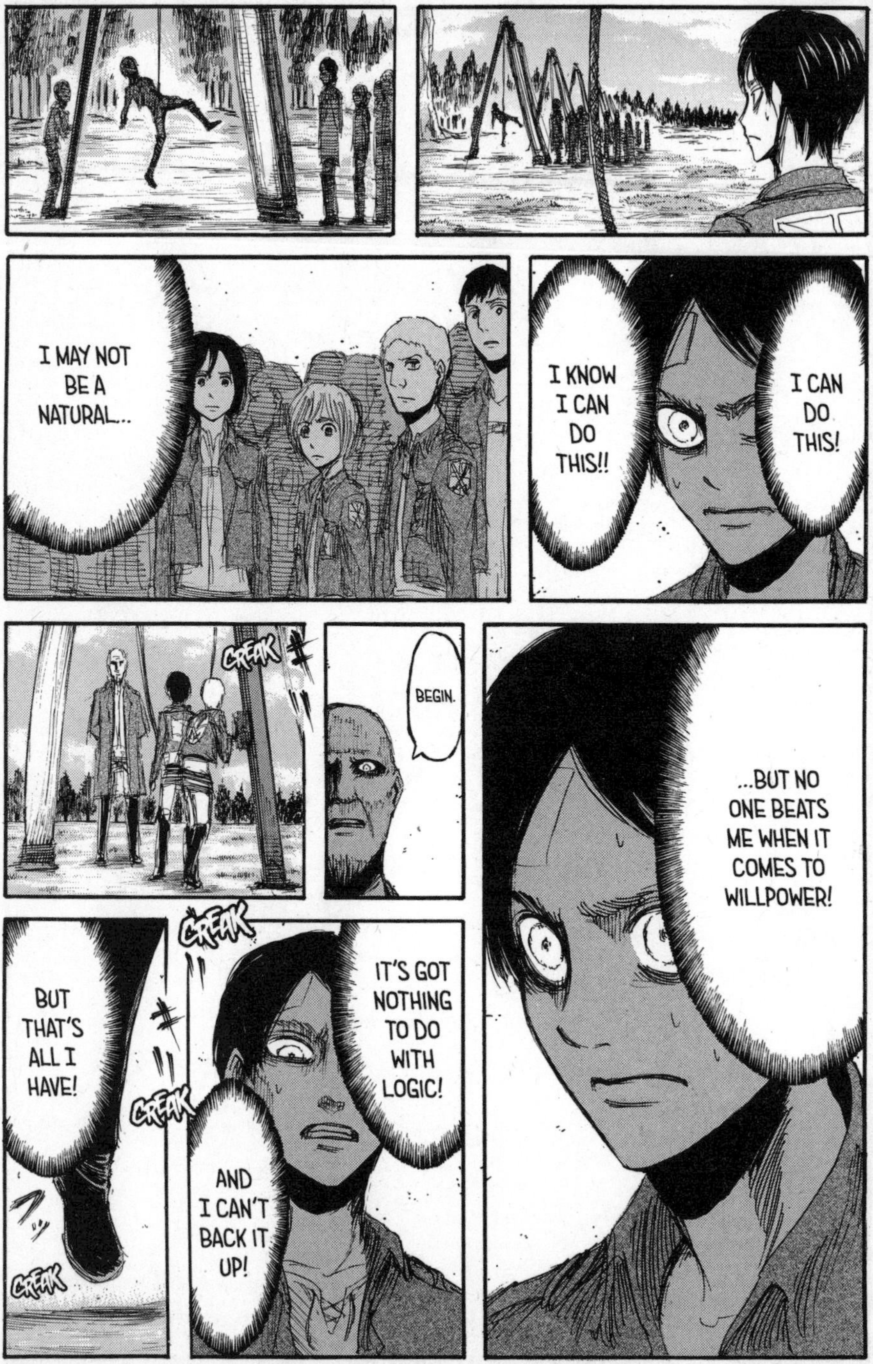
I CAN DO THIS!
I KNOW I CAN DO THIS!!
I MAY NOT BE A NATURAL...
...BUT NO ONE BEATS ME WHEN IT COMES TO WILLPOWER!
BEGIN.
CREAK
IT'S GOT NOTHING TO DO WITH LOGIC!
CREAK
CREAK
AND I CAN'T BACK IT UP!
BUT THAT'S ALL I HAVE!
CREAK

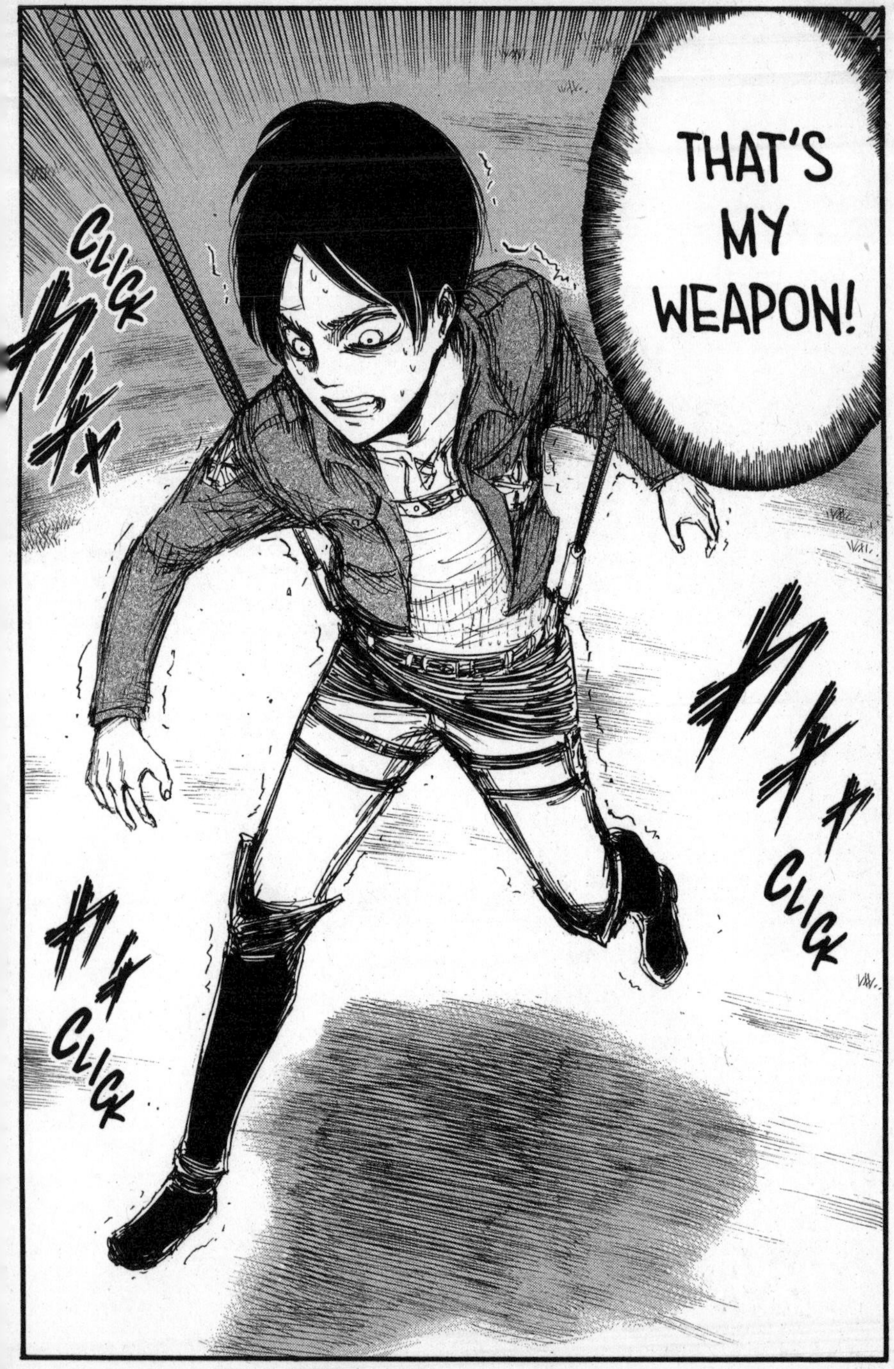
THAT'S MY WEAPON!
CLICK
CLICK
CLICK

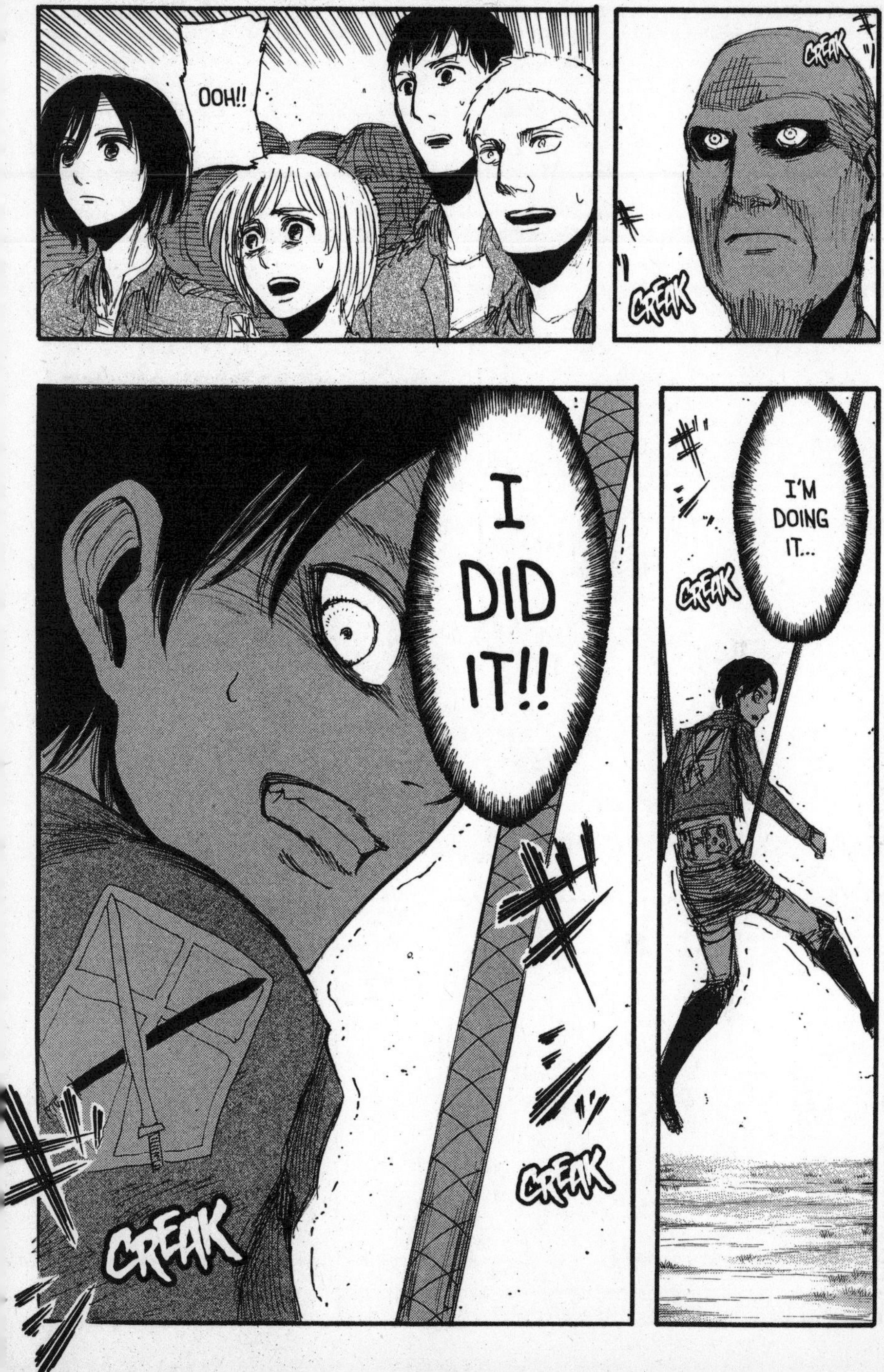
CREAK
CREAK
OOH!!
I'M DOING IT...
CREAK
I DID IT!!
CREAK
CREAK

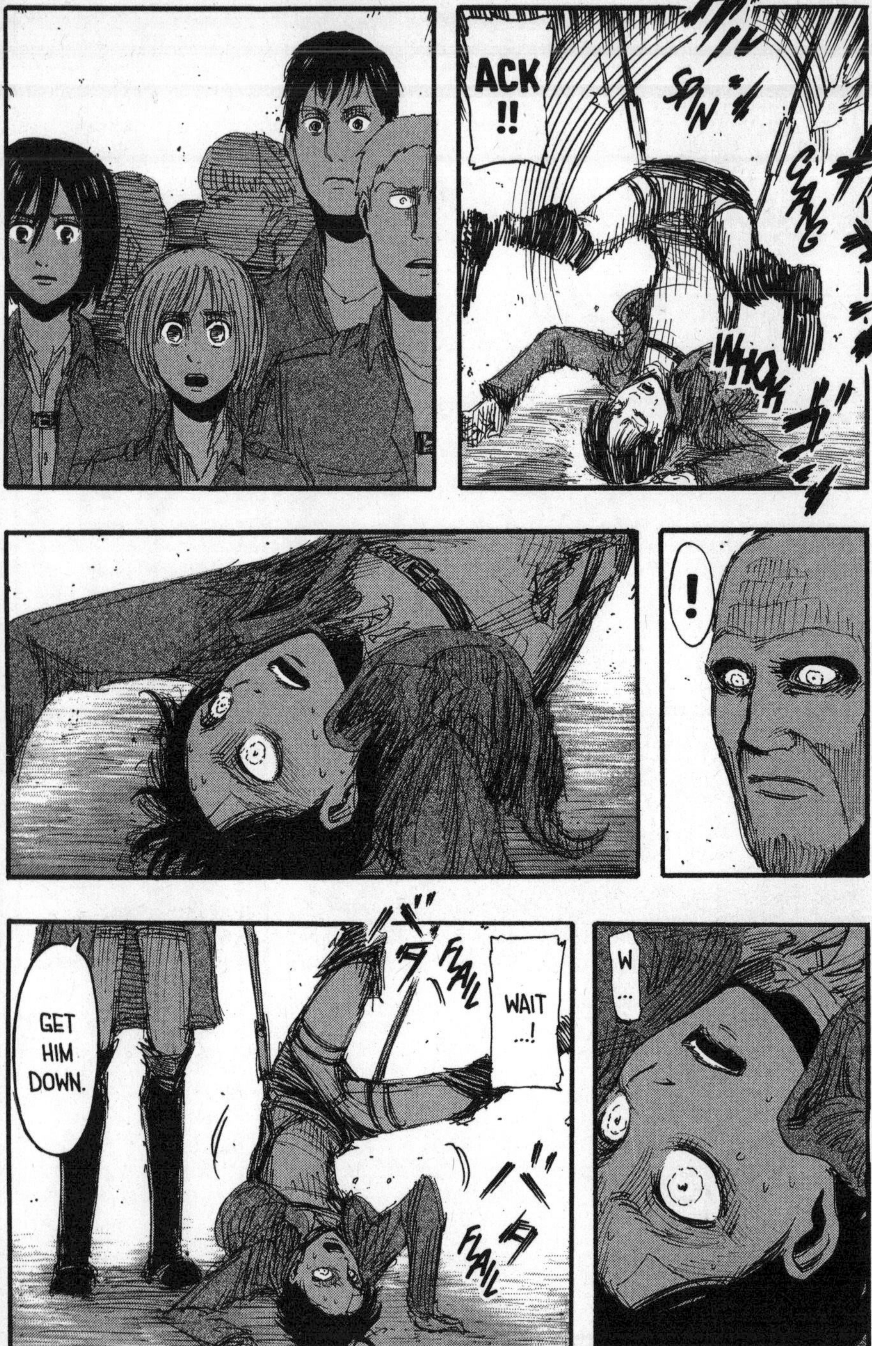
ACK !!
SPIN
CLANG
WHOCK
!
W ...
WAIT ...!
FLAIL
GET HIM DOWN.
FLAIL

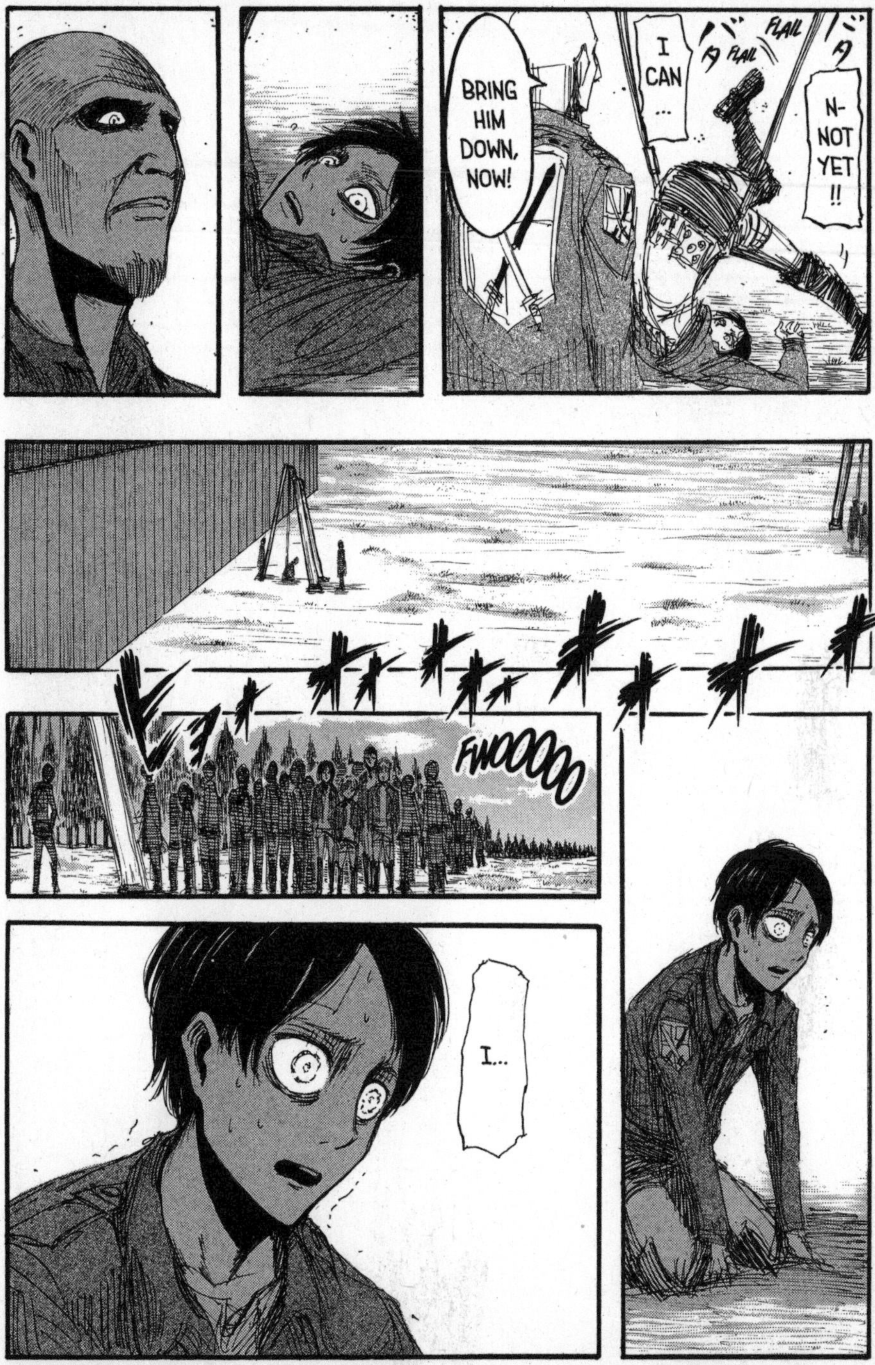

バタ
N-NOT YET!!
FLAIL
FLAIL
バタ
I CAN ...
BRING HIM DOWN, NOW!
FWOOOOO
I...

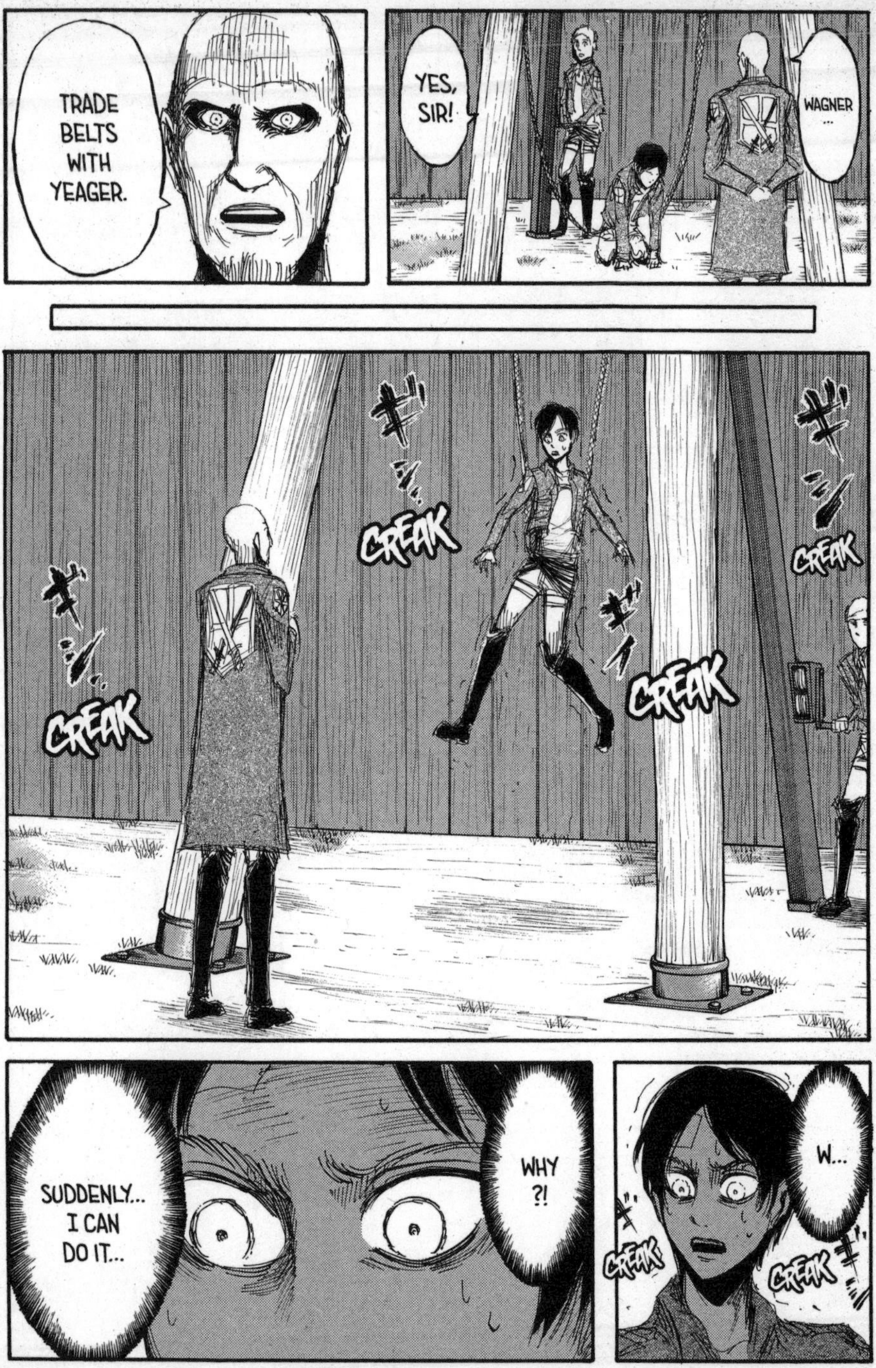
WAGNER...
YES, SIR!
TRADE BELTS WITH YEAGER.
CREAK
CREAK
CREAK
CREAK
W...
CREAK
CREAK
WHY ?!
SUDDENLY... I CAN DO IT...

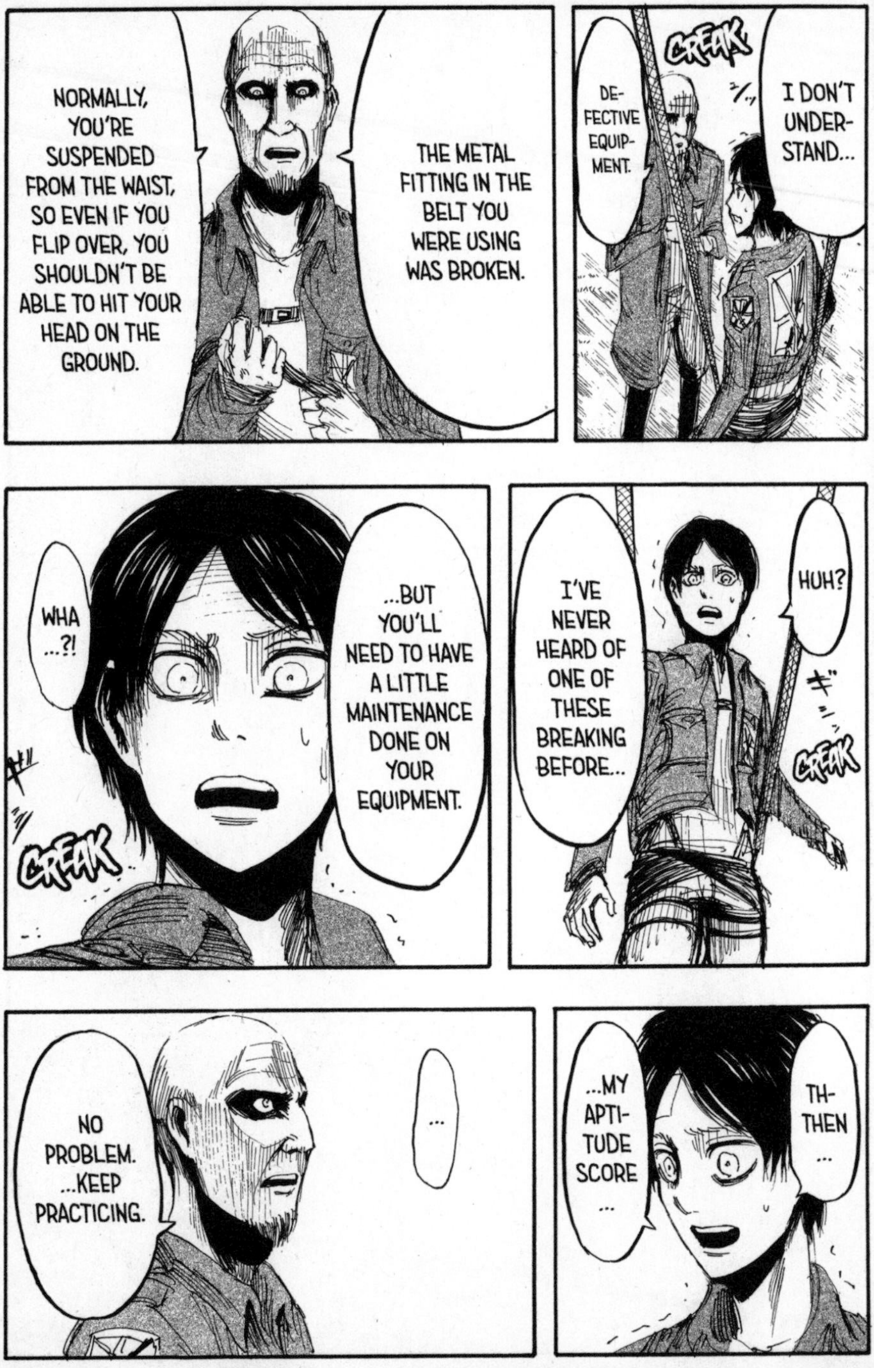
CREAK
I DON'T UNDERSTAND...
DEFECTIVE EQUIPMENT.
THE METAL FITTING IN THE BELT YOU WERE USING WAS BROKEN.
NORMALLY, YOU'RE SUSPENDED FROM THE WAIST, SO EVEN IF YOU FLIP OVER, YOU SHOULDN'T BE ABLE TO HIT YOUR HEAD ON THE GROUND.
HUH?
CREAK
I'VE NEVER HEARD OF ONE OF THESE BREAKING BEFORE...
...BUT YOU'LL NEED TO HAVE A LITTLE MAINTENANCE DONE ON YOUR EQUIPMENT.
WHA...?!
CREAK
TH-THEN...
...MY APTITUDE SCORE...
...
NO PROBLEM. ...KEEP PRACTICING.

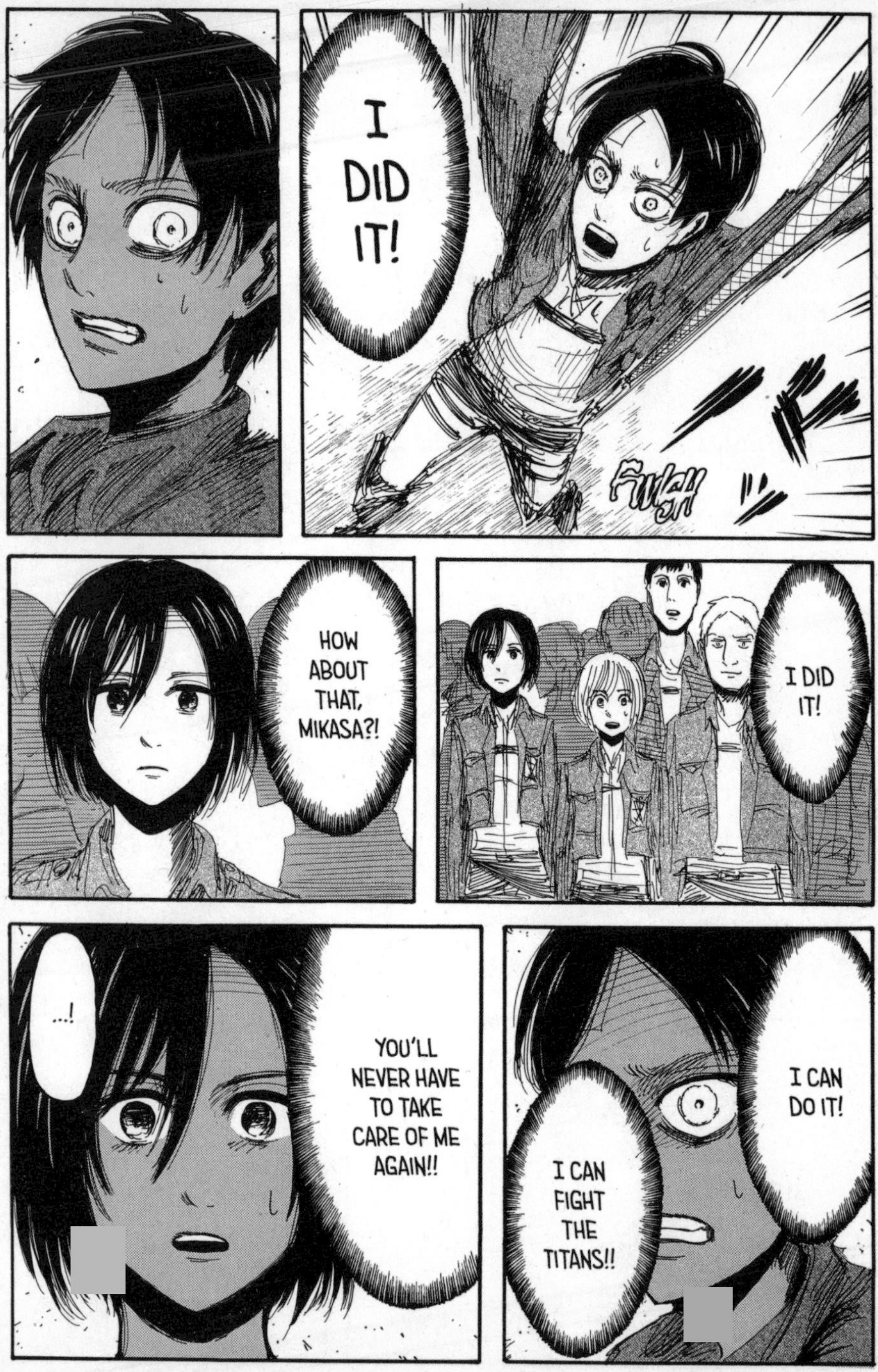
I DID IT!
FWISH
I DID IT!
HOW ABOUT THAT, MIKASA?!
I CAN DO IT!
I CAN FIGHT THE TITANS!!
YOU'LL NEVER HAVE TO TAKE CARE OF ME AGAIN!!
...!

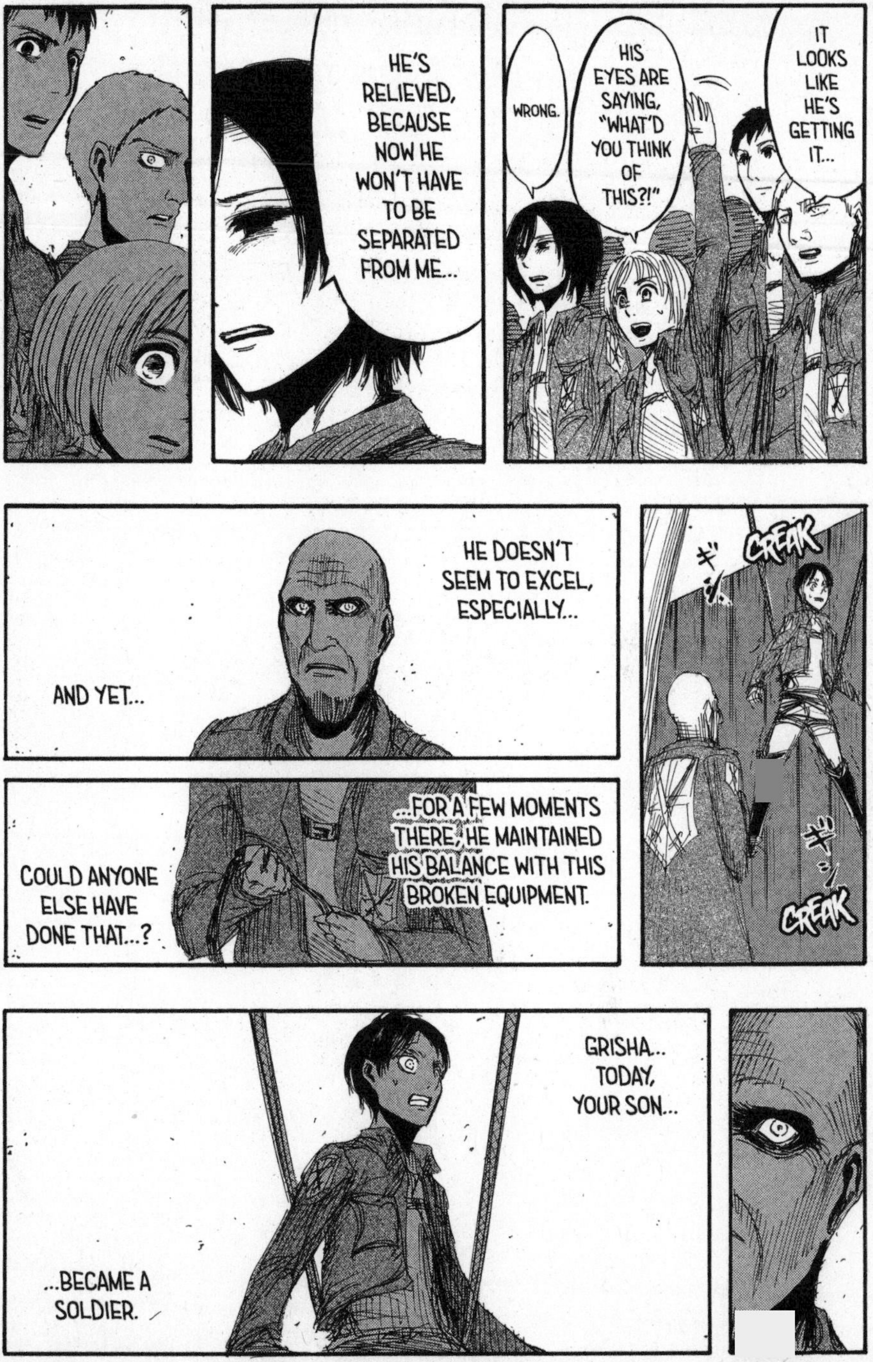
IT LOOKS LIKE HE'S GETTING IT...
HIS EYES ARE SAYING, "WHAT'D YOU THINK OF THIS?!"
WRONG.
HE'S RELIEVED, BECAUSE NOW HE WON'T HAVE TO BE SEPARATED FROM ME...
ギシ
CREAK
ギシ
CREAK
HE DOESN'T SEEM TO EXCEL, ESPECIALLY...
AND YET...
...FOR A FEW MOMENTS THERE, HE MAINTAINED HIS BALANCE WITH THIS BROKEN EQUIPMENT.
COULD ANYONE ELSE HAVE DONE THAT...?
GRISHA... TODAY, YOUR SON...
...BECAME A SOLDIER.

Current Publicly Available Information

8. Vertical Maneuvering Equipment Training

HUMANS MOVE IN TWO DIMENSIONS, SO VERTICAL MANEUVERING EQUIPMENT TRAINING, IN WHICH THEY MUST ADAPT TO THREE DIMENSIONS, IS EXTREMELY DEMANDING. PHYSICAL STRENGTH IS MOST IMPORTANT, ESPECIALLY LEG STRENGTH, THOUGH THE ABILITY TO ADAPT TO G FORCES (WHICH WOMEN PARTICULARLY EXCEL AT) AND A GRASP OF THREE-DIMENSIONAL SPACE ARE ALSO VITAL. WHEN IN MIDAIR, ONE MUST QUICKLY ASSESS THE SITUATION AND SURROUNDINGS, WHILE UNCOMMON WILLPOWER IS REQUIRED TO KEEP FROM PANICKING. THE VARIOUS TRAINING ACTIVITIES INCLUDE BUNGEE JUMPING AND GYMNASTICS WITH EQUIPMENT. AT ONE POINT, THE INSTRUCTOR WILL DELIBERATELY CUT THE LIFELINE (AN "AMBUSH" IN TRAINEE VERNACULAR). AT ANY RATE, IT WOULD BE HARD TO CALL THIS TRAINING "SAFE," BUT ANYONE WHO WOULD DIE DURING THIS PERIOD WOULD NOT STAND A CHANCE IN BATTLE AGAINST A TITAN, AND SOLDIERS WHO MANAGE TO GET THROUGH IT COME OUT WITH A STRONGER FIGHTING SPIRIT AND SELF-CONFIDENCE.

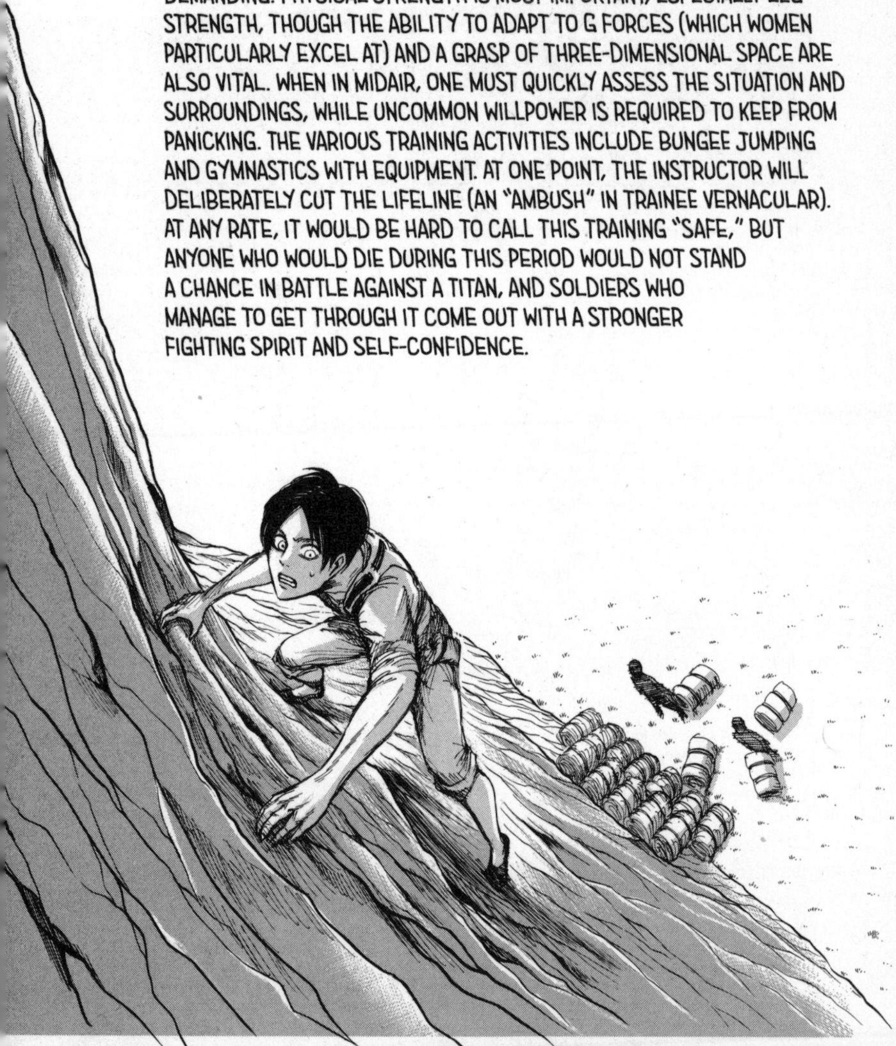

(WITH THANKS TO UKYŌ KODACHI AND KIYOMUNE MIWA)

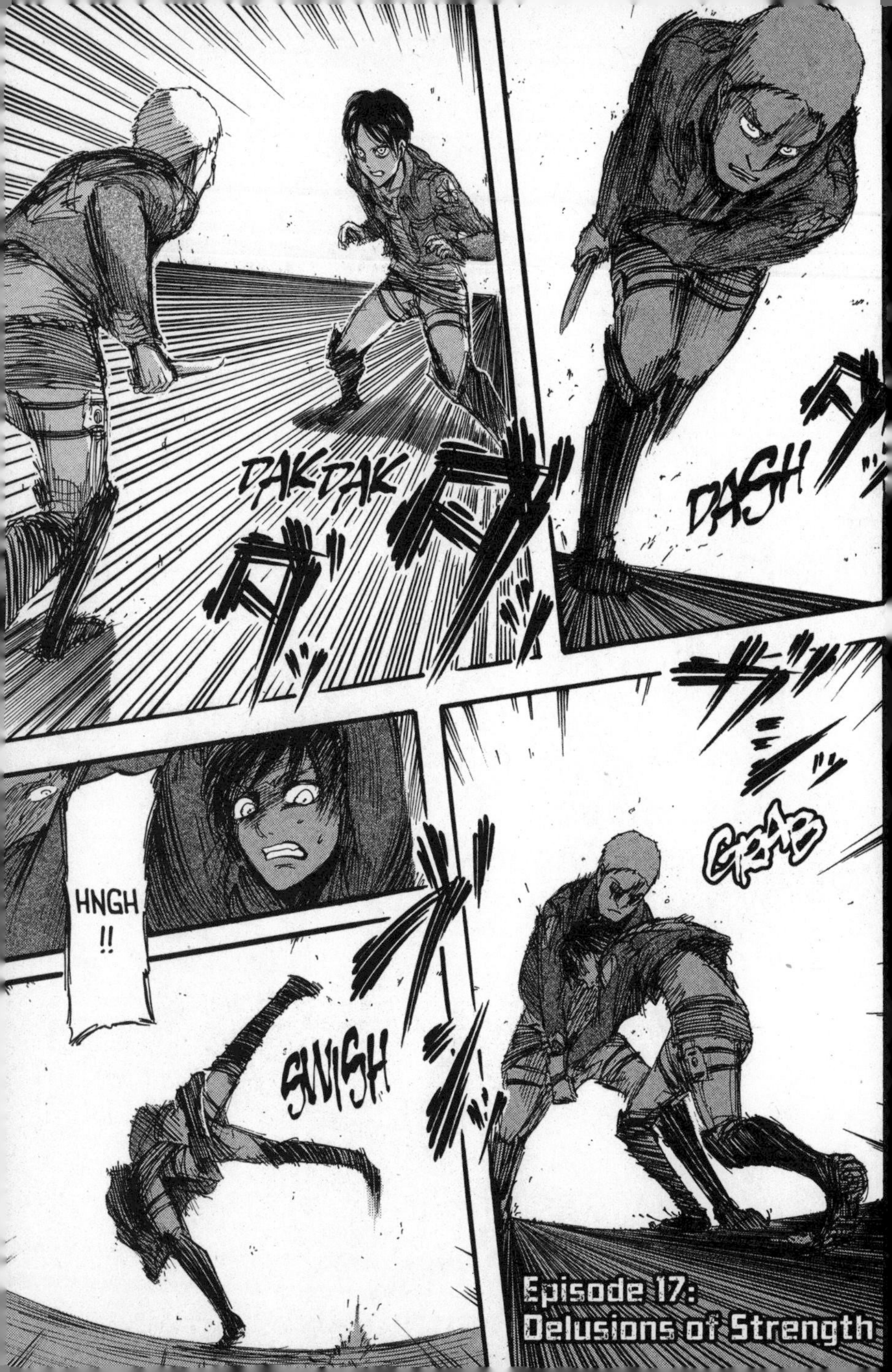
DASH
DAK DAK
GRAB
Episode 17:
Delusions of Strength
HNGH !!
SWISH

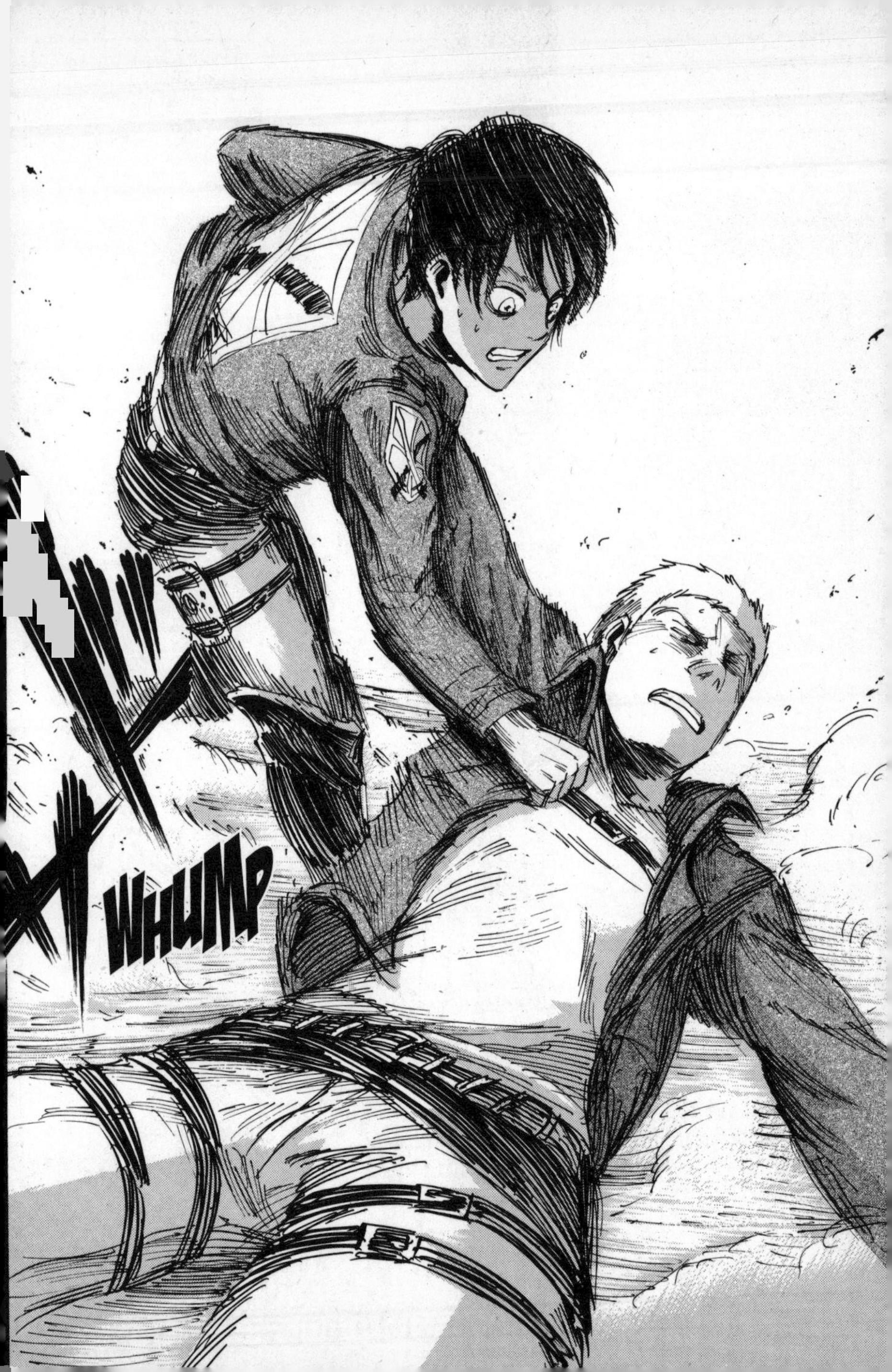
WHUMP

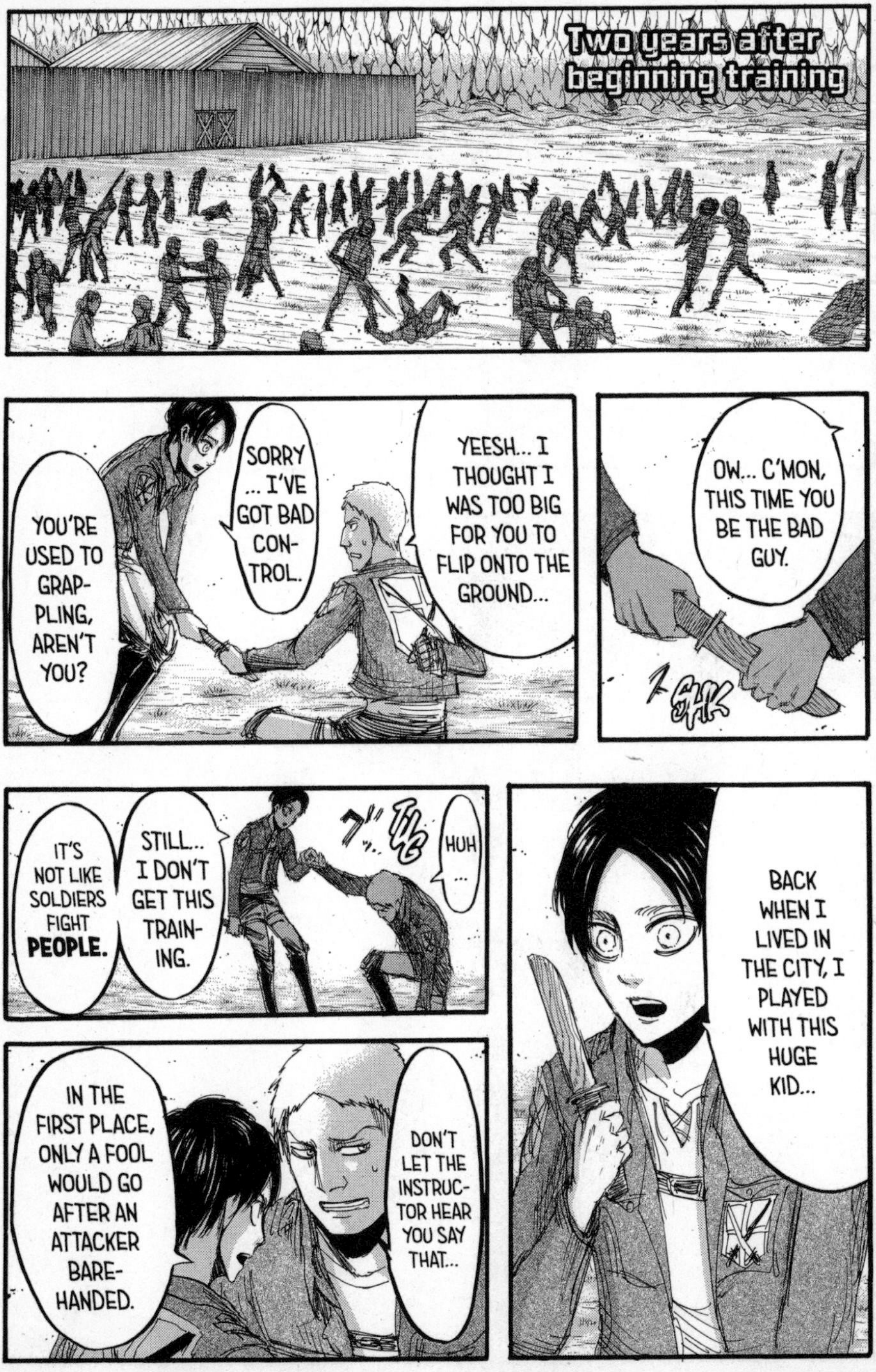
Two years after beginning training
OW... C'MON, THIS TIME YOU BE THE BAD GUY.
SHK
YEESH... I THOUGHT I WAS TOO BIG FOR YOU TO FLIP ONTO THE GROUND...
SORRY ... I'VE GOT BAD CON-TROL.
YOU'RE USED TO GRAP-PLING, AREN'T YOU?
BACK WHEN I LIVED IN THE CITY, I PLAYED WITH THIS HUGE KID...
HUH ...
TUG
STILL... I DON'T GET THIS TRAIN-ING.
IT'S NOT LIKE SOLDIERS FIGHT **PEOPLE.**
DON'T LET THE INSTRUC-TOR HEAR YOU SAY THAT...
IN THE FIRST PLACE, ONLY A FOOL WOULD GO AFTER AN ATTACKER BARE-HANDED.

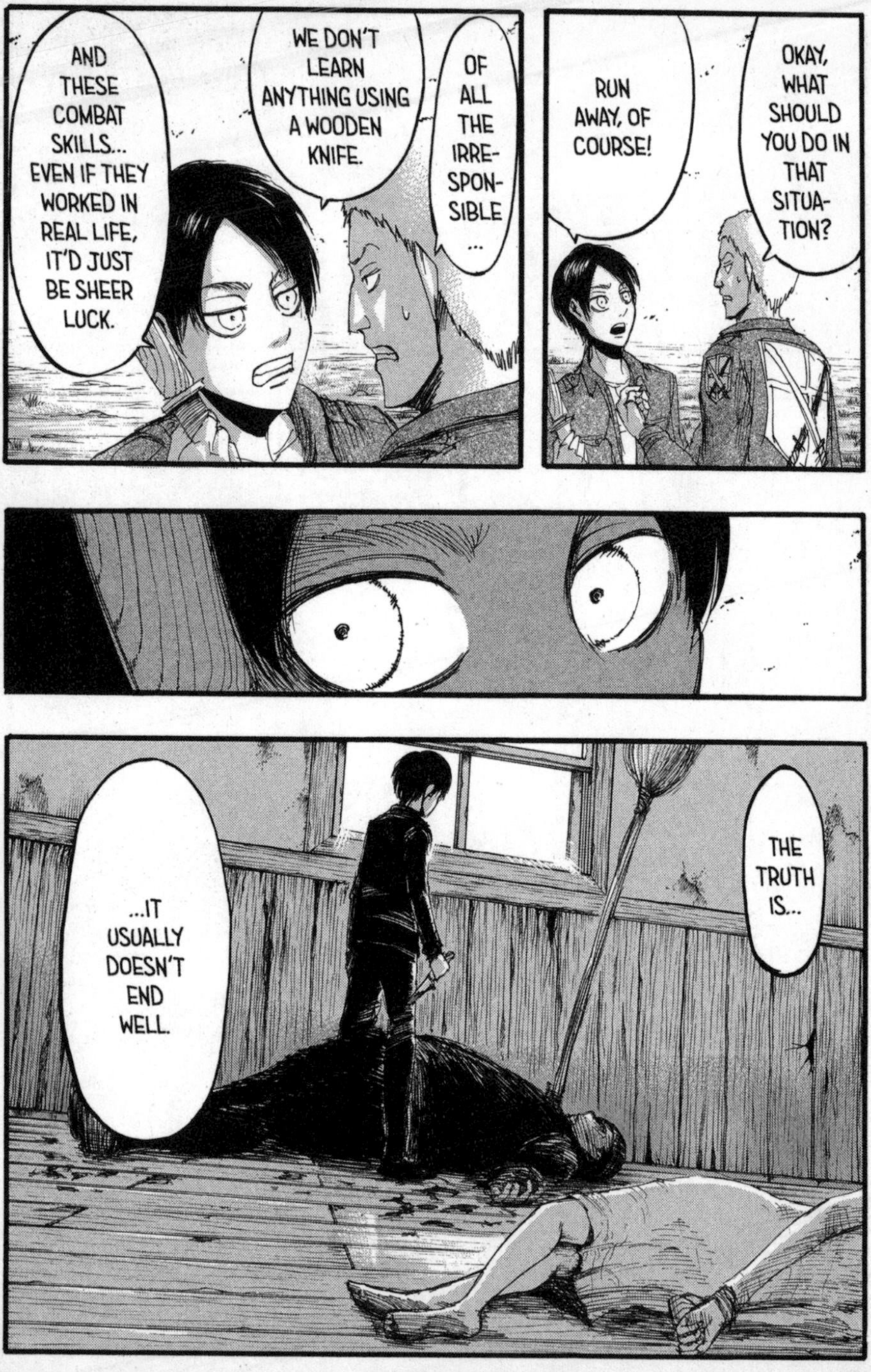
OKAY, WHAT SHOULD YOU DO IN THAT SITUATION?
RUN AWAY, OF COURSE!
OF ALL THE IRRESPONSIBLE...
WE DON'T LEARN ANYTHING USING A WOODEN KNIFE.
AND THESE COMBAT SKILLS... EVEN IF THEY WORKED IN REAL LIFE, IT'D JUST BE SHEER LUCK.
THE TRUTH IS...
...IT USUALLY DOESN'T END WELL.

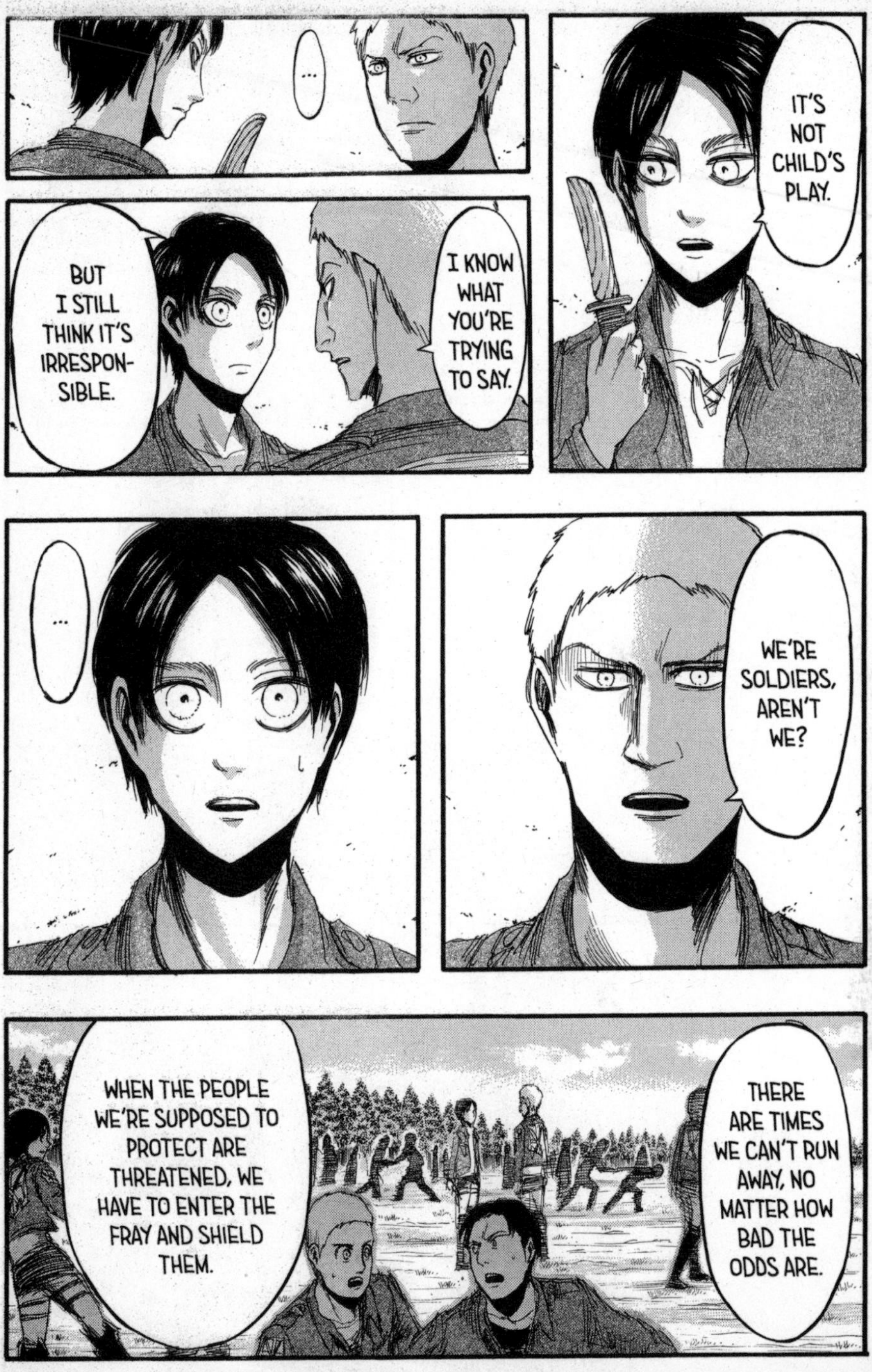
IT'S NOT CHILD'S PLAY.
...
I KNOW WHAT YOU'RE TRYING TO SAY.
BUT I STILL THINK IT'S IRRESPON-SIBLE.
WE'RE SOLDIERS, AREN'T WE?
...
THERE ARE TIMES WE CAN'T RUN AWAY, NO MATTER HOW BAD THE ODDS ARE.
WHEN THE PEOPLE WE'RE SUPPOSED TO PROTECT ARE THREATENED, WE HAVE TO ENTER THE FRAY AND SHIELD THEM.

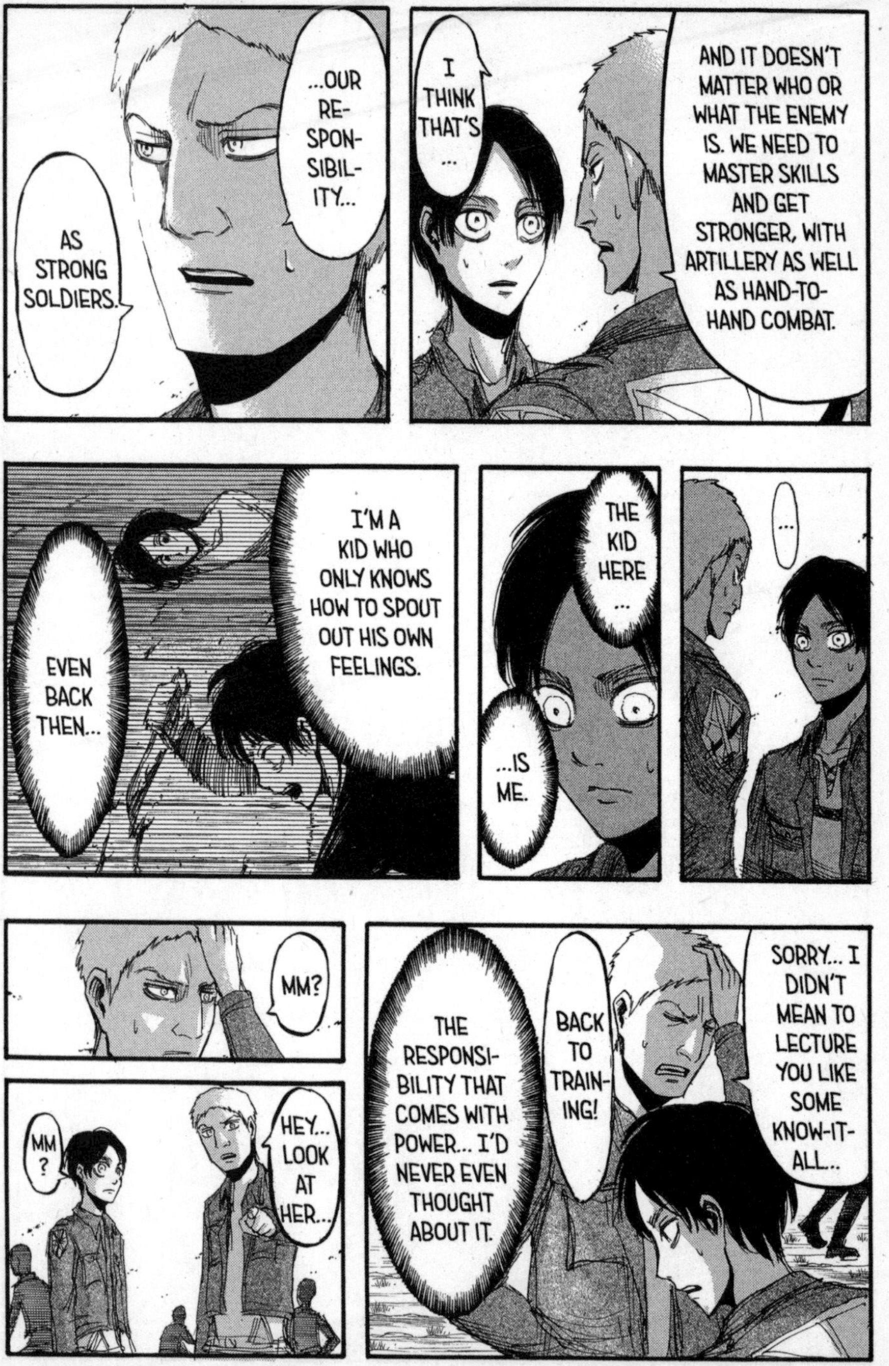
AND IT DOESN'T MATTER WHO OR WHAT THE ENEMY IS. WE NEED TO MASTER SKILLS AND GET STRONGER, WITH ARTILLERY AS WELL AS HAND-TO-HAND COMBAT.
I THINK THAT'S ...
...OUR RESPONSIBILITY...
AS STRONG SOLDIERS.
...
THE KID HERE ...
...IS ME.
I'M A KID WHO ONLY KNOWS HOW TO SPOUT OUT HIS OWN FEELINGS.
EVEN BACK THEN...
SORRY... I DIDN'T MEAN TO LECTURE YOU LIKE SOME KNOW-IT-ALL...
BACK TO TRAINING!
THE RESPONSIBILITY THAT COMES WITH POWER... I'D NEVER EVEN THOUGHT ABOUT IT.
MM?
HEY... LOOK AT HER...
MM ?

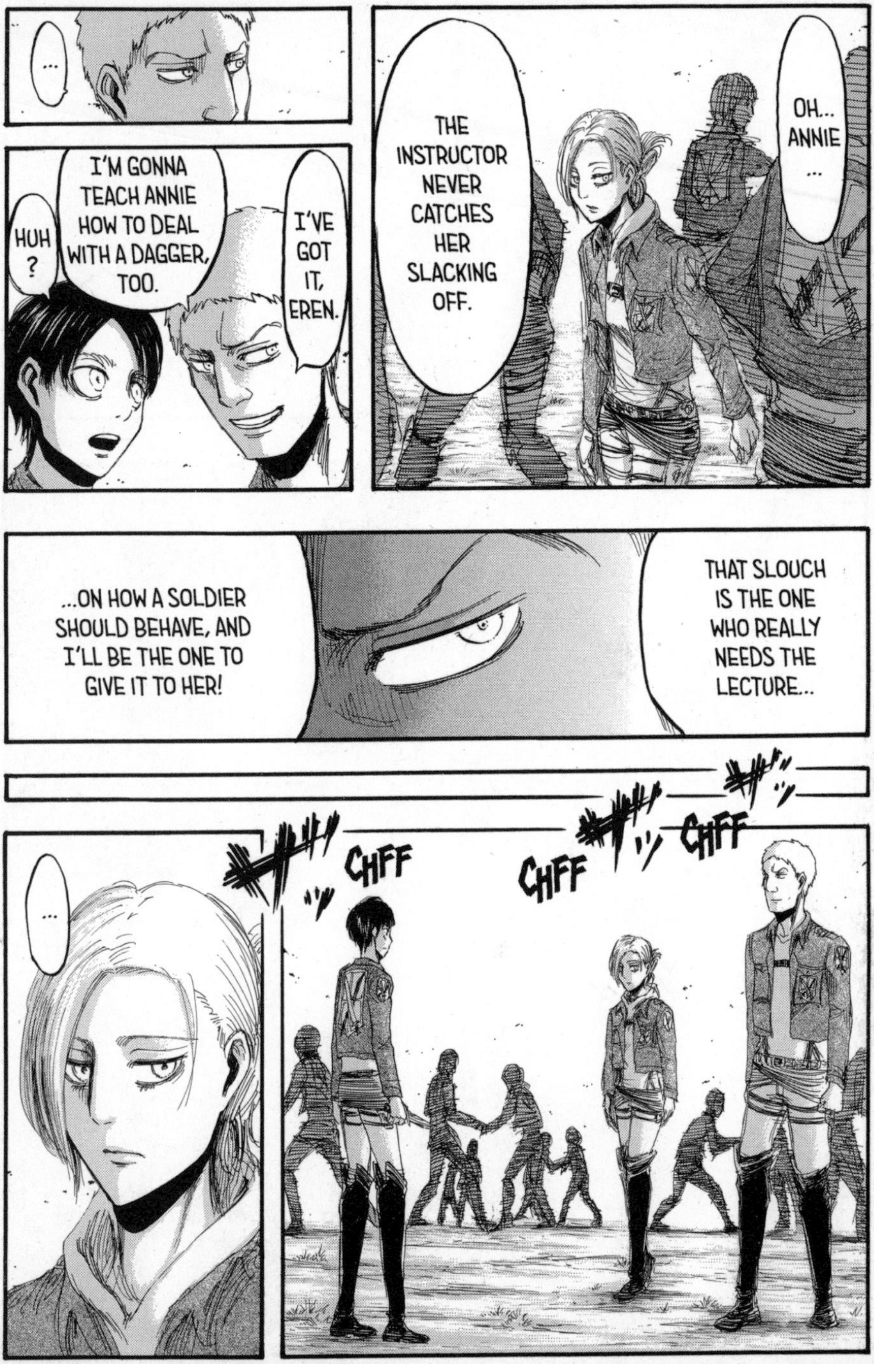
OH... ANNIE ...
THE INSTRUCTOR NEVER CATCHES HER SLACKING OFF.
...
I'VE GOT IT, EREN.
I'M GONNA TEACH ANNIE HOW TO DEAL WITH A DAGGER, TOO.
HUH ?
THAT SLOUCH IS THE ONE WHO REALLY NEEDS THE LECTURE...
...ON HOW A SOLDIER SHOULD BEHAVE, AND I'LL BE THE ONE TO GIVE IT TO HER!
CHFF
CHFF
CHFF
...

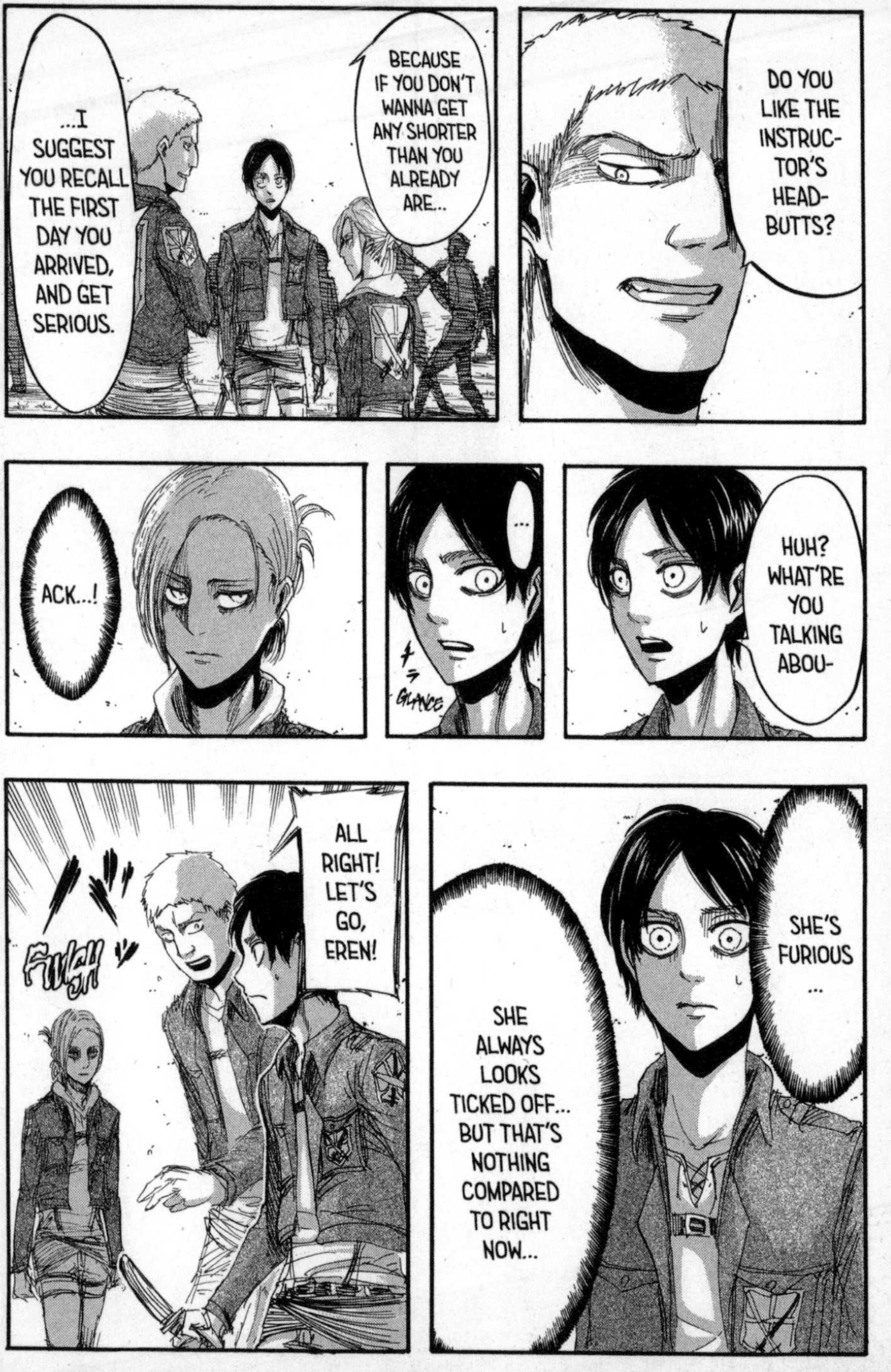
DO YOU LIKE THE INSTRUCTOR'S HEAD-BUTTS?
BECAUSE IF YOU DON'T WANNA GET ANY SHORTER THAN YOU ALREADY ARE...
...
...I SUGGEST YOU RECALL THE FIRST DAY YOU ARRIVED, AND GET SERIOUS.
HUH? WHAT'RE YOU TALKING ABOU-
...
GLANCE
ACK...!
SHE'S FURIOUS ...
SHE ALWAYS LOOKS TICKED OFF... BUT THAT'S NOTHING COMPARED TO RIGHT NOW...
ALL RIGHT! LET'S GO, EREN!
FWISH

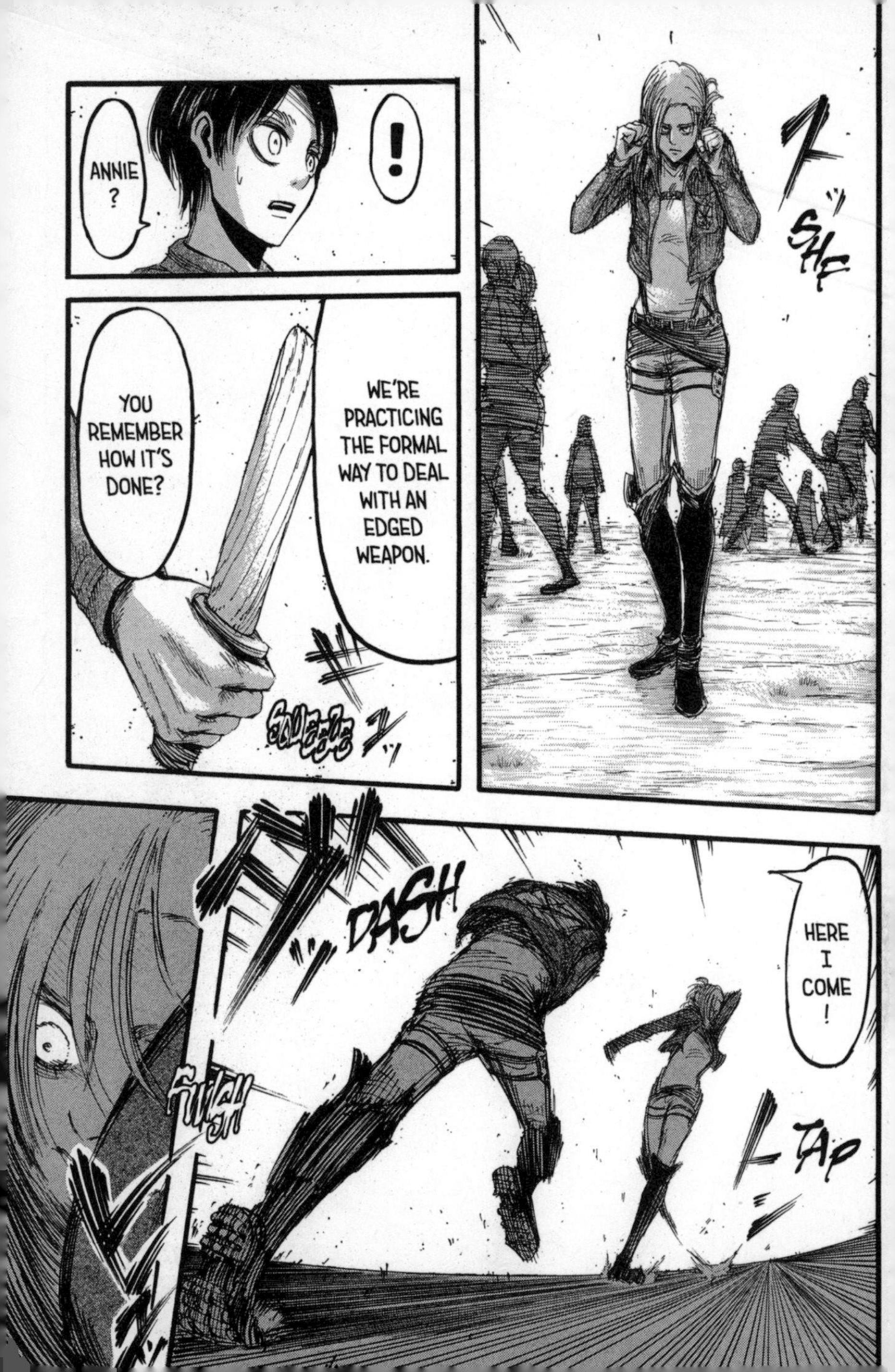

SHF
!
ANNIE ?
WE'RE PRACTICING THE FORMAL WAY TO DEAL WITH AN EDGED WEAPON.
YOU REMEMBER HOW IT'S DONE?
HERE I COME !
TAP
DASH

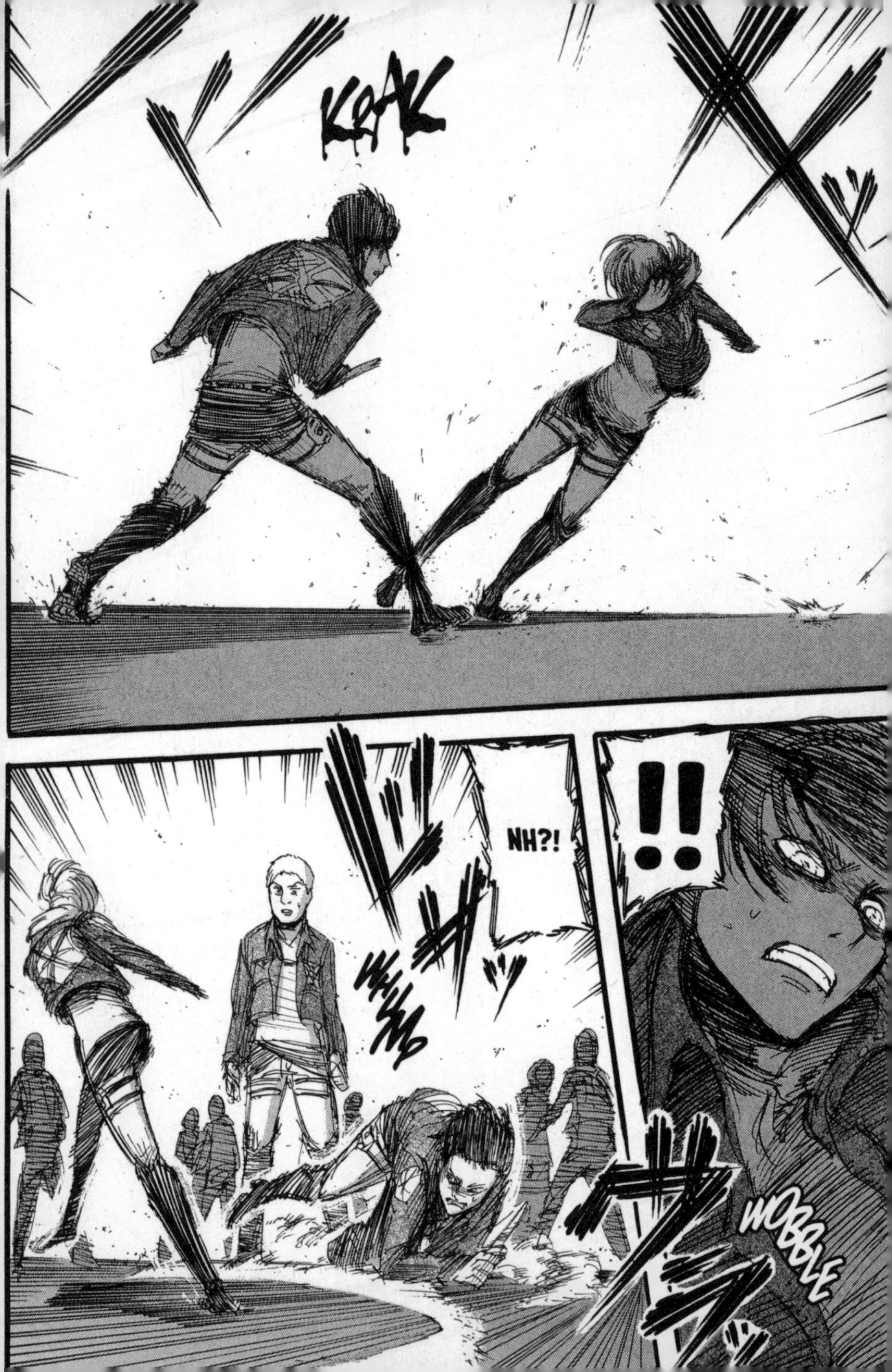
KRAK
!!
WOBBLE
NH?!

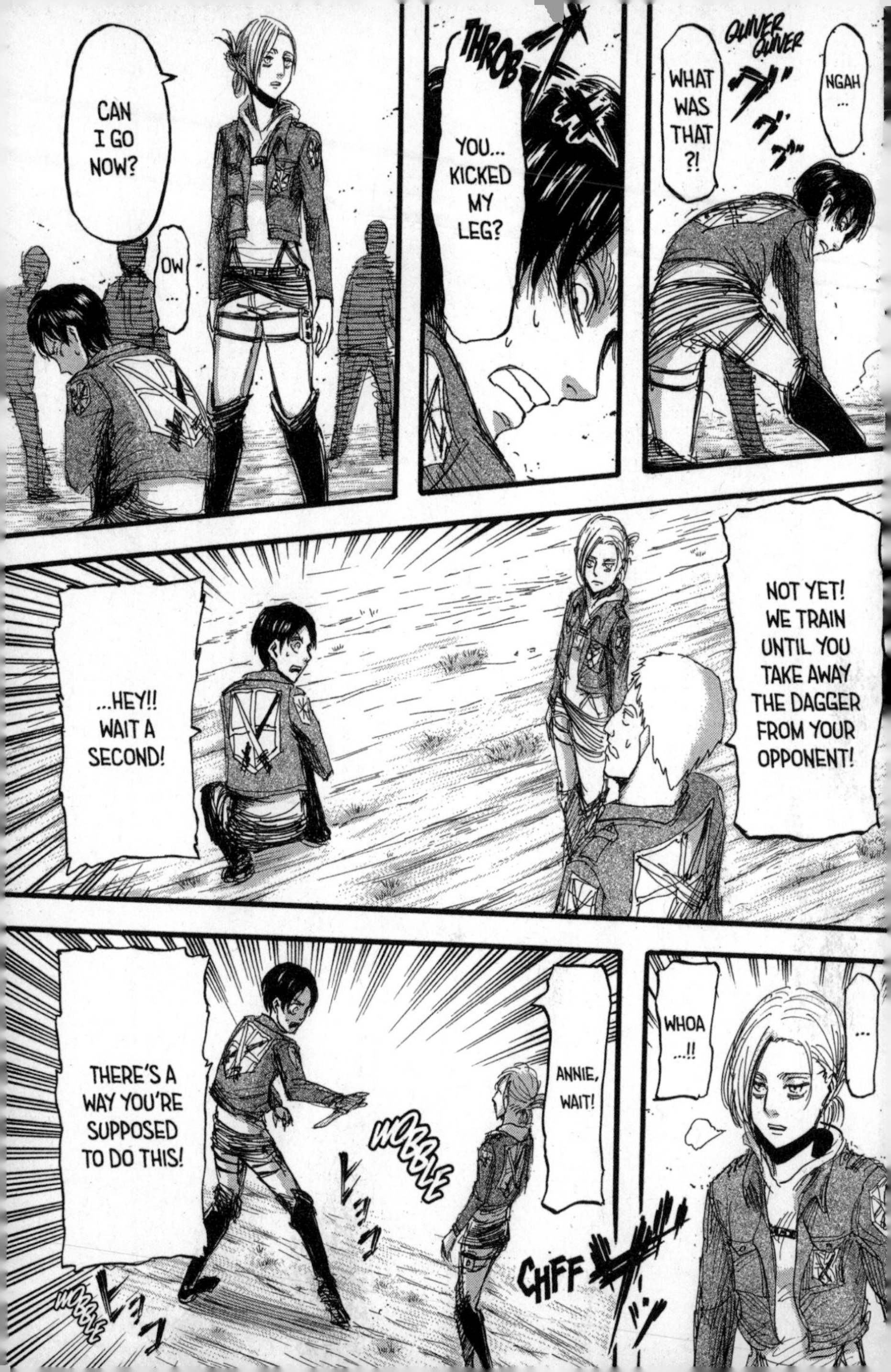
NGAH ...
QUIVER QUIVER
WHAT WAS THAT ?!
THROB
YOU... KICKED MY LEG?
CAN I GO NOW?
OW ...
NOT YET! WE TRAIN UNTIL YOU TAKE AWAY THE DAGGER FROM YOUR OPPONENT!
...HEY!! WAIT A SECOND!
...
WHOA ...!!
CHFF
ANNIE, WAIT!
WOBBLE
THERE'S A WAY YOU'RE SUPPOSED TO DO THIS!
WOBBLE

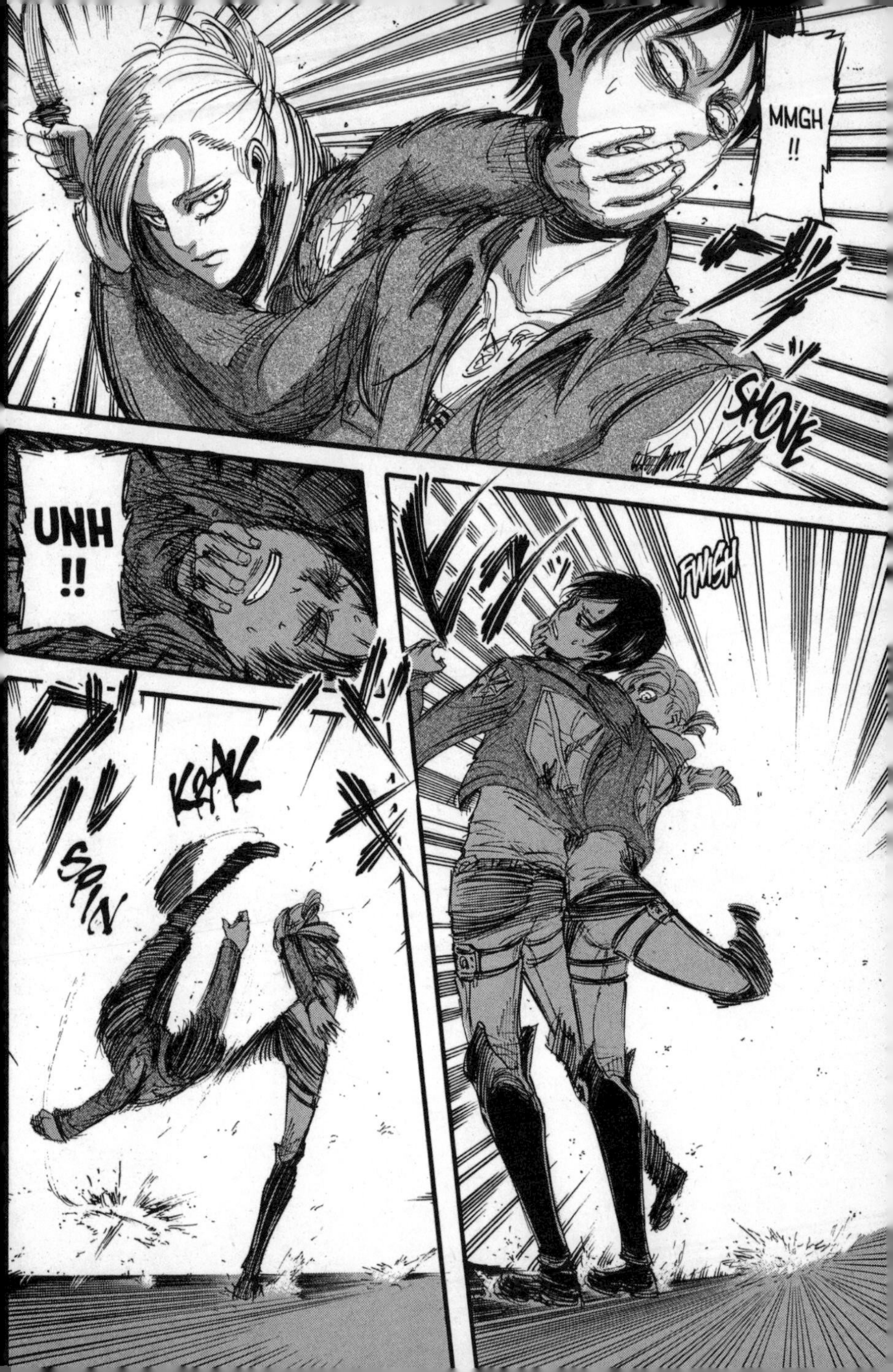
MMGH !!
SHOVE
FWISH
UNH !!
KRAK
SPIN

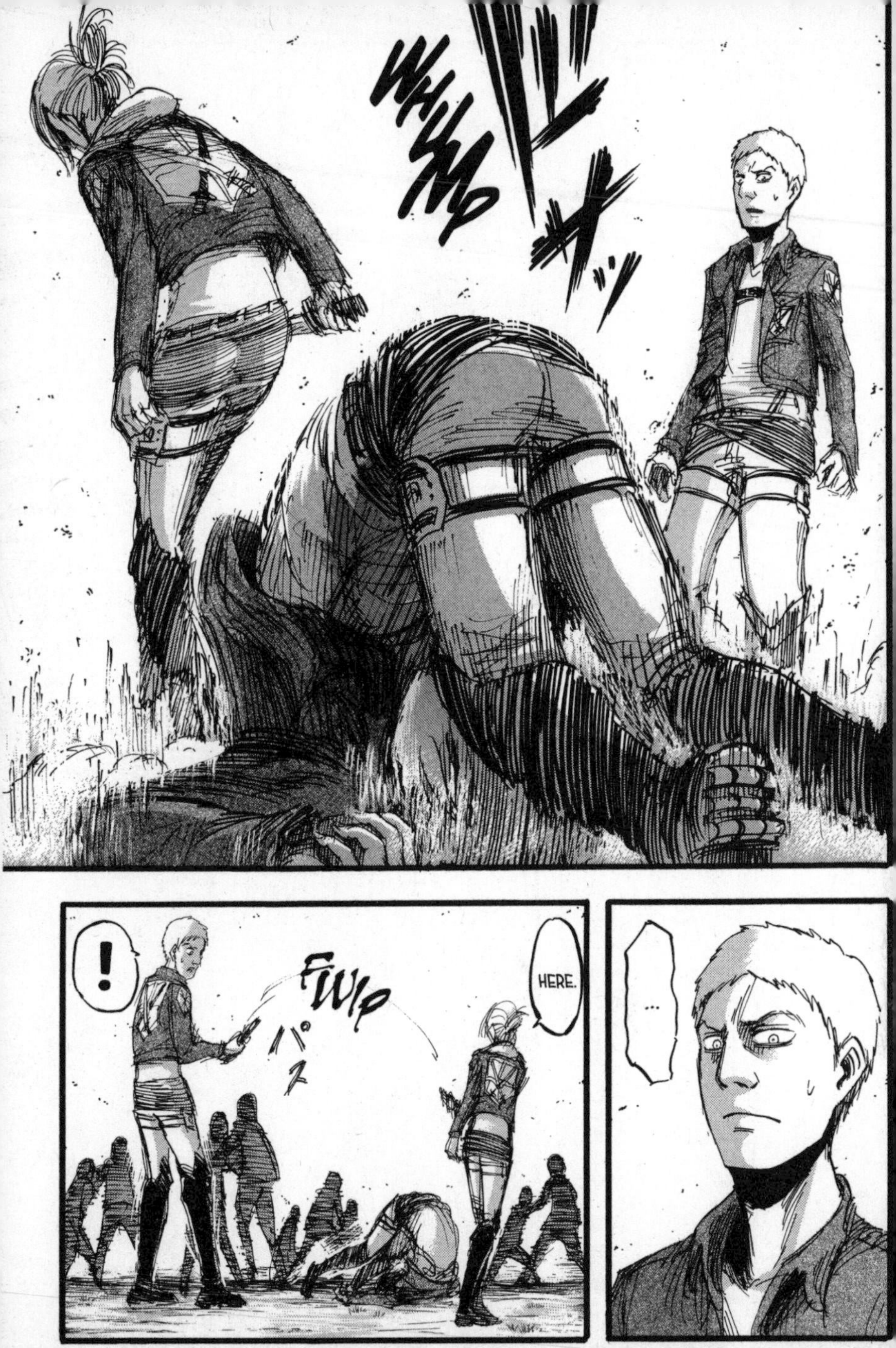
WHUMP
...
HERE.
FWIP
!

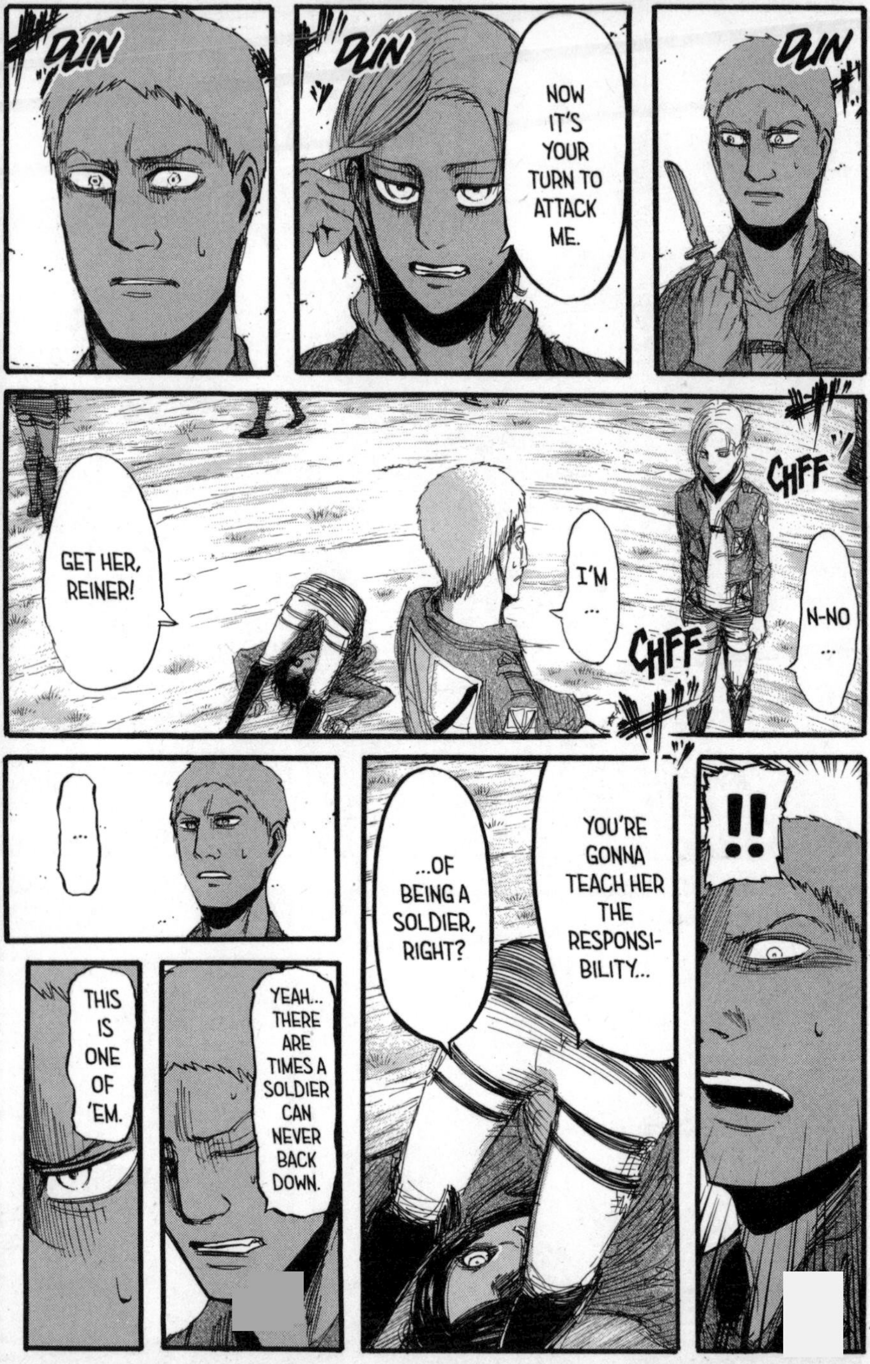
DUN
DUN
NOW IT'S YOUR TURN TO ATTACK ME.
DUN
N-NO ...
CHFF
CHFF
I'M ...
GET HER, REINER!
!!
YOU'RE GONNA TEACH HER THE RESPONSI-BILITY...
...OF BEING A SOLDIER, RIGHT?
...
YEAH... THERE ARE TIMES A SOLDIER CAN NEVER BACK DOWN.
THIS IS ONE OF 'EM.

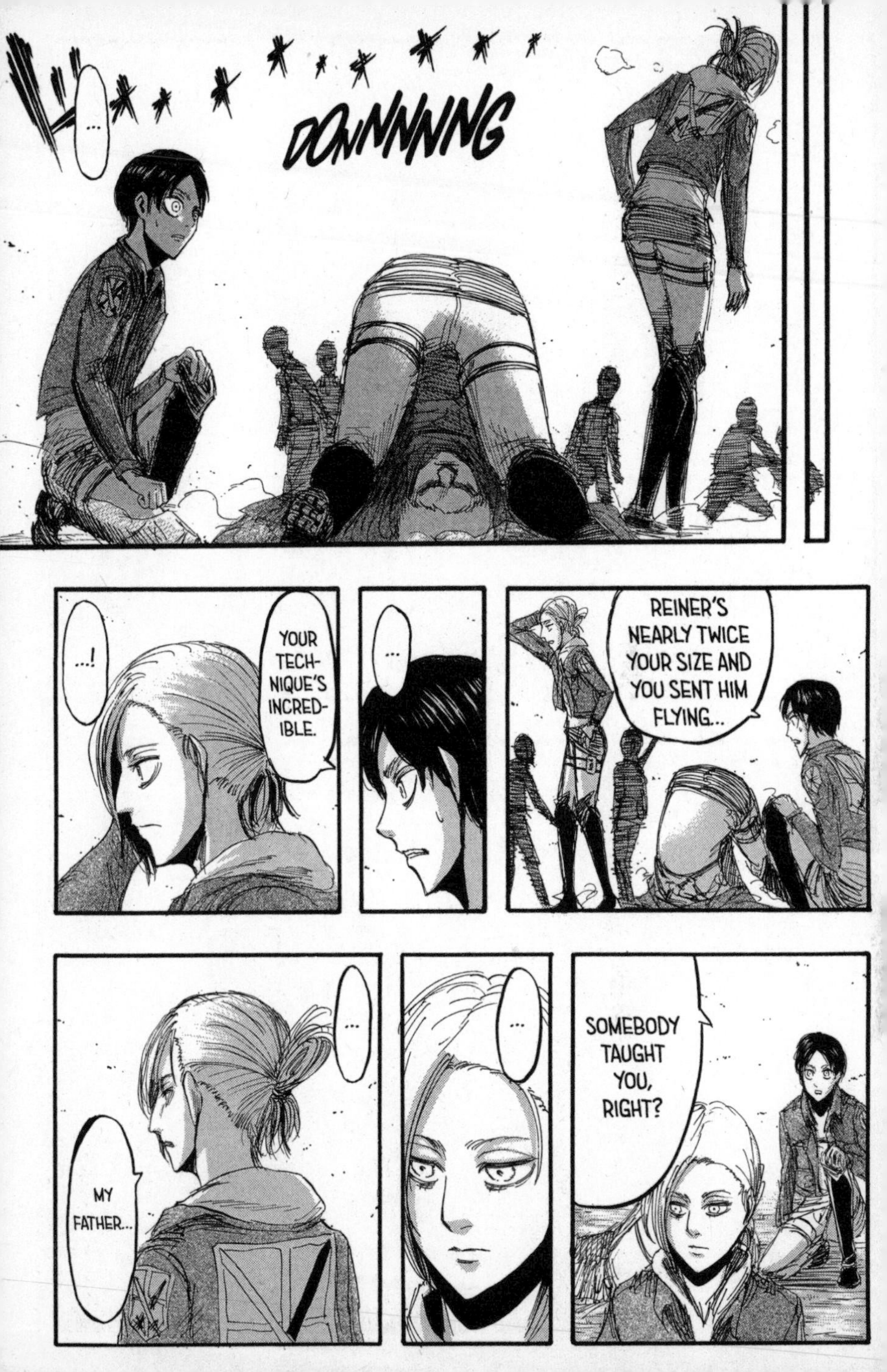
DONNNNG
...
REINER'S NEARLY TWICE YOUR SIZE AND YOU SENT HIM FLYING...
...
YOUR TECH-NIQUE'S INCRED-IBLE.
...!
SOMEBODY TAUGHT YOU, RIGHT?
...
...
MY FATHER...

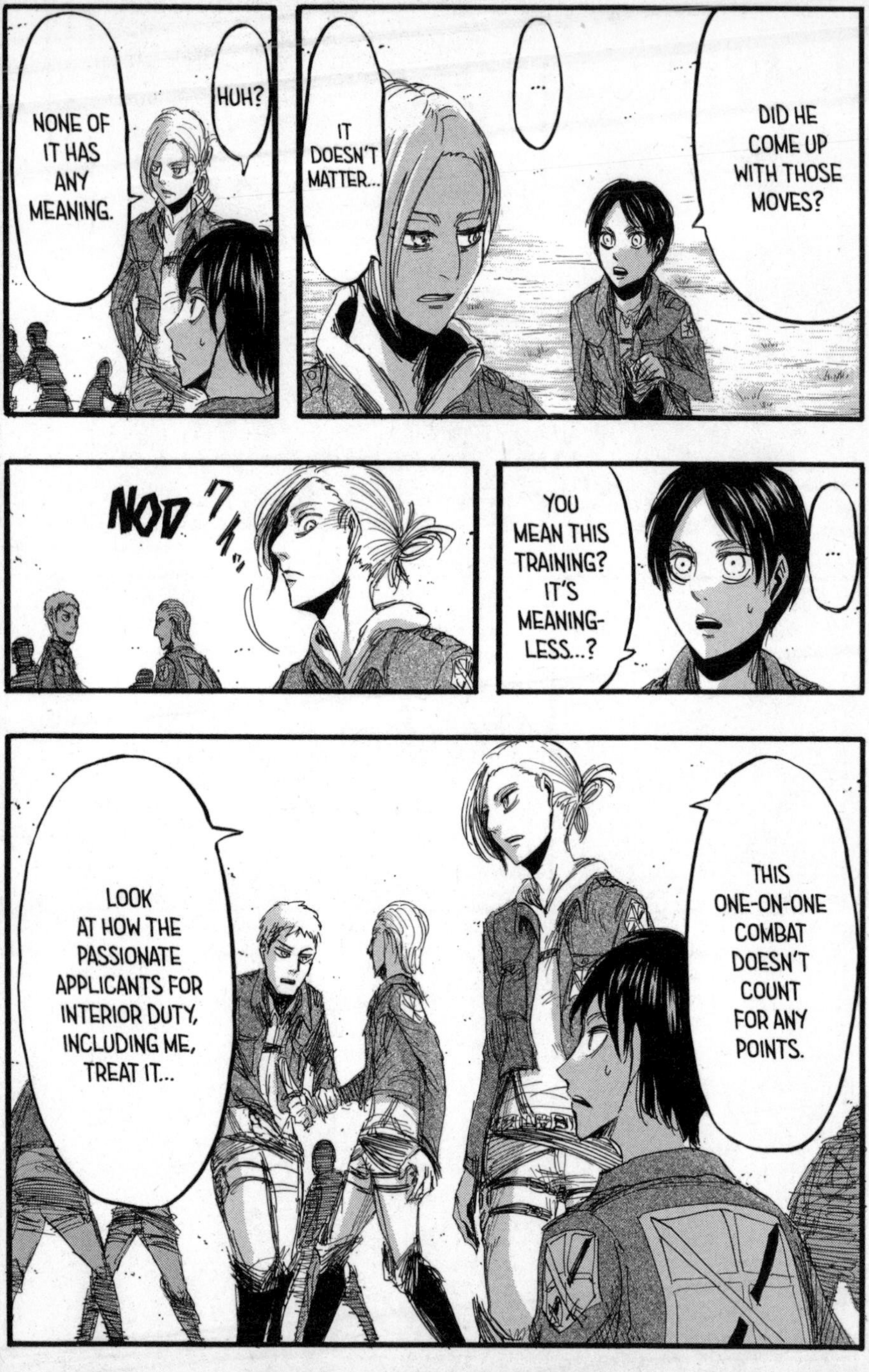
DID HE COME UP WITH THOSE MOVES?
...
IT DOESN'T MATTER...
HUH?
NONE OF IT HAS ANY MEANING.
...
YOU MEAN THIS TRAINING? IT'S MEANING-LESS...?
NOD
THIS ONE-ON-ONE COMBAT DOESN'T COUNT FOR ANY POINTS.
LOOK AT HOW THE PASSIONATE APPLICANTS FOR INTERIOR DUTY, INCLUDING ME, TREAT IT...

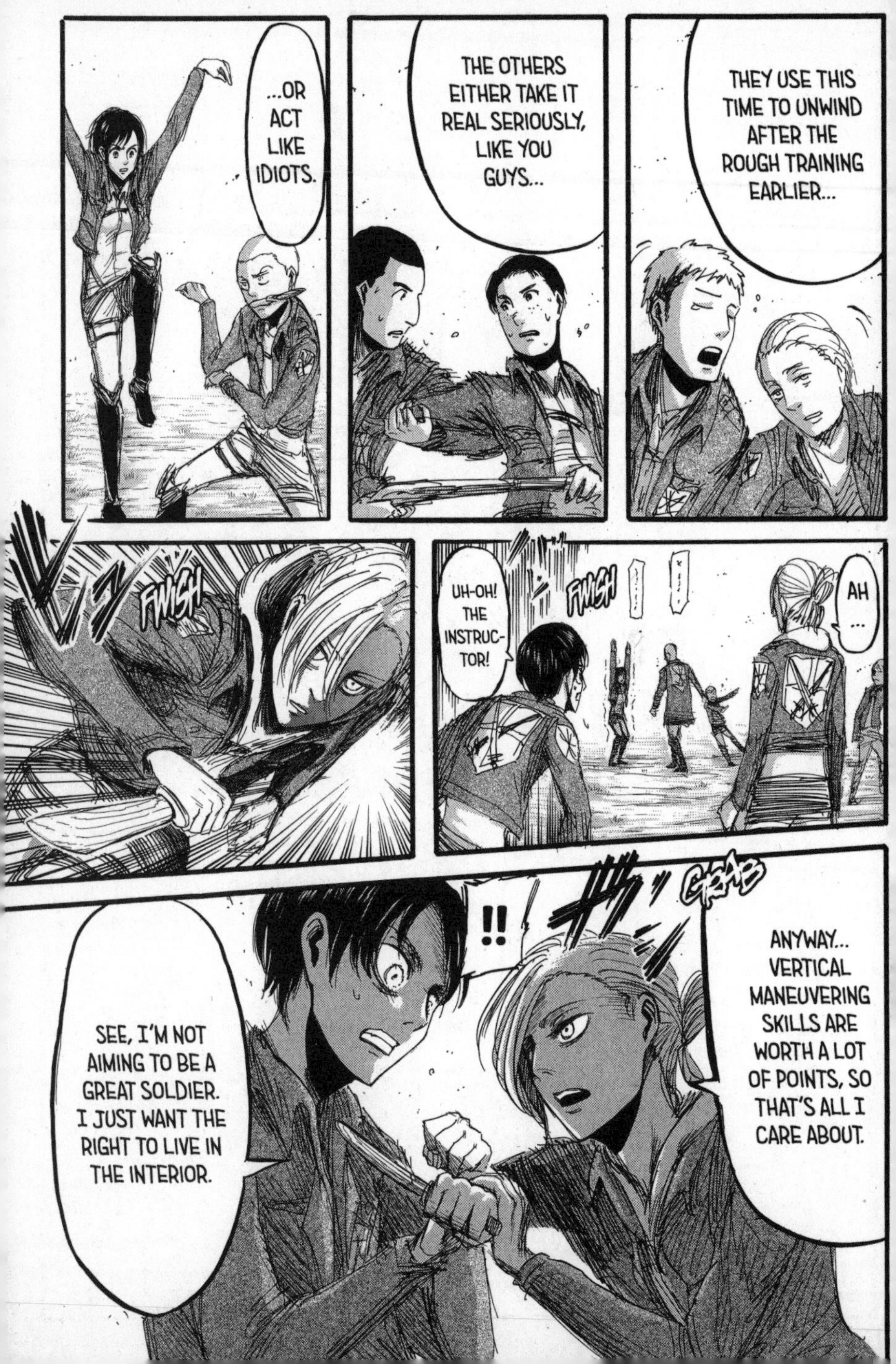
THEY USE THIS TIME TO UNWIND AFTER THE ROUGH TRAINING EARLIER...
THE OTHERS EITHER TAKE IT REAL SERIOUSLY, LIKE YOU GUYS...
...OR ACT LIKE IDIOTS.
AH ...
FWISH
UH-OH! THE INSTRUCTOR!
FWISH
GRAB
ANYWAY... VERTICAL MANEUVERING SKILLS ARE WORTH A LOT OF POINTS, SO THAT'S ALL I CARE ABOUT.
!!
SEE, I'M NOT AIMING TO BE A GREAT SOLDIER. I JUST WANT THE RIGHT TO LIVE IN THE INTERIOR.

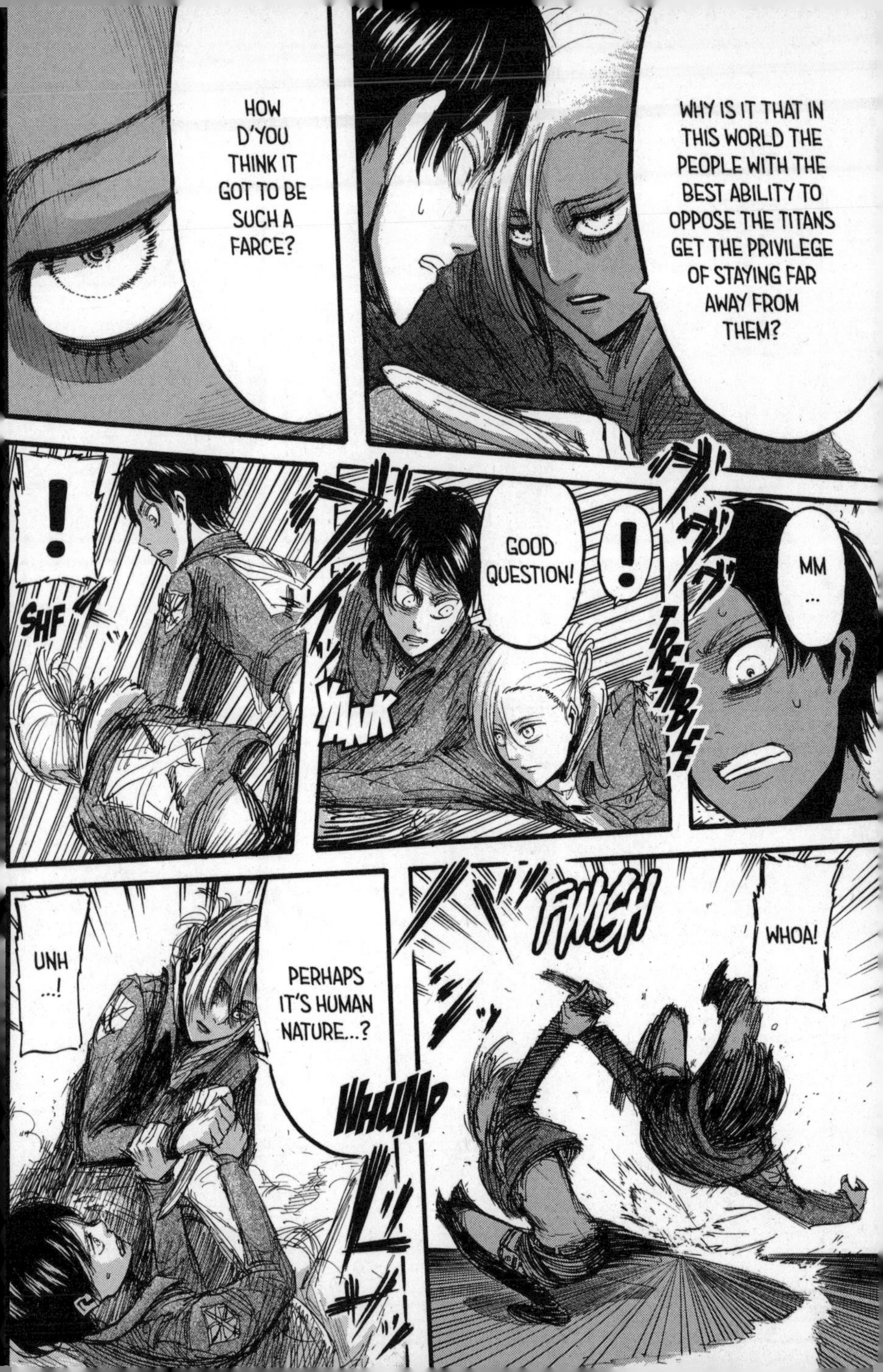
WHY IS IT THAT IN THIS WORLD THE PEOPLE WITH THE BEST ABILITY TO OPPOSE THE TITANS GET THE PRIVILEGE OF STAYING FAR AWAY FROM THEM?
HOW D'YOU THINK IT GOT TO BE SUCH A FARCE?
MM ...
TREMBLE
!
GOOD QUESTION!
YANK
!
SHF
WHOA!
FWISH
PERHAPS IT'S HUMAN NATURE...?
UNH ...!
WHUMP

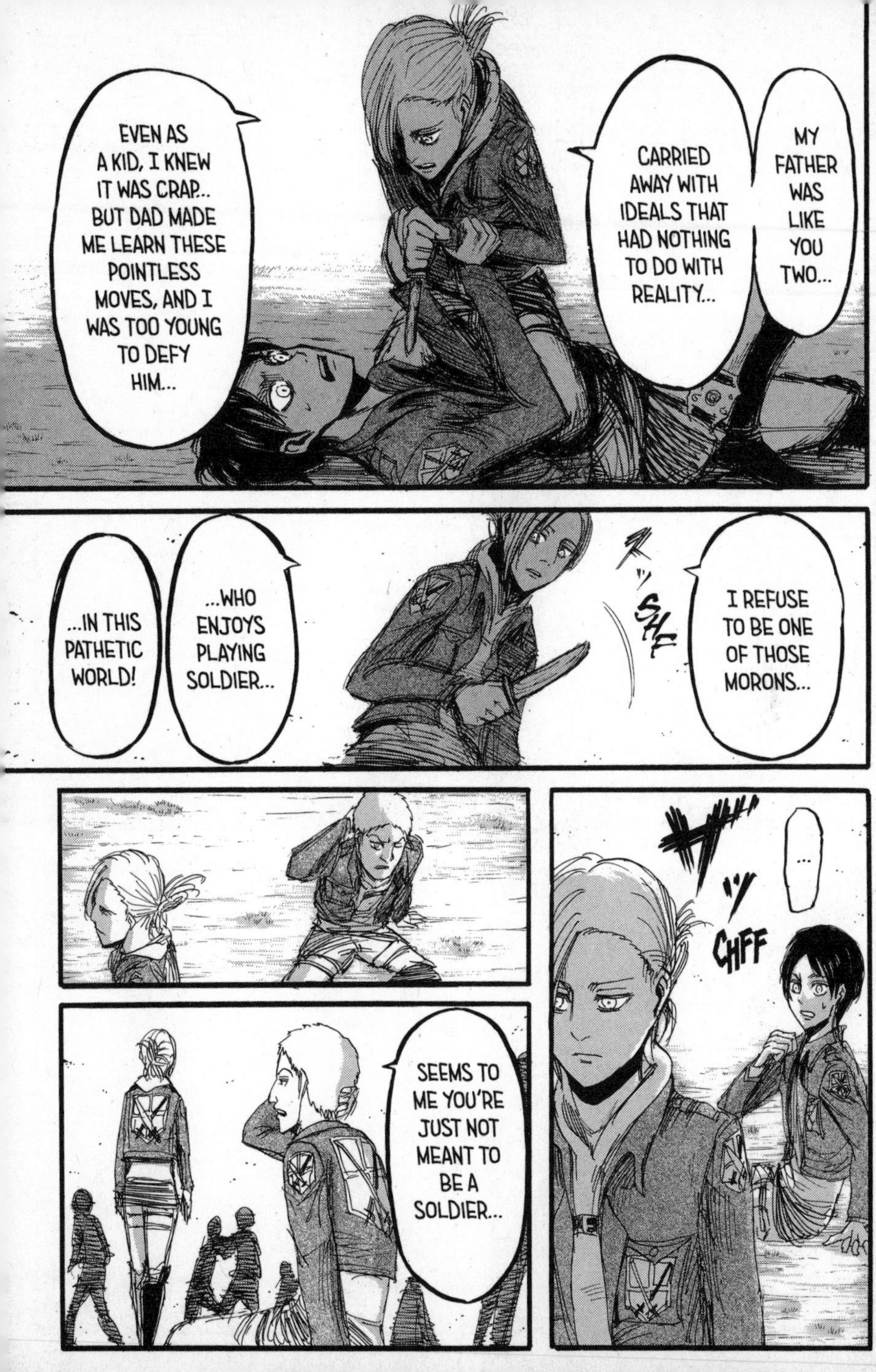

MY FATHER WAS LIKE YOU TWO...
CARRIED AWAY WITH IDEALS THAT HAD NOTHING TO DO WITH REALITY...
EVEN AS A KID, I KNEW IT WAS CRAP... BUT DAD MADE ME LEARN THESE POINTLESS MOVES, AND I WAS TOO YOUNG TO DEFY HIM...
I REFUSE TO BE ONE OF THOSE MORONS...
SHF
...WHO ENJOYS PLAYING SOLDIER...
...IN THIS PATHETIC WORLD!
...
CHFF
SEEMS TO ME YOU'RE JUST NOT MEANT TO BE A SOLDIER...

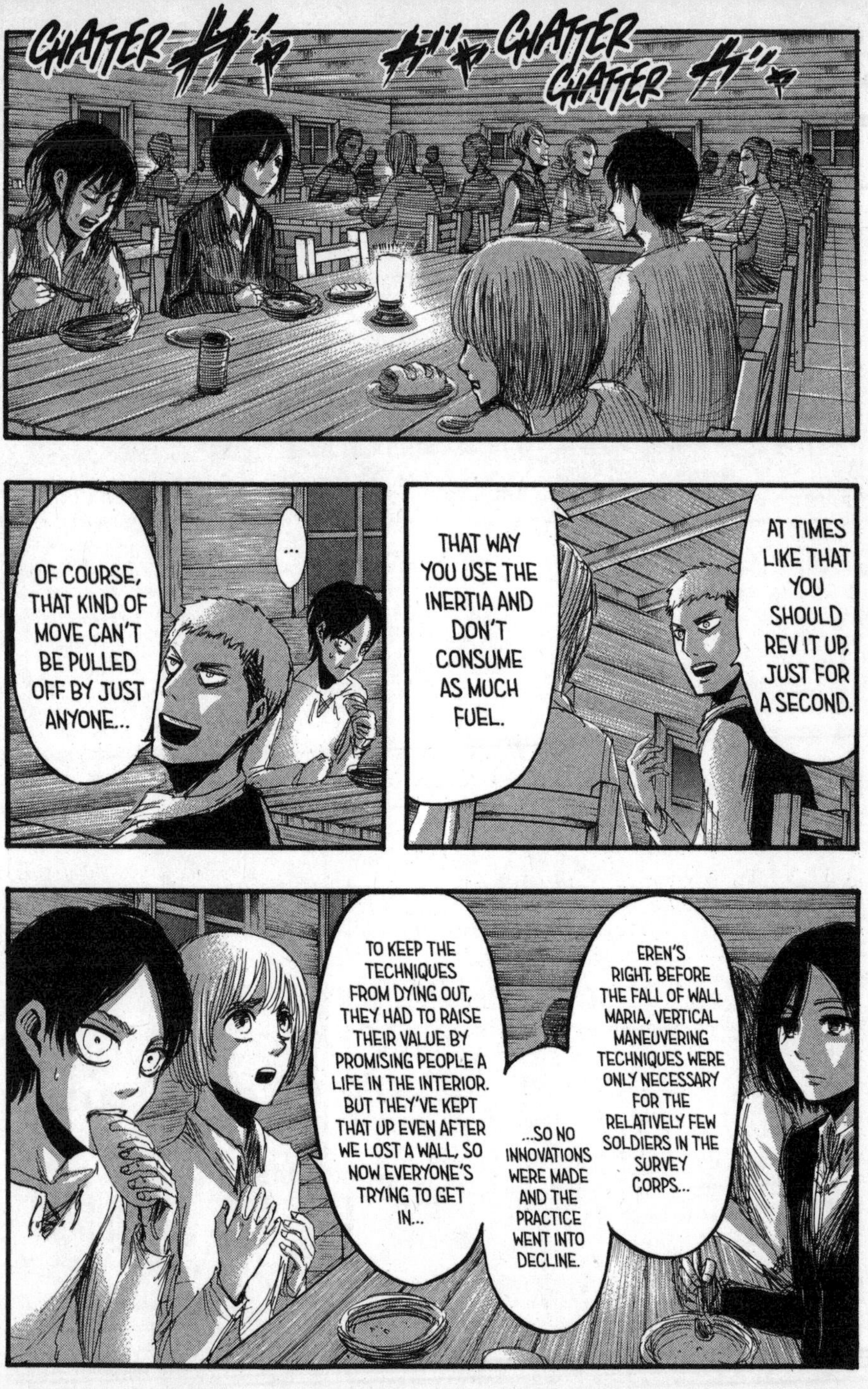
CHATTER
CHATTER
CHATTER
AT TIMES LIKE THAT YOU SHOULD REV IT UP, JUST FOR A SECOND.
THAT WAY YOU USE THE INERTIA AND DON'T CONSUME AS MUCH FUEL.
...
OF COURSE, THAT KIND OF MOVE CAN'T BE PULLED OFF BY JUST ANYONE...
EREN'S RIGHT. BEFORE THE FALL OF WALL MARIA, VERTICAL MANEUVERING TECHNIQUES WERE ONLY NECESSARY FOR THE RELATIVELY FEW SOLDIERS IN THE SURVEY CORPS...
...SO NO INNOVATIONS WERE MADE AND THE PRACTICE WENT INTO DECLINE.
TO KEEP THE TECHNIQUES FROM DYING OUT, THEY HAD TO RAISE THEIR VALUE BY PROMISING PEOPLE A LIFE IN THE INTERIOR. BUT THEY'VE KEPT THAT UP EVEN AFTER WE LOST A WALL, SO NOW EVERYONE'S TRYING TO GET IN...

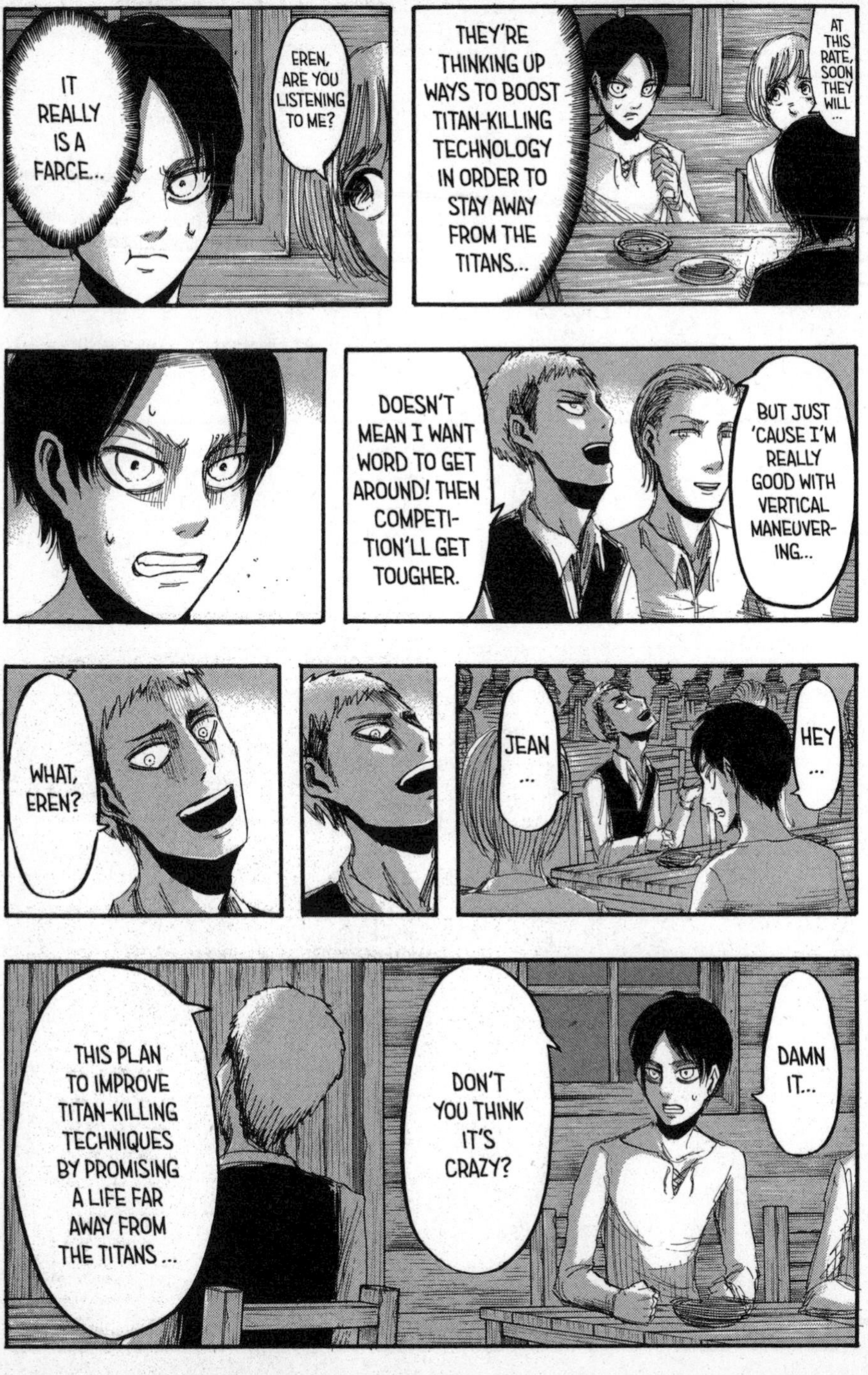
AT THIS RATE, SOON THEY WILL ...
THEY'RE THINKING UP WAYS TO BOOST TITAN-KILLING TECHNOLOGY IN ORDER TO STAY AWAY FROM THE TITANS...
EREN, ARE YOU LISTENING TO ME?
IT REALLY IS A FARCE...
BUT JUST 'CAUSE I'M REALLY GOOD WITH VERTICAL MANEUVER-ING...
DOESN'T MEAN I WANT WORD TO GET AROUND! THEN COMPETI-TION'LL GET TOUGHER.
HEY ...
JEAN ...
WHAT, EREN?
DAMN IT...
DON'T YOU THINK IT'S CRAZY?
THIS PLAN TO IMPROVE TITAN-KILLING TECHNIQUES BY PROMISING A LIFE FAR AWAY FROM THE TITANS ...

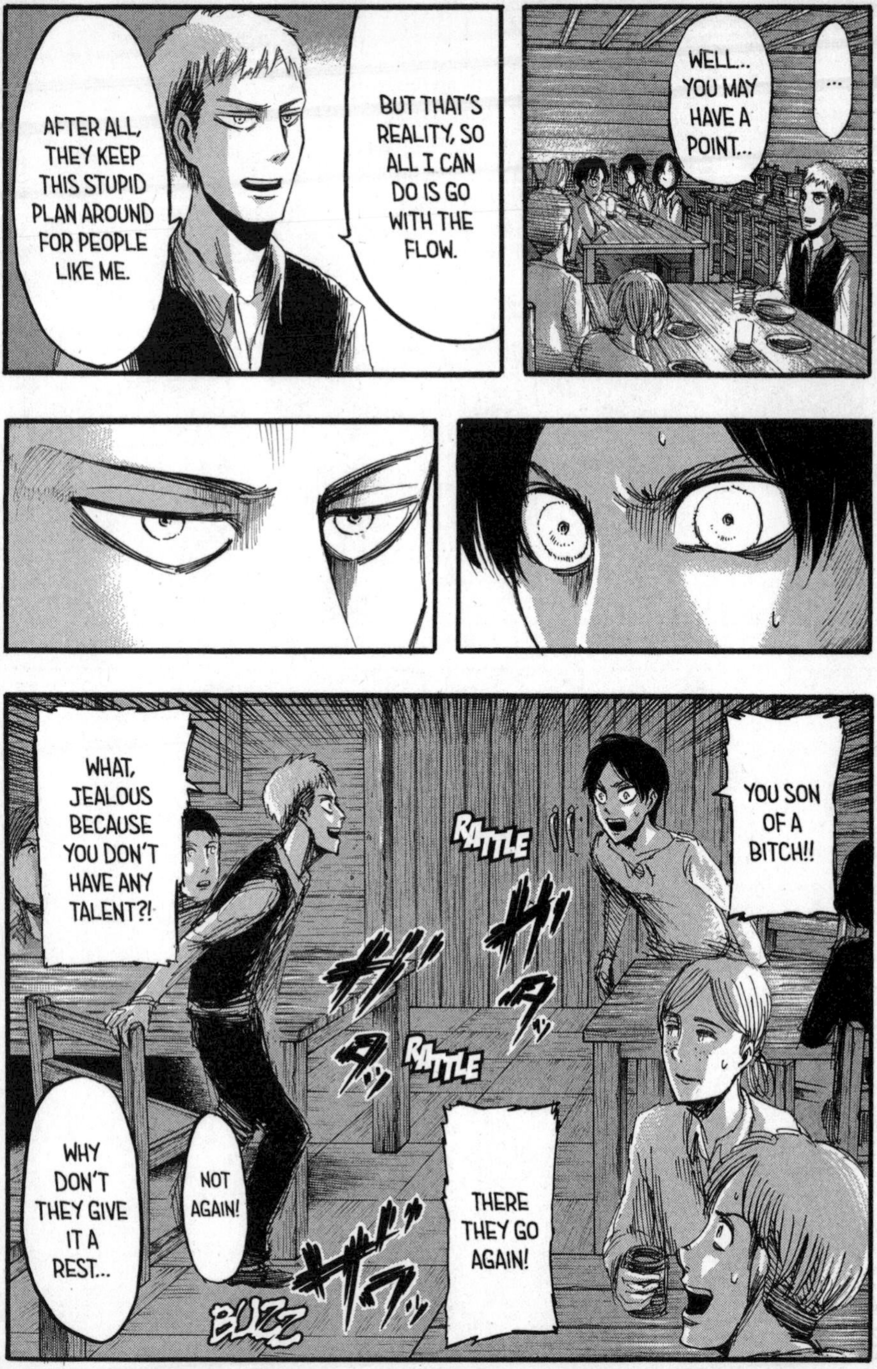
...
WELL... YOU MAY HAVE A POINT...
BUT THAT'S REALITY, SO ALL I CAN DO IS GO WITH THE FLOW.
AFTER ALL, THEY KEEP THIS STUPID PLAN AROUND FOR PEOPLE LIKE ME.
YOU SON OF A BITCH!!
RATTLE
WHAT, JEALOUS BECAUSE YOU DON'T HAVE ANY TALENT?!
RATTLE
THERE THEY GO AGAIN!
NOT AGAIN!
WHY DON'T THEY GIVE IT A REST...
BUZZ

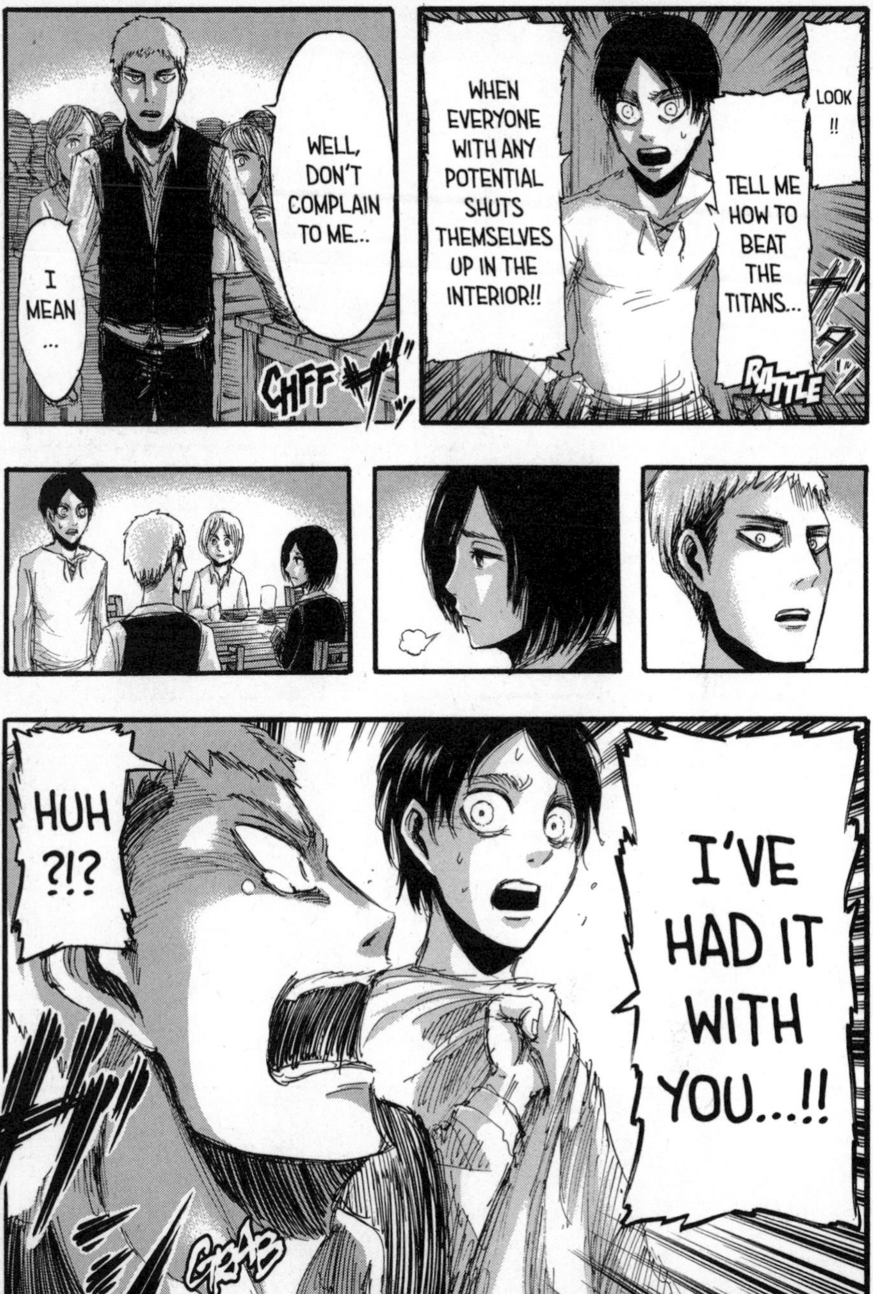
LOOK !!
TELL ME HOW TO BEAT THE TITANS...
WHEN EVERYONE WITH ANY POTENTIAL SHUTS THEMSELVES UP IN THE INTERIOR!!
RATTLE
WELL, DON'T COMPLAIN TO ME...
I MEAN ...
CHFF
I'VE HAD IT WITH YOU...!!
HUH ?!?
GRAB

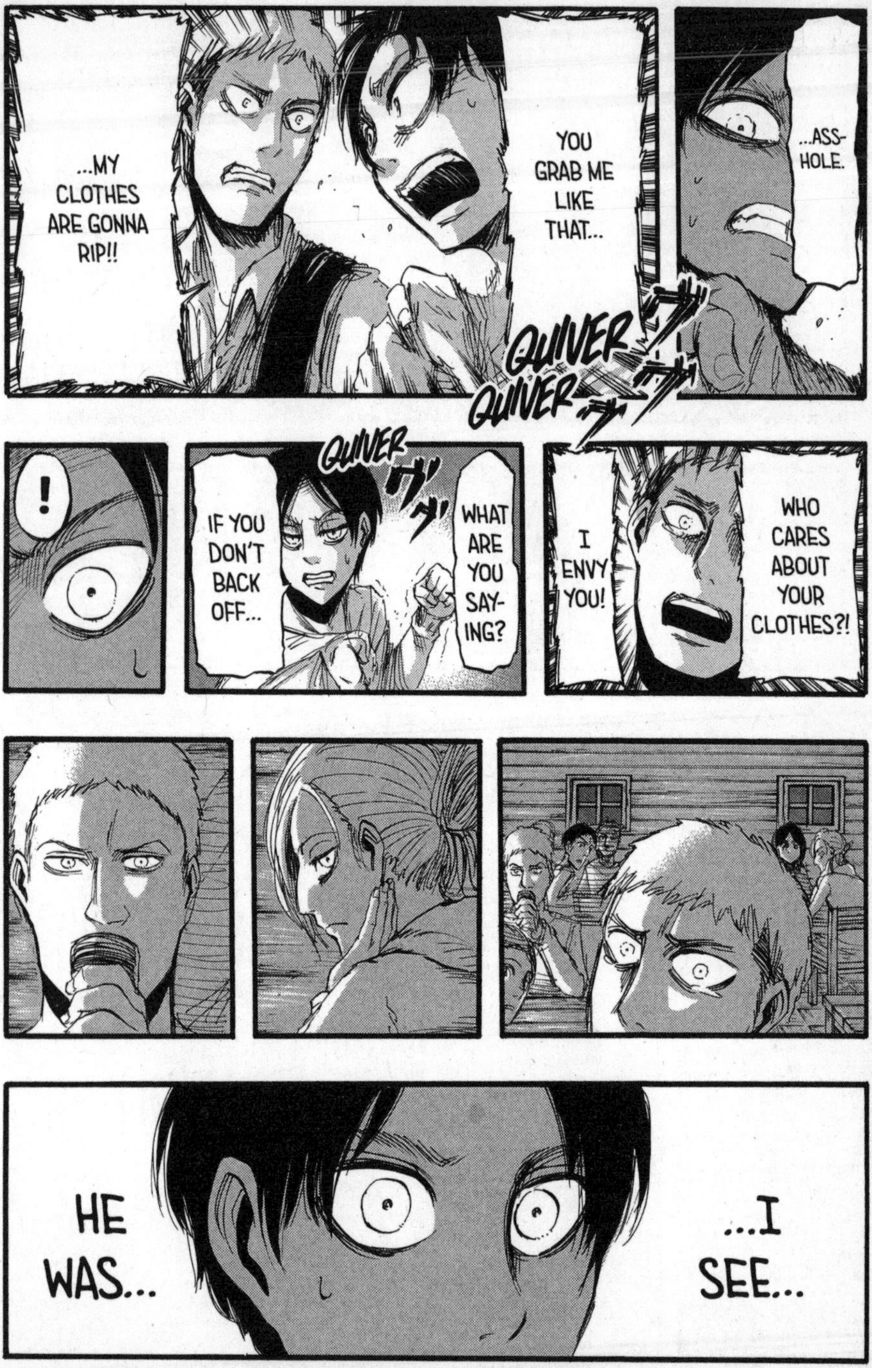
...ASS-HOLE.
YOU GRAB ME LIKE THAT...
...MY CLOTHES ARE GONNA RIP!!
QUIVER
QUIVER
WHO CARES ABOUT YOUR CLOTHES?!
I ENVY YOU!
QUIVER
WHAT ARE YOU SAY-ING?
IF YOU DON'T BACK OFF...
!
...I SEE...
HE WAS...

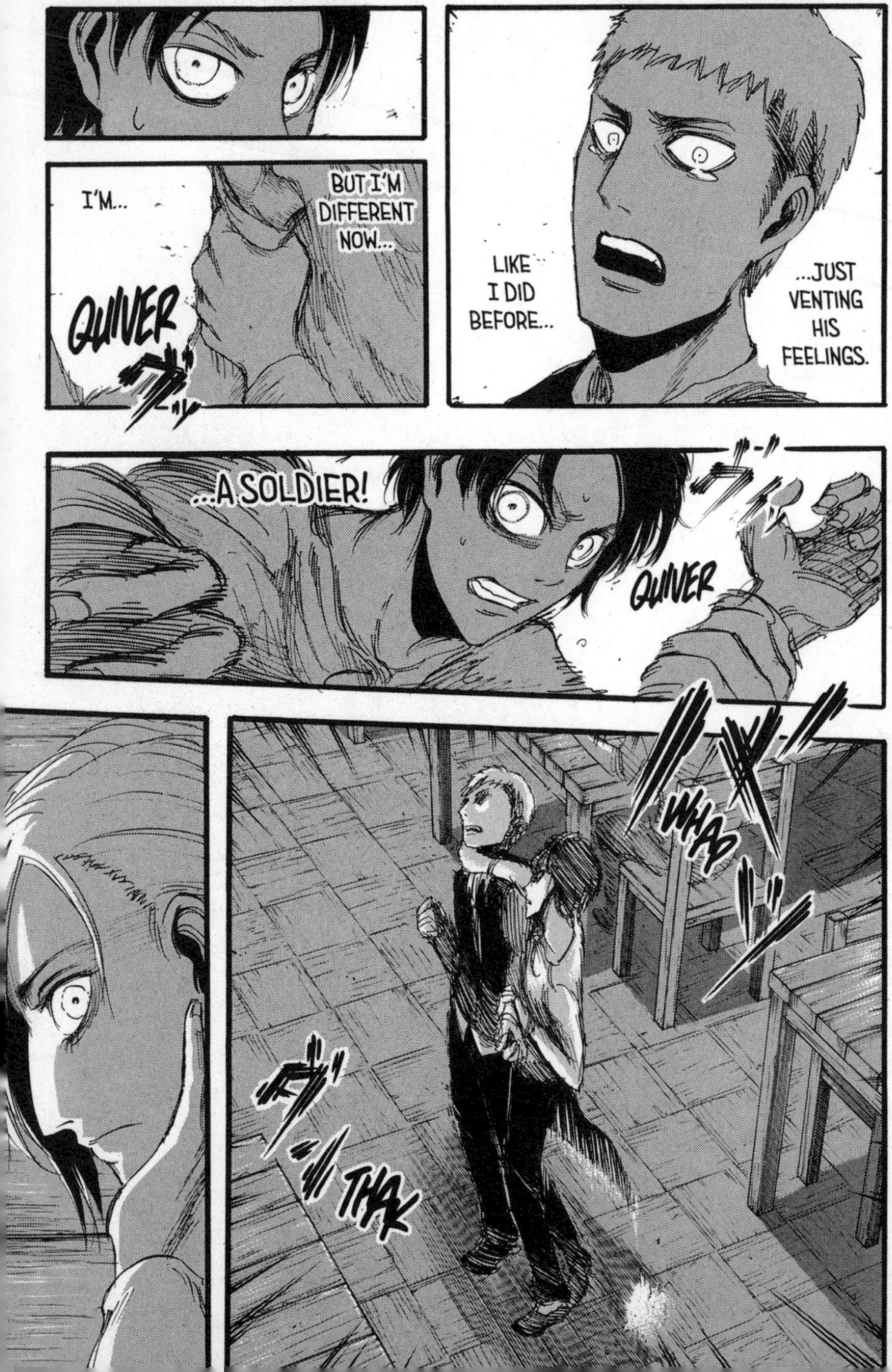
...JUST VENTING HIS FEELINGS.
LIKE I DID BEFORE...
BUT I'M DIFFERENT NOW...
I'M...
QUIVER
QUIVER
...A SOLDIER!
WHAP
THAK

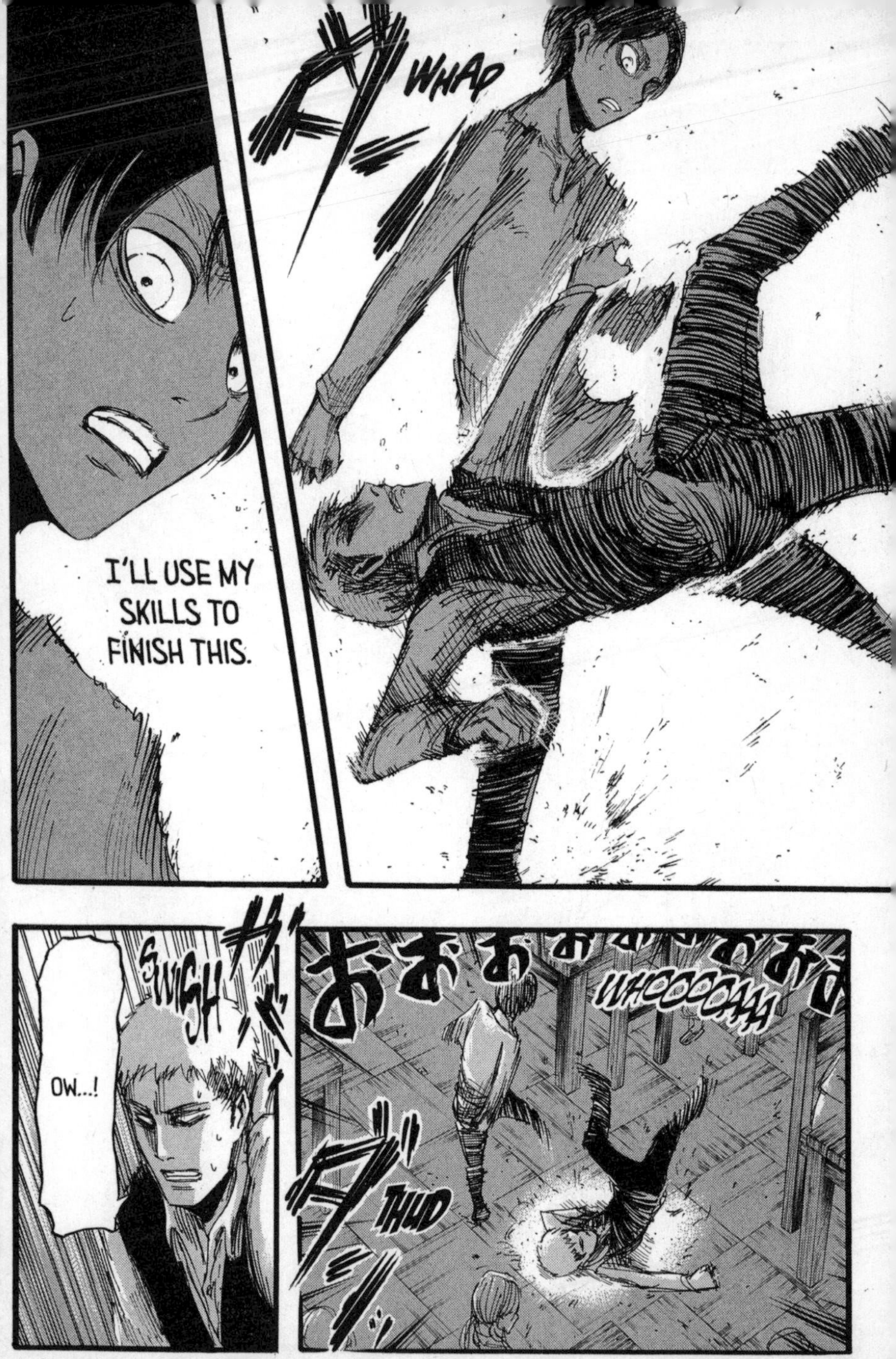
WHAP
I'LL USE MY SKILLS TO FINISH THIS.
WHOOOOAA
THUD
SWISH
OW...!

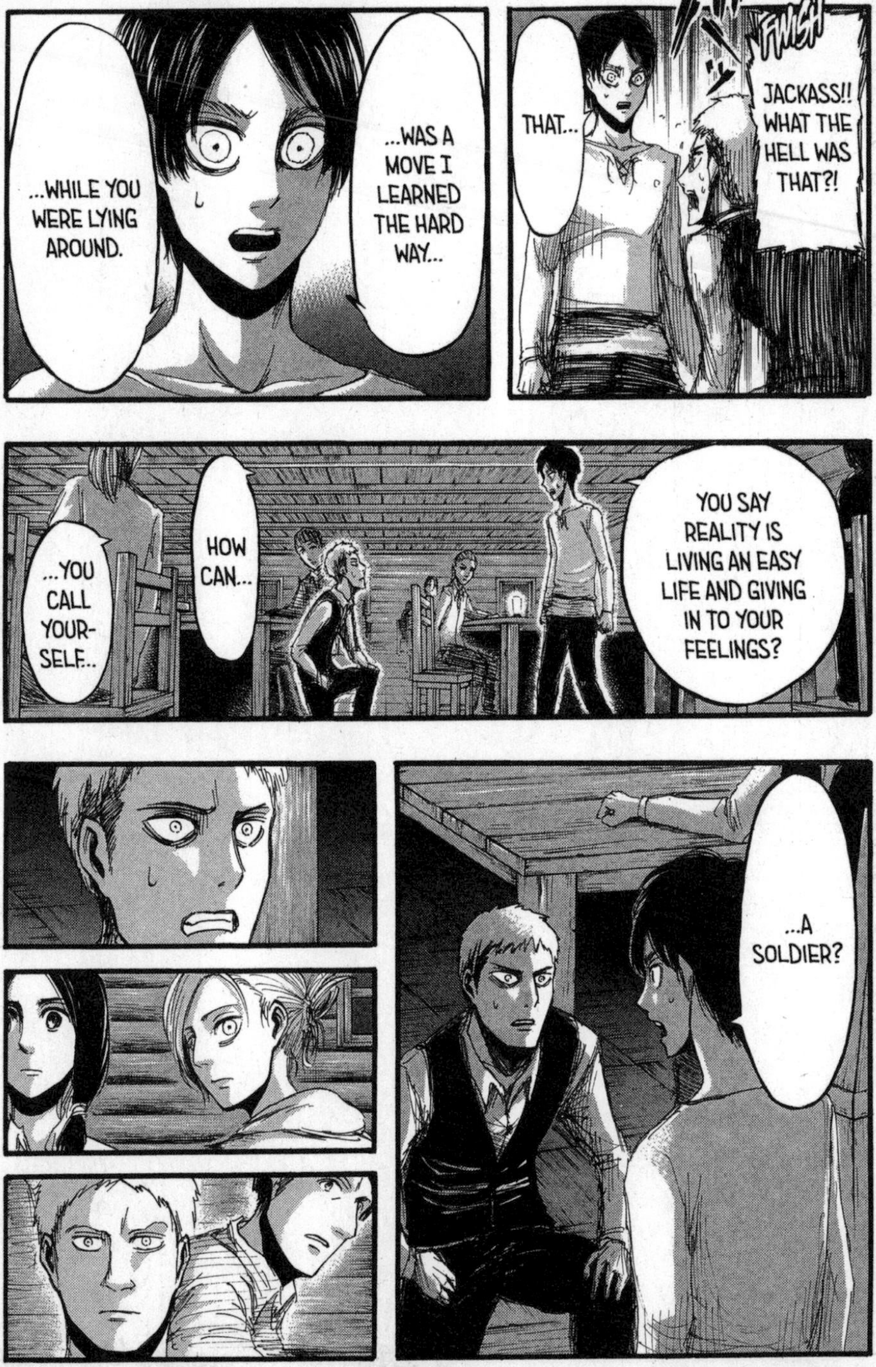
FWISH
JACKASS!! WHAT THE HELL WAS THAT?!
THAT...
...WAS A MOVE I LEARNED THE HARD WAY...
...WHILE YOU WERE LYING AROUND.
YOU SAY REALITY IS LIVING AN EASY LIFE AND GIVING IN TO YOUR FEELINGS?
HOW CAN...
...YOU CALL YOUR-SELF...
...A SOLDIER?

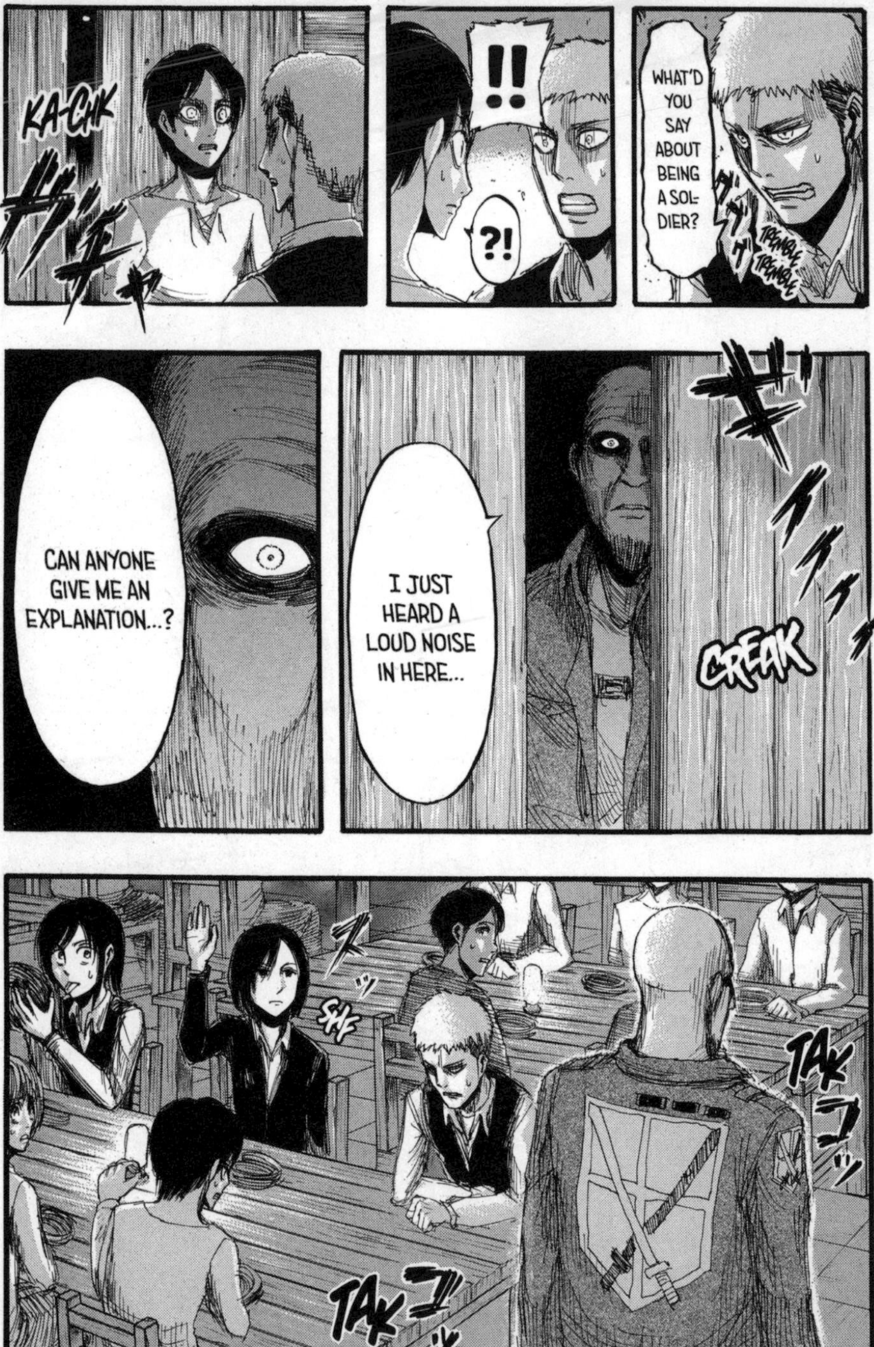
WHAT'D YOU SAY ABOUT BEING A SOL-DIER?
TREMBLE TREMBLE
!!
?!
KA-CHIK
CREAK
I JUST HEARD A LOUD NOISE IN HERE...
CAN ANYONE GIVE ME AN EXPLANATION...?
TAK
SHF
TAK

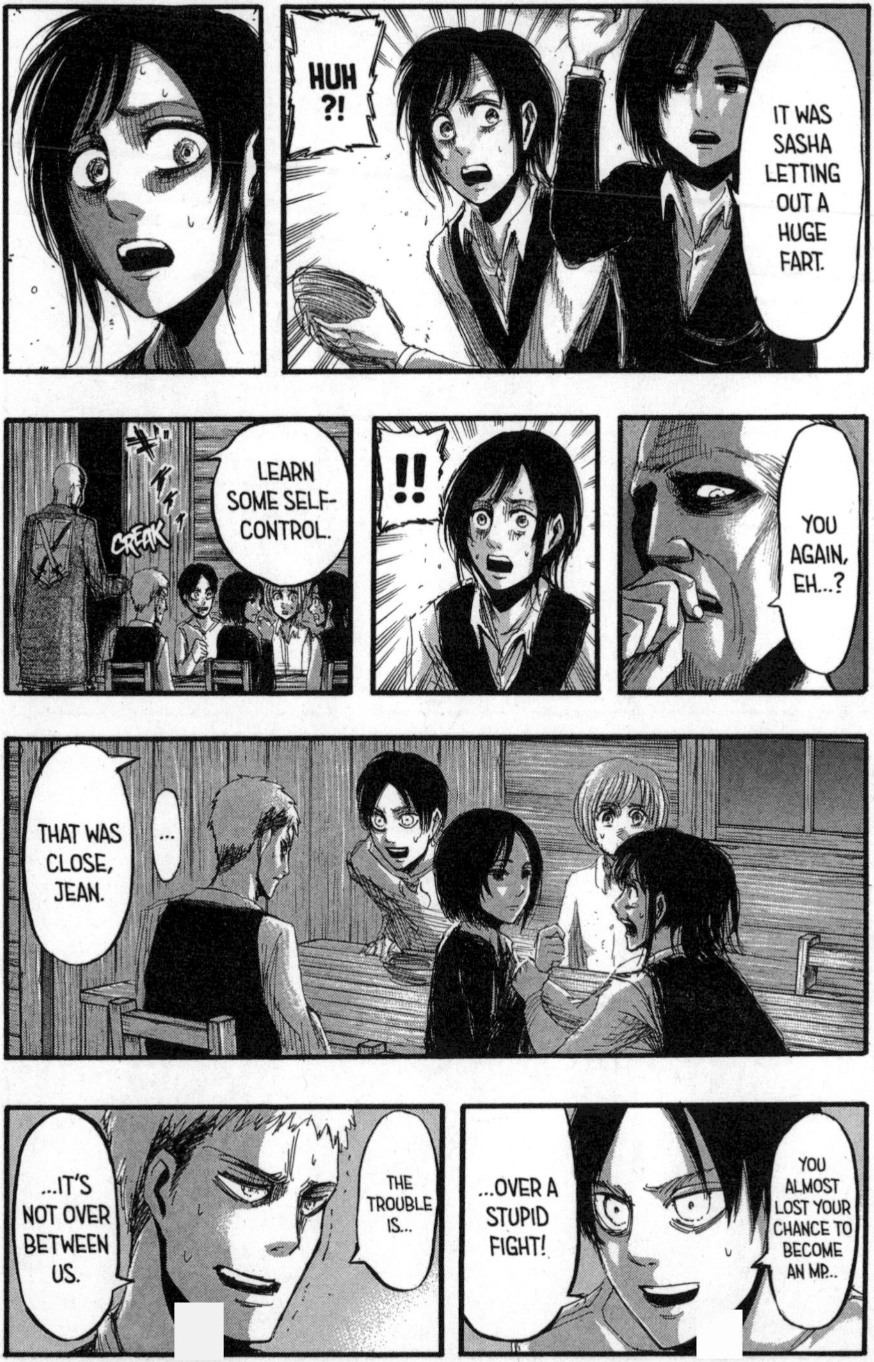
IT WAS SASHA LETTING OUT A HUGE FART.
HUH ?!
YOU AGAIN, EH...?
!!
LEARN SOME SELF-CONTROL.
CREAK
THAT WAS CLOSE, JEAN.
...
YOU ALMOST LOST YOUR CHANCE TO BECOME AN MP...
...OVER A STUPID FIGHT!
THE TROUBLE IS...
...IT'S NOT OVER BETWEEN US.

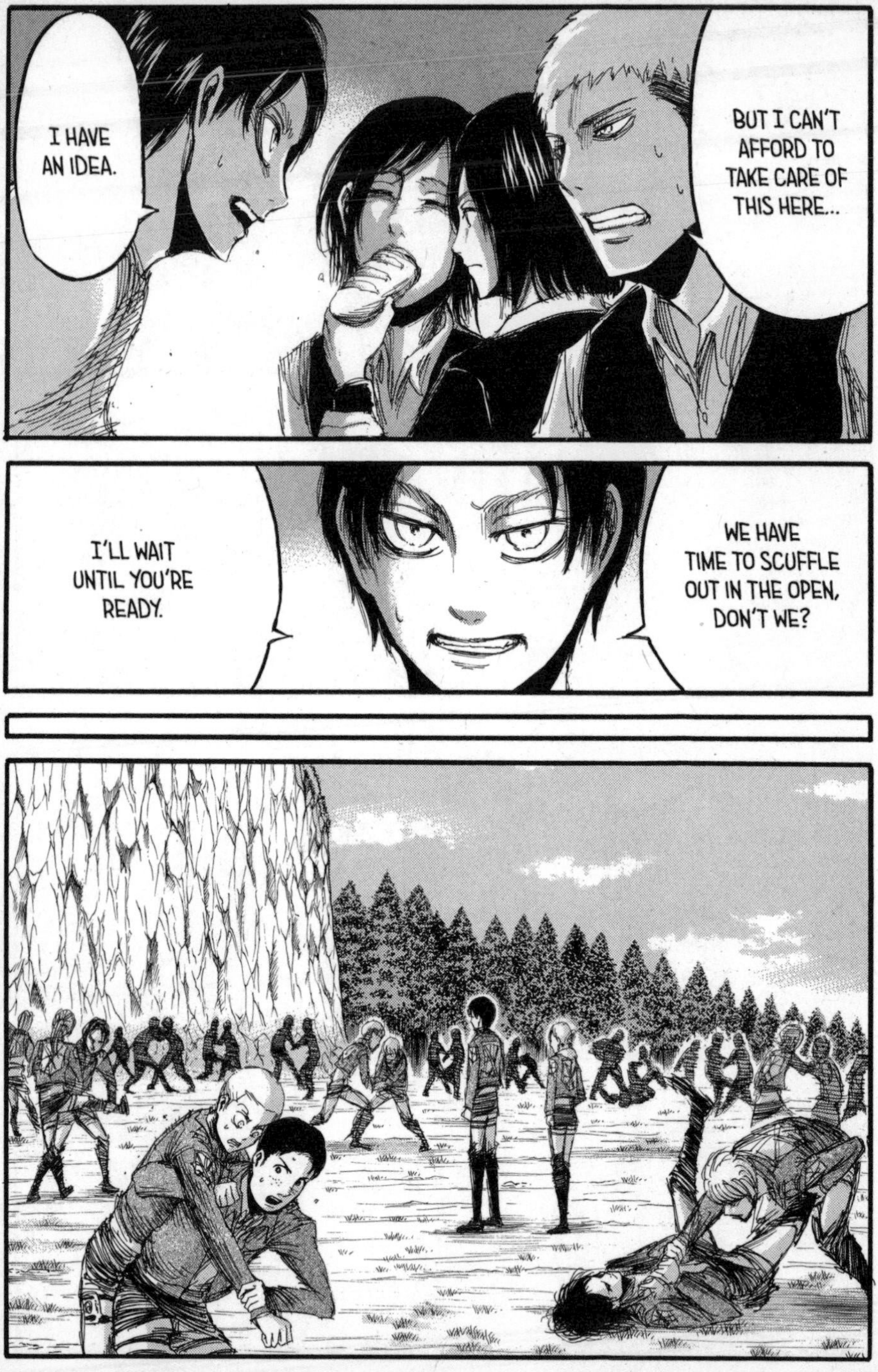
BUT I CAN'T AFFORD TO TAKE CARE OF THIS HERE...
I HAVE AN IDEA.
WE HAVE TIME TO SCUFFLE OUT IN THE OPEN, DON'T WE?
I'LL WAIT UNTIL YOU'RE READY.

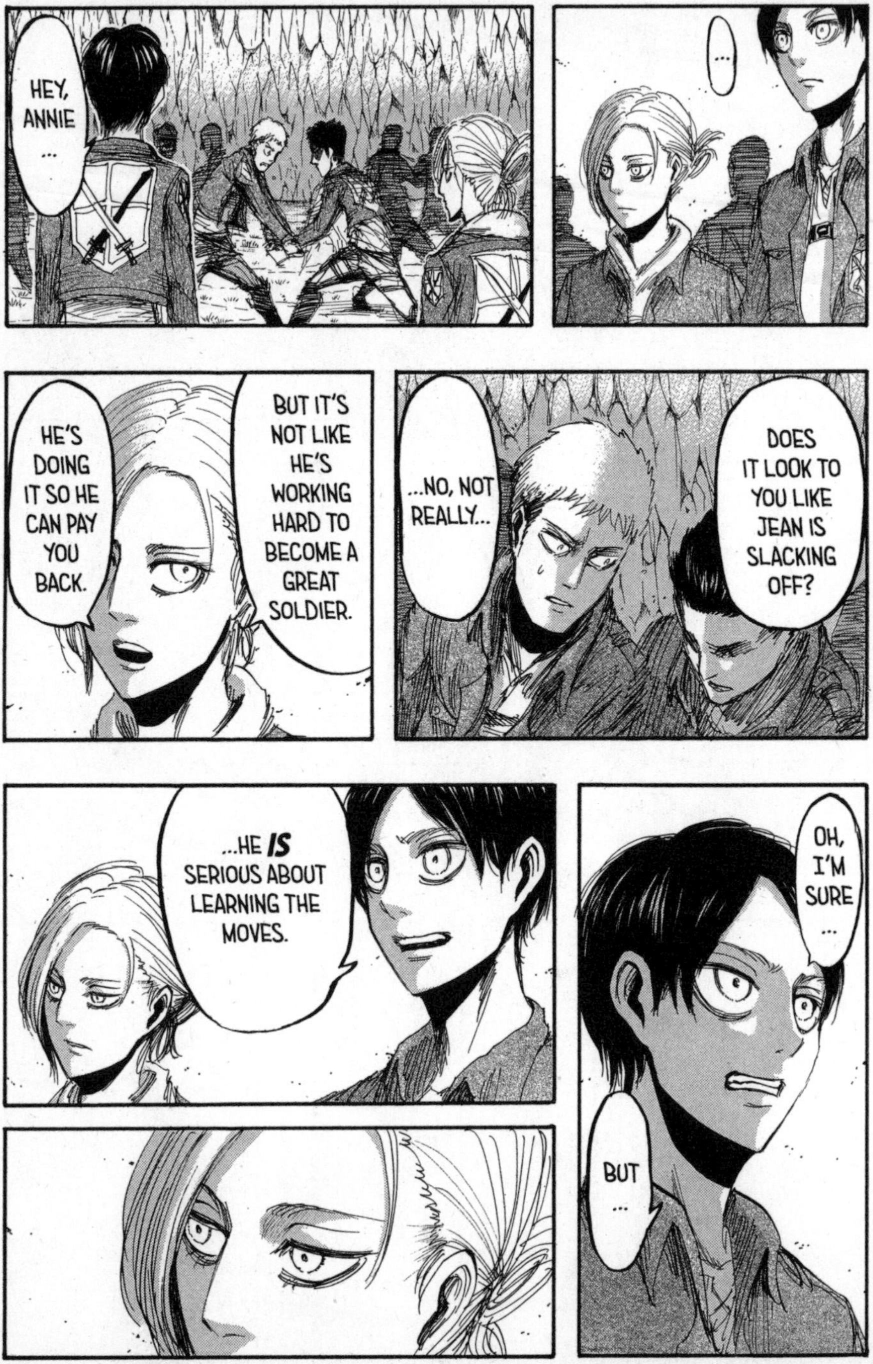
...
HEY, ANNIE ...
DOES IT LOOK TO YOU LIKE JEAN IS SLACKING OFF?
...NO, NOT REALLY...
BUT IT'S NOT LIKE HE'S WORKING HARD TO BECOME A GREAT SOLDIER.
HE'S DOING IT SO HE CAN PAY YOU BACK.
OH, I'M SURE ...
BUT ...
...HE ***IS*** SERIOUS ABOUT LEARNING THE MOVES.

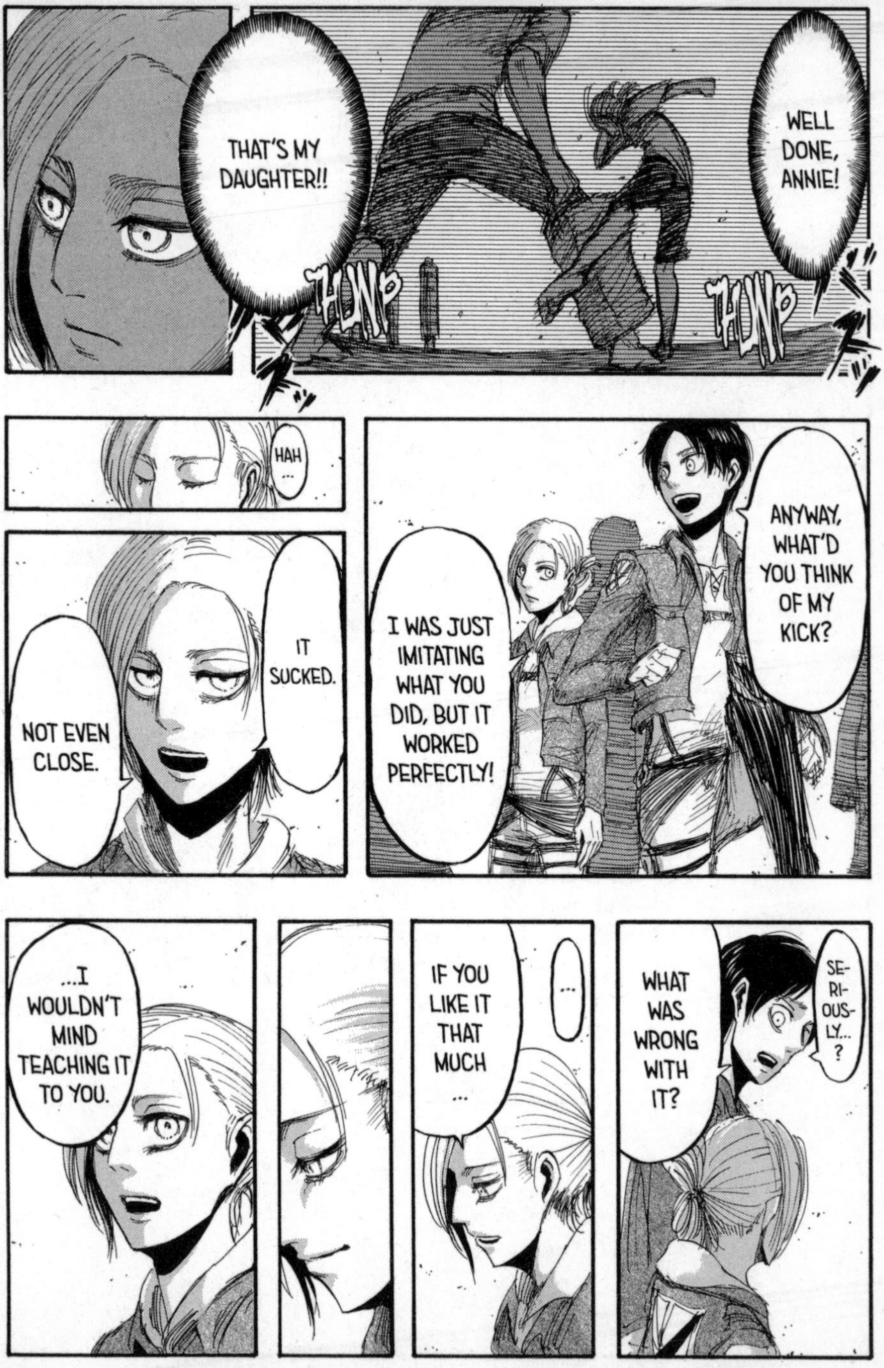
WELL DONE, ANNIE!
THUMP
THUMP
THAT'S MY DAUGHTER!!
ANYWAY, WHAT'D YOU THINK OF MY KICK?
I WAS JUST IMITATING WHAT YOU DID, BUT IT WORKED PERFECTLY!
HAH ...
IT SUCKED.
NOT EVEN CLOSE.
SE-RI-OUS-LY...?
WHAT WAS WRONG WITH IT?
...
IF YOU LIKE IT THAT MUCH ...
...I WOULDN'T MIND TEACHING IT TO YOU.

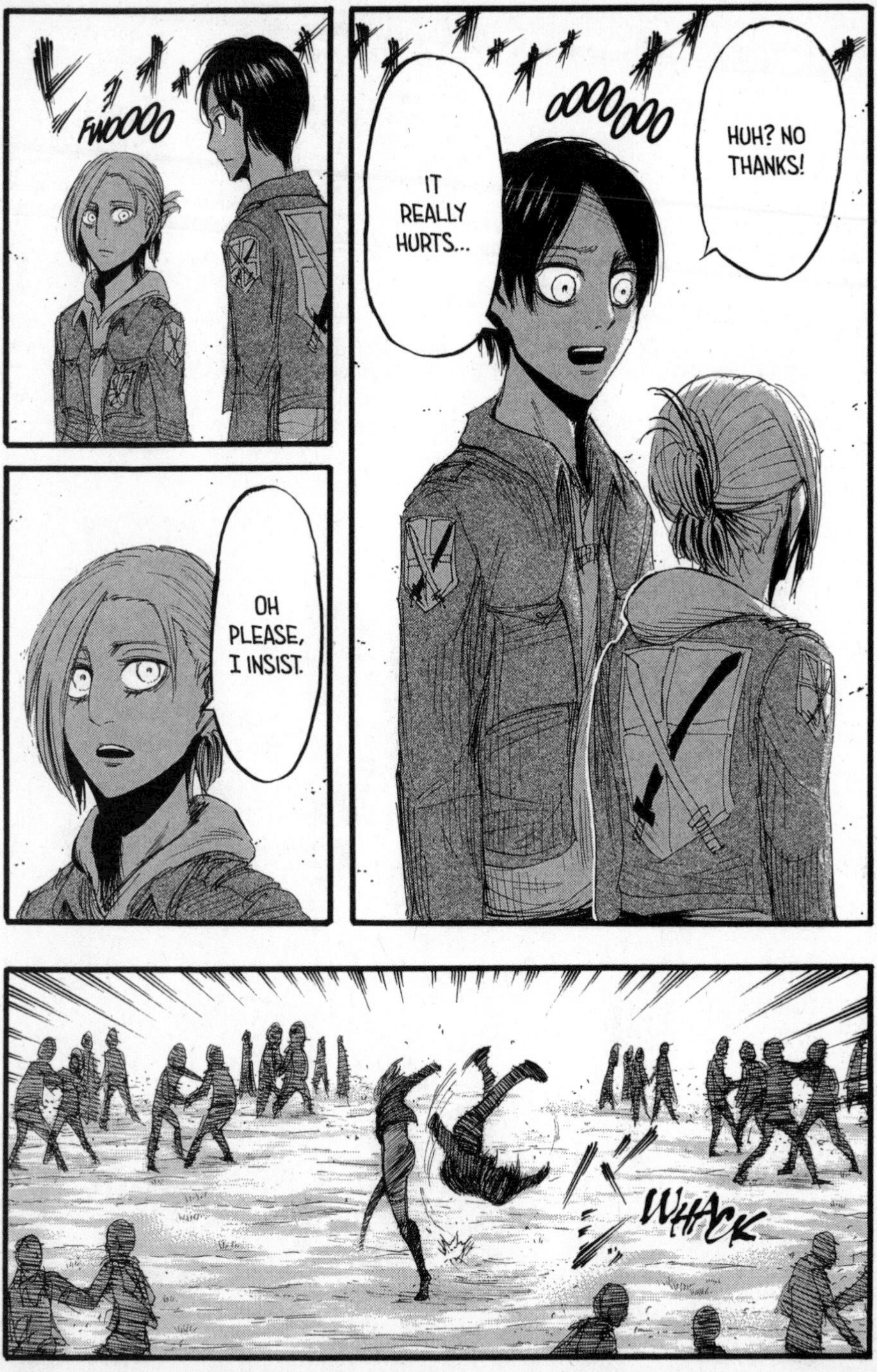
HUH? NO THANKS!
OOOOOO
IT REALLY HURTS...
FWOOOO
OH PLEASE, I INSIST.
WHACK

Current Publicly Available Information
9. Ultrahard Steel

THIS STEEL IS ONLY PRODUCED AT FACTORY TOWNS. IT COMBINES TOUGHNESS AND FLEXIBILITY TO SLICE THROUGH TITAN FLESH, AND IT'S CURRENTLY THE ONLY MATERIAL CAPABLE OF THAT. AS SUCH, THE SINGLE-EDGED SWORD, A SPECIALLY CREASED FORGED BLADE, IS KNOWN FAR AND WIDE AS AN ANTI-TITAN WEAPON. BLAST FURNACES ARE ESSENTIAL TO REFINE "ULTRAHARD STEEL," WHICH IS WHY IT CAN ONLY BE PRODUCED IN FACTORY TOWNS. THE FORGING PROCESS REQUIRES VERY SMALL QUANTITIES OF SEVERAL RARE METALS, BUT EXACTLY WHICH ONES AND IN WHAT RATIOS HAVE BECOME SECRETS KNOWN ONLY TO RESIDENTS OF THOSE TOWNS.

(WITH THANKS TO UKYŌ KODACHI AND KIYOMUNE MIWA)

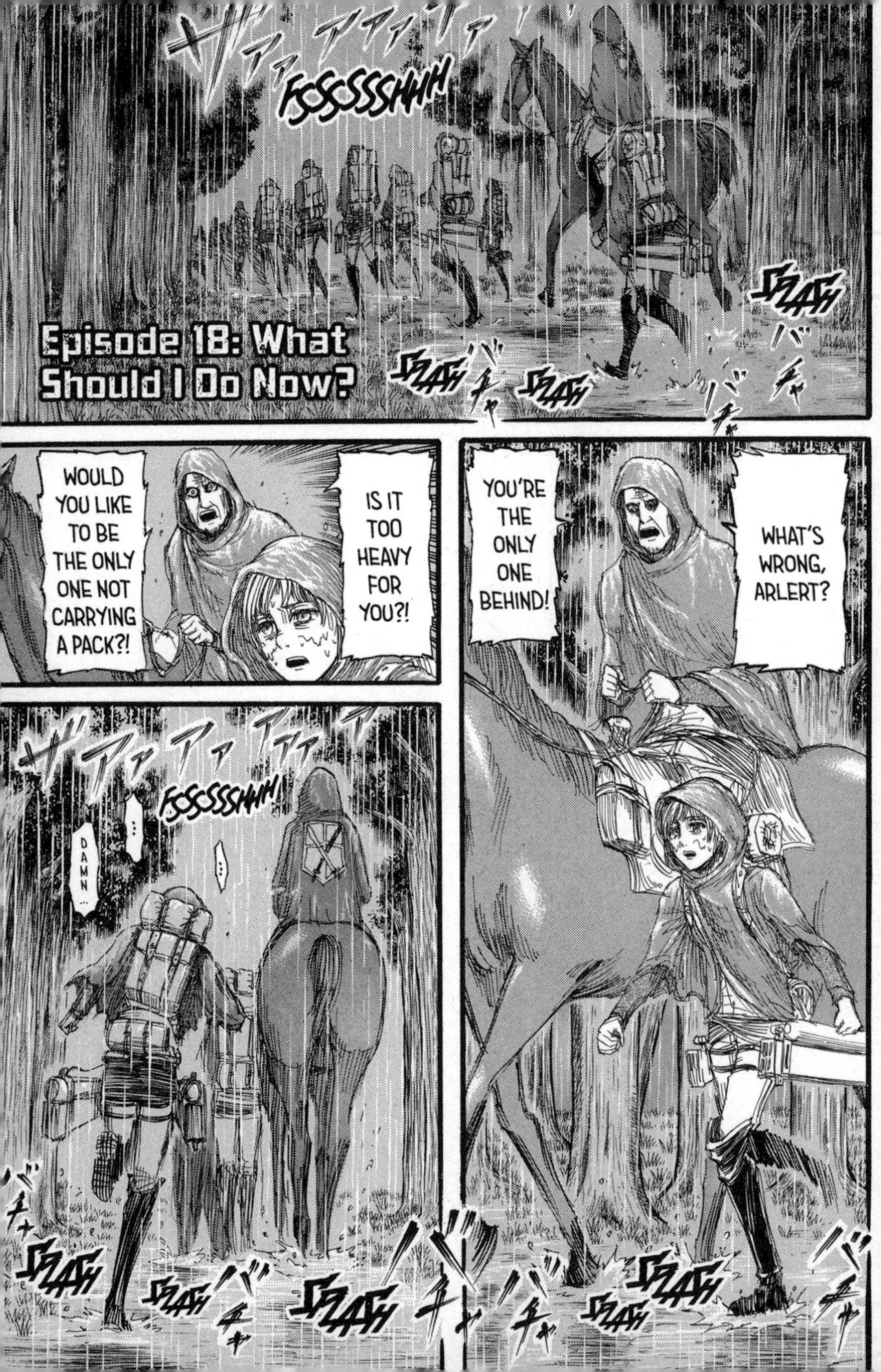
FSSSSSHHH
Episode 18: What Should I Do Now?
SPLASH
SPLASH
SPLASH
WHAT'S WRONG, ARLERT?
YOU'RE THE ONLY ONE BEHIND!
IS IT TOO HEAVY FOR YOU?!
WOULD YOU LIKE TO BE THE ONLY ONE NOT CARRYING A PACK?!
FSSSSSHHH
...
...
DAMN...
SPLASH
SPLASH
SPLASH
SPLASH
SPLASH

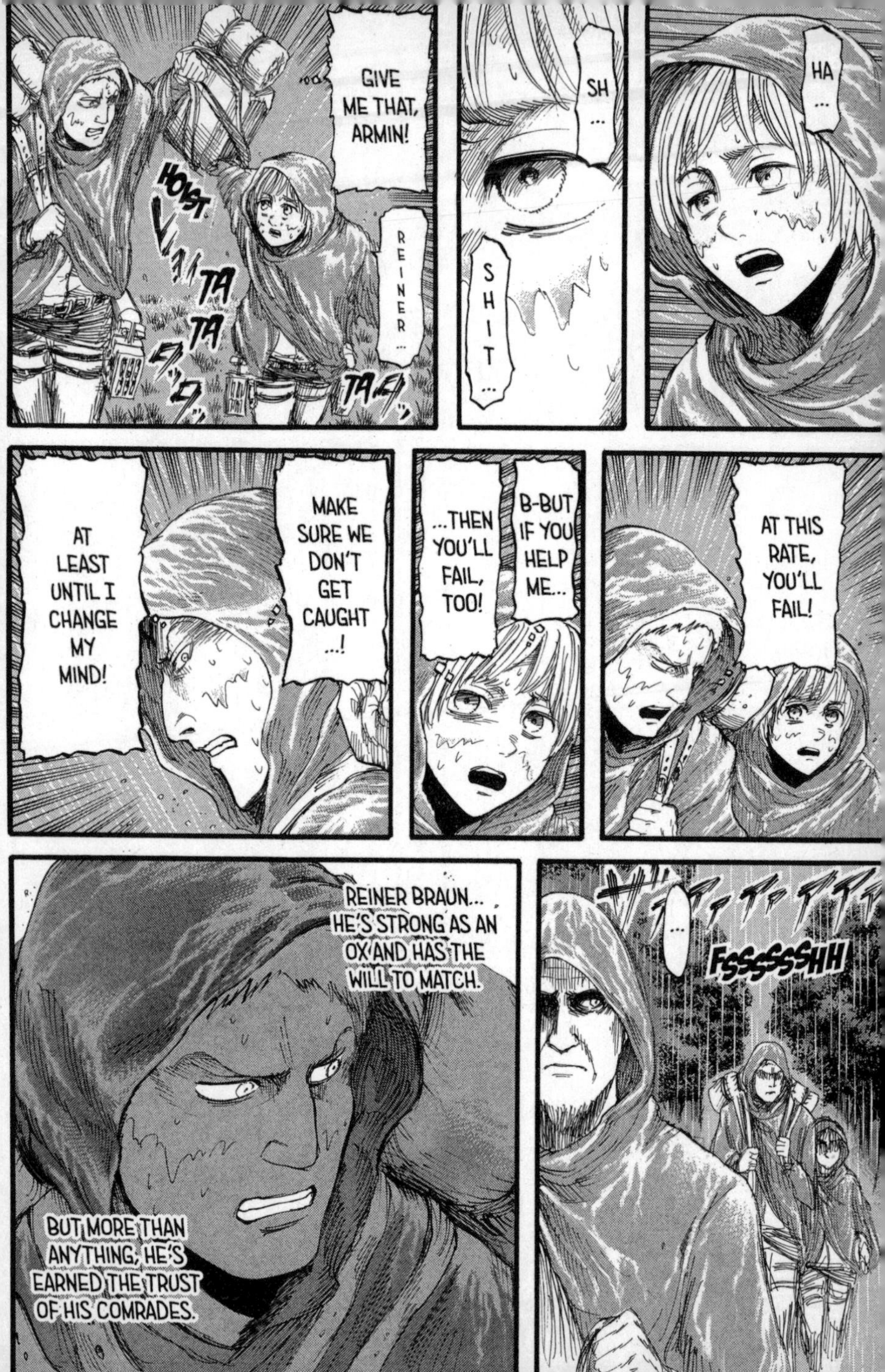
HA ...
SH ...
SHIT ...
GIVE ME THAT, ARMIN!
REINER ...
HOIST
TA TA
TA
AT THIS RATE, YOU'LL FAIL!
B-BUT IF YOU HELP ME...
...THEN YOU'LL FAIL, TOO!
MAKE SURE WE DON'T GET CAUGHT ...!
AT LEAST UNTIL I CHANGE MY MIND!
...
FSSSSSSHH
REINER BRAUN... HE'S STRONG AS AN OX AND HAS THE WILL TO MATCH.
BUT MORE THAN ANYTHING, HE'S EARNED THE TRUST OF HIS COMRADES.

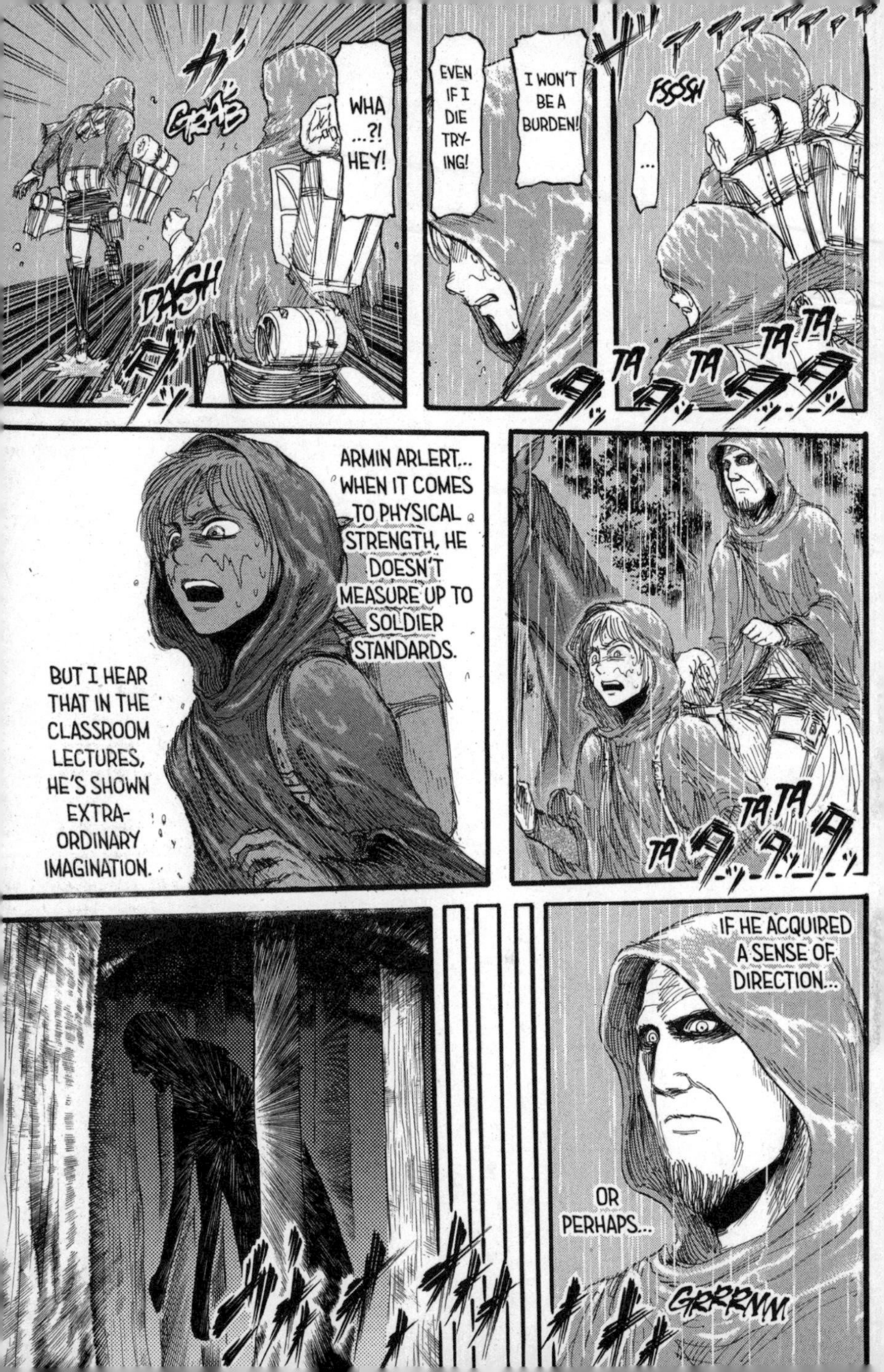
FSSSH
...
TA
TA
TA TA
I WON'T BE A BURDEN!
EVEN IF I DIE TRYING!
WHA ...?! HEY!
GRAB
DASH
TA TA
TA
ARMIN ARLERT... WHEN IT COMES TO PHYSICAL STRENGTH, HE DOESN'T MEASURE UP TO SOLDIER STANDARDS.
BUT I HEAR THAT IN THE CLASSROOM LECTURES, HE'S SHOWN EXTRA-ORDINARY IMAGINATION.
IF HE ACQUIRED A SENSE OF DIRECTION...
OR PERHAPS...
GRRRNN

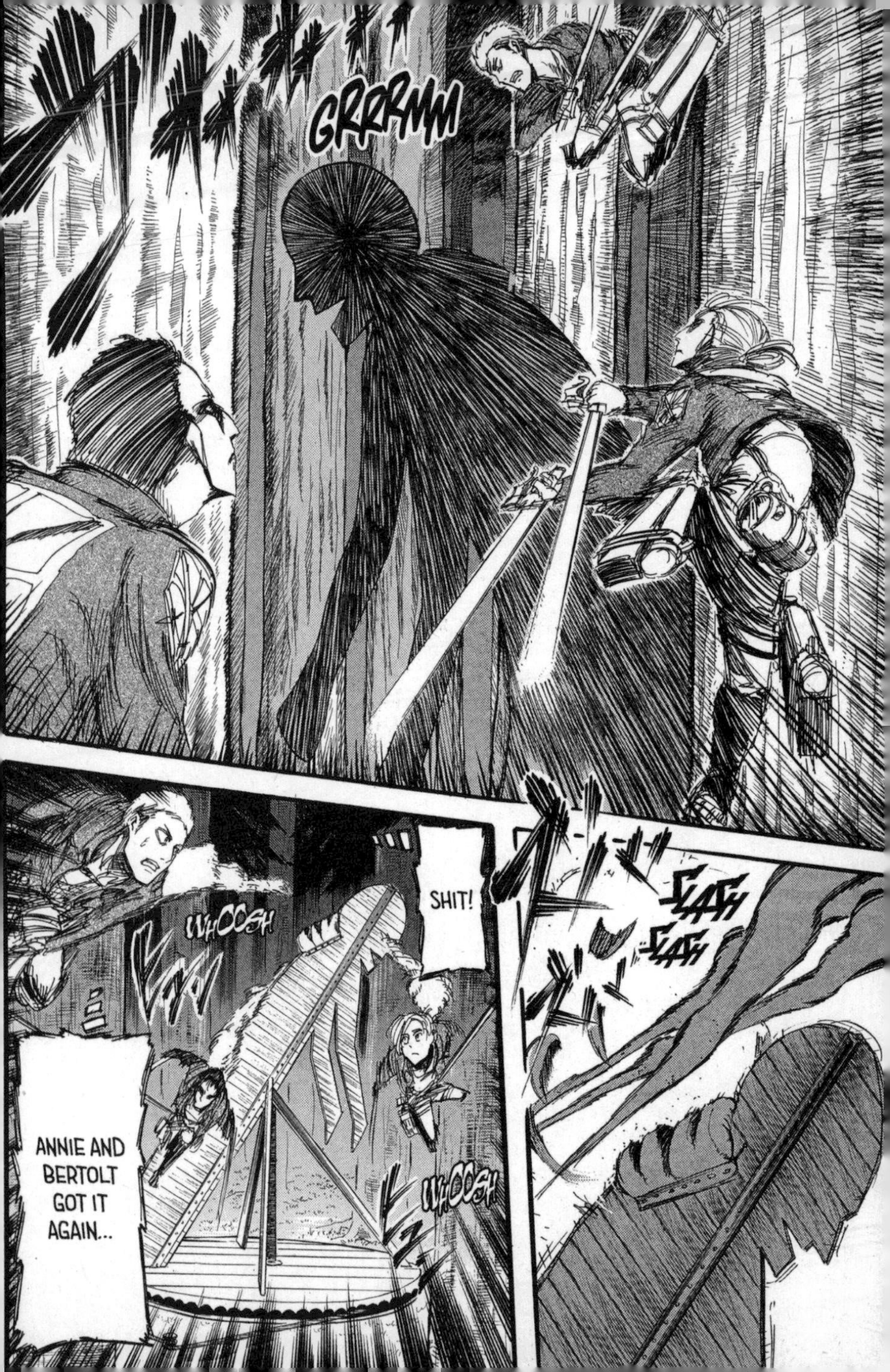
GRRRMM
SLASH
SLASH
SHIT!
WHOOSH
ANNIE AND BERTOLT GOT IT AGAIN...
WHOOSH

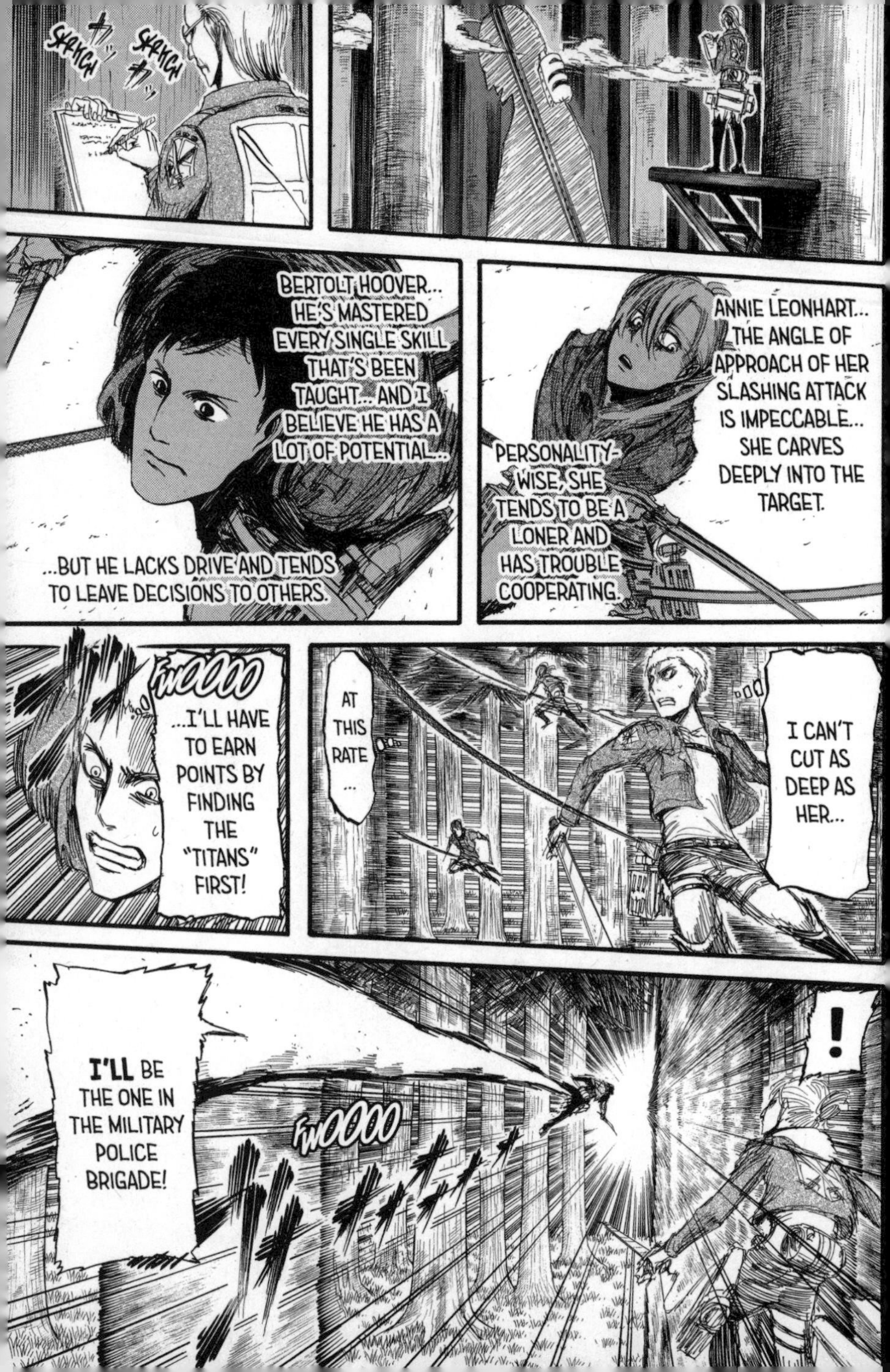
SKRKCH
SKRKCH
ANNIE LEONHART... THE ANGLE OF APPROACH OF HER SLASHING ATTACK IS IMPECCABLE... SHE CARVES DEEPLY INTO THE TARGET.
PERSONALITY-WISE, SHE TENDS TO BE A LONER AND HAS TROUBLE COOPERATING.
BERTOLT HOOVER... HE'S MASTERED EVERY SINGLE SKILL THAT'S BEEN TAUGHT... AND I BELIEVE HE HAS A LOT OF POTENTIAL...
...BUT HE LACKS DRIVE AND TENDS TO LEAVE DECISIONS TO OTHERS.
I CAN'T CUT AS DEEP AS HER...
AT THIS RATE ...
FWOOOO
...I'LL HAVE TO EARN POINTS BY FINDING THE "TITANS" FIRST!
!
FWOOOO
I'LL BE THE ONE IN THE MILITARY POLICE BRIGADE!

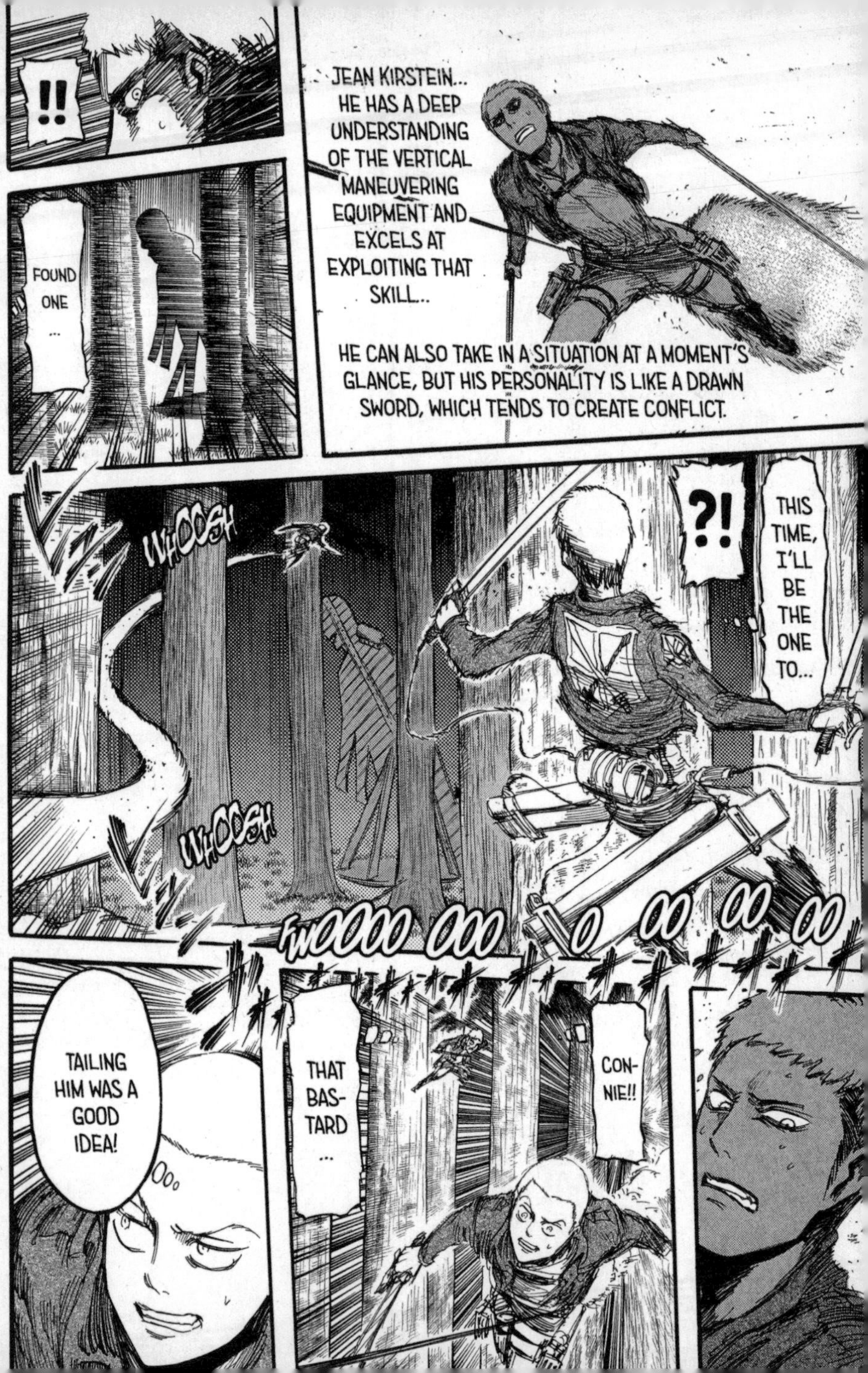
JEAN KIRSTEIN... HE HAS A DEEP UNDERSTANDING OF THE VERTICAL MANEUVERING EQUIPMENT AND EXCELS AT EXPLOITING THAT SKILL...
HE CAN ALSO TAKE IN A SITUATION AT A MOMENT'S GLANCE, BUT HIS PERSONALITY IS LIKE A DRAWN SWORD, WHICH TENDS TO CREATE CONFLICT.
!!
FOUND ONE ...
THIS TIME, I'LL BE THE ONE TO...
?!
WHOOSH
WHOOSH
FWOOOO OOO O OO OO OO
CON-NIE!!
THAT BAS-TARD ...
TAILING HIM WAS A GOOD IDEA!
Ooo

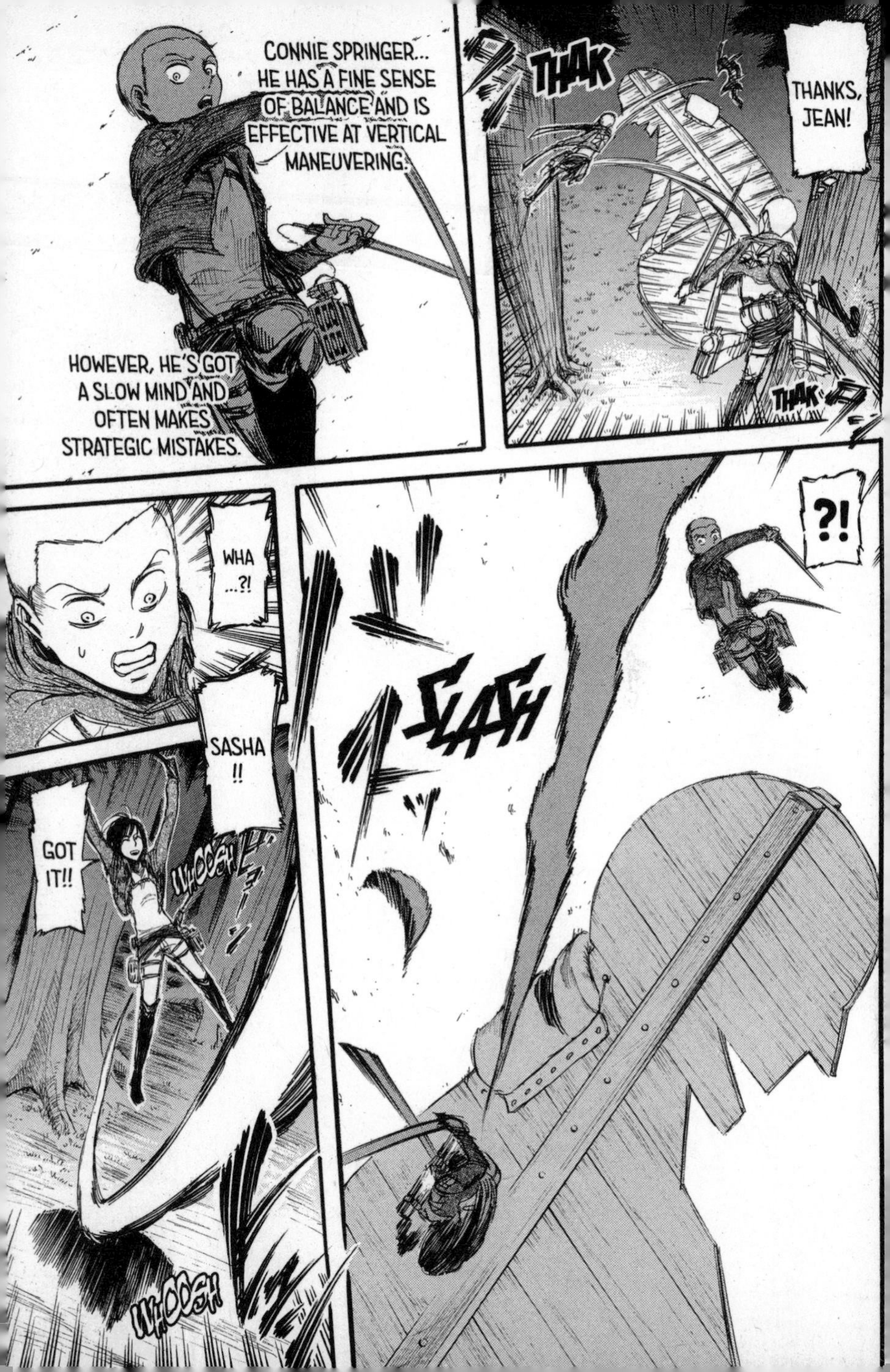

THAK
THANKS, JEAN!
THAK
CONNIE SPRINGER... HE HAS A FINE SENSE OF BALANCE AND IS EFFECTIVE AT VERTICAL MANEUVERING.
HOWEVER, HE'S GOT A SLOW MIND AND OFTEN MAKES STRATEGIC MISTAKES.
?!
SLASH
WHA ...?!
SASHA !!
GOT IT!!
WHOOSH
WHOOSH

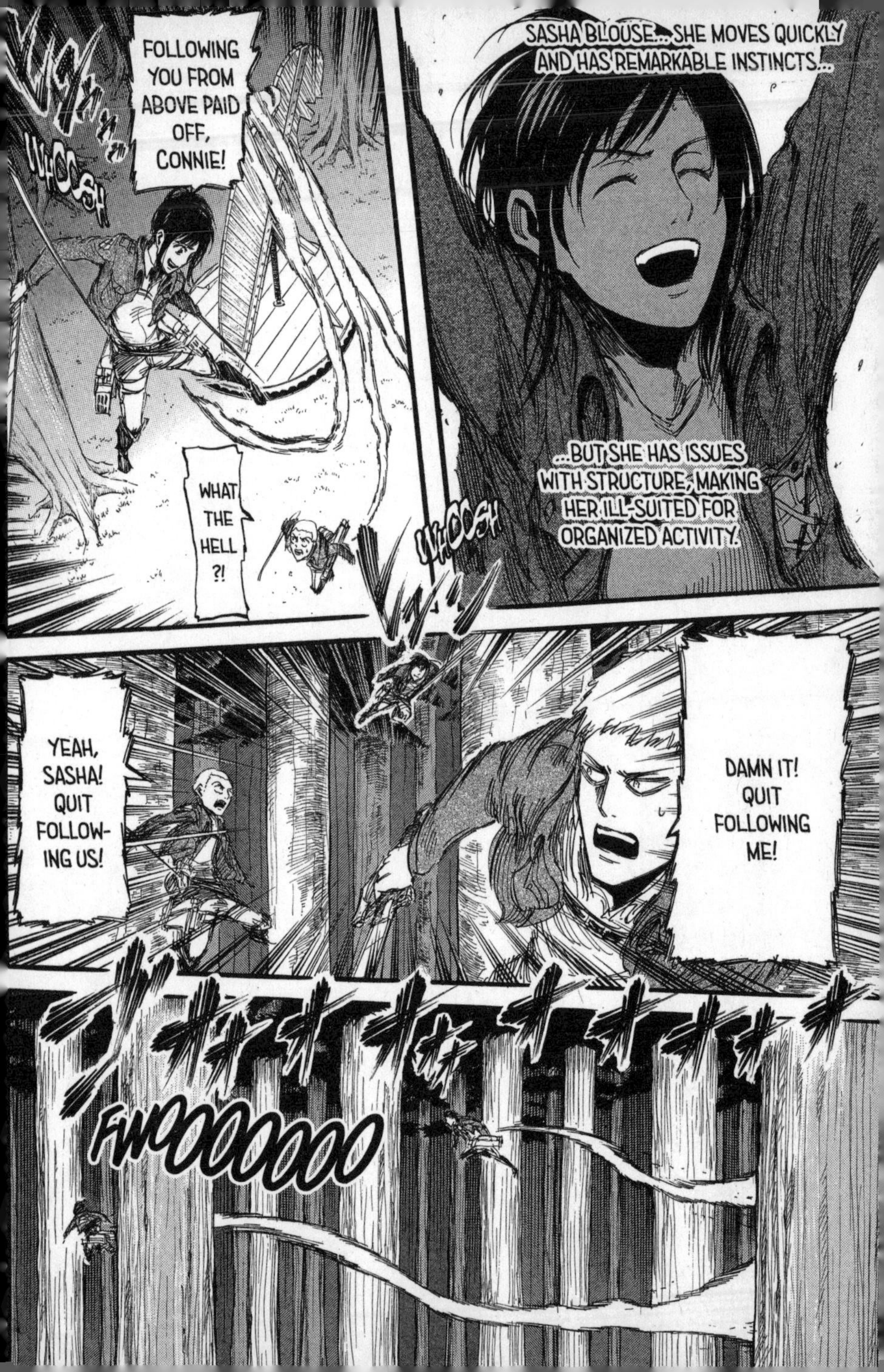
SASHA BLOUSE... SHE MOVES QUICKLY AND HAS REMARKABLE INSTINCTS...
...BUT SHE HAS ISSUES WITH STRUCTURE, MAKING HER ILL-SUITED FOR ORGANIZED ACTIVITY.
FOLLOWING YOU FROM ABOVE PAID OFF, CONNIE!
WHOOSH
WHAT THE HELL ?!
WHOOSH
DAMN IT! QUIT FOLLOWING ME!
YEAH, SASHA! QUIT FOLLOW-ING US!
FWOOOOOOO

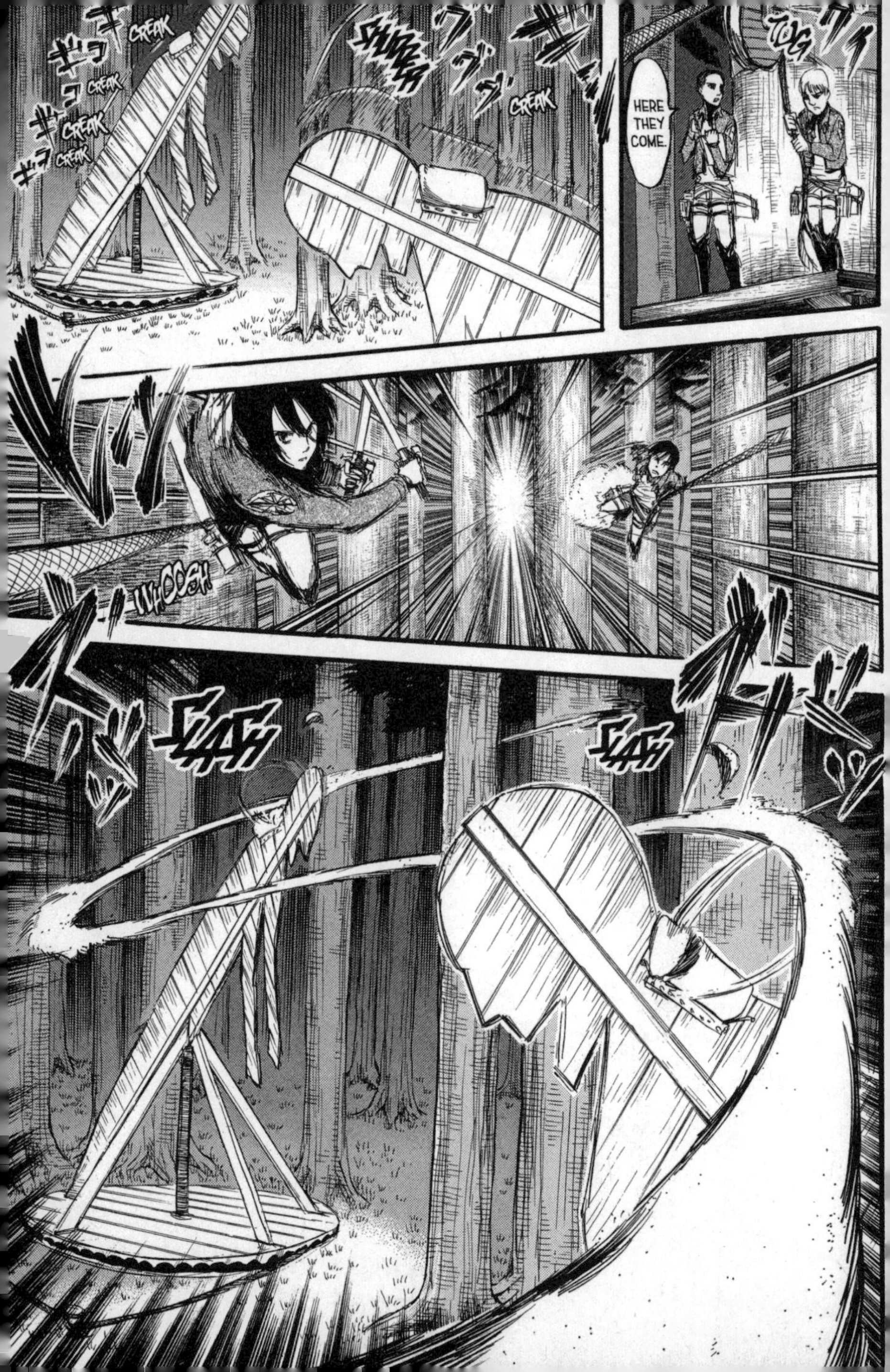
TUG
HERE THEY COME.
CREAK
CREAK
CREAK
CREAK
CREAK
WHOOSH
SLASH
SLASH

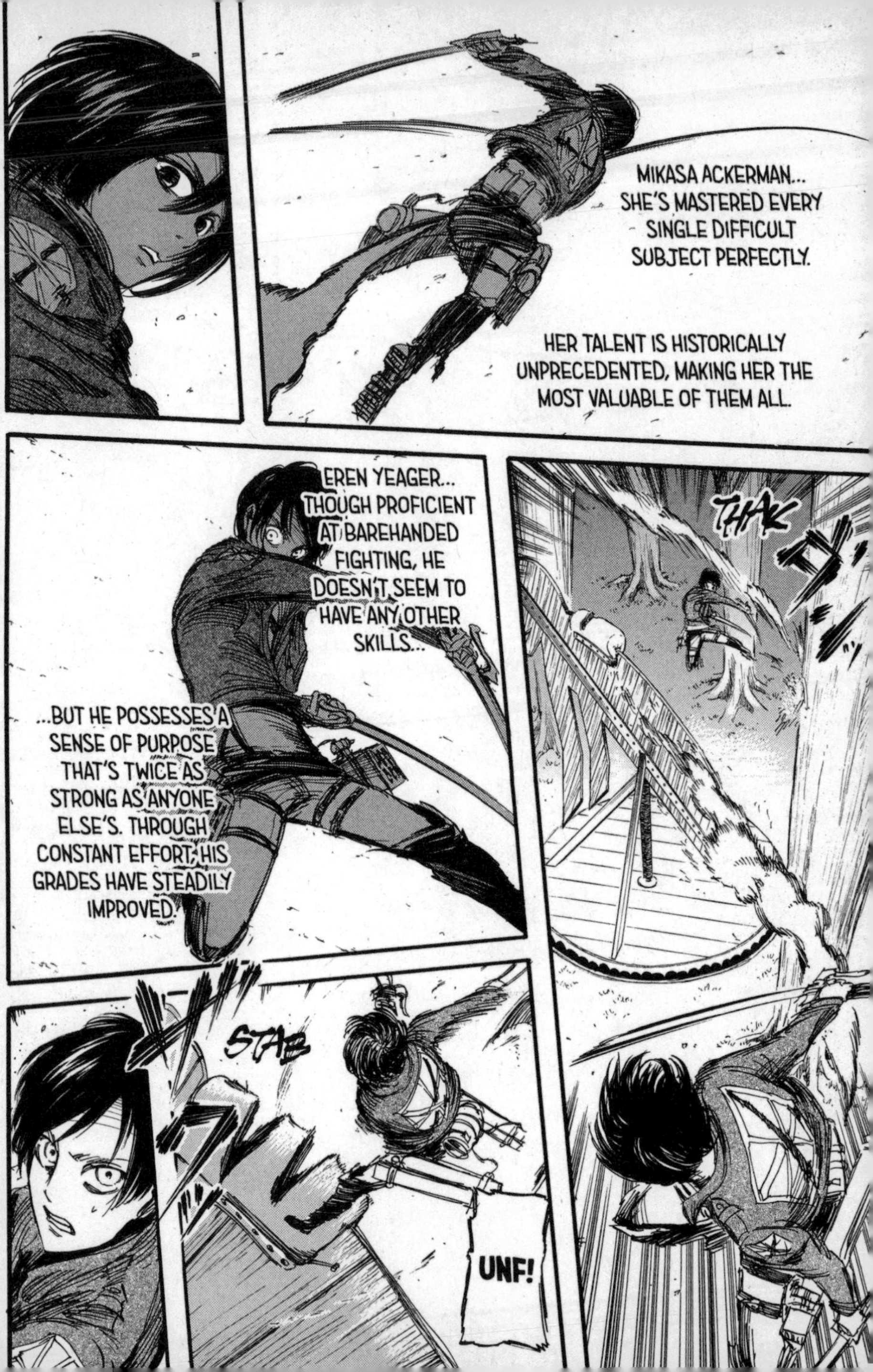
MIKASA ACKERMAN... SHE'S MASTERED EVERY SINGLE DIFFICULT SUBJECT PERFECTLY.
HER TALENT IS HISTORICALLY UNPRECEDENTED, MAKING HER THE MOST VALUABLE OF THEM ALL.
THAK
EREN YEAGER... THOUGH PROFICIENT AT BAREHANDED FIGHTING, HE DOESN'T SEEM TO HAVE ANY OTHER SKILLS...
...BUT HE POSSESSES A SENSE OF PURPOSE THAT'S TWICE AS STRONG AS ANYONE ELSE'S. THROUGH CONSTANT EFFORT, HIS GRADES HAVE STEADILY IMPROVED.
STAB
UNF!

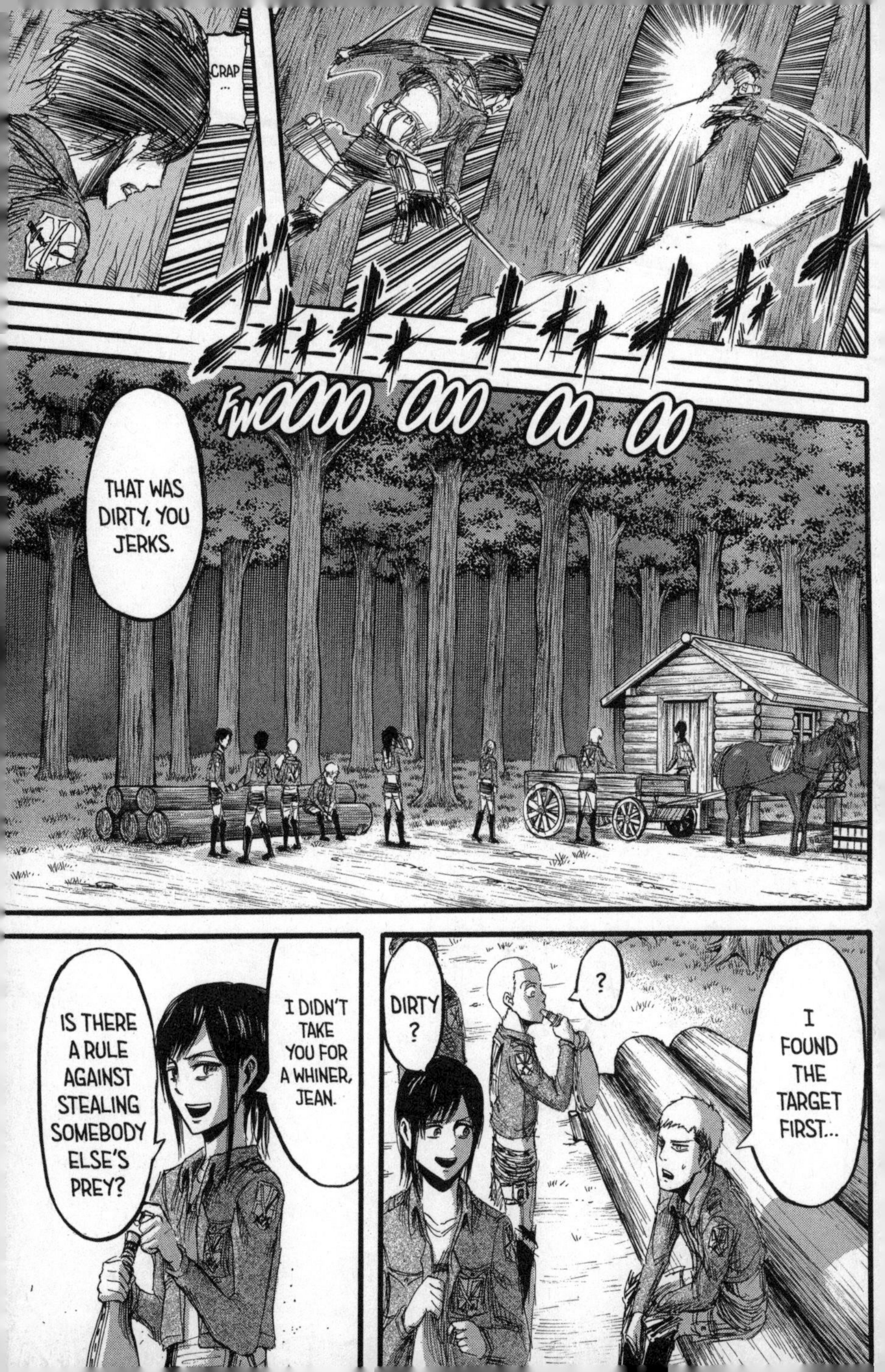
CRAP ...
FWOOOO OOO OO OO
THAT WAS DIRTY, YOU JERKS.
I FOUND THE TARGET FIRST...
?
DIRTY ?
I DIDN'T TAKE YOU FOR A WHINER, JEAN.
IS THERE A RULE AGAINST STEALING SOMEBODY ELSE'S PREY?

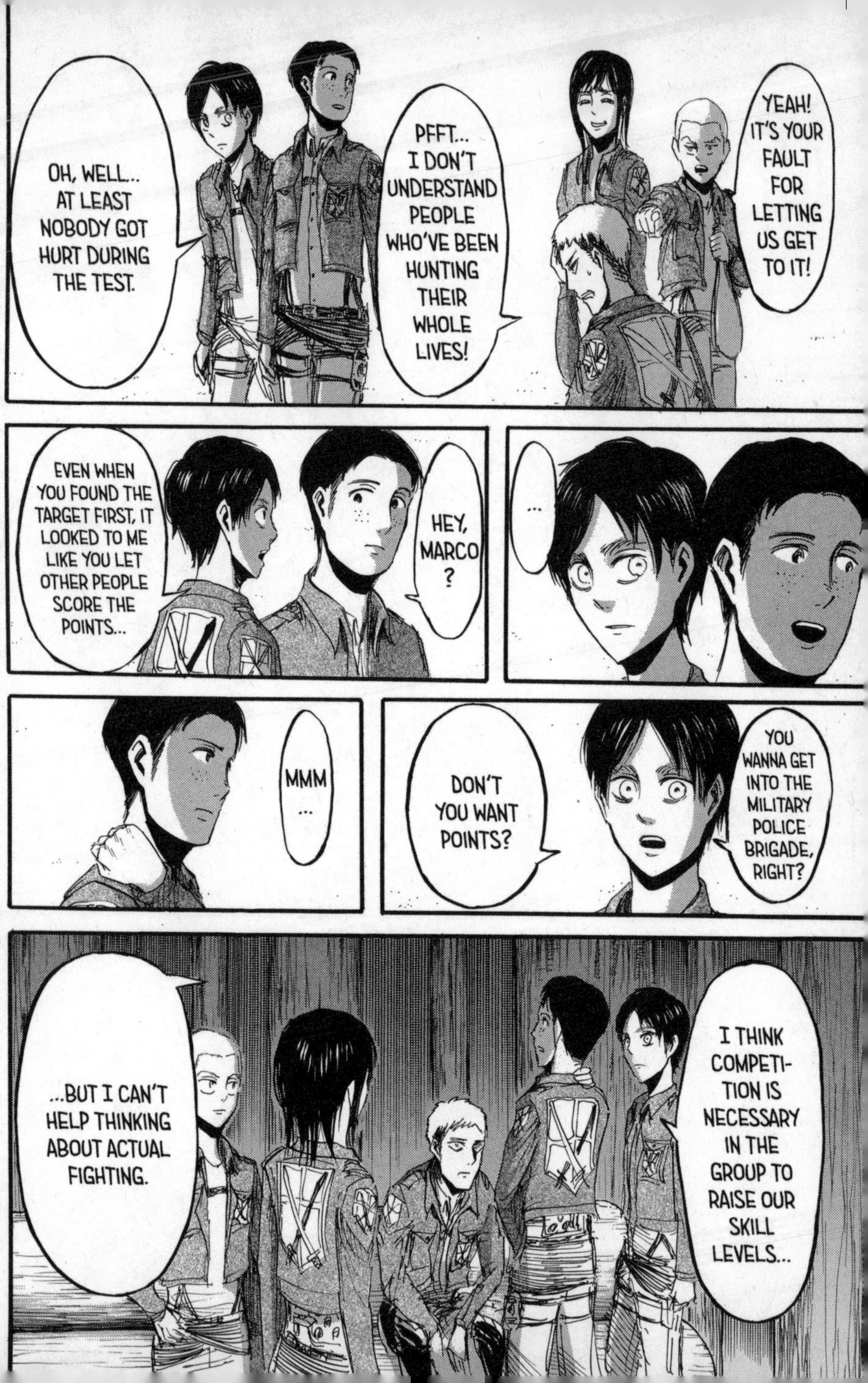
YEAH! IT'S YOUR FAULT FOR LETTING US GET TO IT!
PFFT... I DON'T UNDERSTAND PEOPLE WHO'VE BEEN HUNTING THEIR WHOLE LIVES!
OH, WELL... AT LEAST NOBODY GOT HURT DURING THE TEST.
...
HEY, MARCO?
EVEN WHEN YOU FOUND THE TARGET FIRST, IT LOOKED TO ME LIKE YOU LET OTHER PEOPLE SCORE THE POINTS...
YOU WANNA GET INTO THE MILITARY POLICE BRIGADE, RIGHT?
DON'T YOU WANT POINTS?
MMM...
I THINK COMPETITION IS NECESSARY IN THE GROUP TO RAISE OUR SKILL LEVELS...
...BUT I CAN'T HELP THINKING ABOUT ACTUAL FIGHTING.

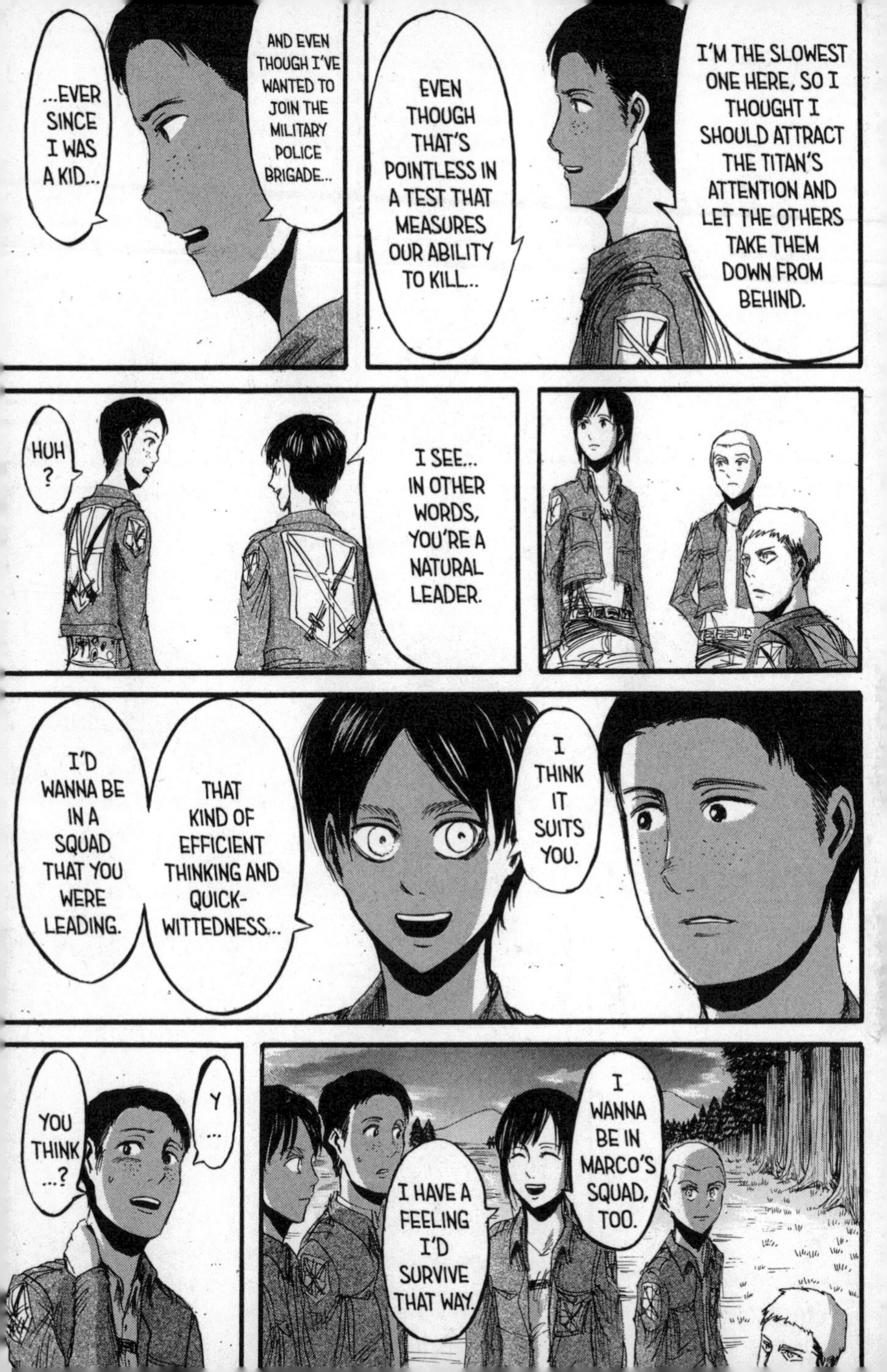
I'M THE SLOWEST ONE HERE, SO I THOUGHT I SHOULD ATTRACT THE TITAN'S ATTENTION AND LET THE OTHERS TAKE THEM DOWN FROM BEHIND.
EVEN THOUGH THAT'S POINTLESS IN A TEST THAT MEASURES OUR ABILITY TO KILL...
AND EVEN THOUGH I'VE WANTED TO JOIN THE MILITARY POLICE BRIGADE...
...EVER SINCE I WAS A KID...
I SEE... IN OTHER WORDS, YOU'RE A NATURAL LEADER.
HUH?
I THINK IT SUITS YOU.
THAT KIND OF EFFICIENT THINKING AND QUICK-WITTEDNESS...
I'D WANNA BE IN A SQUAD THAT YOU WERE LEADING.
I WANNA BE IN MARCO'S SQUAD, TOO.
I HAVE A FEELING I'D SURVIVE THAT WAY.
Y...
YOU THINK...?

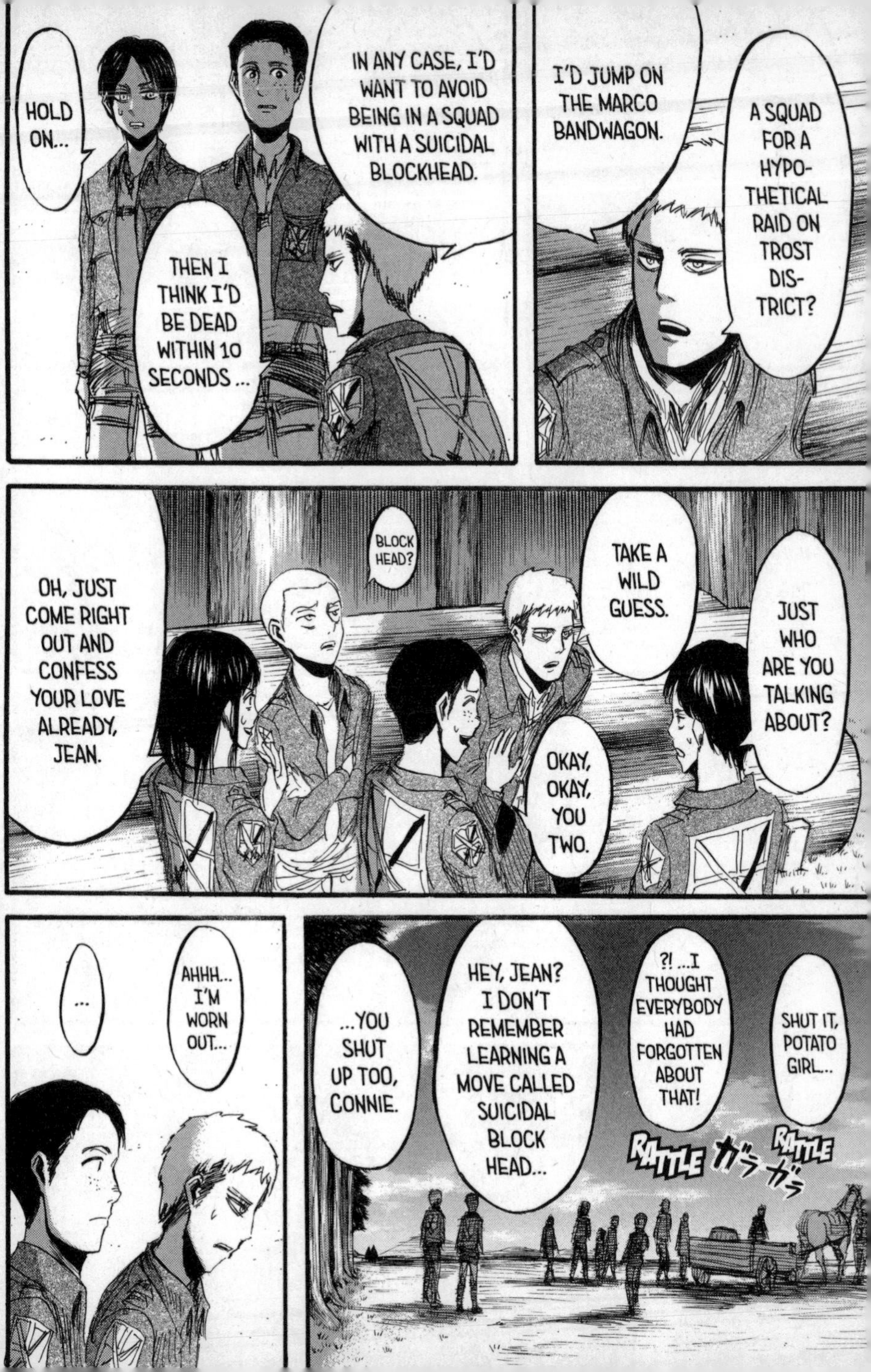
A SQUAD FOR A HYPO-THETICAL RAID ON TROST DIS-TRICT?
I'D JUMP ON THE MARCO BANDWAGON.
IN ANY CASE, I'D WANT TO AVOID BEING IN A SQUAD WITH A SUICIDAL BLOCKHEAD.
THEN I THINK I'D BE DEAD WITHIN 10 SECONDS ...
HOLD ON...
JUST WHO ARE YOU TALKING ABOUT?
TAKE A WILD GUESS.
OKAY, OKAY, YOU TWO.
BLOCK HEAD?
OH, JUST COME RIGHT OUT AND CONFESS YOUR LOVE ALREADY, JEAN.
SHUT IT, POTATO GIRL...
?! ...I THOUGHT EVERYBODY HAD FORGOTTEN ABOUT THAT!
HEY, JEAN? I DON'T REMEMBER LEARNING A MOVE CALLED SUICIDAL BLOCK HEAD...
...YOU SHUT UP TOO, CONNIE.
RATTLE ガラ
RATTLE ガラ
AHHH... I'M WORN OUT...
...

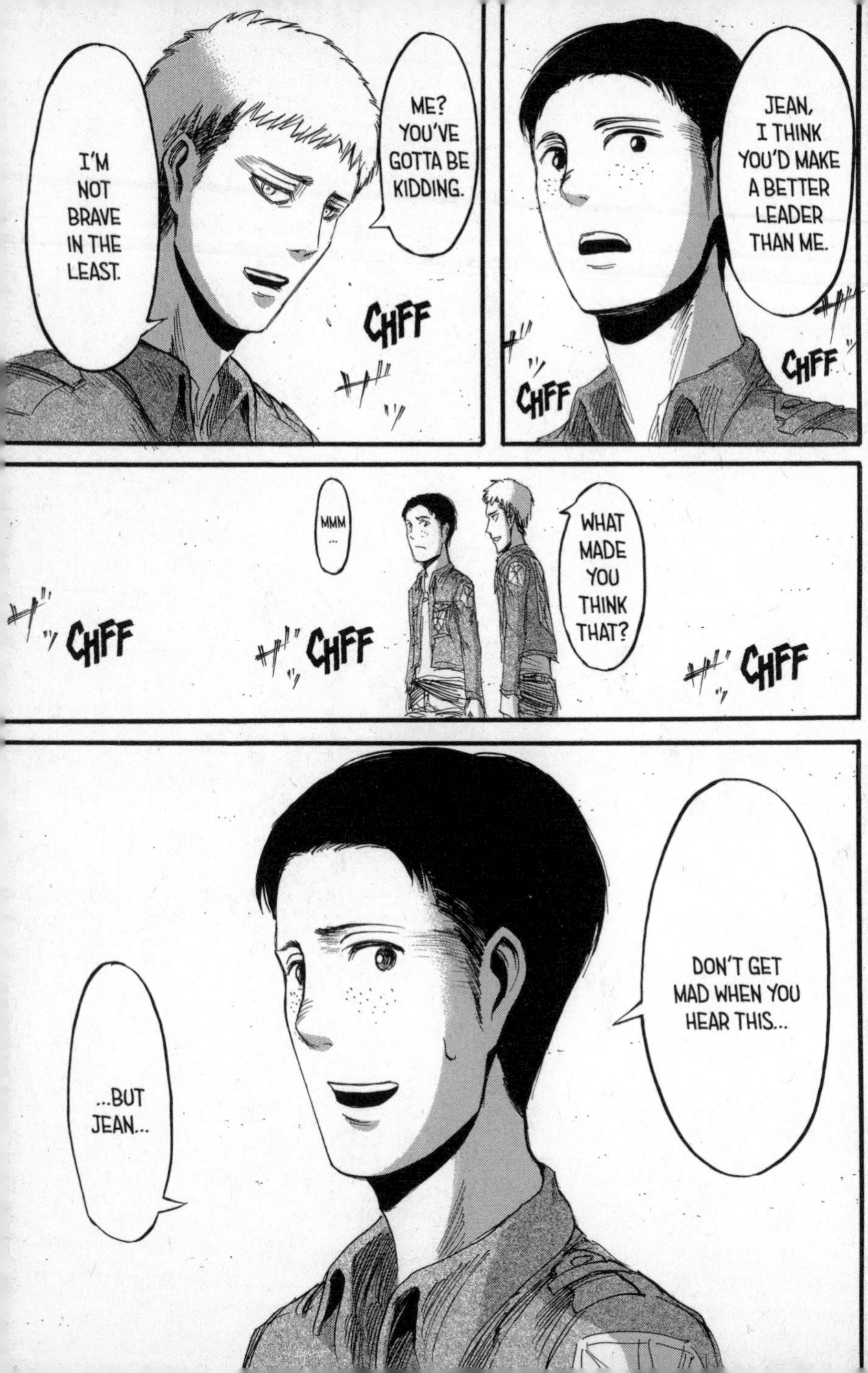
JEAN, I THINK YOU'D MAKE A BETTER LEADER THAN ME.
CHFF
CHFF
ME? YOU'VE GOTTA BE KIDDING.
I'M NOT BRAVE IN THE LEAST.
CHFF
CHFF
WHAT MADE YOU THINK THAT?
MMM...
CHFF
CHFF
DON'T GET MAD WHEN YOU HEAR THIS...
...BUT JEAN...

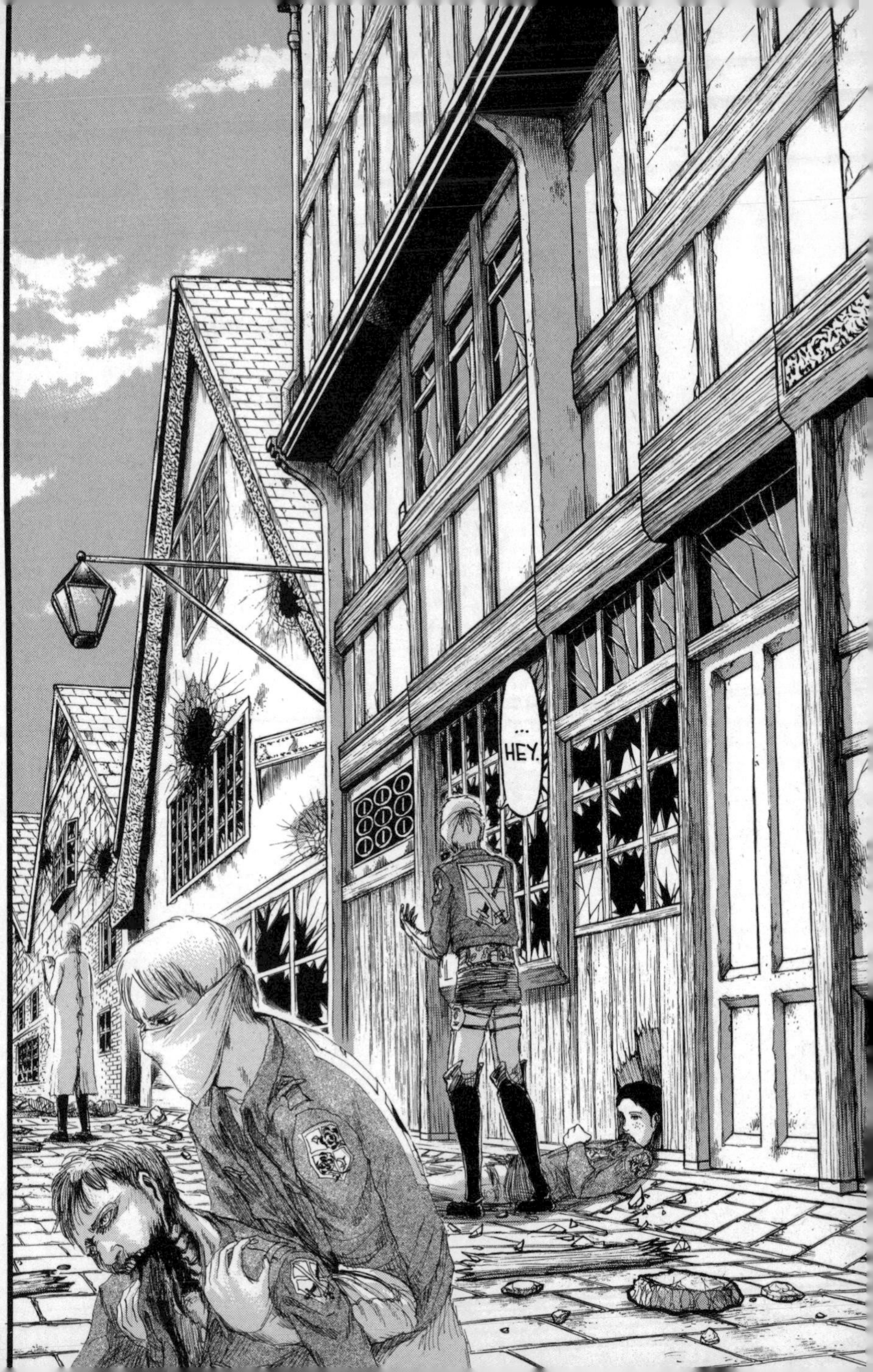
...HEY.

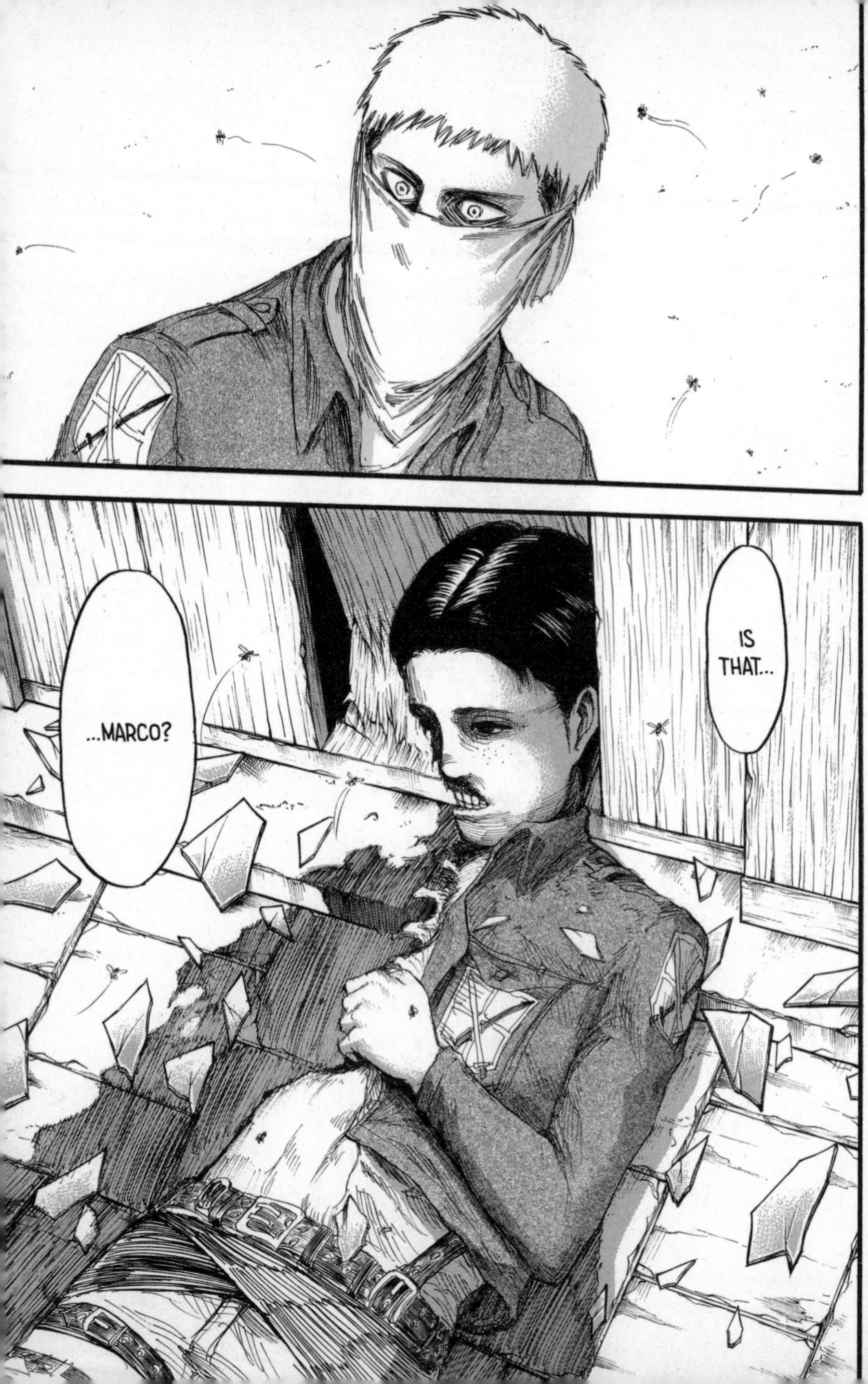
IS THAT...
...MARCO?

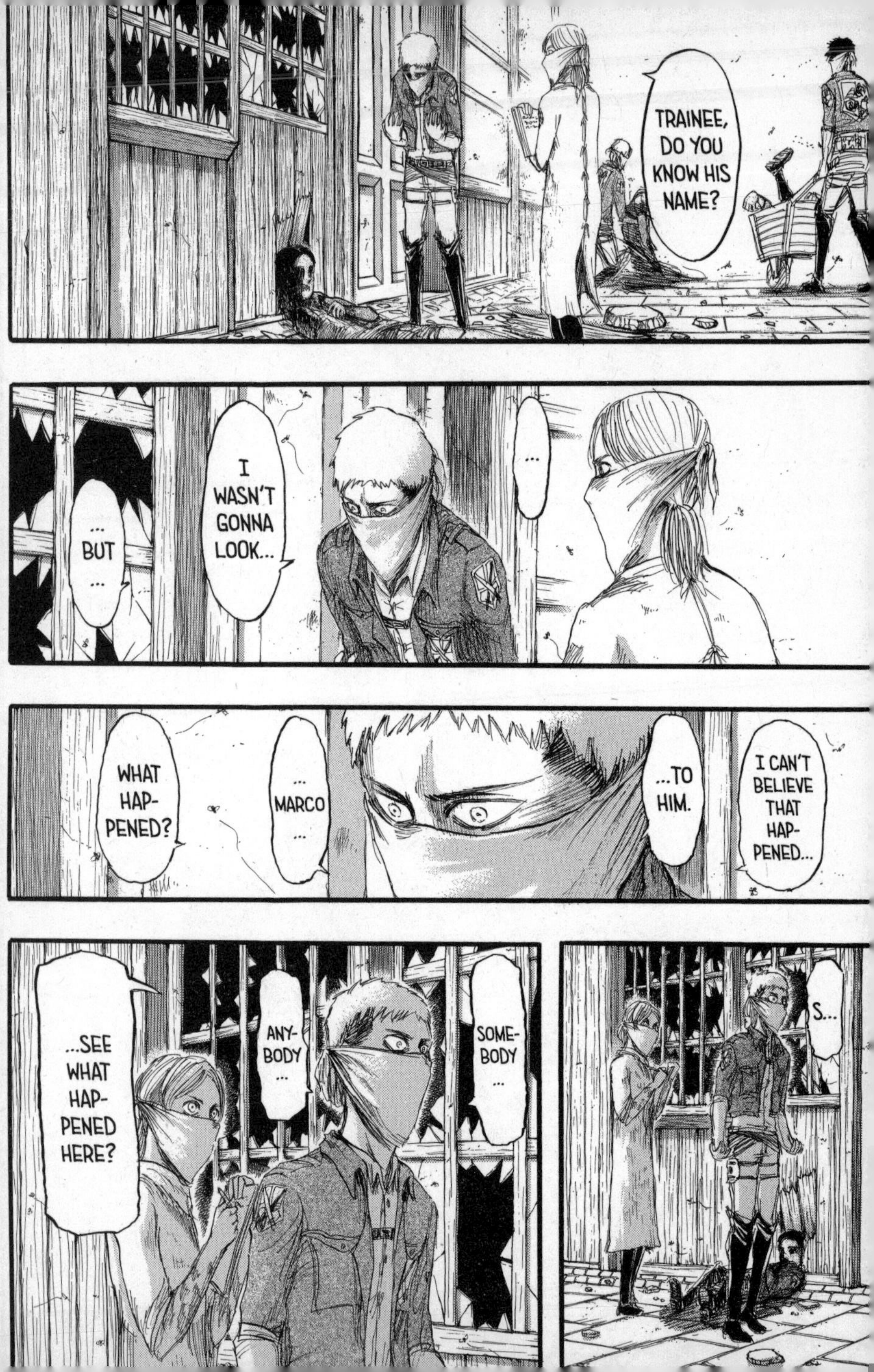
TRAINEE, DO YOU KNOW HIS NAME?
...
I WASN'T GONNA LOOK...
... BUT ...
I CAN'T BELIEVE THAT HAP-PENED...
...TO HIM.
... MARCO ...
WHAT HAP-PENED?
S...
SOME-BODY ...
ANY-BODY ...
...SEE WHAT HAP-PENED HERE?

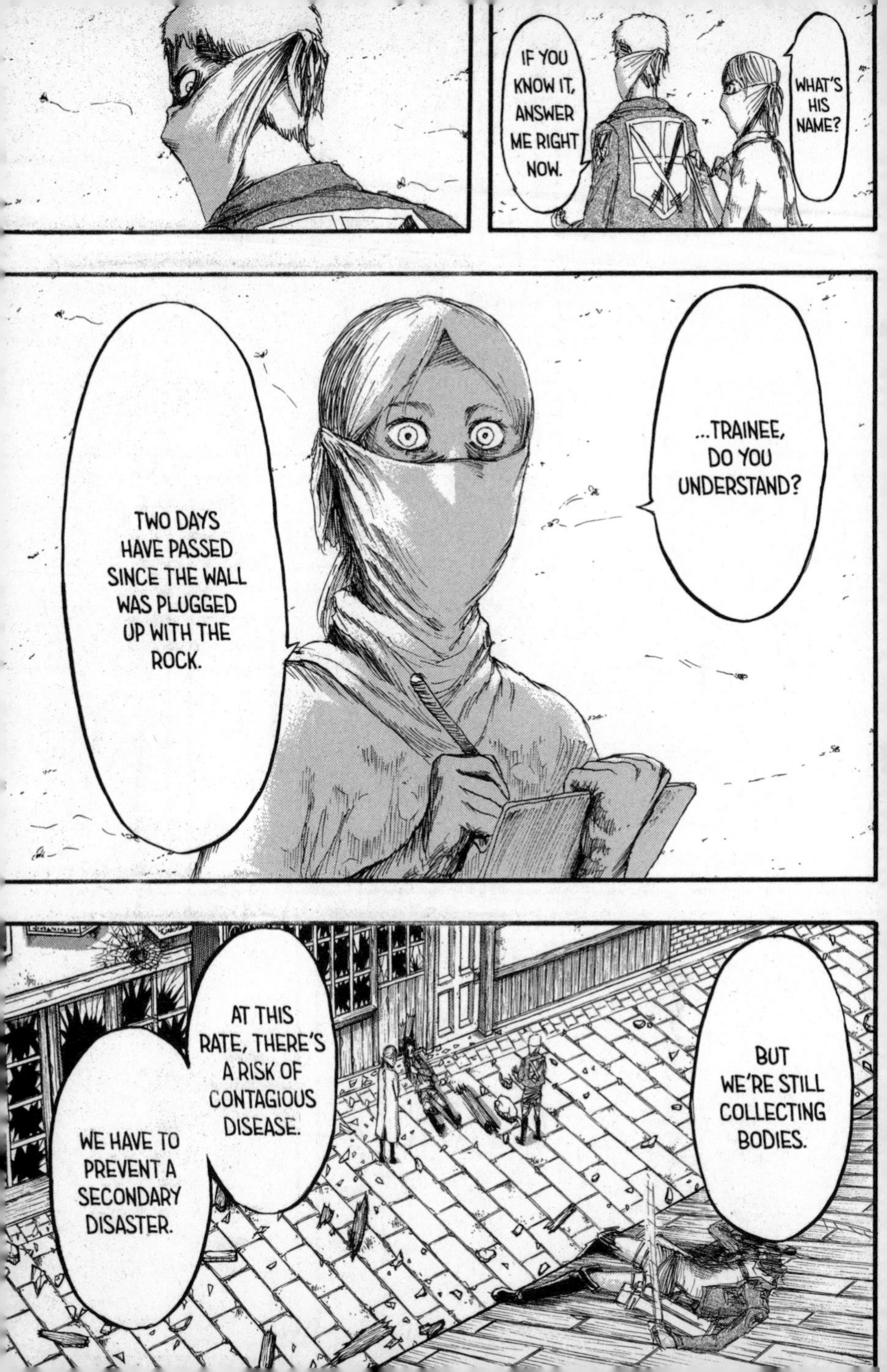
WHAT'S HIS NAME?
IF YOU KNOW IT, ANSWER ME RIGHT NOW.
...TRAINEE, DO YOU UNDERSTAND?
TWO DAYS HAVE PASSED SINCE THE WALL WAS PLUGGED UP WITH THE ROCK.
BUT WE'RE STILL COLLECTING BODIES.
AT THIS RATE, THERE'S A RISK OF CONTAGIOUS DISEASE.
WE HAVE TO PREVENT A SECONDARY DISASTER.

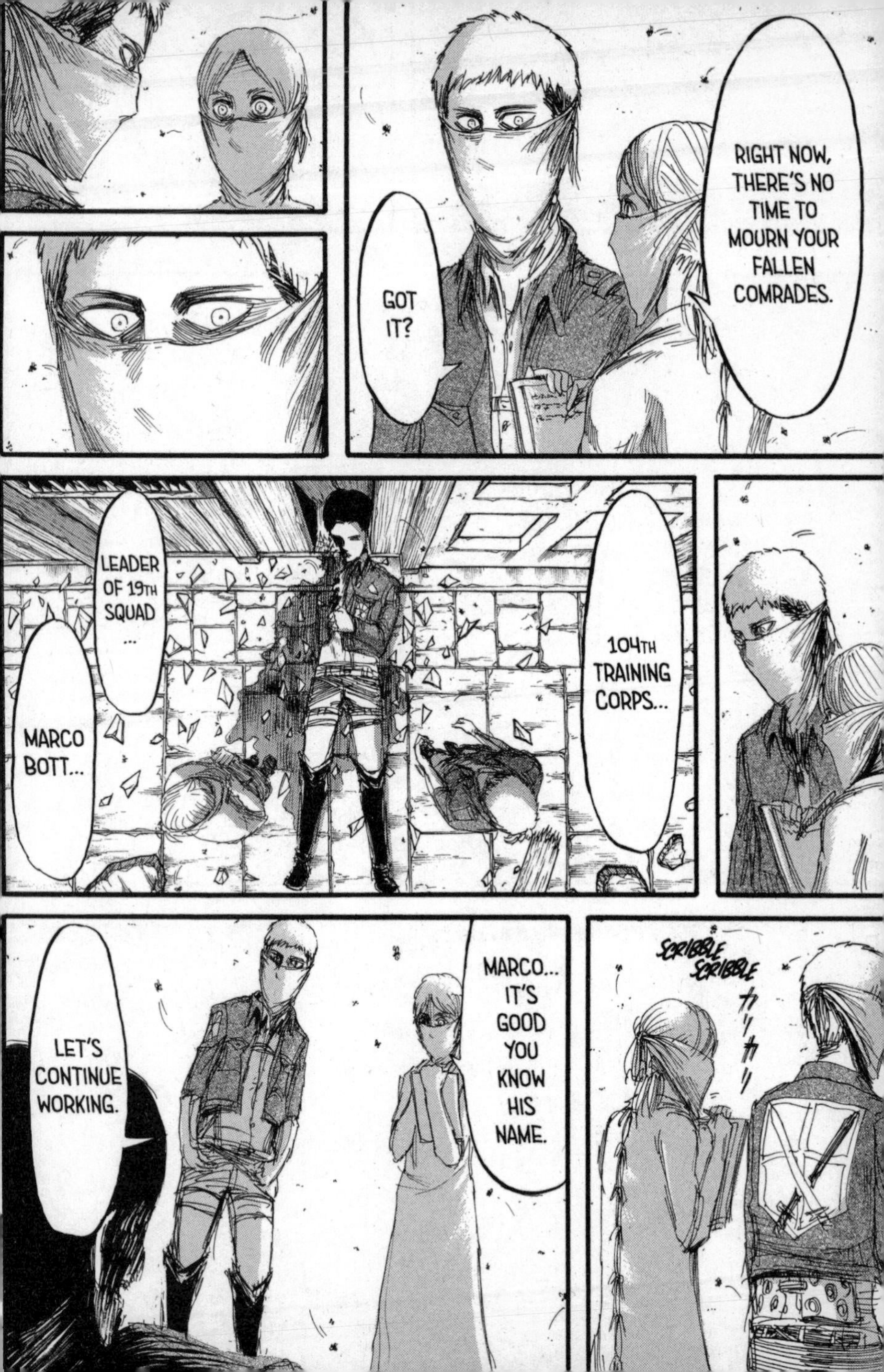
RIGHT NOW, THERE'S NO TIME TO MOURN YOUR FALLEN COMRADES.
GOT IT?
104TH TRAINING CORPS...
LEADER OF 19TH SQUAD ...
MARCO BOTT...
SCRIBBLE SCRIBBLE
MARCO... IT'S GOOD YOU KNOW HIS NAME.
LET'S CONTINUE WORKING.

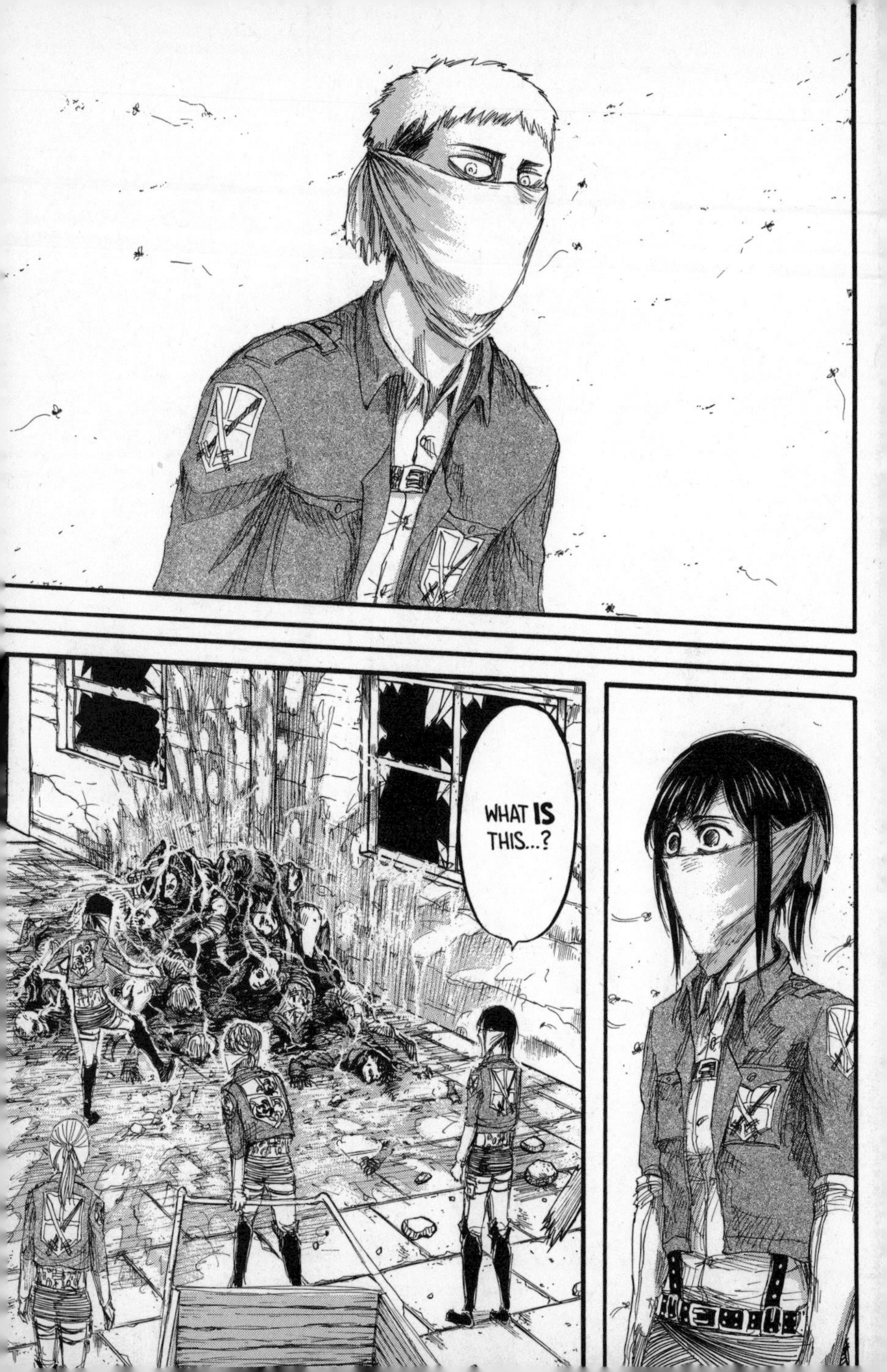
WHAT IS THIS...?

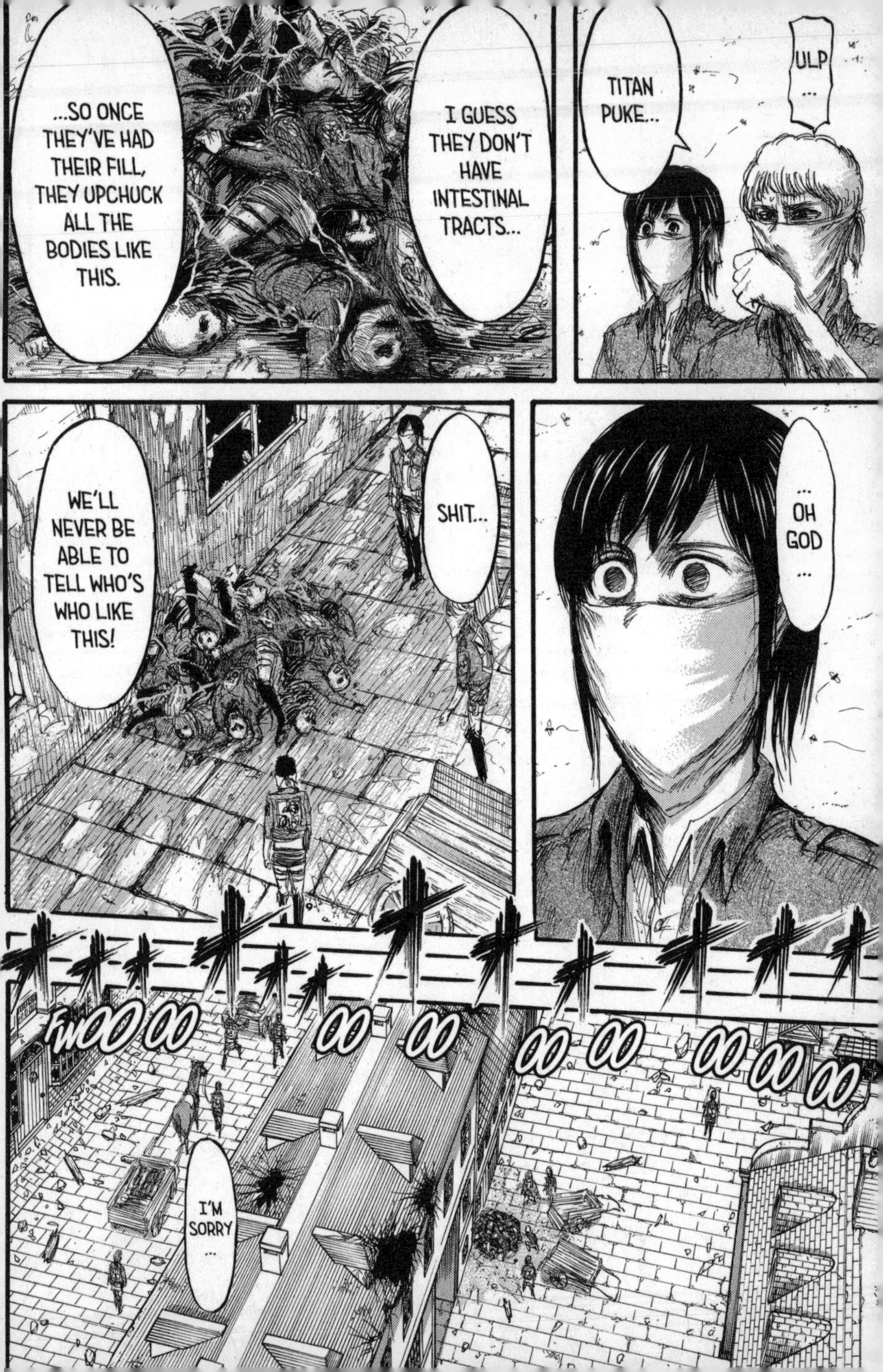
ULP ...
TITAN PUKE...
I GUESS THEY DON'T HAVE INTESTINAL TRACTS...
...SO ONCE THEY'VE HAD THEIR FILL, THEY UPCHUCK ALL THE BODIES LIKE THIS.
... OH GOD ...
SHIT...
WE'LL NEVER BE ABLE TO TELL WHO'S WHO LIKE THIS!
FWOOOO OO OO OO OO OO OO OO OO
I'M SORRY ...

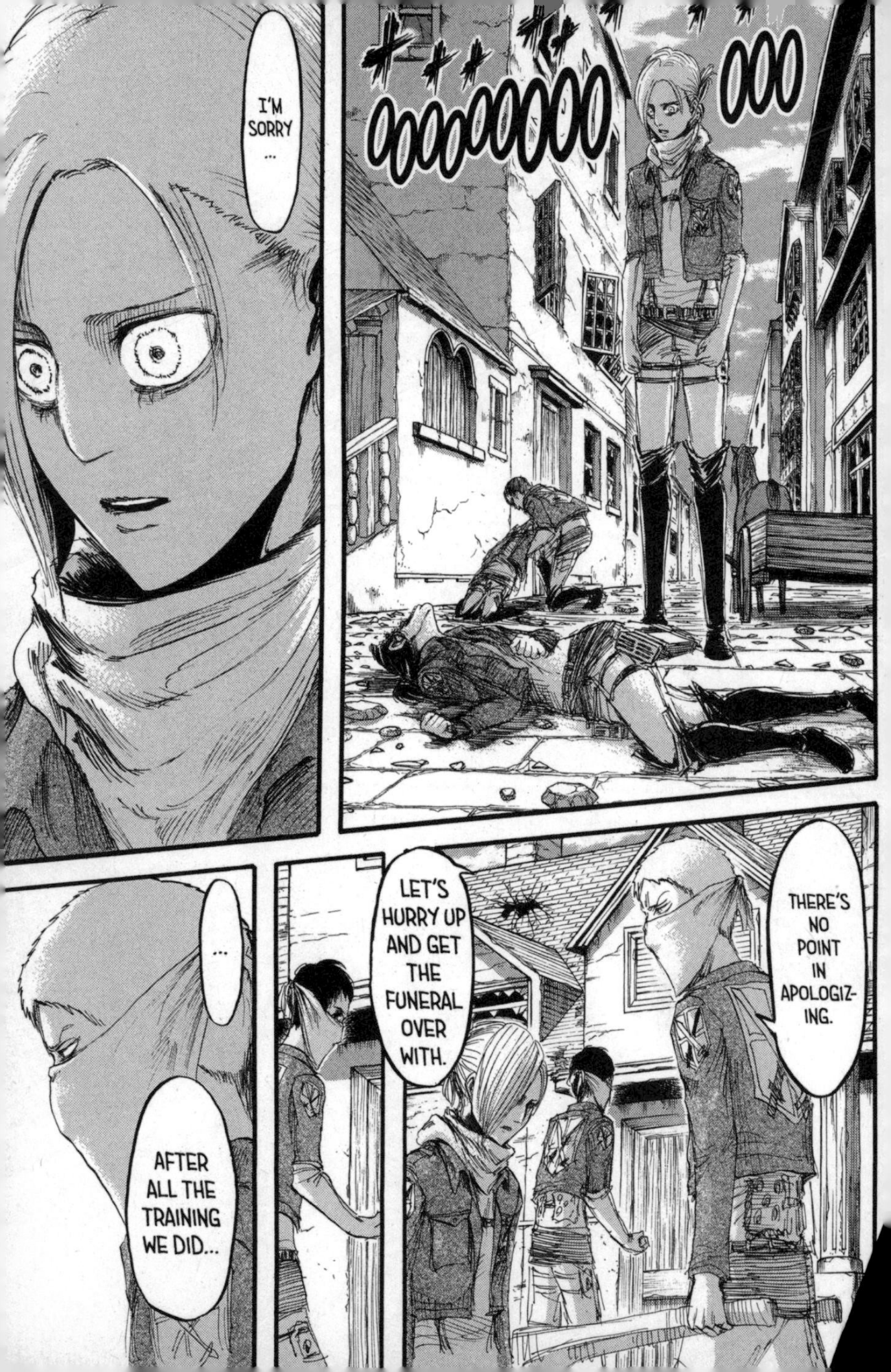
OOOOOOOOOOOO
I'M SORRY ...
THERE'S NO POINT IN APOLOGIZ-ING.
LET'S HURRY UP AND GET THE FUNERAL OVER WITH.
...
AFTER ALL THE TRAINING WE DID...

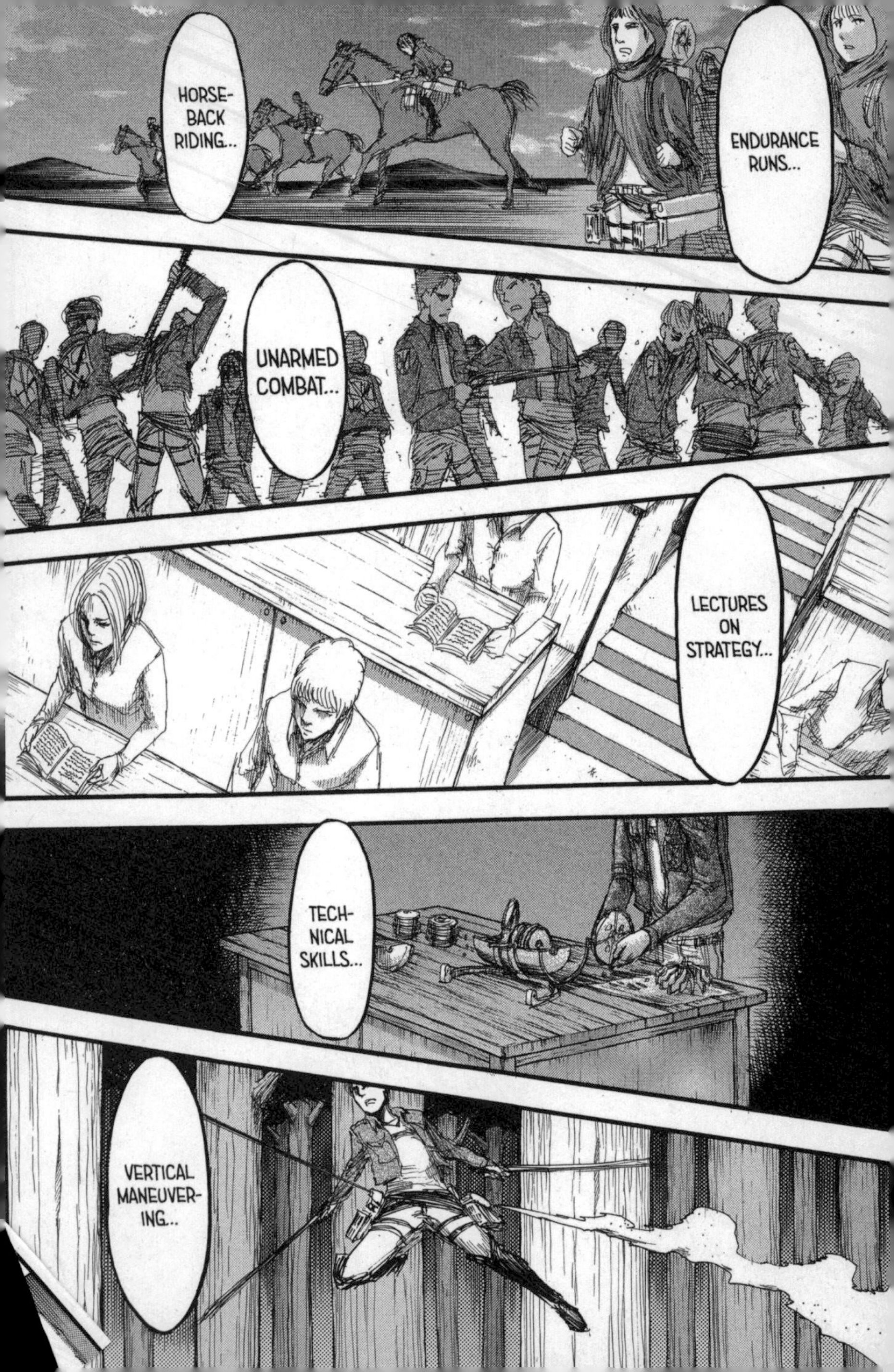
ENDURANCE RUNS...
HORSE-BACK RIDING...
UNARMED COMBAT...
LECTURES ON STRATEGY...
TECH-NICAL SKILLS...
VERTICAL MANEUVER-ING...

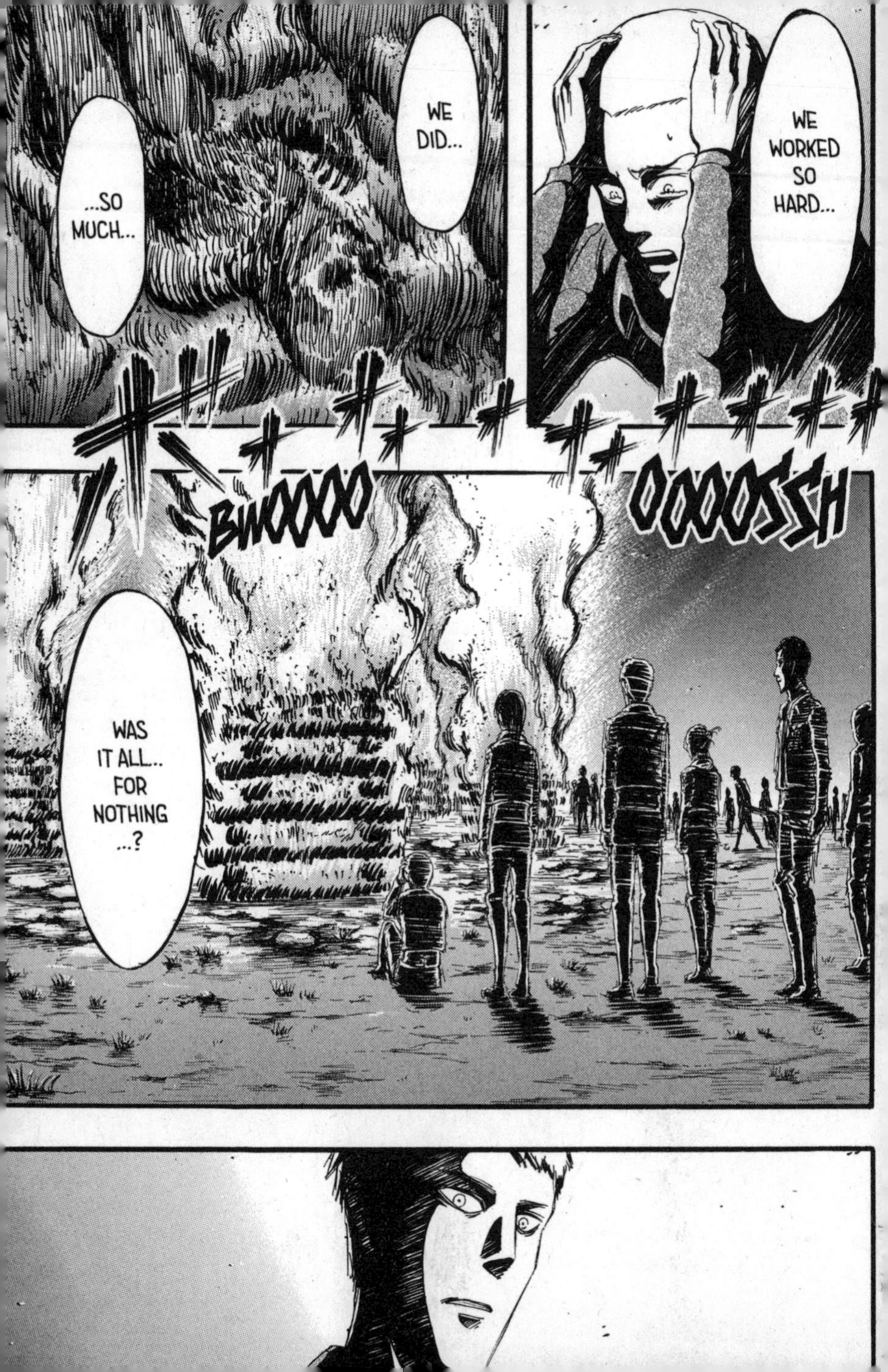
WE WORKED SO HARD...
WE DID...
...SO MUCH...
BWOOOO OOOOSSH
WAS IT ALL... FOR NOTHING ...?

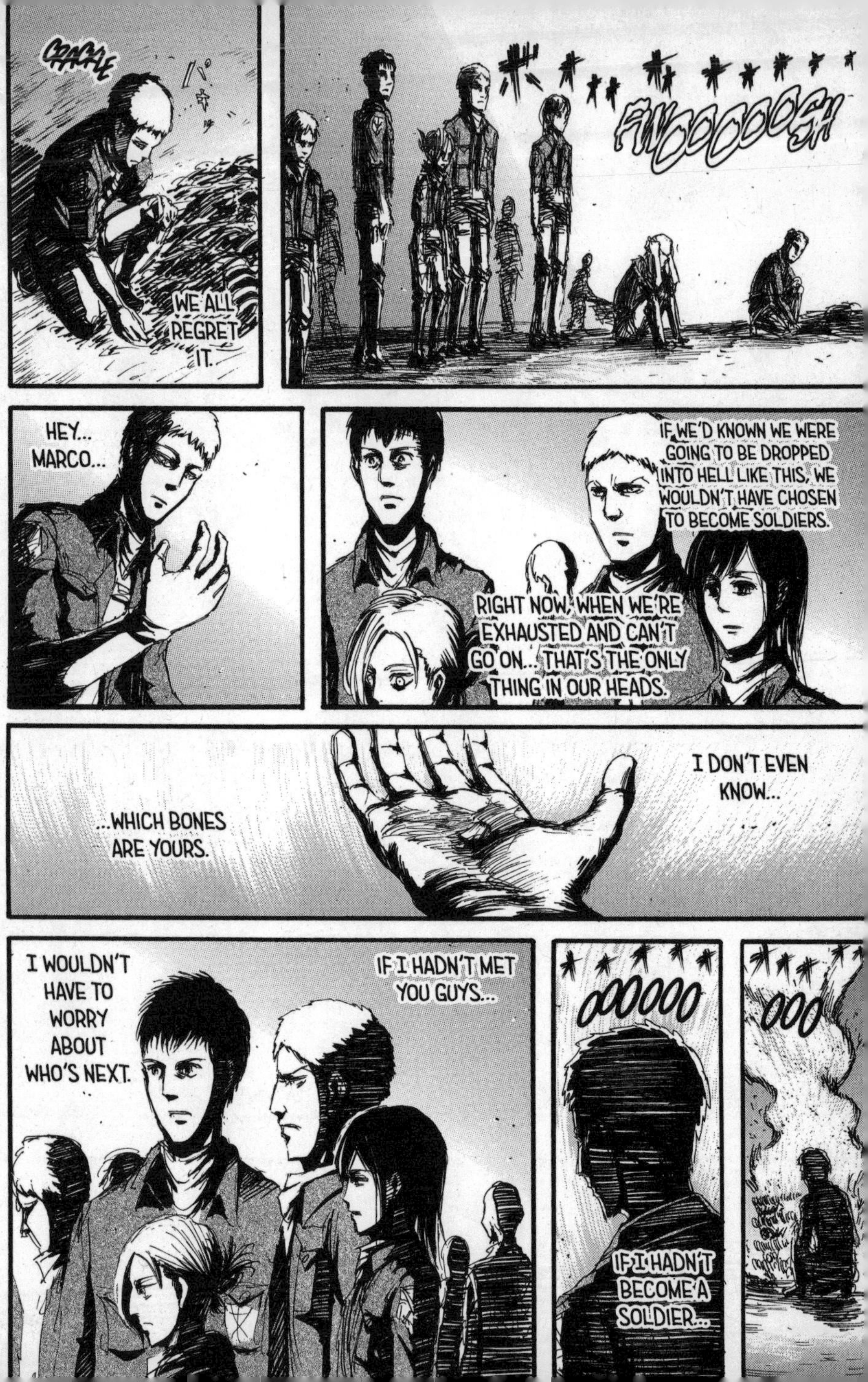
FWOOOOOOSH
CRACKLE
WE ALL REGRET IT.
IF WE'D KNOWN WE WERE GOING TO BE DROPPED INTO HELL LIKE THIS, WE WOULDN'T HAVE CHOSEN TO BECOME SOLDIERS.
RIGHT NOW, WHEN WE'RE EXHAUSTED AND CAN'T GO ON... THAT'S THE ONLY THING IN OUR HEADS.
HEY... MARCO...
I DON'T EVEN KNOW...
...WHICH BONES ARE YOURS.
OOO
OOOOOO
IF I HADN'T BECOME A SOLDIER...
IF I HADN'T MET YOU GUYS...
I WOULDN'T HAVE TO WORRY ABOUT WHO'S NEXT.

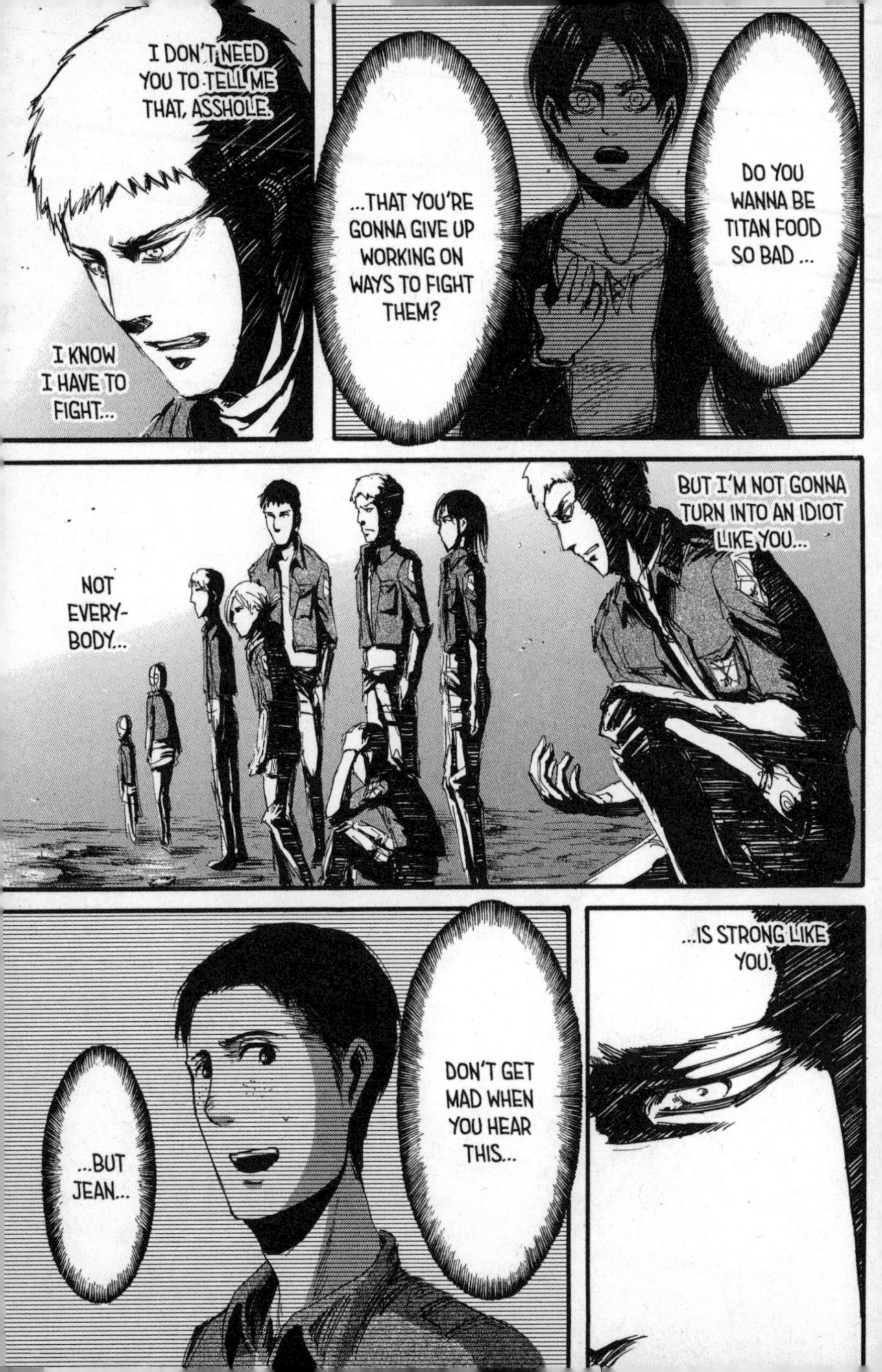
DO YOU WANNA BE TITAN FOOD SO BAD ...
...THAT YOU'RE GONNA GIVE UP WORKING ON WAYS TO FIGHT THEM?
I DON'T NEED YOU TO TELL ME THAT, ASSHOLE.
I KNOW I HAVE TO FIGHT...
BUT I'M NOT GONNA TURN INTO AN IDIOT LIKE YOU...
NOT EVERY-BODY...
...IS STRONG LIKE YOU.
DON'T GET MAD WHEN YOU HEAR THIS...
...BUT JEAN...

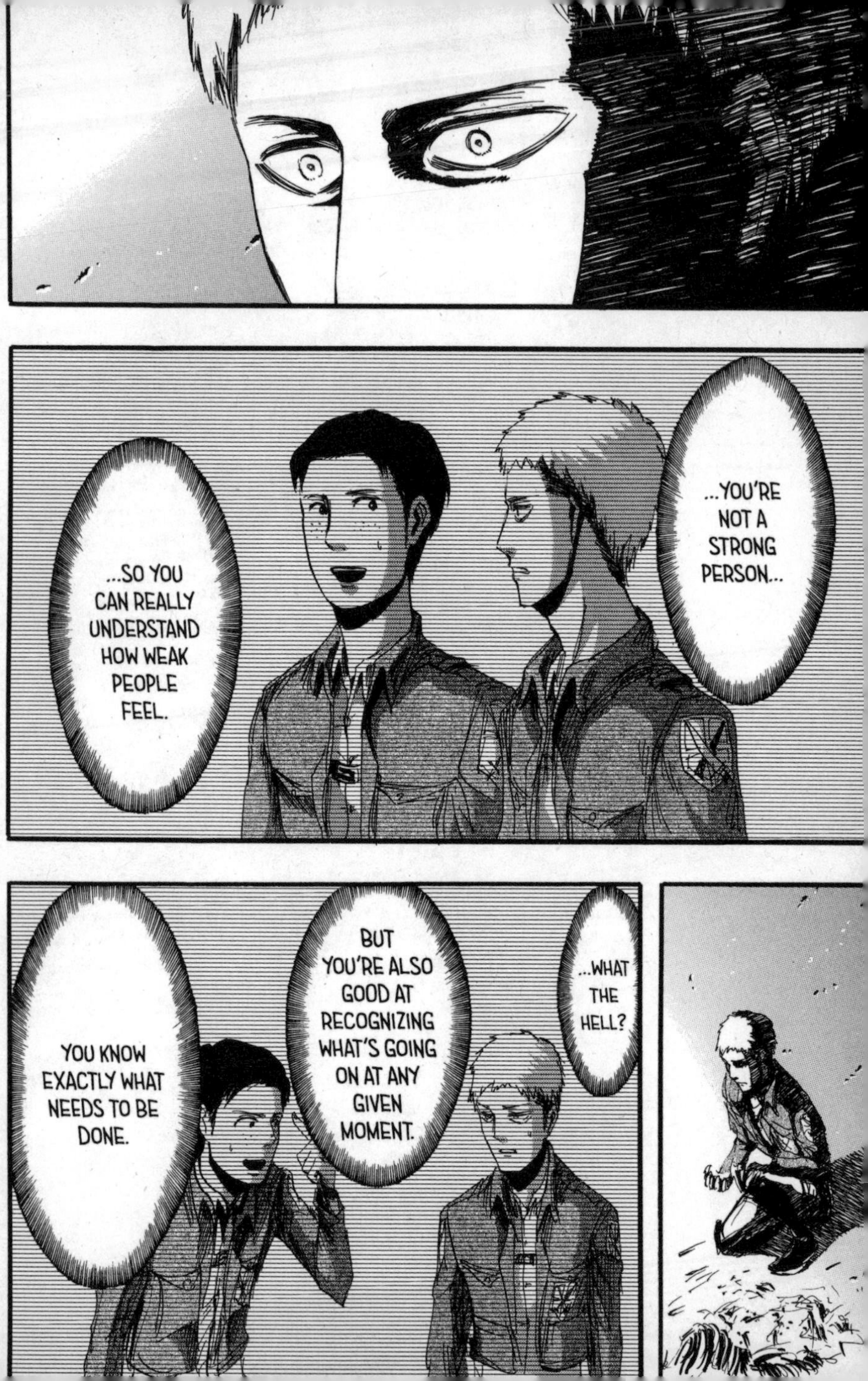
...YOU'RE NOT A STRONG PERSON...
...SO YOU CAN REALLY UNDERSTAND HOW WEAK PEOPLE FEEL.
...WHAT THE HELL?
BUT YOU'RE ALSO GOOD AT RECOGNIZING WHAT'S GOING ON AT ANY GIVEN MOMENT.
YOU KNOW EXACTLY WHAT NEEDS TO BE DONE.

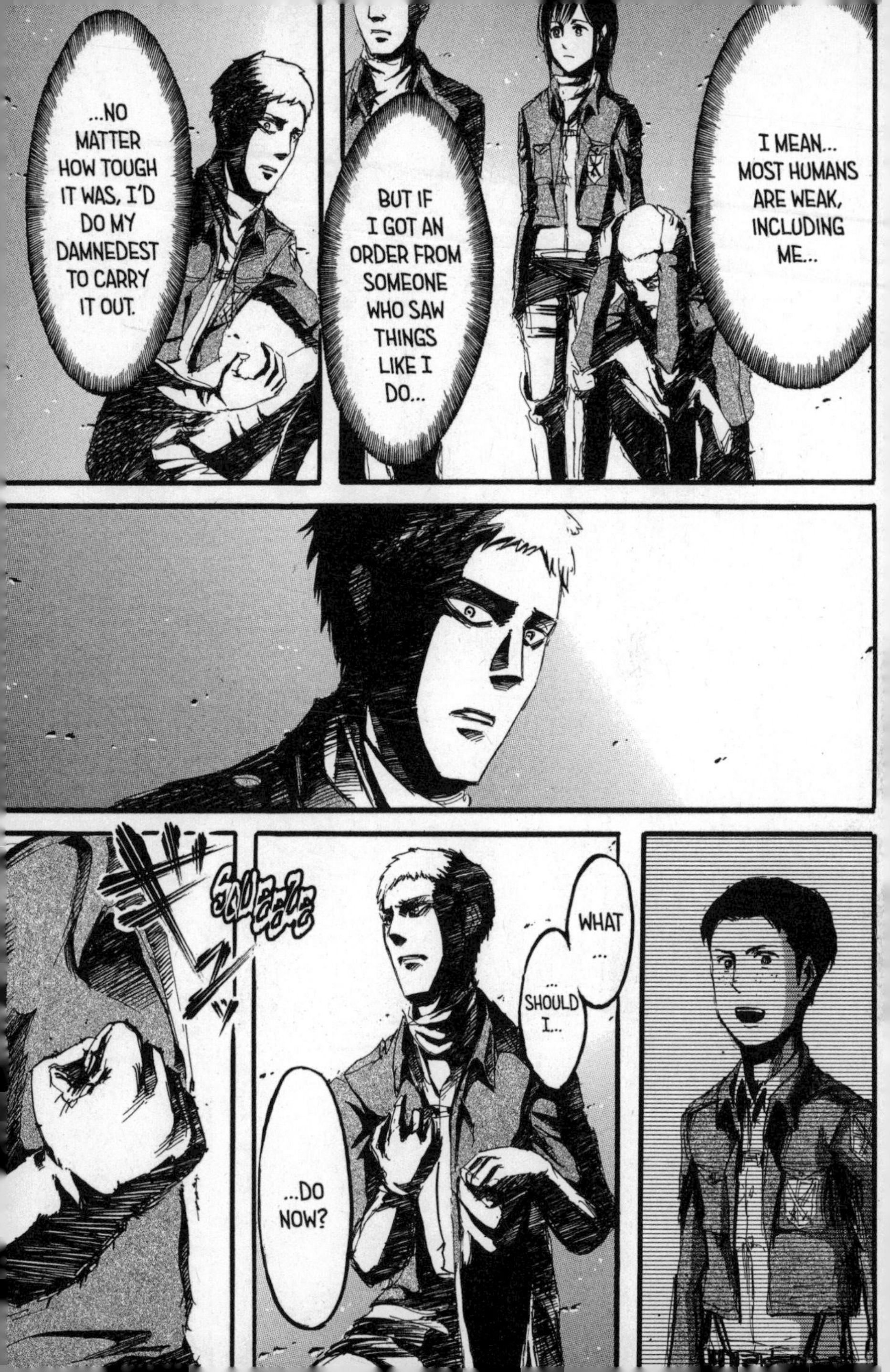
I MEAN... MOST HUMANS ARE WEAK, INCLUDING ME...
BUT IF I GOT AN ORDER FROM SOMEONE WHO SAW THINGS LIKE I DO...
...NO MATTER HOW TOUGH IT WAS, I'D DO MY DAMNEDEST TO CARRY IT OUT.
WHAT ...
... SHOULD I...
...DO NOW?
SQUEEZE

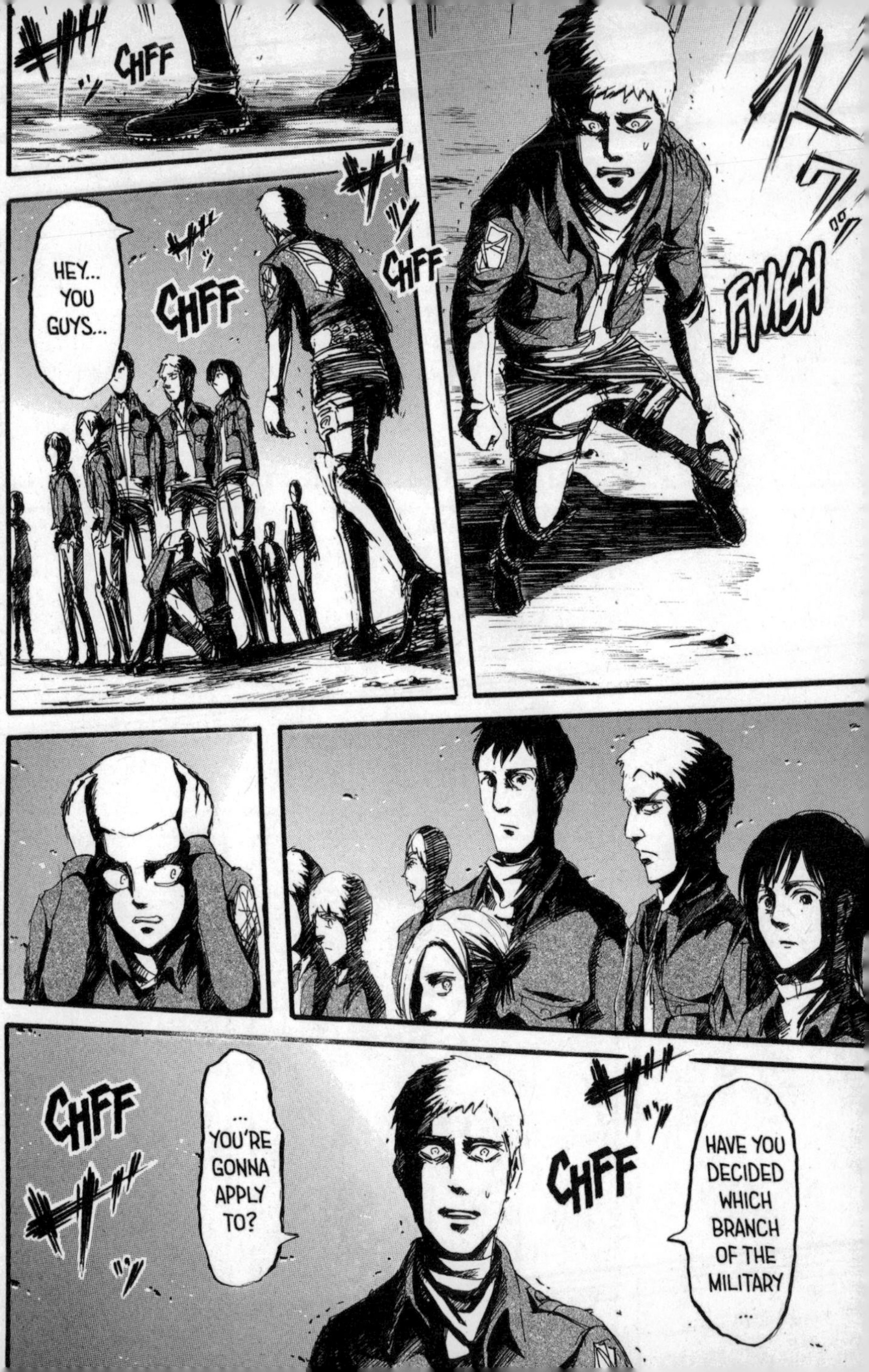
FWISH
CHFF
CHFF
CHFF
HEY... YOU GUYS...
HAVE YOU DECIDED WHICH BRANCH OF THE MILITARY ...
CHFF
... YOU'RE GONNA APPLY TO?
CHFF

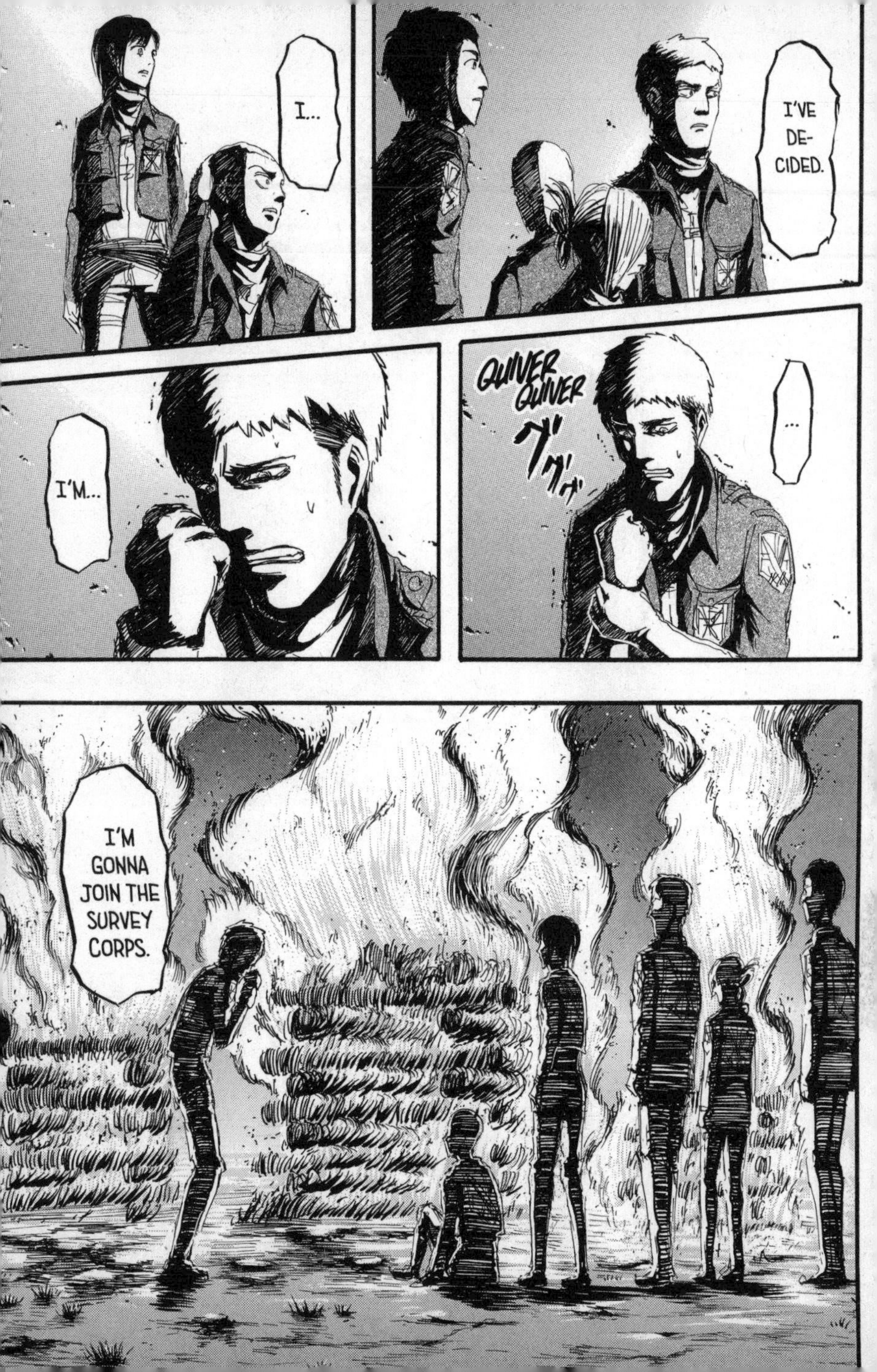
I'VE DE- CIDED.
I...
...
QUIVER QUIVER
ヴヴ
I'M...
I'M GONNA JOIN THE SURVEY CORPS.

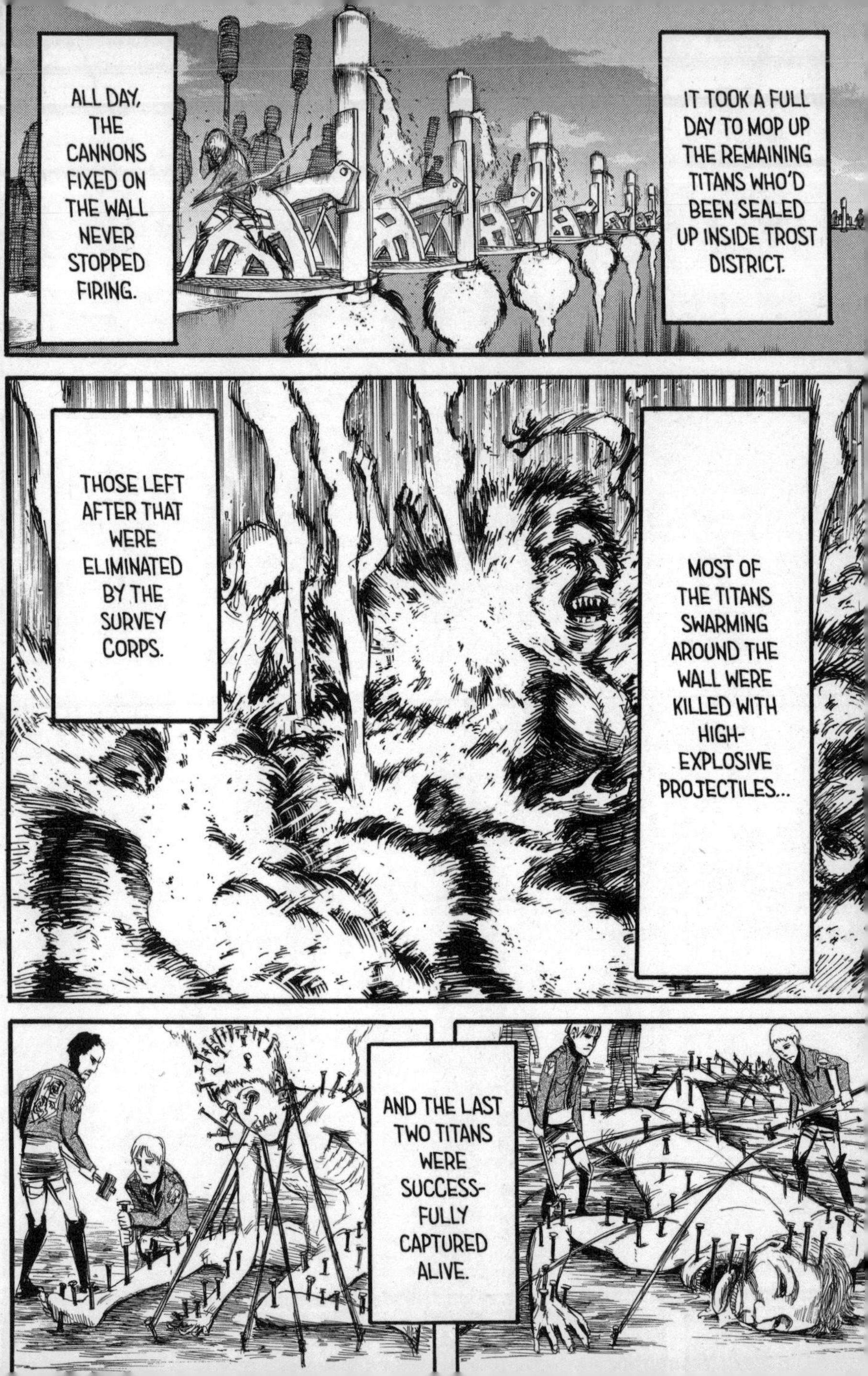
IT TOOK A FULL DAY TO MOP UP THE REMAINING TITANS WHO'D BEEN SEALED UP INSIDE TROST DISTRICT.
ALL DAY, THE CANNONS FIXED ON THE WALL NEVER STOPPED FIRING.
MOST OF THE TITANS SWARMING AROUND THE WALL WERE KILLED WITH HIGH-EXPLOSIVE PROJECTILES...
THOSE LEFT AFTER THAT WERE ELIMINATED BY THE SURVEY CORPS.
AND THE LAST TWO TITANS WERE SUCCESSFULLY CAPTURED ALIVE.

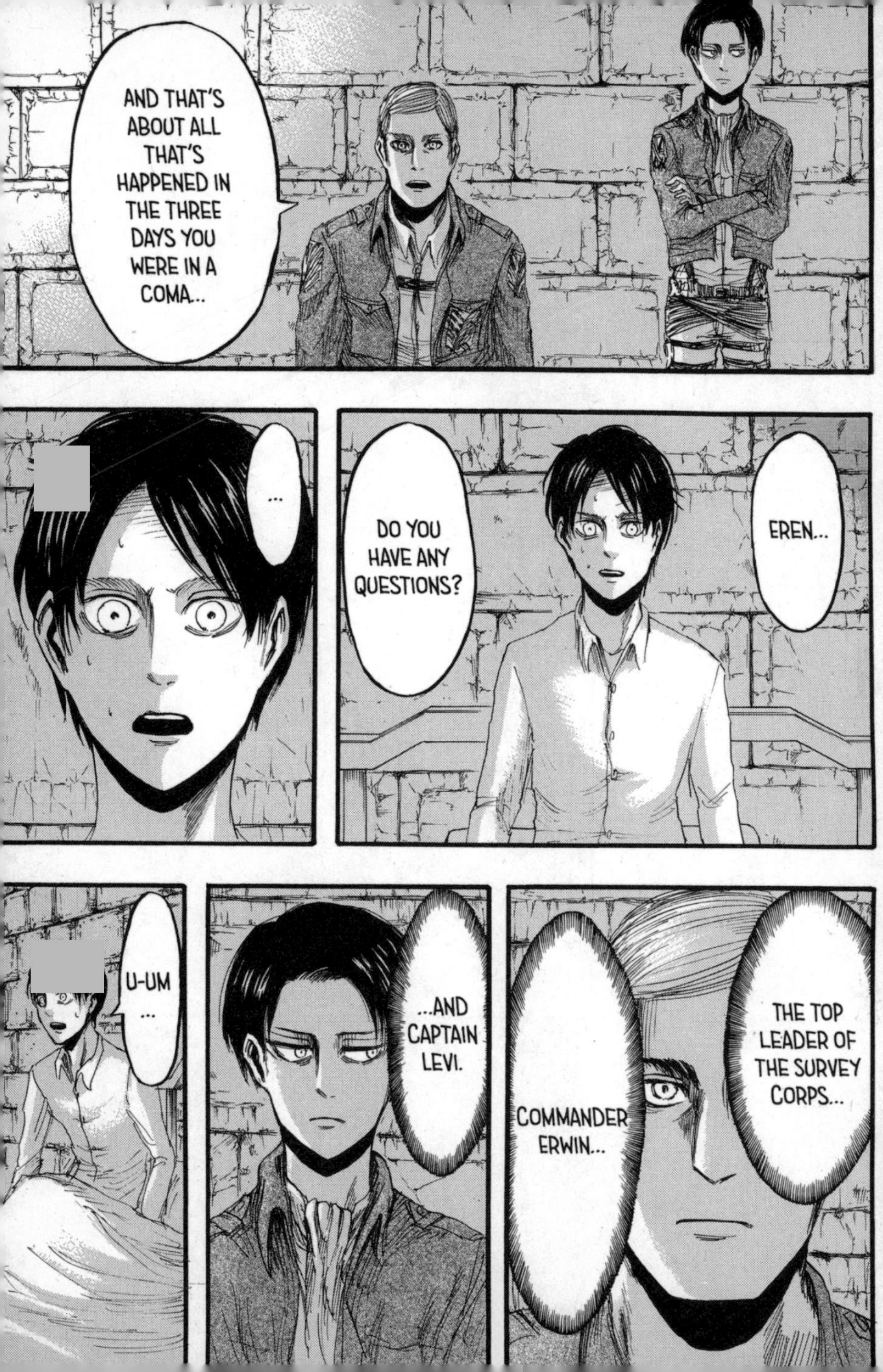
AND THAT'S ABOUT ALL THAT'S HAPPENED IN THE THREE DAYS YOU WERE IN A COMA...
EREN...
DO YOU HAVE ANY QUESTIONS?
...
THE TOP LEADER OF THE SURVEY CORPS...
COMMANDER ERWIN...
...AND CAPTAIN LEVI.
U-UM ...

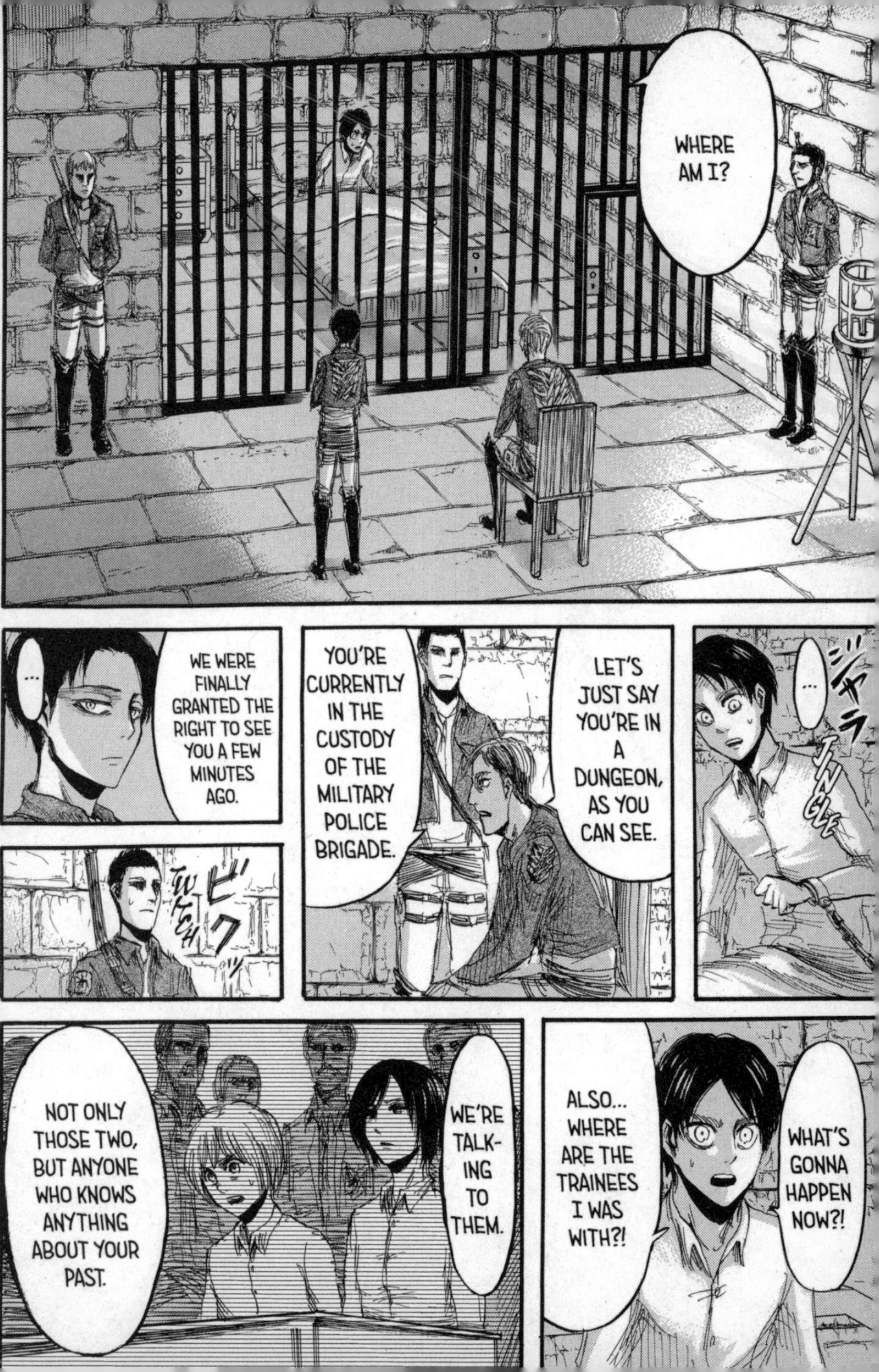
WHERE AM I?
...
ジャラ
JINGLE
LET'S JUST SAY YOU'RE IN A DUNGEON, AS YOU CAN SEE.
YOU'RE CURRENTLY IN THE CUSTODY OF THE MILITARY POLICE BRIGADE.
WE WERE FINALLY GRANTED THE RIGHT TO SEE YOU A FEW MINUTES AGO.
...
ビク
TWITCH
WHAT'S GONNA HAPPEN NOW?!
ALSO... WHERE ARE THE TRAINEES I WAS WITH?!
WE'RE TALKING TO THEM.
NOT ONLY THOSE TWO, BUT ANYONE WHO KNOWS ANYTHING ABOUT YOUR PAST.

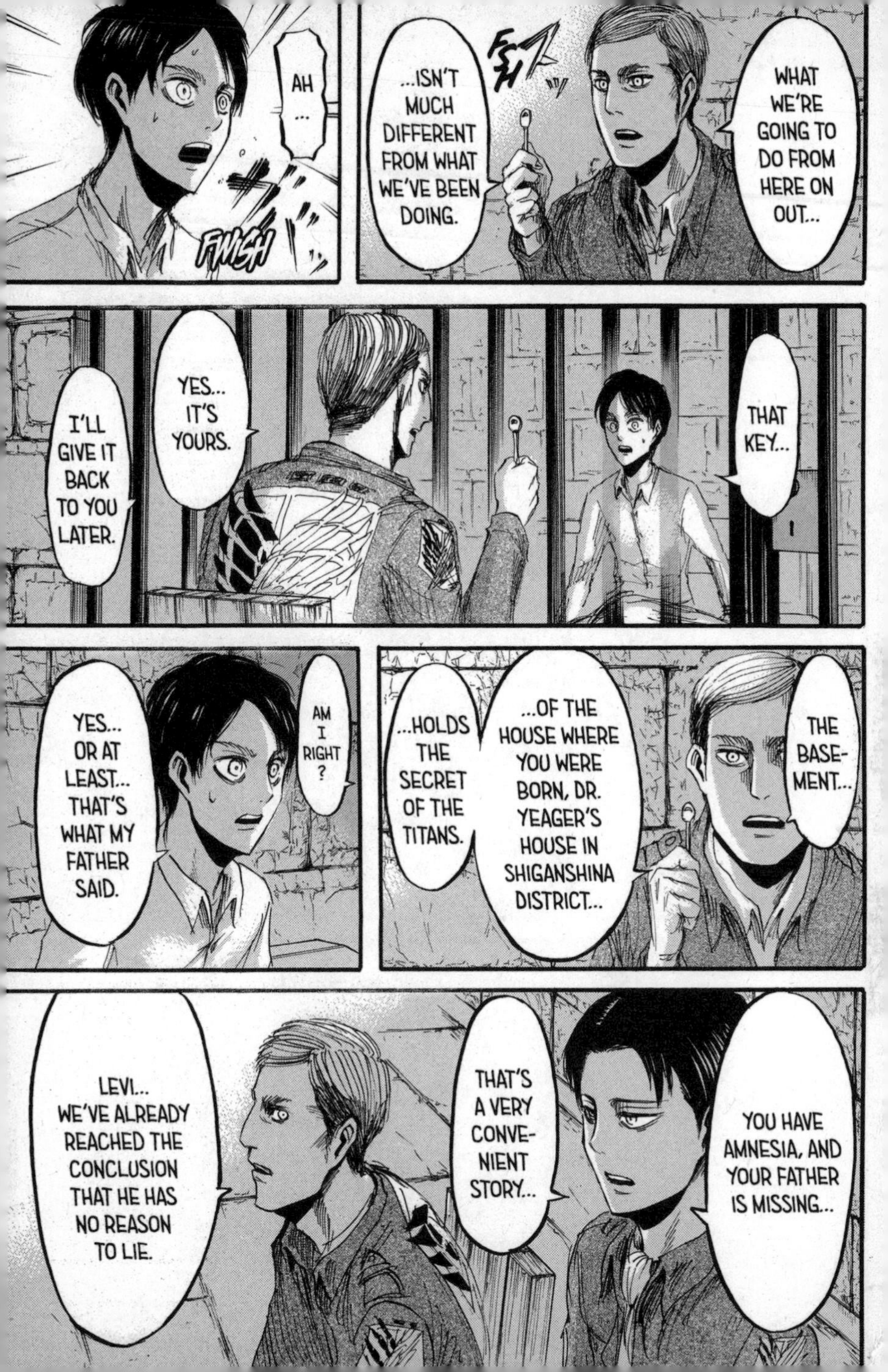
WHAT WE'RE GOING TO DO FROM HERE ON OUT...
FSH
...ISN'T MUCH DIFFERENT FROM WHAT WE'VE BEEN DOING.
AH ...
FWISH
THAT KEY...
YES... IT'S YOURS.
I'LL GIVE IT BACK TO YOU LATER.
THE BASEMENT...
...OF THE HOUSE WHERE YOU WERE BORN, DR. YEAGER'S HOUSE IN SHIGANSHINA DISTRICT...
...HOLDS THE SECRET OF THE TITANS.
AM I RIGHT?
YES... OR AT LEAST... THAT'S WHAT MY FATHER SAID.
YOU HAVE AMNESIA, AND YOUR FATHER IS MISSING...
THAT'S A VERY CONVENIENT STORY...
LEVI... WE'VE ALREADY REACHED THE CONCLUSION THAT HE HAS NO REASON TO LIE.

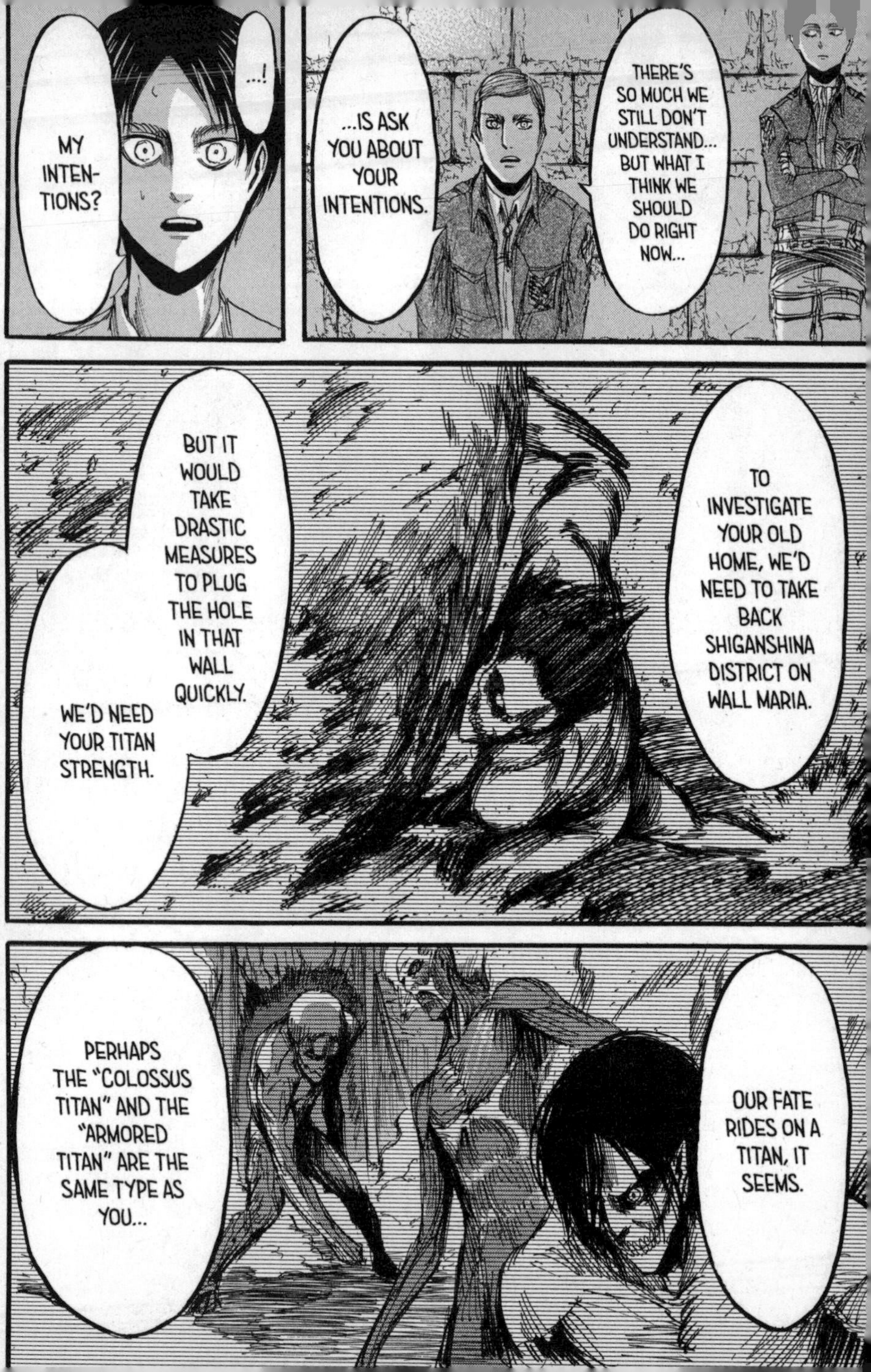
THERE'S SO MUCH WE STILL DON'T UNDERSTAND... BUT WHAT I THINK WE SHOULD DO RIGHT NOW...
...IS ASK YOU ABOUT YOUR INTENTIONS.
...!
MY INTEN-TIONS?
TO INVESTIGATE YOUR OLD HOME, WE'D NEED TO TAKE BACK SHIGANSHINA DISTRICT ON WALL MARIA.
BUT IT WOULD TAKE DRASTIC MEASURES TO PLUG THE HOLE IN THAT WALL QUICKLY.
WE'D NEED YOUR TITAN STRENGTH.
OUR FATE RIDES ON A TITAN, IT SEEMS.
PERHAPS THE "COLOSSUS TITAN" AND THE "ARMORED TITAN" ARE THE SAME TYPE AS YOU...

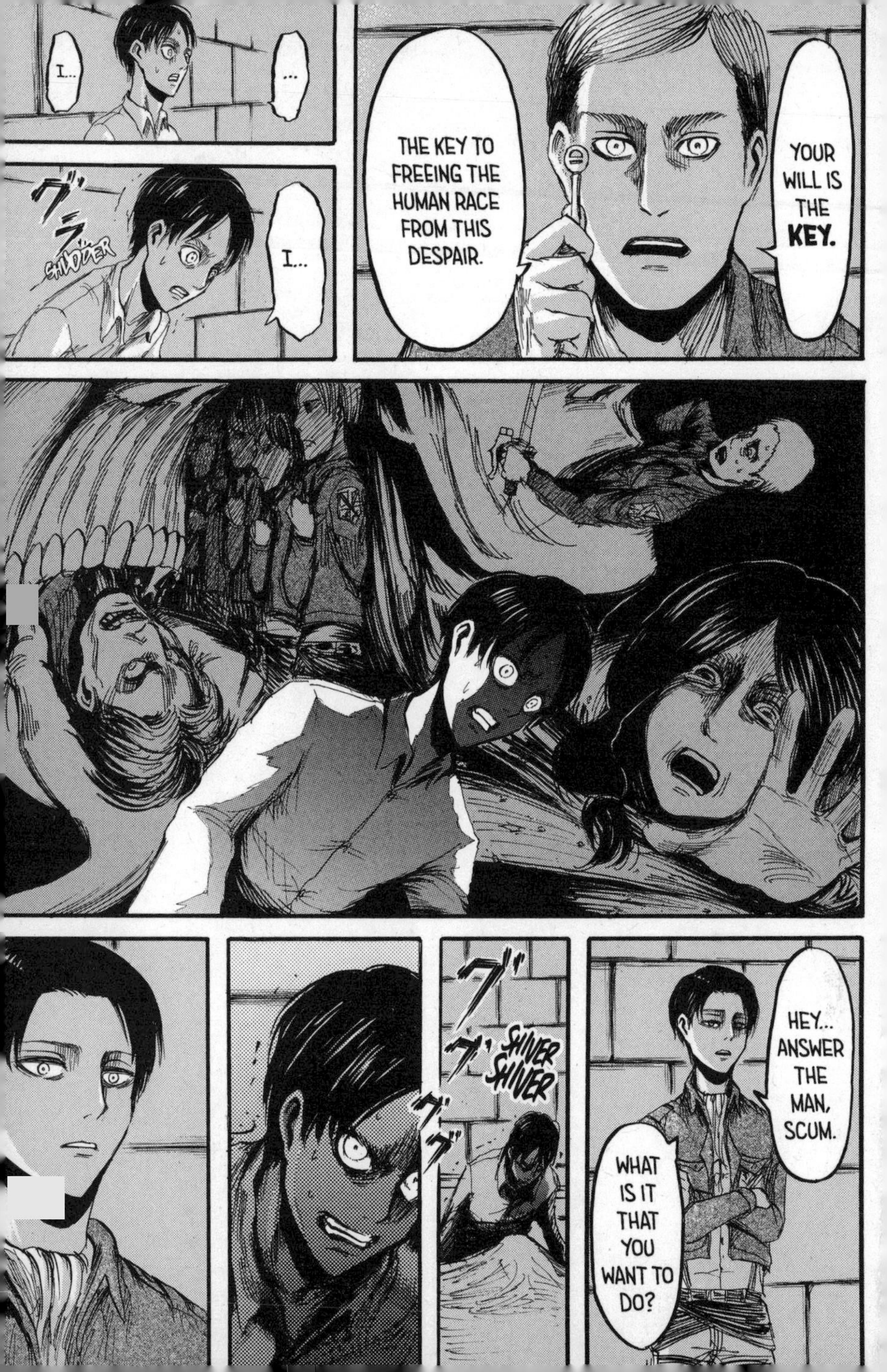
YOUR WILL IS THE KEY.
THE KEY TO FREEING THE HUMAN RACE FROM THIS DESPAIR.
...
I...
I...
SHUDDER
HEY... ANSWER THE MAN, SCUM.
WHAT IS IT THAT YOU WANT TO DO?
SHIVER SHIVER

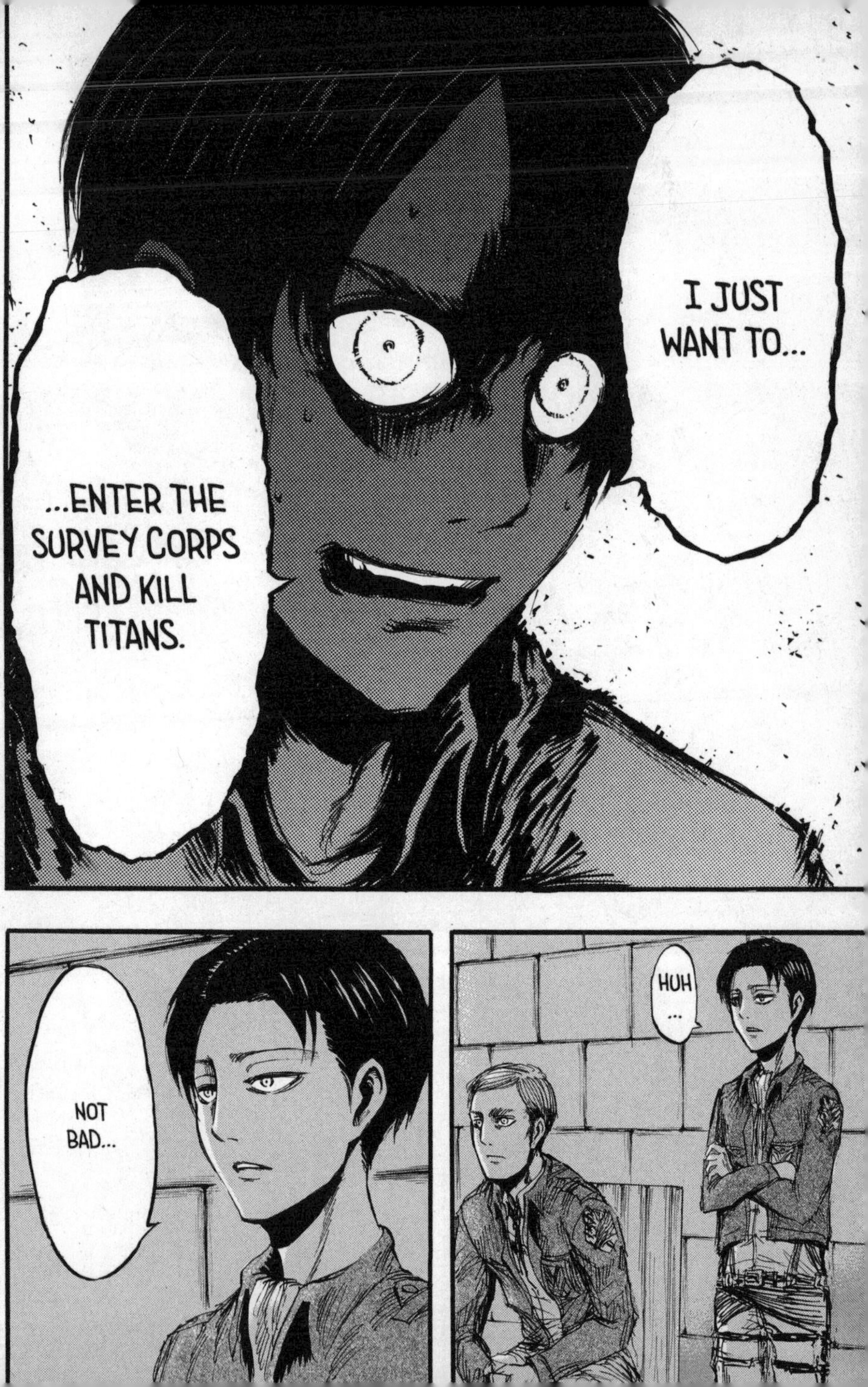
I JUST WANT TO...
...ENTER THE SURVEY CORPS AND KILL TITANS.
HUH ...
NOT BAD...

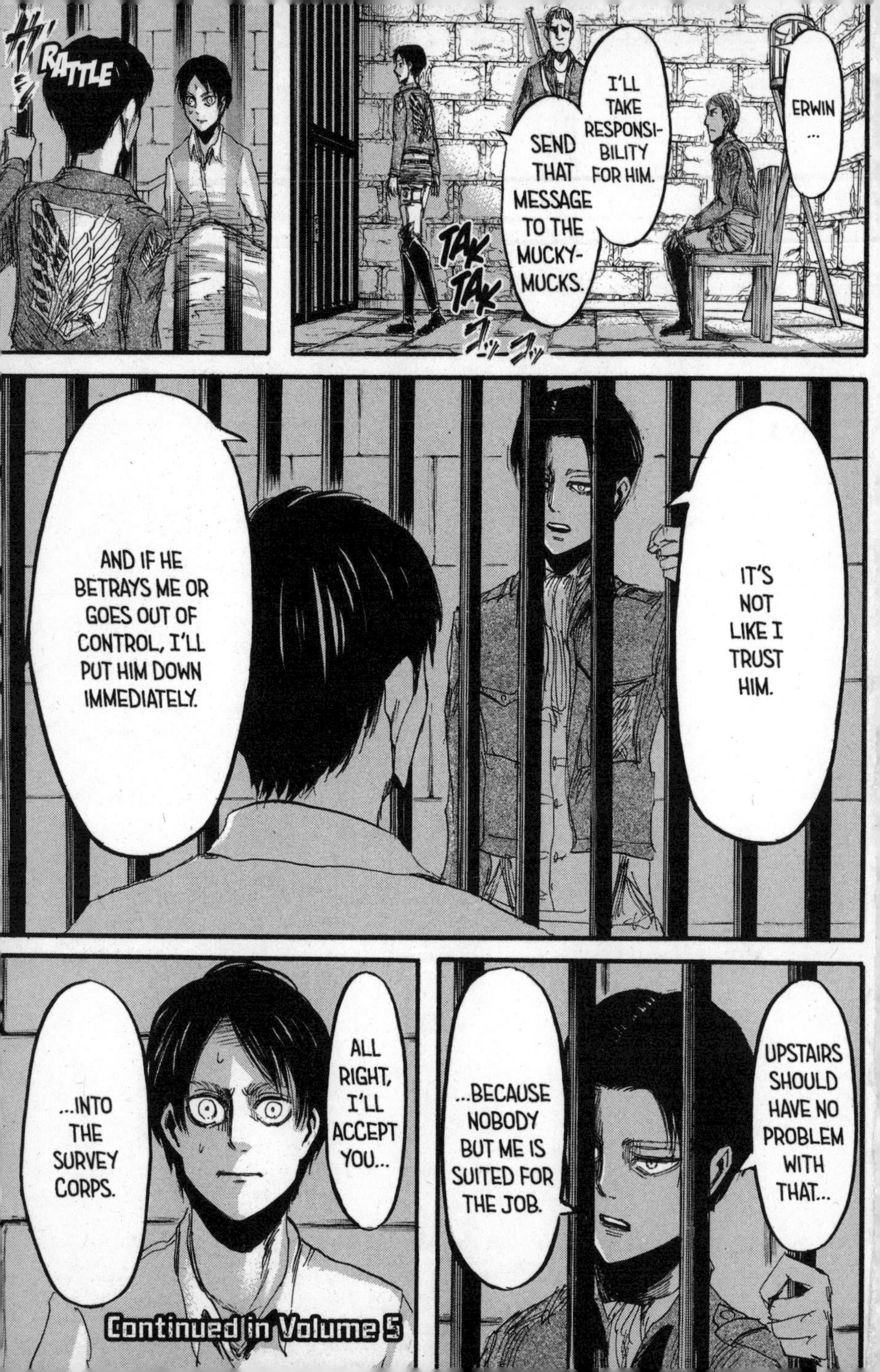
ERWIN...
I'LL TAKE RESPONSIBILITY FOR HIM.
SEND THAT MESSAGE TO THE MUCKY-MUCKS.
TAK TAK
RATTLE
IT'S NOT LIKE I TRUST HIM.
AND IF HE BETRAYS ME OR GOES OUT OF CONTROL, I'LL PUT HIM DOWN IMMEDIATELY.
UPSTAIRS SHOULD HAVE NO PROBLEM WITH THAT...
...BECAUSE NOBODY BUT ME IS SUITED FOR THE JOB.
ALL RIGHT, I'LL ACCEPT YOU...
...INTO THE SURVEY CORPS.
Continued in Volume 5

A Kodansha Comics Trade Paperback Original

Attack on Titan volume 4 copyright © 2011 Hajime Isayama
English translation copyright © 2013 Hajime Isayama

All rights reserved.

Published in the United States by Kodansha Comics, an imprint of Kodansha USA Publishing, LLC, New York.

Publication rights for this English edition arranged through Kodansha Ltd., Tokyo.

First published in Japan in 2011 by Kodansha Ltd., Tokyo as *Shingeki no Kyojin*, volume 4.

ISBN 978-1-61262-253-8

Original cover design by Takashi Shimoyama (Red Rooster)

Printed in the United States of America.

www.kodanshacomics.com

9 8 7 6
Translator: Sheldon Drzka
Lettering: Steve Wands